The Shell Guide to the Birds

of Britain and Ireland

James Ferguson-Lees
Ian Willis
J.T.R. Sharrock

Michael Joseph

*To the memory of the late Bernard W. Tucker who began modern
field identification techniques; to Roger Tory Peterson
who started the concept of field guides; and to Bruce Campbell
who suggested this one.*

First published in Great Britain by
Michael Joseph Limited
44 Bedford Square, London WC1
April 1983
Reprinted 1986

ISBN 0 7181 2220 8

This book was designed and produced by
George Rainbird Limited
40 Park Street, London W1Y 4DE

Editors: David Burnie
Duncan J. Brooks
Design: Rod Josey Associates
Cartographer: Richard Natkiel
Production: Elizabeth Winder
Indexer: Lorna Gradden

Text filmset by Oliver Burridge and Company Limited, Crawley, Sussex
Illustrations originated by Aragorn Colour Reproduction, London
and Bridge Graphics Limited, Hull
Printed and bound by Brepols s.a., Turnhout, Belgium

The Author

JAMES FERGUSON-LEES, who planned and wrote this book, is one of Britain's foremost ornithologists. He has studied birds throughout the world, and has first-hand experience of all but a few species covered in this book. For many years, he was executive editor of the monthly magazine *British Birds*. A past president of the British Trust for Ornithology, he was awarded its Bernard Tucker Medal for his work in connection with *The Atlas of Breeding Birds in Britain and Ireland* (1976), and is now chairman of the working group currently organising the forthcoming atlas of winter birds. He has been chairman of the education and conservation committees of the Royal Society for the Protection of Birds, and was for two years its deputy director for conservation. He is currently chairman of the Records Committee of the British Ornithologists' Union, which maintains the official list of British birds. He has been co-author, collaborator or editor of a number of books, including the revised editions of *A Field Guide to the Birds of Britain and Europe* (1965, 1974) and the first volume of *The Birds of the Western Palearctic* (1977).

The Artist

IAN WILLIS, who painted all the plates in this guide, began his career as a wildlife illustrator and writer in 1968. He has had extensive experience of birdwatching, not only in the British Isles, but also further afield. He has travelled widely to study birds and flowers throughout Europe, North Africa, the Middle East and Siberia. His illustrations have appeared in many books and articles, ranging from children's books to more specialist publications, including *Flight Identification of European Raptors* (1974), a comprehensive study of raptor plumages. This has subsequently become a standard reference work. He has also produced the colour plates of raptors for the second volume of *Birds of the Western Palearctic* (1980). Much of his field knowledge for his works on birds of prey was gained in 1966, when, with several colleagues, he undertook a six-month expedition to Turkey mainly to study the migrations of raptors and other soaring birds. He is also particularly interested in owls and Middle Eastern birds, and has illustrated *The Barn Owl* (1982) and *Owls of Europe* (1983) as well as the forthcoming guide *Birds of North Africa and the Middle East*.

The Map Consultant

Dr J. T. R. SHARROCK, who compiled all the maps, is managing editor of the monthly magazine *British Birds*, which has been published continuously since 1907. Formerly a botanist, he has since become an ornithologist of international standing. His strong interest in bird distributions is reflected by his holding the position of chairman of the European Ornithological Atlas Committee since its formation in 1971. During 1969–76 he was national organiser of the project which led to the publication in 1976 of *The Atlas of Breeding Birds in Britain and Ireland*. He has been author or co-author of a number of other books on the birds of Britain and Ireland.

Preface

The last forty years have produced an enormous increase in interest in birds and a corresponding proliferation of books about them. With the development of travel and the growth of international scientific cooperation, books on bird identification have tended to cover whole continents. Thus, most of the current field guides deal not just with Britain and Ireland, but with Europe as a whole, sometimes extending to adjacent parts of northwest Africa and southwest Asia. As a result, a large number of species have had to be described in a limited space, and in many cases only adult plumages have been illustrated. For people watching birds in Britain and Ireland this has meant looking through pages of often irrelevant pictures.

By contrast, this new field guide is confined to the species which have actually been recorded in Britain and Ireland and it aims to show as many of the main plumages as possible. Just over 500 species have now been seen here and, of these, 263 may be classed as the 'regulars' which make up the bulk of this book: many of them nest and the others appear every year in appreciable numbers, either as winter visitors or as passage migrants between their breeding areas to the north and winter quarters to the south. The remainder are 'vagrants', wanderers from other parts of Europe and Asia or even America and Africa: some of these have been recorded here only once or twice (although for every one seen it is likely that more have been missed), while others turn up every year in very small numbers. This book contains all vagrants noted up to the end of 1980, except 14 species which have not reappeared since 1930.

Acknowledgments

Planning, research, writing and painting have taken the best part of three years. Various people have given a great deal of help. Karen Goldie-Morrison, of Rainbird, put much work into setting up the project. Lars Svensson and D. I. M. Wallace read the whole text in proof and made many suggestions. Others who similarly read sections were D. J. Britton (waders), Dr Bruce Campbell (habitat spreads), P. J. Grant (gulls, terns), Peter Harrison (seabirds), J. H. Marchant (waders), J. R. Mather (divers, grebes, ducks, skuas), Dr I. C. T. Nisbet (American vagrants), M. A. Ogilvie (swans, geese, ducks) and R. F. Porter (diurnal birds of prey). P. J. Grant also produced the topographical charts on page 11 from his drawings in *British Birds* for June 1981; and J. H. Marchant and M. A. Ogilvie, as well as Peter Colston, Martin Robinson and Donald Watson, gave additional help with specific problems by looking at skins, providing references to publications or advising on certain plates. Invaluable references were also turned up by Dr I. H. J. Lyster of the Royal Scottish Museum. Dr D. W. Snow, I. C. J. Galbraith and the staff of the Ornithological Section of the British Museum (Natural History) at Tring gave permission and help over examining skins. Heather Angel's photographs are well up to her own remarkable standard.

James Ferguson-Lees and Ian Willis owe much to their wives, Karen and Diane, for encouragement and understanding; Karen Ferguson-Lees also typed the entire manuscript. But our greatest single debts are to Duncan J. Brooks who not only read all the proofs and commented on many of the plates, but earlier helped to revise and reduce about half of the text drafts to an acceptable length; and David A. Burnie, of Rainbird, who went to great pains to help, advise, encourage, comment and check. If this book serves to engender a wider understanding of the identification, sexing and ageing of birds, and their place in Britain and Ireland, we shall be well satisfied.   I.J.F-L., I.W., J.T.R.S.

Contents

The bird families appear in this book in a sequence as close as practicable to the scientifically established taxonomic order. However, there are a few places where the sequence has been altered slightly to aid identification, allowing similar birds – for example the Swift and the Swallow – to appear on the same page. The page numbers for the bird families are in two columns; the first refers to **regulars**, and the second (in italics) to **vagrants**.

How to use this book	8	
Annotations	9	
Map key	10	
Bird topography	11	

BIRD HABITATS

Towns, gardens and parks	12
Fields and hedges	14
Lowland broadleaved woods	16
Upland broadleaved woods	18
Coniferous woods and plantations	20
Caledonian forest	22
Heaths and brecks	24
Downs and grasslands	26
Moors and mountains	28
Rivers and streams	30
Lakes, reservoirs and gravel pits	32
Marshes, fens and reedbeds	34
Estuaries and saltings	36
Sand, shingle and dunes	38
Rocky coasts and islands	40

BIRD FAMILIES

Gaviidae	DIVERS	42	*250*
Podicipedidae	GREBES	44	*250*
Diomedeidae	ALBATROSSES		*250*
Fregatidae	FRIGATEBIRDS		*250*

Sulidae	GANNETS	48	
Procellariidae	PETRELS, SHEARWATERS	48	*252*
Hydrobatidae	STORM-PETRELS	52	*252*
Phalacrocoracidae	CORMORANTS	54	
Ardeidae	BITTERNS, HERONS	56	*254*
Ciconiidae	STORKS		*256*
Threskiornithidae	IBISES, SPOONBILLS	56	*256*
Anatidae	SWANS, GEESE, DUCKS	58	*258*
Accipitridae	KITES, HARRIERS, HAWKS, BUZZARDS, EAGLES	92	*264*
Pandionidae	OSPREYS	102	
Falconidae	FALCONS	104	*264*
Tetraonidae	GROUSE	108	
Phasianidae	PARTRIDGES, PHEASANTS	112	
Rallidae	RAILS, CRAKES, GALLINULES	116	*268*
Gruidae	CRANES		*270*
Otididae	BUSTARDS		*270*
Haematopodidae	OYSTERCATCHERS	120	
Recurvirostridae	AVOCETS, STILTS	120	*272*
Burhinidae	STONE-CURLEWS	120	
Glareolidae	COURSERS, PRATINCOLES		*272*
Charadriidae	PLOVERS	122	*274*
Scolopacidae	TYPICAL WADERS	128	*272/6*
Stercorariidae	SKUAS	148	
Laridae	GULLS	152	*282*
Sternidae	TERNS	164	*284*
Alcidae	AUKS	168	*286*
Pteroclididae	SANDGROUSE		*288*
Columbidae	PIGEONS, DOVES	172	*288*
Cuculidae	CUCKOOS	174	*288*
Psittacidae	PARAKEETS	174	
Tytonidae	BARN-OWLS	176	
Strigidae	OWLS	176	*290*
Caprimulgidae	NIGHTJARS	180	*292*
Meropidae	BEE-EATERS		*290*
Coraciidae	ROLLERS		*290*
Alcedinidae	KINGFISHERS	180	*290*
Upupidae	HOOPOES	180	
Picidae	WRYNECKS, WOODPECKERS	180	*292*
Alaudidae	LARKS	184	*294*

Apodidae	SWIFTS	186	*292*
Hirundinidae	SWALLOWS, MARTINS	186	*292*
Motacillidae	PIPITS, WAGTAILS	188	*296*
Bombycillidae	WAXWINGS	194	
Troglodytidae	WRENS	194	
Cinclidae	DIPPERS	194	
Prunellidae	ACCENTORS	196	*296*
Mimidae	THRASHERS		*298*
Turdidae	CHATS, THRUSHES	196	*298*
Sylviidae	WARBLERS, KINGLETS	208/20	*306*
Muscicapidae	FLYCATCHERS	218	*312*
Timaliidae	REEDLINGS	220	
Aegithalidae	LONG-TAILED TITS	220	
Paridae	TITS	222	
Sittidae	NUTHATCHES	226	
Tichodromadidae	WALLCREEPERS		*314*
Certhiidae	TREECREEPERS	226	*314*
Remizidae	PENDULINE TITS		*314*
Oriolidae	ORIOLES	226	
Laniidae	SHRIKES	228	*314*
Corvidae	CROWS	228	*316*
Sturnidae	STARLINGS	234	*316*
Passeridae	SPARROWS	234	*316*
Fringillidae	FINCHES	236	*318*
Parulidae	AMERICAN WARBLERS		*320*
Vireonidae	VIREOS		*322*
Thraupidae	TANAGERS		*324*
Emberizidae	BUNTINGS, AMERICAN SPARROWS	244	*324*
Icteridae	AMERICAN ORIOLES		*328*

Bibliography   330

Index   331

How to use this book

REGULARS and VAGRANTS (see page 4) are
arranged in separate sections, each in the
same sequence of families. This sequence
and that of the species within the families,
as well as the scientific names, follows the
List of Recent Holarctic Bird Species by
Professor Dr K. H. Voous (1977), with
only minor modifications to suit the layout
of the plates. To identify a bird, the reader
should first consult the REGULARS section
and then, if necessary, refer to the
VAGRANTS. The treatment of regulars is
intentionally fuller, with usually only two
or three species on each plate to allow
more text and a wider range of illustrated
plumages. The less detailed treatment of
vagrants often excludes plumages not seen
in Britain and Ireland.

Text

Species texts are set out as follows:

Name Both English and scientific names
are given. Although the latter may seem
rather off-putting at first, they have the
advantages of precision and of showing
relationships: the family is a grouping of
related genera, and the genus (the first of
the two words in the individual Latinised
name) is a grouping of related species (the
second word being the name of the
species). Sometimes, within the text, other
names are used in conjunction with the
initials of the scientific name: these refer
to subspecies, or 'races', with distinctive
characters (note, however, that there is
often no sharp dividing line between races,
which tend to grade into one another).

Size Birds vary as much as any other
animals in size. The extremes of the main
range of length are given in centimetres,
with an approximate mean in inches.

Field characters The first sentence of the
text gives the general characters of the
species, concentrating on shape and only
the more obvious plumage features, such
as contrasting colours, white rumps and
pale wing-bars.

Behaviour The second sentence describes
flight, gait and other actions, as well as
flocking.

Plumages and moults Under separate
headings, attention is drawn to the
characters and differences of males and
females, winter and summer plumages,
and immature stages; for some species
these differences are very marked, for
others slight. Certain of the passerines (the
'song-birds', from larks to buntings) are
indistinguishable from the adult by their
first winter, while many larger birds, such
as Gannets, eagles and gulls, take several
years to acquire adult plumage. The terms
used are 'juvenile' for the first covering of
true feathers; '1st winter' for the plumage
following a moult in the first autumn and
'1st summer' for that worn when the bird
is approaching one year old (or '1st year'
for these two combined); and so on
through second winter and second summer
if different from the adult. All species
moult once a year, many twice (at least
partially), and a few three times; some
also change appearance, even quite
strikingly, by wearing away through
abrasion the often duller tips and edges of
feathers moulted in autumn, to reveal
brighter colours or clearer patterns by
spring. Moult from one stage to another
may take weeks or even months through
many (often blotchy) mixtures of two
plumages and, even if the plumages are
similar, there is usually a contrast between
new well-pigmented and old faded
feathers: these mixtures cannot really be
described or illustrated, but the duration
of moult is given as far as possible to show
when such intermediates may be expected.

Voice Brief descriptions or renderings are
attempted for songs and main calls. These
are often characteristic, and so important
in identification, but notoriously difficult
to express phonetically; most species also
have wider vocabularies than can be
covered in a line or two. They become
familiar through experience rather than
by what is written in field guides.

Habitat A crucial basis for identification is
knowing where to expect a species, and the

typical habitats are briefly summarised (but migrants may turn up in strange surroundings). Some idea of the birds likely to be found in particular habitats is also given under broad groupings on pages 12–41.

Nest For the species which breed in Britain and Ireland, brief details are noted of nest site, clutch size, season, and number of broods; if breeding is in colonies, this is also stated. The season shown is that during which the nest is usually occupied: for most birds this means by either eggs or nestlings, but the downy young of divers, grebes, swans, geese, ducks, grouse, partridges, pheasants, rails, crakes, moorhens, coots, waders, gulls and terns leave the nest soon after hatching, and in their cases the season covers eggs only.

Food The main foods are listed, but generally just in very broad categories.

Range For the regulars, this complements the maps with the months of arrival/departure and the destinations of summer visitors, and the seasons and origins of winter visitors and passage migrants. For the vagrants, it gives the total of records to the end of 1980, as an indication of likelihood of further sightings, with a brief summary of the months and counties or regions of occurrence in Britain and Ireland; the continents where the species breeds (but not necessarily winters) are set out at the end. Throughout, where additional months appear in brackets without the emphasising 'esp', these are the extremes of the period concerned.

Comparisons Under the regulars, there are often cross-references, either in the body of the text or at the end, to similar species and related vagrants (especially those which might be confused with them).

Annotations

♂ male
♀ female
ad adult
juv juvenile
imm immature

Sexes are given only if distinguishable ('ad' indicates either).

An **oblique** is used between any two plumages that are indistinguishable, *eg*
ad/juv either adult or juvenile
1st winter/ad either 1st winter or adult
ad/1st winter either adult *winter* or 1st winter

A **dash** indicates a transitional stage, *eg*
juv–1st winter between juvenile and 1st winter plumages

10

Maps

Each of the 263 species in the main section of birds classed as 'regulars' has a map designed to show both population sizes and distribution at a glance. The 'vagrants' do not have maps as they by definition, do not occur in predictable numbers or locations.

Population sizes

The figures at the top right-hand corner of each map relate to the numbers of each species estimated to be breeding (B), or present during winter (W), spring (S) or autumn (A), in Britain and Ireland as a whole. The numbers are expressed as simple orders of magnitude, and refer to individuals, not pairs:

0	=	usually none
1	=	1–10
2	=	11–100
3	=	101–1,000
4	=	1,001–10,000
5	=	10,001–100,000
6	=	100,001–1,000,000
7	=	1,000,001–10,000,000
8	=	over 10 million

The order of magnitude is easily converted by thinking of it as the number of figures in the population size (or the number of zeros in the maximum). Thus, B5 shows a 5-figure breeding total (in the ten thousands) or at most 100,000; W6 indicates a 6-figure wintering total (in the hundred thousands) or at most 1,000,000. Although readers may find it helpful to refer to the above conversion table at first, the orders will quickly become familiar. This system has the advantages of ease of comparison

and lack of spurious accuracy associated with definite figures.

It should be borne in mind that these orders of magnitude are for an 'average' year. The populations of some birds vary considerably from year to year, through such factors as hard winters, weather effects on migration, food supplies, and breeding success; the numbers of many species are highest in autumn through the summer's production of young. It should also be realised that 'B0' does not necessarily mean that a species is absent in summer: small numbers of some waders, for example, are often present then without breeding.

Distribution

Breeding areas are shown in blue, winter quarters are hatched, and regions where a species is found only on passage or wandering are stippled. The breeding distributions are based on the 1968–72 survey carried out by the British Trust for Ornithology and the Irish Wildbird Conservancy, as published in *The Atlas of Breeding Birds in Britain and Ireland* (1976), but updated to include major changes during 1973–80. For the sake of clarity (and also to conceal the precise localities of certain rare breeders), some small areas of distribution have been enlarged. As data for birds at sea are much less detailed than those for land species, the distributions of essentially marine species are shown in exaggerated coastal strips, indicating the shores from which these birds may often or sometimes be seen.

Bird topography

A knowledge of the superficial features of the body, or topography, is essential to describe birds fully and to understand identification, ageing and sexing. The diagrams below show all the main areas of the plumage and 'bare parts' (bill, eyes, legs) on a whole bird, a head and an underwing. In this book, however, the dictates of space and simplicity, coupled with the fact that the positions of the markings are usually clear on the facing plate, have made it more convenient often to adopt looser and more graphic terms with a human analogy, such as 'face', 'spectacles', 'cheeks', 'moustaches', 'shoulders' and even 'armpits' and 'trousers', as well as 'arms' and 'hands' for the inner and outer parts of the wings; also, 'upperparts' (or 'above') and 'underparts' (or 'below') are used for the upper and under surfaces of the bird, and 'back' is sometimes loosely applied to the whole upper body. The 'speculum' (not illustrated) is the term for a patch of different colour found on the wings of certain ducks.

HEAD

UNDERWING

Towns, gardens and parks

Though our cities and bigger towns may seem the dullest of habitats, more than 50 species regularly appear in towns, gardens and urban parks and others occur on passage or in hard weather. Among the commonest are Feral Pigeons (descendants of the coastal Rock Dove) and, of course, Starlings and House Sparrows. Starlings form vast noisy roosts in some cities in winter; in contrast, on fine summer days they glide gracefully high overhead hawking insects. The real aerial insect-feeders in summer, however, are the Swifts and House Martins; both nest under eaves in towns, the Swifts using holes, and crevices in large buildings, and the House Martins building conspicuous mud cups. Swallows, on the other hand, penetrate only as far as the suburbs.

Gulls also hawk insects overhead and feed at town rubbish tips; they roost on urban reservoirs. Among other larger birds, Kestrels often nest in city centres, and Tawny Owls in gardens and parks. Ponds may hold Moorhens and Mallards (the latter often semi-domesticated) and larger lakes Coots and Tufted Ducks. Woodpigeons breed in town squares with trees, and Collared Doves have become a familiar suburban sight since the 1950s. Jackdaws, Rooks and, more locally, odd pairs of Carrion Crows nest in towns, while even Magpies and Jays appear in the suburbs and some central city parks.

But it is the small birds which the garden watcher sees most closely. Blackbirds, Song Thrushes, Robins, Wrens, Dunnocks, Chaffinches and Greenfinches are all common in urban gardens and parks. Blue Tits are the most numerous of the tits, and in winter they come to bird tables with Great and Coal Tits for nuts

and scraps: although only two or three Blue Tits may be seen at a time, a garden may well be visited by 30 or 40 in a day. Creepers on houses provide nesting places for Spotted Flycatchers, and for Pied Wagtails. A much more local city nester, the Black Redstart, usually first attracts attention over the traffic by its 'gravelly' song. Willow Warblers, Chiffchaffs, Whitethroats and Blackcaps wander through gardens on spring and autumn passage, while Blackcaps (and to a lesser extent Chiffchaffs) have now become regular in winter in small numbers. Other garden visitors include Bullfinches, Linnets, Redpolls and, in the latter part of the winter, Siskins. And almost anything may turn up: Long-tailed Tits or a Treecreeper; Redwings, Reed Buntings or even a Sparrowhawk in severe weather.

Fields and hedges

In 1950, the total length of field and roadside hedges in Britain was nearly four million kilometres. Today, although some parts of lowland Britain and Ireland are still a patchwork of arable and grass with these ancient dividing boundaries, sadly, many of these hedges have been grubbed out, to be replaced by wire fences or just larger fields. This drastically reduces the variety and numbers of birds.

In large fields Skylarks are often almost the only nesting birds, though Corn Buntings favour extensive arable and corn if there are wires from which to sing. Grey Partridges are widespread, although often outnumbered in lowland England by the introduced Red-legged; both usually need hedge-bottoms to nest in. Pheasants also feed in open fields, but mainly near woods. A gamebird which does breed in hay and corn is the Quail, a scarce summer visitor seldom seen and mainly heard at night. Another nocturnal caller, the Corncrake, is now confined largely to parts of Ireland and Scotland where the hay is cut later.

Lapwings nest early on ploughed land or short grass. Other waders that breed in fields include Oystercatchers in north Britain, Stone-curlews on flinty arable in the southeast, Ringed and even Little Ringed Plovers locally on stony patches in fallow and young crops, and Redshanks, Snipe or Curlews in water meadows, but none of these is typical of this habitat.

Many birds feed in fields, some taking seeds and shoots, others insects and worms. Woodpigeons, along with Stock Doves and Feral Pigeons, are familiar sights, as are flocks of Rooks and Jackdaws, and Carrion or Hooded Crows. Starlings are seen as parties of plain brown juveniles from June onwards and later in large flocks. In winter, too, come flocks of Lapwings and sometimes Golden Plovers, of gulls (especially Black-headed and Common), and of thrushes, finches and buntings. Locally, particularly in the north, Pink-footed and Greylag Geese feed on stubble and young crops. Other field birds in winter include Moorhens, Meadow Pipits and Pied Wagtails, while in summer Swifts and Swallows hunt insects over the grass.

But any real diversity depends on hedges, and the wider and taller the better. Many of the common birds of gardens and wood-edges also breed in hedgerows, especially thrushes, Dunnocks and Chaffinches. Really thick hedges house Long-tailed Tits and, in southern Britain, Turtle Doves and Lesser Whitethroats, as well as Greenfinches, Bullfinches and Linnets. Those on banks or with dense bases attract Yellowhammers and Robins; if there are trees in them, Blackcaps, Redpolls, Goldfinches and, locally, Cirl Buntings enter the picture. Even Moorhens, Sedge Warblers and Reed Buntings will breed in hedges well away from water. Magpies build in high thorns, and Carrion Crows in large hedgerow trees (as do Buzzards in Wales), their old nests in turn providing sites for Kestrels, occasional Hobbies, and Stock Doves. The last also breed in cavities in mature hedgerow trees, as do Tawny, Little and even Barn Owls. Smaller holes make homes for Blue and Great Tits and Tree Sparrows (House Sparrows more usually building untidy domed structures in rank hedges). Green Woodpeckers often excavate their holes in timbered hedgerows and these may be taken over by Starlings or even Nuthatches.

In winter, Redwings, Fieldfares and other thrushes, and sometimes Waxwings, flock where berries are plentiful. Hedges are also important as connecting 'lanes' along which many birds, such as Great Spotted Woodpeckers, Jays, Treecreepers and tits, will travel from wood to wood.

Lowland broadleaved woods

Birds are often hard to see in woods and so it is important to learn their songs and calls. The largest areas of lowland broadleaved woods are in England and Wales, and here pedunculate oak, ash and beech are among the dominant trees. The richest woods are those where oaks are common, as these support huge numbers of invertebrates on which insect-eating birds feed.

The best time to see and hear woodland bird life is in late spring and early summer, when the annual chorus of bird song reaches its climax. Perhaps the most famous of woodland songsters is the Nightingale, a summer visitor to southern Britain: despite its name, it also sings by day and may be silent on cold nights;

it is hard to see in its dense thickets. Garden Warblers and Blackcaps, whose songs are often confused, are also found in these tangles, although the Blackcaps are confined more to the parts with taller trees, as are Chiffchaffs and Spotted Flycatchers. Willow Warblers, on the other hand, are heard in scrubby clearings and at wood edges, where there may also be the occasional pair of Whitethroats. Wood Warblers are found locally in lowlands, often in beech woods with little ground cover. Redstarts are dependent on old trees with cavities, while Tree Pipits use more open trees as song-posts and nest on the ground. Cuckoos are a typical spring sound of open woodland: only the male actually 'cuckoos'; the female, here laying her eggs in the nests of Dunnocks, Robins and Tree Pipits, gives a very different bubbling chuckle.

Among resident birds, Wrens, Robins,

Dunnocks, Blackbirds, Song and Mistle Thrushes, Great and Blue Tits, Chaffinches and Greenfinches account for most of the rest of the spring song. Redpolls are noisy in scrub areas, and Nuthatches call loudly in old trees. Distinctive too are Green and Great Spotted Woodpeckers. Unless their calls are known, Lesser Spotted Woodpeckers, Marsh and Willow Tits, Treecreepers, Tree Sparrows and Hawfinches are likely to be overlooked.

Lowland broadleaved woods have their share of larger birds as well. These may include Kestrels, Sparrowhawks and, very locally, Buzzards, Hobbies and a few Goshawks and Honey Buzzards, while Pheasants, Woodpigeons, owls and crows are well distributed throughout. But without doubt one of the most fascinating woodland birds is the Woodcock, with its squeak-and-croak call during its 'roding' or display flight at dusk.

From July to September, when song is all but over and many birds are moulting, the woods are much duller for the birdwatcher, and odd calls give just a tantalising hint of the species that are present. But the arrival of winter brings with it better conditions for watching birds as the last leaves fall. The resident birds are augmented by winter visitors, especially Bramblings in open beech woods and Siskins in birches and alders. Flocks of mixed tits, Goldcrests, Nuthatches and Treecreepers are then often to be seen as they flutter between the trees in search of food.

Upland broadleaved woods

Woods on the hillsides and valley slopes of the west and north have a charm of their own. Here sessile oaks are often dominant, mixed with birch, alder, rowan and holly. Small birds still include the familiar Chaffinches, Robins, Wrens, Dunnocks, Starlings and various thrushes and tits, but fewer warblers. Coal Tits, elsewhere associated more with conifers, often outnumber the Blue and Great, and in Ireland, another conifer species, the Goldcrest, is one of the commonest birds of sessile oak woods. Nuthatches become scarce or absent except in Wales and southwest England, but Treecreepers are well distributed and Long-tailed Tits often nest in birch-forks.

The dominant summer visitors in more open parts are Willow Warblers. There are also Chiffchaffs, and the sessile oak woods of west Britain are a main haunt of Wood Warblers, which have recently also colonised similar places in one or two parts of eastern Ireland. Other warblers are scarce. There are no Nightingales, but at least visually their absence is compensated by the comparative abundance of Redstarts in old upland birch and oak woods. In west Britain, another delightful and characteristic bird of open oak woodland is the Pied Flycatcher, whose numbers are increased by the provision of nestboxes. Spotted

Flycatchers are also well distributed, as are Tree Pipits (in Britain only) where there is open ground.

Mature woods on steep hillsides in Wales are the special habitat of our now rather healthier remnant population of Red Kites: it is a marvellous sight to see one of these magnificent birds of prey circling over a valley. Other raptors of the scrub-woods are Sparrowhawks and, in west Britain, Buzzards, as well as Kestrels. Tawny Owls are common in broadleaved woods throughout Britain, but absent from Ireland where Long-eared Owls, normally linked with conifers, take over. Black Grouse are found in open upland birch, and Woodcocks anywhere with adequate cover. The only other larger birds of the upland broadleaved woods are Pheasants, Woodpigeons and some Stock Doves, Cuckoos, Green and Great Spotted Woodpeckers in Britain, and the inevitable members of the crow family, which here include some Ravens.

Coniferous woods and plantations

The only indigenous conifers are Scots pine, yew and juniper. Most conifer woods consist of about ten introduced species that have been extensively planted since the First World War. Obvious exceptions include the ancient yews of Kingley Vale in Sussex and the remnants of the Caledonian pine forest. Patches of indigenous conifers also occur in mixed woods.

The birds of conifers vary a great deal, depending particularly on geography and the age and spacing of the trees. In close plantations, when the trees are about 15 years old, they form a thick canopy, and this and the forestry practice of lopping off the lower branches and leaving them to lie destroys the undergrowth. They are then usually dull places for birds. Canopy-nesting Goldcrests, Chaffinches and perhaps Mistle Thrushes, together with Coal Tits that breed in mouse holes, are the main songsters. The spread of the Siskin, however, has been greatly aided by older plantations. The rest of the bird fauna consists largely of Wood-pigeons; Jays, Carrion or Hooded Crows and, more at the edge, Magpies; Tawny and especially Long-eared Owls; and Sparrowhawks as well as some Buzzards and, very locally, Goshawks. A few Blackbirds and Wrens persist in ground debris, while the provision of nestboxes adds Blue and Great Tits and, more patchily, Redstarts to the population. Crossbills may be quite widespread in invasion years, feeding on the cones along with Great Spotted Woodpeckers. It is true that there are some colonies of Grey Herons and Rooks in plantations and that Kestrels, Hobbies and even Merlins will breed in old crow nests at the edges; also that in Scotland a few Capercaillies and Golden Eagles nest in such places, while in southeast England Stone-curlews have tried to adapt to wide fire-breaks. But, in general, older plantations have little interest for the birdwatcher.

It is a different story, however, when these areas are newly planted. In the first stages they provide homes for Nightjars and, in the north, for Black Grouse. As the trees develop in association with brambles, heather and other growth, the birds of low cover, such as Willow and Grasshopper Warblers, Whitethroats, Tree Pipits, Dunnocks, Wrens and Yellowhammers, move in. Sometimes there are occasional pairs of Sedge Warblers and Reed Buntings which are normally associated with water. Locally, too, Hen and Montagu's Harriers, Short-eared Owls, Woodcocks and even Dartford Warblers nest among the young trees. When the trees are several years old, Blackbirds and Song Thrushes, Linnets, Greenfinches and Bullfinches, Garden Warblers and Lesser Whitethroats take over, followed later by Redpolls and Goldfinches, Blackcaps and Turtle Doves. By this stage, Tree Pipits are confined to edges and rides. Red-backed Shrikes used to nest in young conifers and some Firecrests do now in tall spruce or fir.

Caledonian forest

The remnants of the indigenous pine
forests of the Scottish Highlands are
among the most fascinating of woodland
habitats. They are often much more open
than artificially planted conifers, under-
grown with heather, cowberry and bilberry
as well as the ubiquitous bracken, and
frequently mixed with scrubby birch,
alder, rowan and juniper. This openness
is shown by such birds of rough ground
as Meadow Pipits and Whinchats.

Here there are not only Sparrowhawks,
Kestrels and Buzzards, but also Golden
Eagles and now a few Goshawks and
Ospreys, as well as Peregrines where there
are crags. Other predators include Tawny
and Long-eared Owls; Ravens are often
rather scarce away from cliffs, but there
are Carrion and Hooded Crows and many
intermediates between the two. Among
other larger birds, this is one of the best
areas to see Black Grouse displaying at
their 'lek', a most exciting spectacle for the
early riser who visits one of the traditional
sites, often in rushy areas at the edge of
pines and scrub, between March and May
(and to a lesser extent in autumn). Another
spectacular grouse is the huge Capercaillie,

reintroduced here in the 19th century,
which holds sway in the hillside woods
with its remarkable strutting display and
'cork-pulling' song. Woodcocks can be
seen and heard on their 'roding' flights at
dusk, but Nightjars have now all but
disappeared from the Highlands.

The typical small birds of coniferous
trees are common, including Goldcrests,
Chaffinches, Greenfinches, Coal Tits and,
because there are holes and crevices in the
mature trees, other tits, Redstarts and
Treecreepers. Holes are also provided by
the spread of Great Spotted Woodpeckers
up through the Highlands in the early part
of this century. The scrub among the pines
also holds Redpolls and provides song-

posts for Tree Pipits and Willow Warblers. Other warblers are rather scarce, but Wrens, Robins, Dunnocks and the commoner thrushes and finches are widespread.

But it is the specialities of these areas that the birdwatcher will particularly be looking for among the small birds. Above all, the Caledonian forest is the home of Britain's one endemic bird, the Scottish Crossbill, now regarded as a separate species distinct from both the widespread Crossbill of Europe (which breeds regularly elsewhere in Britain) and the Parrot Crossbill of Fenno-Scandia (which is a rare vagrant here): its beak is intermediate in size and, like the Parrot Crossbill, it is found in pines, and feeds almost exclusively on pine seeds, rather than spruce and larch. This is also the traditional breeding habitat of the Siskin, a finch which has now spread to conifers in other parts of Britain and Ireland over the last 150 years, and of the Crested Tit which, though widespread on the Continent, remains confined here to old pines with rank heather and decaying stumps. Finally, it is this region that some Scandinavian birds are colonising: a few Redwings, Fieldfares and possibly Bramblings breed here, as well as Wrynecks and now even Red-backed Shrikes – two species that have declined so disastrously in England.

Heaths and brecks

Heaths are flattish, sandy or gravelly areas overlying a layer of peat. Their soils are acidic, but usually much drier than moorland which they sometimes resemble. Extensive growths of heathers, gorse and broom, as well as scattered clumps of birches and pines, form a habitat that offers birds a good supply of food together with a certain amount of shelter. In the west and north, they are typically coastal, but in England they extend well inland. The Brecks are a comparable region of some thousand square kilometres in East Anglia. Also sandy and flat or undulating, they vary from calcareous grassland like that of downland to more acidic sands with cover similar to that on heaths. Depending on the vegetation, both heaths and brecks share many of the common scrub birds of lowland areas, but the larger heaths and breckland of southern and eastern England also hold certain species which are particularly characteristic.

Dartford Warblers in Britain are confined to the lowland heaths of the southernmost counties of England, notably Dorset and Hampshire, and are found typically in a mixture of heather and gorse. (These are our only truly resident warblers, apart from the newly colonising Cetti's Warblers of wetland tangles.) They share the habitat particularly with Stonechats, which otherwise have a much wider distribution in coastal scrub. Whinchats are also present, but prefer grassier areas. These southern heathlands, like downland, hold a good proportion of our rarest breeding falcon, the Hobby, and here both it and the Kestrel use the old nests of Carrion Crows. Other raptors of wooded heaths include Buzzards and Sparrowhawks, while the occasional pair of the now rare Montagu's Harrier nests on gorse-clad areas. Two other predatory species, Rough-legged Buzzards and Great Grey Shrikes, are scarce winter visitors. Red-legged Partridges, which prefer drier habitats, outnumber the Grey. During this century the spreading Curlew has colonised some heaths, while the declining and very different Stone-curlew can be found in only the sandiest and most open parts. Another decreasing species, the Nightjar, is perhaps now most typical of dry heathland with scattered trees.

Curlews, Stone-curlews and Nightjars are also typical of the Brecks. Some marginal heathland birds, such as

Lapwings and Wheatears, are commoner on the breckland grass. Two species which have declined drastically this century may be seen in these areas. The Woodlark, which used to breed in many parts of England and Wales, and also in Ireland, is now reduced to perhaps two hundred pairs, mainly in the extreme south and southwest of England and in the Brecks where it inhabits short grass with scattered trees. Similarly, the Red-backed Shrike once had a wide distribution in Britain but is now largely confined to dry heathland with thorn bushes and brambles in East Anglia. The open breckland also holds the remnants of a formerly much larger inland-nesting population of Ringed Plovers, while the pine woods of the Brecks and of the New Forest heathlands are the two well-established breeding areas of Crossbills.

Apart from these mainly scarce or local species, various other small birds can be found on heaths and brecks. Depending on the vegetation and the season, these include most of the common species of grasslands and scrub.

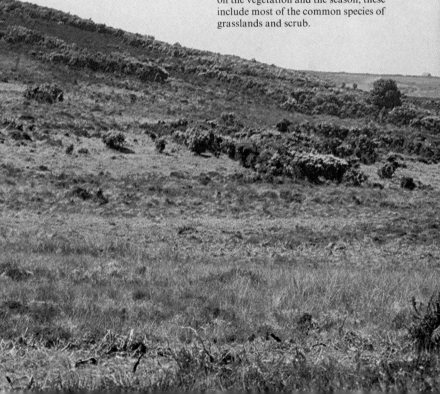

Downs and grasslands

Grasslands are found in both upland and lowland areas, and many of them overlap other broad habitat types, especially grass fields and grass moorlands. Calcareous grassland, however, is confined to the alkaline soils over limestone formations, particularly on the low undulating chalk hills of southern and eastern England from east Dorset to Yorkshire. This is the rolling 'downland' typified by the North and South Downs, Chilterns, Berkshire Downs and Salisbury Plain. Although these places are often naturally rich in plants and, for example, butterflies, they have a limited but interesting variety of birds. Sadly, the spread of cultivation and widespread use of herbicides and fertilisers have done much damage to this special habitat.

Open downland in particular holds few nesting species, some of them the same as in large grass fields. Skylarks of course are everywhere. Meadow Pipits are scarcer and patchily distributed, as are Corn Buntings which need either wires or tall plants from which to sing. Lapwings are scattered over the flat and rolling grassland, but not on the steeper slopes. Grey Partridges nest in grass tufts, and Red-legged Partridges make their scrapes in some surprisingly open places; downland corn is also a favoured habitat of Quails. Stock Doves and Little Owls are two other birds of ordinary farmland that have adapted to the open downs: scattered pairs of both nest in rabbit burrows. Wheatears, which also breed in burrows, have never been as common here as on stony uplands, grass moors and rocky islands; also, being adapted to life on short grass, they began to decrease with the decline in downland sheep grazing and, later, with the reduction in rabbits through myxomatosis, but some still persist. Apart from the brecks, this was at one time also the main habitat of Stone-curlews. Indeed, often it still is, but they need open ground, short turf and solitude: longer grass, increased cultivation and greater disturbance have reduced the total to perhaps a quarter of what it was.

The growth of low scrub, gorse and thorn enables many other birds typical of hedges, young conifer plantations and heaths to move in, including Dunnocks, Wrens, Blackbirds, Yellowhammers and Linnets; Whitethroats and Willow and Grasshopper Warblers; Stonechats or perhaps the odd pair of Whinchats; and, in taller cover, Chaffinches, Tree Pipits and Magpies. Nightjars nest on chalky patches among scrub in downland valleys. Sheltered southern slopes with thorn bushes and small trees are still favoured by Cirl Buntings and Woodlarks, both of which have greatly decreased, but Red-backed Shrikes have all but disappeared from this habitat. Clumps of trees provide nesting sites for Carrion Crows, and the Hobbies and Kestrels which use their old nests; a building may house Barn or Little Owls.

Many of the birds that feed in grass fields in winter may also be seen on the downs at other seasons, such as flocks of Lapwings, gulls, Rooks, Jackdaws and Starlings. Characteristic, too, are parties of Mistle Thrushes and Goldfinches. Migrant predators include Kestrels, Hen Harriers and, in less exposed parts, Short-eared Owls and sometimes also the odd Peregrine, Merlin or Montagu's Harrier.

Moors and mountains

The uplands of Scotland, and also of north and southwest England, Wales and various parts of Ireland, provide some of our most spectacular scenery and birds. Some species are associated with water, such as the Greylag Geese, Teal and Wigeon of moorland lochs and pools, and the Dippers and Grey Wagtails of mountain streams, but others are found among the crags and the open heather. At the top of the food chain are the predators: Buzzards, Hen Harriers, Peregrines, Merlins, Kestrels and Short-eared Owls, and, in the Scottish Highlands, one of Europe's strongest remaining stocks of

the magnificent Golden Eagle. Equally typical are the grouse, although only the widespread Red Grouse, with its characteristic *gobak-gobak* call, is found in Ireland. In Britain the Black Grouse is restricted mainly to wooded moorland edges and the Ptarmigan to the higher slopes and hill tops of Scotland.

Uplands are also the breeding places of a number of waders that we normally associate with marshes and mudflats on spring and autumn passage and in winter. There are Curlews with their ringing cries and bubbling songs, Snipe with their constant chippering calls and drumming displays, Golden Plovers and Dunlins resplendent in summer plumage and, in north Scotland, the elusive Greenshank. There are also Lapwings and Redshanks, usually on grass moors and bogs, and

Oystercatchers and Ringed Plovers, especially on grass and river shingle. In contrast, sparsely covered mountain tops are the home of another plover, the rare Dotterel, one of rather few species where the male does all the work of incubating the eggs and rearing the young. One more wader, the tittering Whimbrel, breeds on moorland in the Northern Isles, especially Shetland, sharing the habitat there with two other very local birds of Britain, the predatory and aggressive Great and Arctic Skuas. Various gulls breed locally on moors and moorland bogs, including Great and Lesser Black-backed, Herring, Common and Black-headed, although the last is mainly found near rushy pools which it sometimes shares with Common Terns. In north Scotland there are also colonies of Arctic Terns on dry moorland a kilometre or two from the sea.

Small birds are few in species, although some are very common in summer, especially Meadow Pipits (the main foster parents here for Cuckoos), Skylarks in the drier areas, and Wheatears among rocks and short turf. Stonechats need gorse or long heather, and Whinchats coarse growth in boggy places. Ring Ouzels are not uncommon on steep slopes with rocky outcrops, replacing Blackbirds and Song Thrushes which penetrate up valleys and to scrubby patches at moorland edges. Similarly, the Twite of moorland replaces the Linnet of scrub grassland. But the ubiquitous Wren will occupy a dry peat-face or any patch of rocks, and Pied Wagtails nest on crags. Rarer nesters include a few Snow Buntings on the barer mountain tops (joined by immigrants from Greenland and Scandinavia on the hills in autumn and winter) and, in the last decade, even fewer Lapland Buntings and Shore Larks.

In winter the moors become bleak and inhospitable with few birds.

Rivers and streams

Rivers and streams cut through a range of habitats and the birds associated with them to some extent reflect their surroundings. The shallow, fast-flowing, rocky streams and burns of the uplands are the special habitat of Dippers and Grey (as well as Pied) Wagtails; these also inhabit lower and slower reaches with weirs, mill-races and other artificial falls. Upland streams are the particular summer home, too, of Common Sandpipers. In contrast, lowland rivers and streams with suitable banks provide nest-sites for Kingfishers and Sand Martins, while open stretches hold many of our Mute Swans.

The bird life of rivers and streams includes a variety of waterfowl, waders, gulls and, in summer, smaller insect-eating species (although many of our commonest songsters, such as Wrens, Blackbirds and Chaffinches, often also nest in waterside tangles and trees). In particular, Grey Herons are commonly seen standing in river shallows, ready to strike at fish. Ducks, though much less numerous than on lakes and reservoirs, include Mallards everywhere. Teal nest by streams, Wigeon by moorland rivers. In the north, Goosanders breed near larger wooded rivers to a height of about 500m and Red-breasted Mergansers by both open and wooded rivers from around 300m down to the sea. Tufted Ducks and Pochards both nest by slow lowland rivers and small parties are sometimes seen on them in winter. Moorhens are widespread, but Coots are mostly seen on the slowest rivers with extensive reeds and really prefer the still waters of lakes and reservoirs. The Water Rail is a related and secretive bird of thick waterside vegetation. Among waders, both Ringed and Little Ringed Plovers are sometimes found on upland river shingle, while Oystercatchers commonly nest there as well as on adjacent fields and moorland. Lapwings, Snipe, Curlews and Redshanks also breed in water meadows and other riverside areas, along with Black-tailed Godwits and Ruffs in East Anglia. Various other waders, such as Green and Common Sandpipers, occur by rivers on passage. Gulls, especially Black-headed and Herring, are opportunist feeders over any wetland areas. Common Terns also nest on upland river islets and shingle beds.

Many insects are found by rivers and Swifts, Swallows and House Martins, as well as Sand Martins, congregate there to feed on them, as they do over lakes and reservoirs. Reed and Sedge Warblers nest in stands of waterside vegetation, where they may often find themselves fostering Cuckoos. The rare and very local Marsh Warbler typically inhabits dry osiers with nettles or meadowsweet. Other summer birds of riverside water meadows include Yellow Wagtails and often the occasional pair of Whinchats, while Pied Wagtails and Reed Buntings may be seen there the year round. Streamside birches and alders often attract Redpolls and Siskins in winter, and riverside willows are favoured as nesting places by Little Owls and Redstarts.

Lakes, reservoirs and gravel pits

Natural and man-made stretches of fresh water vary greatly in size, from flooded gravel workings and the smaller lakes or reservoirs to the vast expanse of Lough Neagh, over 250 km² in area. The variety and numbers of birds on these fresh waters depends not only on size and location, but also on depth and, above all, on the quality of the water. The acid and often deep waters of upland Wales, north Britain and northern and extreme western parts of Ireland are oligotrophic, or nutritionally poor. They have little plant and invertebrate life, and therefore little shelter and food to offer to birds. In contrast, the alkaline and often shallow waters of the lowlands are eutrophic, or rich in nutrients, supporting a mass of plants ranging from algae to reeds and a profusion of invertebrate foods.

The breeding birds of oligotrophic lakes are very few in number. They are largely fish-eaters such as Red-throated and Black-throated Divers, Red-breasted Mergansers and Goosanders. Other waterfowl may roost there, and Common Gulls and Common Terns, for example, may nest at the edges, but sometimes the only birds to be seen are a pair of Common Sandpipers on a stony shore. In spring and autumn, the scene is enlivened by a few migrant waterfowl or waders pausing for a brief rest, but in winter these lakes are largely deserted.

At the other extreme, eutrophic lowland lakes with good stands of emergent vegetation at the edges are well stocked with nesting birds. There may be Great Crested and Little Grebes; sometimes a colony of Grey Herons in the trees; a variety of waterfowl, including Mute Swans, Canada Geese, Tufted Ducks,

33

Pochards, possibly Shovelers and Teal; many Coots and Moorhens, and perhaps Water Rails; Snipe and Redshanks close by if there are marshy areas; and Reed and Sedge Warblers, and Reed Buntings. Gulls, terns and waders may turn up on passage, even Little Gulls, Black Terns and Greenshanks, as well as Green and Common Sandpipers. In winter, such lakes and reservoirs can often provide a marvellous spectacle, with any of about a dozen dabbling-ducks, diving-ducks and sawbills – Wigeon, Teal, Pochards and Tufted Ducks, but also perhaps Gadwalls,

Pintails, Shovelers, Goldeneyes, Smews and Goosanders – and rafts of Coots. There will also be grebes and gulls, perhaps Cormorants and Bewick's or Whooper Swans, possibly the odd diver.

Gravel pits also have many of the birds of eutrophic lakes, but, being open, silty, shallow and often in a wide variety of stages of flooding and plant growth, they have a character of their own. Little Ringed Plovers have spread over lowland Britain since the 1940s in this habitat, and some pits are favoured by colonies of Black-headed Gulls and Common Terns.

Marshes, fens and reedbeds

Marshes are wetlands where standing water covers just part of the surface. They tend to be eutrophic – rich in nutrients – and develop a thick growth of submerged plants and reeds, rushes, club-rushes and sweet-grass, making an attractive habitat for birds. Fens occur on peat where nutrients brought in by water from outside also promote rich vegetation.

Reeds and rushes may form narrow belts by rivers, at most 2–3 m wide and confined to sheltered corners, but in shallow lakes they are often extensive and in flooded marshes may cover many hectares. All these types of wetland hold much of interest to the birdwatcher, but the thickness of the vegetation often makes the more secretive species difficult to see.

Although it is not easy, nor desirable in the nesting season, to penetrate into reeds by wading or by boat, many of the characteristic birds can be seen feeding at the edges. Some marshes with extensive reedbeds and areas of open water, such as Minsmere (Suffolk), Stodmarsh (Kent)

and Leighton Moss (Lancashire), are reserves for several rare species, with hides from which to watch them. Conservation of such areas has had much to do with maintaining our tiny populations of Black-necked Grebes, Bitterns and Marsh Harriers, with the recovery of Bearded Tits from a handful in 1947 to about 400 pairs, with the return of Savi's Warblers since 1960 after an absence of 100 years, and with the colonisation of Cetti's Warblers since 1972.

Plenty of common birds breed in or around reedbeds. Great Crested and Little Grebes anchor their floating nests there. Gadwalls, Tufted Ducks and Pochards lay their eggs in grass or sedge tussocks. Water Rails may be heard 'sharming'. Coots and Moorhens are numerous. Among the smaller birds, the nests of Reed and Sedge Warblers attract Cuckoos. In autumn, reedbeds are roosting sites for Swallows and both martins, Yellow and Pied Wagtails, and Starlings, often in large numbers, and these in turn may draw falcons and Sparrowhawks looking for prey. In winter, Grey Herons (which sometimes nest in reeds), various ducks, Snipe and Kingfishers may be seen wading, swimming or fishing in the shallows, and many Wrens and Blue Tits make temporary homes there.

More open marshes, of which the winter-flooded Ouse Washes (on the borders of Cambridge and Norfolk) are a prize example, provide nesting places for other ducks of water meadows and muddy shallows, including Shovelers and a few Garganeys and Pintails. Among breeding waders are Snipe, Redshanks, Curlews, and now Black-tailed Godwits and a few Ruffs. Pheasants nest here in something like their original reedy habitats in Asia. Many waders arrive on passage, and large numbers of ducks and swans winter.

Estuaries and saltings

On sheltered coasts, where the action of
waves is minimal, silts settle in the
intertidal zone to form flats of mud mixed
with sand. Vast numbers of marine
invertebrates inhabit this area and at low
tide provide an enormous food resource
for waders and other shore birds. Over 30
of the estuaries and sheltered bays of
Britain and Ireland, such as Morecambe
Bay, the Wash, Solway, Ribble, Dee,
Thames, Shannon/Fergus and North Bull,
are of international importance as
wintering grounds for waders and wild-
fowl, some holding hundreds of thousands
of birds. The estuarine mudflats are often
backed by saltmarshes, or saltings, a
transitional zone between the sea and the
land, where geese, seed-eating ducks and
small numbers of waders that prefer the
greater shelter of creeks are found.

For the birdwatcher, estuaries are at
their best in winter. The commonest
waders then are Dunlins, and, more
locally, Knots, which roost and fly in huge
dense packs. There are also large
concentrations of Oystercatchers,
Lapwings and Redshanks, slightly smaller
numbers of Golden Plovers, Curlews and
Bar-tailed Godwits, and a good scattering
of Ringed and Grey Plovers, Turnstones,
Snipe, Black-tailed Godwits and
Sanderlings. Many other waders such as
Greenshanks and Spotted Redshanks also
occur on passage in autumn and spring.

The special goose of estuarine areas in
winter is the Brent, which feeds
particularly on eelgrass. Around half the
world population of the dark-bellied form
from arctic USSR winters in Britain, and
the Greenland population of the pale-
bellied race winters in Ireland. Barnacle
Geese come in thousands to the salt-

marshes and adjacent pastures of the Solway and parts of Ireland and the Hebrides. Greylag and Pink-footed Geese feed inland and roost at night on estuarine flats and sandbanks, while many White-fronted Geese winter on lowland pastures and to a lesser extent on saltings. Mute and Whooper Swans also use estuaries, but Bewick's Swans show a preference for inland waters. Among ducks, large numbers of Wigeon, Pintails and Shelducks winter on estuaries. Mallards, Teal and Shovelers are rather scarcer, but some hundreds of Pochards and Goldeneyes are found in a few places, while there are concentrations of Scaups in the Firth of Forth and of Eiders in the Firth of Tay. Long-tailed Ducks and Common and Velvet Scoters are generally farther offshore, although they gather in a few, mainly northern estuaries. Red-breasted Mergansers and, especially on the Beauly

Firth, Goosanders may also be seen.

Cormorants are often in estuaries, and there are always big concentrations of all the commoner gulls with the exception of the Kittiwake. Divers and grebes may sometimes be seen on the water, and occasional raptors, such as Peregrines and Merlins, winter here for the plentiful supply of prey available. The small birds of the saltings then are mainly Skylarks, pipits, wagtails, and Twites and other finches.

By summer, the bird life is relatively reduced. Shelducks, Mallards and Red-breasted Mergansers are often the only ducks. The main waders then are Oyster-catchers, Lapwings, Ringed Plovers and Redshanks, along with a few non-breeders of other species. Gulls and terns feed in estuaries and may be nesting nearby. Small birds include feeding pipits, wagtails and Starlings.

Sand, shingle and dunes

Compared with muddy and rocky coasts, sand and shingle are often rather barren for the birdwatcher. Beaches built up by the constant pounding of waves have a greatly restricted invertebrate fauna and so less food for birds; there is also little vegetation until marram and other grasses stabilise the dunes behind. Such beaches are found on many parts of our coastline. Some of the largest shingle areas are on the Kent and East Anglian coasts, as well as in Dorset, Wales, Cumbria and parts of Scotland. There are major dune complexes in Devon, in various sections of both the east and west coasts of Britain, and in east and south Ireland.

In summer, these habitats are essential to our five breeding species of terns – Common, Arctic, Roseate, Sandwich and Little – all of which are at risk from greatly increased human disturbance of what often used to be comparatively wild areas. The Little Tern, indeed, is almost restricted to coastal sand and shingle, and the Sandwich Tern largely to dunes and shingle, although it nests too on rocky and grassy islets like the Roseate. Herring and Lesser Black-backed Gulls also breed in these areas, notably on the dunes at Walney (Lancashire), and all the commoner gull species rest and roost on beaches. A few waders are characteristic nesters here, especially Oystercatchers, Ringed Plovers and, sometimes, Redshanks. Locally, Stone-curlews may occur on dunes and shingle, while stony islets in brackish lagoons hold many of the nests of our carefully nurtured population of Avocets. Mallards, Eiders and especially Shelducks nest in dune areas, as

well as, very locally, Pintails. A few
Merlins breed in dunes. Grey and Red-
legged Partridges, Stock Doves, Short-
eared Owls and Nightjars are also
marginal dune species. The small birds of
marram-covered dunes are mainly Skylarks, Meadow Pipits, Wheatears and
Linnets.

Exposed sand and shingle beaches are
generally poor for waders, but one species,
the Sanderling, is adept at running along
the tideline, so fast as to seem on wheels,
darting to and fro with the advancing and
retreating waves to snatch up sandhoppers; a few non-breeders stay the
summer, but most are passage and winter
visitors. Apart from Oystercatchers and
Ringed Plovers, various other waders will
sometimes feed or rest on these beaches,
often singly or in small parties, particularly
Dunlins, Curlews, Grey Plovers, Bar-
tailed Godwits and Turnstones.

In autumn, especially on the east and
south coasts, the combination of onshore
winds overnight and drizzle at dawn are
ideal conditions for seeing falls of chats,
thrushes, warblers, flycatchers and other
migrants. Many of these quickly move
inland to the nearest scrub, but often a
Bluethroat or a Redstart, or any of a
variety of warblers, will spend the day
sheltering in the marram of the dunes.

High dunes are often good places from
which to watch the passage movements
of shearwaters, skuas, terns and auks
along the sea. Sadly some of these birds,
especially Guillemots, are all too often
seen dead or dying after being fouled by
oil and swept on to beaches. In winter,
divers, grebes and sea-ducks swim offshore. Otherwise, the main inhabitants
of the open beaches then are gulls and
scavenging crows and Starlings.

40

Rocky coasts and islands

Few sights are more spectacular for the birdwatcher than thousands of seabirds wheeling around their cliff colonies in a cacophony of sound. The cliffs and rocky islands of north and west Britain, and of many parts of Ireland, hold some of the largest seabird concentrations in Europe. Most numerous and conspicuous are the stiff-winged Fulmars, the gentle-looking but noisy Kittiwakes, and the tightly packed and vociferous Guillemots, from which the crevice-nesting Razorbills have to be picked out. Cormorants and Shags are also easily seen (but often confused by the beginner) and the clown-faced Puffins stand outside their burrows among the sea-thrift on the turf-clad slopes. Herring and Lesser Black-backed Gulls circle around the upper slopes, while each headland often holds the odd pair of the more solitary Great Black-backed Gulls.

Also rather solitary, a few Black Guillemots may be found near the foot of the cliff or on the sea close by, with their bold white shoulders and bright red gapes and legs: unlike many of the seabirds, they stay all the year round. Difficult to see because they enter and leave their underground burrows only at night, are Manx Shearwaters, Storm Petrels and, on a few north and west Scottish islands, Leach's Petrels. A visit to a colony after dark when the air is full of their screaming, cackling, churring, laughing and crooning calls is an experience to remember. But most impressive of all, because of their size and gleaming whiteness, their powerful flight and spectacular plunges, must be the Gannets: over 200,000 pairs, or three-quarters of the world population, nest in just 15 colonies around our coasts.

Several birds of prey also nest on sea-cliffs, notably Peregrines, Kestrels, Buzzards, and a few of our Golden Eagles in west Scotland; attempts are now being made on Rhum, in the Inner Hebrides,

to reintroduce the White-tailed Eagle. The north and west coasts of Ireland and Scotland are the last bastions of the wild Rock Dove population, while Irish coasts are the main stronghold of the Chough. Ravens, Jackdaws and Carrion or Hooded Crows also nest on coastal crags. Closer to the water, Eiders make their downy nests among the rocks and swim sedately near the shore even in rough seas. The widespread Turnstone and the much more local Purple Sandpiper are two waders seen at their best on rocky coasts in autumn and winter; Common Sandpipers, Dunlins, Redshanks and Whimbrels feed there on passage; and Ringed Plovers often nest on rock slabs.

Although small birds are usually few around rocky shores, the ubiquitous Wren manages to make a home for itself in all but the barest cliffs, sharing the habitat with Rock Pipits and Pied Wagtails. Starlings and, more locally, Swifts and House Martins also breed on cliffs, while a few pairs of Black Redstarts annually nest there in southeast England. Wheatears are common on rocky islands, and Stonechats where there is gorse at the cliff-top. Autumn winds and drizzle can bring big falls of migrants; then thrushes and warblers may be seen looking for food in scrubby patches of vegetation.

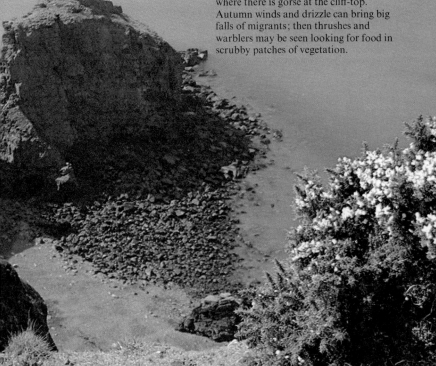

DIVERS (Gaviidae)

Red-throated Diver *Gavia stellata* 53–59
cm (*c*22 in). Smallest diver, with slender
uptilted bill, small head, thinnish neck.
Flies with fast beats of long thin wings,
usually low but also high, with sagging
neck, trailing legs, white underwings as
all divers; swims low, turns on side when
preening, dives often; takes off easily;
awkward on land, heaving jerkily with
feet. *Ad summer* Dull red throat looks
black at distance; head and sides of neck
grey, hindneck striped; upperparts
uniform slate-brown. *Ad winter* White of
lores defined above by dark grey cap;
white extends round eyes; largely white
neck looks very thin; upperparts with
small white spots (mantle paler than wing
coverts). *Juv* As ad winter, but browner
above, with fewer, larger, less white spots
(mantle often darker than coverts);
forehead darker, sides of neck speckled;
bill paler grey; moults in Dec–Jul. VOICE
Flight-cackle *kwuk-kwuk-kwuk* when
nesting; mewing wail. barking croak; song

harsh throaty cooing, rising and falling,
often in duet. HABITAT Breeds at lochs,
moor pools; winters mainly off coasts.
NEST On islets or loch-sides, or built up
in shallows, 2 eggs, mid May–mid Jul; 1
brood. FOOD Fish, also frogs, invertebrates. RANGE Breeding areas Apr–Sep;
coastal Sep–May, inc many from N
Europe, also Greenland.

Black-throated Diver *Gavia arctica* 56–69
cm (*c*24½ in). Bulkier than Red-throated,
with straight bill, heavier head; smaller
than Great Northern, with more slender
bill, thinner neck, often sloping forehead.
Wing-beats shallower, slower than Red-
throated; rises from water less easily. *Ad
summer* Black throat bordered by stripes;
grey head and hindneck; upperparts
black with 4 sets of squarish white spots;
bill black. *Ad winter* Darker than other
divers; forehead and upperparts uniform
black-brown, crown and hindneck paler;
often bold white patch on rear flanks; bill
grey. *Juv* As ad winter, but upperparts
browner with much pale scaling; bill blue-

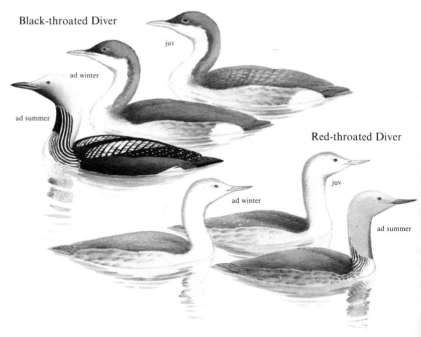

Black-throated Diver

juv

ad winter

ad summer

Red-throated Diver

juv

ad winter

ad summer

white; moults to look as ad winter Jan–Jun. VOICE Usually silent in flight; song loud rhythmic wailing *tlooeet-to-tlooeet-to-tlooeet . . .*; also short wails, croaks. HABITAT Breeds at freshwater lochs; winters off coasts. NEST On islets, 2 eggs, May–Jun; 1 brood. FOOD As Red-throated. RANGE Breeding areas Apr–Sep; coastal Sep–May, inc many from N Europe.

Great Northern Diver *Gavia immer* 69–81 cm (*c*29½ in). Bulky, with deep heavy bill, steep forehead and thick neck; usually looks much bigger than Black-throated. Powerful wing-beats slow and shallow; takes off laboriously. *Ad summer* Glossy black head and neck, striped part-collars; upperparts black with white spots, large and square on scapulars; bill black. *Ad winter* Crown/hindneck darker than mantle and pale-edged scapulars; pale eye-rings; jagged division of dark/light on neck-sides; bill grey with dark culmen. *Juv* As ad winter, but paler above and very distinctly scaled; throat and sides of neck speckled brown; bill blue-white, but

culmen dark; moults throughout 1st year. VOICE Moaning calls from autumn flocks. HABITAT Winters mainly off coasts. RANGE Winter visitor from Iceland/?Greenland, Oct–May (mid Aug–Jun); has bred NBr, at least in 1970.

COMPARE White-billed Diver (250), also swimming Cormorant (54).

Red-throated Diver	B4 W5 S5 A5

Black-throated Diver	B3 W4 S4 A4

Great Northern Diver	B0 W4 S4 A4

Great Northern Diver

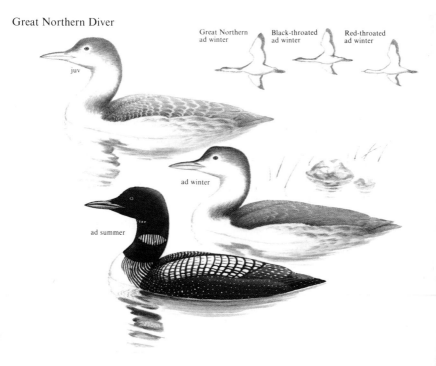

Great Northern ad winter Black-throated ad winter Red-throated ad winter

juv

ad winter

ad summer

GREBES (Podicipedidae)

Red-necked Grebe *Podiceps grisegena*
40–46 cm (*c*17 in). Stocky, with thick neck
and bulbous head, black and yellow bill;
crown down to eyes always dark; well-
defined cheeks and throat. Flight as Great
Crested, but shape less attenuated, no
white along scapulars; more secretive in
summer, usually close to cover; walks
more easily. *Ad summer* Bill black with
bright yellow base; black cap down to
brown eyes, short double crest; pale grey
cheeks and throat outlined in white;
foreneck and upper breast chestnut, flanks
mottled grey. *Ad winter* Bill greyer, with
dull yellow base; crown and upperparts
paler grey-brown, cheeks and throat white
but for grey patch just under eyes; front
and sides of neck greyish, upper breast
and flanks mottled grey. *Juv* Bill paler with
more yellow, eyes yellow; resembles ad
summer, with paler chestnut-buff
foreneck, but crown and upperparts
browner, sides of head striped blackish,
and flanks mottled paler grey-brown.

1st winter After moult in Sep–Jan, as ad
winter, but bill stays paler and eyes yellow.
VOICE Generally silent except when
breeding. HABITAT Breeds on smaller
waters with more cover than Great
Crested; winters mainly along coasts and
estuaries, rarely on lakes and reservoirs.
FOOD Insects, also small fish, molluscs,
crustaceans, worms, tadpoles. RANGE
Winter visitor from Baltic region, Oct–
Mar (Aug–Apr); since 1974 single ads
or pairs have summered, even displayed
or built nest, mainly in NBr.

Great Crested Grebe *Podiceps cristatus*
45–51 cm (*c*19 in). Large, with long-slender
neck, pinkish dagger-like bill; face and
supercilia white. Flies little, extended
neck and feet hanging lower than humped
back, showing white on forewings, secondaries and scapulars; like all grebes,
rises awkwardly, pattering along surface;
swims with body low and neck erect, or
rests with neck sunk into shoulders and
bill often buried in neck-feathers; dives
expertly; usually not shy; seldom on land,

Red-necked Grebe

juv

ad winter

ad winter

ad summer

waddling awkwardly or flopping along on breast; like all grebes, covers eggs if leaving nest, later carries chicks on back; often loosely gregarious in winter. *Ad summer* Black crown extending to double crest, chestnut and black tippets erected in complex head-waggling and other displays; white face and supercilia divided by black line from bill to red eyes; rufous tinge to sides of neck and flanks. *Ad winter* Crown grey-brown, crest smaller, no tippets, less rufous on neck and flanks; head, neck and underparts otherwise boldly white, but for dark line down hindneck, black in front of eyes, and chestnut and blackish marks on rear cheeks. *Juv* Head and neck with broken stripes of black-brown and rufous; upperparts browner, bill paler, eyes orange. *1st winter* After moult in Jul-Jan, as ad winter, but almost no crest, sides of head whiter without chestnut and blackish marks. VOICE When breeding, harsh or guttural croaks, growls, snarls, also mooing; quiet *kek* and *gung*; song barking *rah-rah-rah*; young pipe persistently.

HABITAT Breeds on lakes, reservoirs and gravel pits, locally also rivers, among reeds, sedges; winters on reservoirs, estuaries, coasts. NEST Sometimes loosely colonial; soggy heap floating among reeds or weeping branches, or built up from bottom, 3-5 eggs, Apr-Jul (Feb-Aug); 1-2 broods. FOOD Fish, also insects, crustaceans, molluscs, tadpoles, frogs. RANGE Leaves smaller lakes Aug-Feb; many along coasts Sep-Apr, inc some from Low Countries/Denmark.

COMPARE Smaller grebes (46, 250).

Red-necked Grebe — B0 W3 S2 A2 | Great Crested Grebe — B4 W5 S4 A5

Great Crested Grebe

ad winter

juv

ad winter

1st winter

ad summer

Slavonian Grebe *Podiceps auritus* 31–36 cm (*c*13 in). Small and snaky-headed, with stubby bill, flat crown, and often erect neck (*cf* Black-necked). Flies readily, showing white secondaries and forewing-wedge; not shy; often dives with forward jump; usually seen in ones and twos. *Ad summer* Head and tippets black, with golden 'horns' back from eyes; neck, upper breast and flanks chestnut. *Ad winter* Black cap (grey spot before each eye), demarcated at eye-level from white of cheeks which almost meets across nape; thin blackish hindneck. *Juv* Until moult in Oct–Jan, blacks browner, border between cap and more mottled cheeks ill-defined, flanks whiter. VOICE When nesting, nasal descending *yaaarr*; trills in duet like Little Grebe. HABITAT Breeds on lochs with sedges, mare's-tails, reeds; winters in bays, estuaries, also lakes, reservoirs. NEST Soggy floating heap anchored to vegetation, 4–5 eggs, mid May–Jul; 1–2 broods. FOOD Insects, fish, also some crustaceans, molluscs, worms. RANGE Breeding lochs Mar–Sep; winter visitor Nov–Feb (Sep–May), esp from Iceland/ Scandinavia.

Black-necked Grebe *Podiceps nigricollis* 28–33 cm (*c*12 in). Small, with thin uptilted bill, high rounded crown, and often curved neck (*cf* Slavonian). Flies little (white only on rear wings, reaching inner primaries); shy, likes cover; often skims insects off surface, usually dives without jump; gregarious in winter. *Ad summer* Head, neck and upper breast black, with golden fan behind eyes; flanks chestnut, mottled black. *Ad winter* Like Slavonian (*cf* juv), but duller cap (no grey spot) diffusely down to cheeks, dark hindneck broader. *Juv* Until moult in Aug–Dec, upperparts browner, cheeks duskier, sides of upper neck tinged buff, dusky collar above breast, flanks paler. VOICE When breeding, soft fluty *poo-ee*, harsh chatter. HABITAT Breeds on shallow lakes and meres with reeds or sedges; winters on estuaries, reservoirs, lakes. NEST Often colonial; small soggy floating heap in vegetation, 3–5 eggs, Mar–early Jul; 1–2

Slavonian Grebe

Slavonian
ad winter

Little
ad winter

Black-necked
ad winter

juv

ad winter

ad summer

broods. FOOD As Slavonian, but few fish.
RANGE Breeding areas Apr–Sep; passage/
winter visitor from Continent, Aug–May.

Little Grebe *Tachybaptus ruficollis* 25–29
cm (*c*10$\frac{1}{2}$ in). Dumpy, with blunt fluffy
brown-grey stern (can look whitish), and
short bill and neck. Flies readily (plain
wings), often dives on touch-down; swims
buoyantly; shy when nesting; perches,
walks, even runs, more easily than other
grebes; gregarious in winter. *Ad summer*
Bright yellow-green gape-patch; mainly
blackish but for chestnut panel on cheeks
and foreneck, rufous patches at sides of
rump, brown flanks. *Ad winter* Bill more
yellowish at base, but bright gape lost;
dull brown above, sandy-buff below with
greyer flanks and stern. *Juv* Stripy head;
darker above than ad winter, deeper buff
below with browner-grey flanks; much as
ad after moult in Sep–Dec. VOICE Main
breeding call high whinnying trill, often
in duet; sharp *wit wit* in alarm. HABITAT
Breeds on ponds, lakes, reservoirs, rivers,
marshes, with reeds, sedges, submerged
bushes; winters on lakes, reservoirs,
estuaries. NEST Soggy floating heap in
cover or anchored in open, 4–6 eggs,
Apr–mid Aug (late
Feb–early Sep); 2–3
broods. FOOD As
Slavonian; less fish,
more molluscs.
RANGE Disperses to
open waters Aug–
Apr; some from
Continent. COMPARE
Pied-billed Grebe
(250).

Slavonian Grebe	B2 W4 S4 A4

Black-necked Grebe	B2 W4 S4 A4

Little Grebe	B5 W5 S5 A5

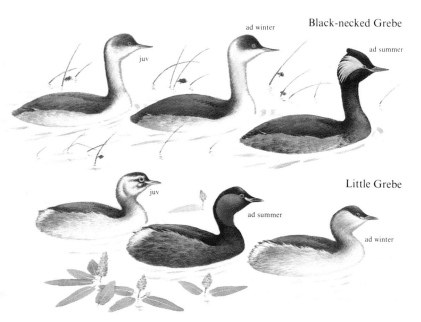

ad winter

Black-necked Grebe

juv

ad summer

Little Grebe

juv

ad summer

ad winter

GANNETS (Sulidae)

Gannet *Sula bassana* 86–96 cm (*c*36 in). Largest indigenous seabird, with long narrow wings; spear-bill (often pointing down), long body and pointed tail give distinctive 'cigar-shape'; ad mainly white with black wing-tips, imms range from blackish to pied. Flight powerful: deep beats mixed with glides on angled wings and, in stronger winds, banks and soars like shearwater, esp Cory's (50), for which imms sometimes mistaken at long range; characteristically plunges for food, wings folded back, from heights of 5–40 m; swims with head and tail up, sometimes immersing head and diving from surface; take-off laboured, flapping over water; waddles awkwardly on land; often singly at sea. *Ad* Shining white, but for creamy-yellow head and neck, black wing-tips; bill blue-white with dark lines; feet grey-black, with yellow-green lines on ♂, blue-green on ♀. *Juv* At distance, looks black with paler breast and belly, whitish V above tail: mainly black-brown speckled with white, but lower breast and belly whiter, mottled dark, most of underwings silvery-grey; bill and legs dark. *Imm* Much variation in timing, but over *c*4 years turns increasingly white: first to whiten are lower underbody and axillaries; next, head and neck, also losing dark breast-band in 2nd autumn; then upper mantle and, by 3rd autumn, upperbody, smaller wing-coverts; last dark areas are some secondaries and tail-centre. VOICE Noisy at colonies, esp barking *urrah*, groans, croaks, and yapping of young; otherwise silent unless several feeding together. HABITAT Essentially marine, breeding on rocky stacks, islands and cliffs. NEST Colonial; on cliff-ledges, island slopes, 1 egg, Apr–Sep. FOOD Fish, offal. RANGE Nesting areas Jan–Oct; some inshore all year, but others disperse, esp in 1st year, south to W Africa. COMPARE Larger shearwaters (50).

PETRELS, SHEARWATERS (Procellariidae)

Fulmar *Fulmarus glacialis* 44–50 cm (*c*18½ in). Rather gull-like petrel with stout tube-nosed bill, dumpy bull-necked body and long, centrally set, narrow wings; usually white with grey back and upperwings (but light patch on inner primaries), paler rump and tail, dark eyes emphasised by blackish patch in front, and yellow bill with green to blue-grey base. Flight powerful, with glides, neat turns and banking on stiff wings, mixed with more frequent and persistent flapping than shearwaters; often follows trawlers; swims buoyantly, but seldom dives; take-off awkward, pattering along surface; unlike shearwaters, diurnal at colonies, wheeling about cliffs, often close to people, and making several dummy runs before settling; on land shuffles on tarsi, but can stand; when alarmed, ads and young both spurt oil; abundant, gregarious. *Ad/juv* Head, neck and underparts usually white or tinged yellow, with contrasting grey upperparts (browner when worn) and dusky edges to underwings; some have pale grey crown, hindneck and often also belly; fewer show darker grey crown and pale grey breast (but almost uniform dark grey 'Blue Fulmars' mainly vagrants from Arctic.) VOICE At nest, chuckling or cackling, as well as thin whine when regurgitating food for young and squeaky growl when about to spurt oil; soft croon in flight, and feeding flocks grunt and cackle. HABITAT Oceanic, but breeds on cliffs, locally on dunes, scree, ruins, even crags several km inland. NEST Colonial; on ledges or in recesses, 1 egg, mid May–mid Sep; 1 brood. FOOD Crustaceans, cephalopods, fish, offal. RANGE Some stay inshore all year, even visiting nesting cliffs; others disperse as far as Greenland. COMPARE Larger shearwaters (50).

| Gannet | B6 W5 S6 A6 | Fulmar | B6 W5 S6 A6 |

Gannet

ad

3rd year

2nd year

1st year

juv

ad

ad

ad

Fulmar

ad/juv

grey ad/juv

ad/juv

ad/juv

SHEARWATERS (Procellariidae)

Cory's Shearwater *Calonectris diomedea*
43–48 cm (*c*18 in). Heavy and big-headed,
with thick pale bill, and long, comparatively broad wings; brown above,
white below, with distinctive greyish hood
(*cf* Great Shearwater). Flight not unlike
Fulmar (48) but glides and banks on more
bowed wings; in light winds, alternates
glides with several deep, slow, loose flaps;
in rough weather, soars as Gannet (48) or
towers; may swim in rafts; feeds at surface or plunges. *Ad/juv* Bill yellow; head
and hindneck grey-brown merging into
white of throat, no pale collar; rest of
upperbody brown with, in new plumage,
distinct grey feather-fringes and whitish-
tipped tail-coverts sometimes forming
pale horseshoe (*cf* Great); wings and tail
dark brown; underparts all white, but for
grey-brown or dark wing-border, faint
grey mottling on lower·flanks. VOICE Silent
at sea. HABITAT Oceanic, occasional
inshore. FOOD Fish, cephalopods,
crustaceans, offal from fishing boats.
RANGE Scarce visitor from Mediterranean/
Cent Atlantic, Jul–Sep (Apr–Nov); sometimes in numbers (17,000+ in 1980 was
exceptional and 10 times previous total).

Great Shearwater *Puffinus gravis* 42–49 cm
(*c*18 in). Narrow-headed with slender dark
bill and moderately long wings; brown
above, with well-defined dark cap, and
white below, boldly marked with dark
brown on underwings (*cf* Cory's Shearwater). Flight more like Manx Shearwater
(52) than Cory's, gliding and banking
mixed with rapid beats of straight, stiff
wings; gregarious and often swimming in
large rafts; feeds both at surface and by
plunging. *Ad/juv* Bill blackish; cap black-
brown, contrasting with white of throat
and pale greyish collar; upperbody brown
to grey-brown with distinct light feather-
fringes and white-tipped tail-coverts
usually forming pale horseshoe; wings
darker than back, and primaries and tail
dark brown; underwings white, boldly
blotched and streaked dark brown and
with darker wing-border than Cory's;
underbody white, but grey-brown patch on

belly (often obscure), smaller patches at
chest-sides, and brown-spotted flanks and
undertail-coverts. VOICE Sometimes
raucous squawks from feeding flocks.
HABITAT Oceanic. FOOD Fish, cephalopods,
offal from fishing boats. RANGE Annual
visitor from S Atlantic, Jul–Oct (Mar–
Nov), rare winter.

Sooty Shearwater *Puffinus griseus* 39–44
cm (*c*16½ in). Heavy-bodied but with thin
head and long slender bill; narrow wings
appear set far back; all dark but for pale
strip along underwings (*cf* dark Balearic
Shearwater, 50, which is smaller, slimmer,
shorter-winged). Flight usually direct and
powerful, more 'mechanical' than Manx
(52), with more backswept wing-beats;
swims readily; feeds at surface by
plunging; usually singly or in small parties.
Ad/juv Wholly sooty-brown above, but
for paler tinge to scapulars and wing-
coverts in some lights; greyer-brown
below, not quite so dark, offset by whitish
chin, greyer flight-feathers and esp pale
wing-coverts which catch the sun at long
range in banking flight; bill blackish.
VOICE Silent at sea. HABITAT Oceanic,
sometimes inshore. FOOD Cephalopods,
crustaceans, fish. RANGE Annual visitor
from S oceans,
Aug–Sep (Jul–Oct),
rare rest of year.

COMPARE Fulmar
and imm Gannet
(48), Manx Shear-
water (52), Little
Shearwater (252).

Cory's Shearwater — B0 W0 S1 A3

Great Shearwater — B0 W0 S0 A4

Sooty Shearwater — B0 W0 S2 A5

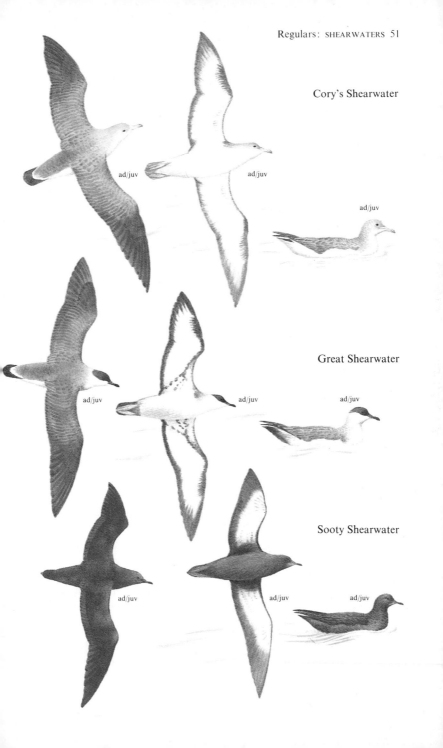

Cory's Shearwater

ad/juv

ad/juv

ad/juv

Great Shearwater

ad/juv

ad/juv

ad/juv

Sooty Shearwater

ad/juv

ad/juv

ad/juv

Manx Shearwater *Puffinus puffinus* 30–38 cm (*c*14 in). Medium-sized shearwater (but smaller runts occur), with a smallish head, long thin bill; black and white (but note that Balearic race all browner). Banks on stiff wings, now looking black, now white, with periodic rapid beats; often in flocks, at distance like lines of wheeling black or white crosses; swims readily and feeds also by hovering, with paddling feet, or plunging; shuffles awkwardly on land. *Ad/juv (P.p. puffinus)* Black above, extending down under eyes; white below but for dark wing-borders, mottling on sides of neck, breast, flanks and axillaries. *Balearic Shearwater (P.p. mauretanicus)* Dark brown above; tinged grey-brown below, sometimes entirely, but often centre of body and underwings whitish; looks all-dark in poor light (*cf* Sooty Shearwater, 50). VOICE Silent at sea; raucous caws, weird croons and screams at night at colonies. HABITAT Breeds on turf-topped islands, headlands, also scree-slopes; otherwise oceanic. NEST Colonial; in burrows, 1 egg, May–Sep; 1 brood. FOOD Fish, also cephalopods, crustaceans, offal. RANGE Breeding areas Feb–Oct, otherwise at sea ranging to S America; Balearic Shearwater scarce visitor, Jun–Oct (Mar–Jan), off Channel coast and rarer north to Scotland. COMPARE Other shearwaters (50, 252).

STORM-PETRELS (Hydrobatidae)

Storm Petrel *Hydrobates pelagicus* 14–16 cm (*c*6 in). Small, shortish-winged; feet do not project beyond squarish tail; black with white rump, band on underwings. Bat-like fluttering and short glides; patters on surface, wings raised; follows ships, to and fro across wake; sometimes settles on sea; flutters on land, or shuffles on tarsi. *Ad/juv* Sooty, but for white rump curving down to lower flanks, variable whitish band on underwings and, in new plumage, thin whitish line on upperwings (broader on juv). VOICE Silent at sea; *turr-chik*, *wik-wik-wik* and *pee-pee-pee* at night at colonies; sustained purring on nest ends in hiccup. HABITAT Breeds on rocky or turfy islands and headlands; otherwise

oceanic. NEST Colonial; under boulders, in rock-crevices, stone walls or burrows. 1 egg, Jun–mid Oct; 1 brood. FOOD Plankton, tiny fish, offal scraps. RANGE Breeding areas Apr–Oct; rarely storm-driven inshore or inland in autumn or spring; otherwise at sea, ranging south to S Africa.

Leach's Petrel *Oceanodroma leucorhoa* 19–22 cm (*c*8 in). Larger, more attenuated than Storm Petrel, with longer wings and forked tail; also browner, with less defined rump, pale bar on upperwings only. Flight buoyant, bounding with sudden direction changes, now gliding and banking, now hovering, now flapping with deep beats; glides with wings arched in flattened M; patters on surface, wings slightly raised; seldom follows ships. *Ad/juv* Dark brown, but for white rump bisected by faint grey strip, pale bar on upperwings. VOICE Usually silent at sea; chatters and screeches at night at colonies; churrs on nest, interspersed with indrawn *whee* or chatter. HABITAT Breeds on turfy islands; otherwise oceanic. NEST Colonial; in burrows or under boulders, 1 egg, Jun–mid Oct; 1 brood. FOOD As Storm Petrel. RANGE Breeding areas Apr–Nov; rarely storm-driven inshore in numbers in autumn; otherwise at sea, ranging south to S Africa.

COMPARE Vagrant petrels (252).

Manx Shearwater

puffinus ad/juv

puffinus ad/juv

puffinus ad/juv

mauretanicus ad/juv

mauretanicus ad/juv

mauretanicus ad/juv

Storm Petrel

ad/juv

ad/juv

underwing variations

Leach's Petrel

ad/juv

ad/juv

CORMORANTS (Phalacrocoracidae)

Shag *Phalacrocorax aristotelis* 72–80 cm
(*c*30 in). Smaller, slighter than Cormorant,
with slender bill, steeper forehead and
thinner neck; ad all dark and imms also
more uniformly brown on underparts, with
less bare facial skin than Cormorant.
Flight and behaviour as Cormorant, but
wing-beats faster, glides more, flies high
less often; dives with more marked
forward spring; mainly on or near rocks.
Ad summer Glossy green-black; upcurved
crest in spring; mantle, scapulars and
wing-coverts purplish and scaled black;
bill black with elongated yellow gape-
patch, eyes green. *Ad winter* Duller, less
glossy, with paler, mottled throat; no
crest, less gape-patch. *Juv* Brown above
with only faint gloss, mantle and scapulars
scaled darker; buff-tipped wing-coverts
tend to form pale wing-patches (*cf* juv
Cormorant); underparts buff-brown, typically more uniform than Cormorant (esp
breast), but chin white; bill pink-brown
eyes yellow-white. *1st year* Slow moult to

glossier upperparts scaled with black as
ad, black-brown throat and foreneck with
paler speckling, and darker brown underparts. *2nd year* As ad winter above, but
dark brown below, only speckled, glossy
green down to breast. VOICE At nest, main
sound throat-clicking; ♂ also grunts, ♀
hisses. HABITAT Rocky coasts, islands.
NEST Colonial; on rock ledges, often in
sea-caves, or under boulders, 3 eggs, mid
Mar–Aug; 1 brood. FOOD Fish, some
crustaceans. RANGE Disperses Sep–Mar;
some, esp 1st year, cross to coasts between
Norway and Biscay, few reach SBr from
NW France; prolonged onshore winds
cause food shortages and so movements to
flat coasts or inland (esp imms).

Cormorant *Phalacrocorax carbo* 84–98 cm
(*c*36 in). Long-necked with heavy bill
(but thin as Shag on some juvs); dark,
but ad has white on face (also on thighs
in summer) and imms often whitish below;
face always shows obvious bare yellow
skin. Flight goose-like, with neck
extended in kink, but primaries separated

Shag

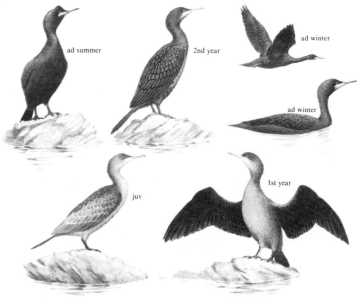

ad summer

2nd year

ad winter

ad winter

juv

1st year

on downstroke of measured beats; sometimes glides; usually low over water, but often at some height, when flocks may be in echelon; swims low in water, resembling diver (42), but bill more raised, neck more erect; dives from surface, swims underwater; take-off laboured, with much flapping; rests on rocks, banks, posts or trees, often with wings hanging open; on land, waddles awkwardly. *Ad summer* Head and body glossy blue-black, but for white cheeks, throat and thigh-patch; scapulars and wing-coverts bronze, scaled black; bill grey and yellow, eyes green; in spring, long white feathers on crown and upper neck, often few and soon wearing off, but sometimes over most of head like Continental race (*P.c. sinensis*). *Ad winter* Less glossy, white of cheeks and throat mottled brown, no white on thighs. *Juv* Mainly dark brown above, flecked blue-black; bronzy wing-coverts also look dark (*cf* juv Shag); variable below from sooty with light spots to, more usually, white on central throat, breast and belly; bill mainly yellow, eyes grey-brown. *1st year*

As juv, but glossier above, often whiter below. *2nd year* As ad winter, but less glossy, variously mottled whitish below. VOICE When nesting, variety of guttural croaks. HABITAT Breeds mainly on sea-cliffs, rocky islets, locally by fresh water (esp Ir); winters on all coasts, estuaries, tidal rivers, large lakes, reservoirs. NEST Colonial; on cliffs or rocks, or usually dead trees by fresh water, 3–4 eggs, end Mar–Aug; 1 brood. FOOD Fish. RANGE Disperses to all coasts Sep–Mar, locally inland, some south to Iberia; some immigrants from Low Countries/Denmark.

Cormorant

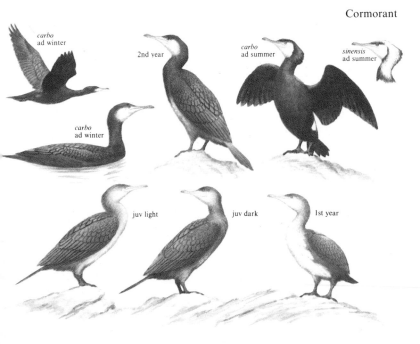

BITTERNS, HERONS (Ardeidae)

Bittern *Botaurus stellaris* 70–80 cm (*c*30 in). Stocky, thick-necked; buff, but more rufous on flight-feathers, all marked with black. Flight owl-like; very skulking and usually crepuscular; walks deliberately with lowered head and hunched shoulders, or clambers in reeds; if alarmed, stretches neck, points bill up, and sways with the reeds, eyes swivelled forward. *Ad* Golden-brown and buff, mottled, barred and striped with blackish and brown; black crown and moustaches; bill yellowish, legs green. *Juv* Paler, with browner crown, moustaches and breast-stripes; as ad after moult in Jul–Nov. VOICE Harsh *kau-kau* in flight; ♂ foghorn-like boom *upwoomp* in spring audible for 2–5 km. HABITAT Large reedbeds; reedy patches by lakes or rivers in winter. NEST In old reeds, 4–6 eggs, Apr–Jul; 1 brood. FOOD Fish, frogs, insects. RANGE Some winter dispersal and immigration from Continent, Nov–Feb (Aug–Apr). COMPARE American Bittern, imm Night Heron (254).

Grey Heron *Ardea cinerea* 90–100 cm (*c*37 in). Tall, with heavy bill, long neck and legs; grey and white marked with black. Flight slow, with deep flaps of bowed wings, neck retracted in bulge and legs extended; walks deliberately, often stands motionless in or near water, with neck erect or hunched; not shy. *Ad* Blue-grey upperbody, contrasting white head and neck to belly, with black crest and markings; yellow bill and brown legs turn orange or red in spring. *Juv* More compact; generally dark grey (some mainly brownish), inc top of head, with little white on face, foreneck and underbody, and lacking clear black marks; bill browner, legs dark grey. *1st year* After moult in Sep–Feb, bluer-grey above (inc forehead and crown), whiter cheeks and underbody, some black on foreneck, slight crest. *2nd–3rd year* Variable: more as ad, but duller, greyer, with mainly grey forehead and crown; black crest and markings, pale neck and bill/leg colours assumed gradually. VOICE Harsh *frarnk* in flight; much noise and bill-snapping at

Bittern

Spoonbill

juv

ad

ad

ad

ad winter

ad winter

ad summer

juv

nest. HABITAT Rivers, lakes, marshes, estuaries; nests may be far from water. NEST Colonial; in trees, locally in bushes, reeds, long heather or on cliff-ledges or rocks, 3–5 eggs, Feb–Aug; 1–2 broods. FOOD Fish, frogs, voles, insects. RANGE Much post-breeding dispersal, also immigration from Norway/Low Countries, Aug–Apr. COMPARE Brown juv with Purple Heron (256); albinos stockier than Great White Egret (256), with less snaky neck.

IBISES, SPOONBILLS (Threskiornithidae)

Spoonbill *Platalea leucorodia* 80–90 cm (*c*34 in). White, heron-like, with unmistakable spatulate bill, long neck and legs. Flies slowly, also glides, with sagging neck and trailing legs; sweeps bill-tip from side to side in shallows. *Ad summer* White with loose crest, yellowish gorget; yellow-tipped blackish bill, bare yellow throat, black legs. *Ad winter* No crest or gorget. *Juv* As ad winter, but black tips to primaries; pink bill, throat and legs. *1st year* Bill mainly yellow with blackish base;

legs olive-grey, then slate; but no crest or gorget, some black on wing-tips. VOICE Silent. HABITAT Marshes, estuaries. FOOD Insects, fish, crustaceans, molluscs. RANGE Scarce visitor from Netherlands, all months, esp May–Jul in E Anglia, Sep–Mar elsewhere; bred in Br to *c*1650. COMPARE Egrets (256), swans (58).

Bittern B2 W3 S3 A3

Grey Heron B5 W5 S5 A5

Spoonbill B0 W1 S2 A2

Grey Heron

imm   ad spring   ad   brown juv   grey juv   ad

SWANS, GEESE, DUCKS (Anatidae)

Mute Swan *Cygnus olor* 145–160 cm (*c*60 in). Very large, with rounded head, curved neck, longish tail, wings often arched; orange bill has black base and knob. Loud rhythmic throbbing of slow powerful wing-beats; swims with bill slanted downwards; immerses head and neck to feed, or up-ends; waddles clumsily on land; takes off with laboured flaps, pattering feet; often gregarious; not shy. *Ad* All white, some stained rusty on head or belly by ferrous water; bill pink to red-orange, with black knob (larger on ♂ in spring), basal triangle and edges; legs black (pink or grey on 'Polish' variety). *Juv* Unevenly dingy grey-brown and whitish ('Polish' all white); bill grey with black base, no knob. *1st year* Slowly whitens, but juv wings and tail kept until Jun–Aug; bill turns pink, then dull orange, grows knob. *2nd winter* Until Jan or later, some show brown spots and shaft-streaks on head, wings, rump. VOICE Snorts and hisses near nest. HABITAT Any fresh or salt water from rivers and lakes to marshes, estuaries, bays; also fields nearby. NEST By water on banks, islets, marshes, or among reeds, 2–9 eggs, end Mar–Jun; 1 brood. FOOD Water-plants; also grazes on land. RANGE Resident, but much local movement.

Bewick's Swan *Cygnus columbianus* 116–128 cm (*c*48 in). Resembles Whooper Swan, but smaller, stockier, with shorter and thicker neck, more rounded head, slightly concave culmen and truncated yellow base to bill. Flight more goose-like, with faster beats; swims and walks easily with neck less stiffly erect; equally gregarious; less shy. *Ad* All white, but some stained rusty (*cf* Mute); bill black with yellow base rounded, jagged or squared at front behind nostrils. *Juv* Slightly paler and greyer above than Whooper, with browner head; bill darker pink towards tip. *1st–2nd winter* Changes as Whooper, but body whitens more quickly. VOICE Repeated honking, sharper, more abrupt than Whooper, more baying in chorus; herds produce musical babble.

Mute Swan

ad

♂ ♀

juv

juv 'Polish'

1st winter

HABITAT Floods and lakes, adjacent fields.
FOOD As Whooper; digs for roots. RANGE
Winter visitor from N Russia/NW Siberia,
Nov–Mar.

Whooper Swan *Cygnus cygnus* 145–160
cm (*c*60 in). Size of Mute Swan, but
distinguished by long flat profile of head
and stiffly erect neck; wings not arched,
tail short; bill black with pointed yellow
base. Wings make only swishing noise in
flight; swims with neck straight, bill
horizontal; feeds as Mute, but forages
more on land, walking easily with neck
straight or kinked back; highly gregarious;
wary. *Ad* All white, but often stained rusty
(*cf* Mute); bill black with yellow base
extending in wedge usually to below or
beyond nostrils. *Juv* Brown-grey and
whitish; bill dirty pink with dark tip. *1st
year* Body whitens somewhat in Jan–Mar;
bill turns black at tip, whiter and then
yellowish at base, developing ad pattern.
2nd winter Usually some brown feathers
on head or wings, dark shaft-streaks on
scapulars. VOICE Loud *whoop-whoop*,

trumpet-like in flock. HABITAT Winters on
bays, estuaries, floods, large lakes,
adjacent fields. NEST On loch banks or
islets, marsh hummocks, 3–5 eggs,
mid May–Jun; 1
brood. FOOD Water-
plants, also grass,
grain, potatoes.
RANGE Winter
visitor from Iceland/
?N Eurasia, Oct–
Apr; few summer
in NBr/Ir.

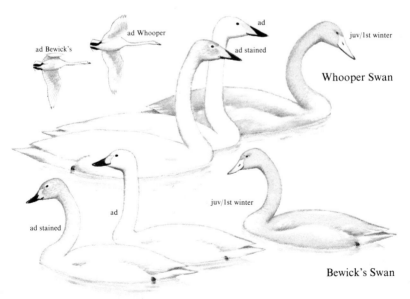

Whooper Swan

Bewick's Swan

Bean Goose *Anser fabalis* 71–89 cm (28–35 in). Larger, taller, longer-necked than Pink-footed, slimmer than Greylag; brown with dark head/neck, longish black and orange bill, orange legs; in flight, all dark (forewings hardly paler) with long head, thin neck. Actions much as Greylag; often among other geese; shyer than Pink-footed, feeds more slowly, seldom on stubble. *Ad W race (A.f. fabalis)* Head and neck dark brown, blacker on forehead, but some show white by base of bill (*cf* White-fronted, 62); otherwise, dull brown above with bold pale bars, and buff-brown below with obscurely banded darker flanks and belly; bill orange with black nail, variable black at base. *Juv/1st winter* Duller with less clear pattern on back/flanks, grey-orange on bill/legs; as ad with moult in Oct–Apr. *Ad W tundra race (A.f. rossicus)* Smaller, bill and neck shorter, forehead steeper; bill black with narrow orange band. VOICE Not noisy: *ung-unk* or *ow-ow*, lower and more braying than Pink-footed. HABITAT Winters in wet pastures. FOOD Grass, grain, crops. RANGE Scarce winter visitor from N Europe, end Dec–Mar (Oct–Apr).

Pink-footed Goose *Anser brachyrhynchus* 61–76 cm (24–30 in). Compact, with round head and short neck; pinkish-brown with dark head/neck, short blackish and pink bill, and pink legs; forewings ash-grey in flight. Flight faster than Greylag, and more buoyant and tumbling; walks/feeds much more quickly; often large flocks. *Ad* Head and upper neck dark brown, but some show white by base of bill (*cf* White-fronted, 62); otherwise, pinkish-grey above with pale bars, and pinkish-brown below with obscurely banded darker flanks and belly; bill pink with black nail, variable blackish at base, legs pink. *Juv/1st winter* Darker, browner, with less clear pattern on back; as ad with moult in Oct–Feb. VOICE High yelp *wink-wink*, cackling *ang-ang-ank*. HABITAT Winters on stubble, pastures, crops, locally saltmarshes, roosting on lakes, estuaries, sand-banks. FOOD Grass, grain, cereals, potatoes. RANGE Winter visitor from esp Iceland/Greenland, mid Sep–May.

Greylag Goose *Anser anser* 76–89 cm (30–35 in). Bulky, with big head and thick neck; all brown-grey with triangular orange bill, orange eye-rings and pink legs; forewings bold blue-grey in flight. Flight direct, strong, fast, with glides; flocks in Vs or lines, at times plunging or banking; takes off with short run, or flapping and pattering on water; planes down to land, braking with wings turned forward and tail spread, dropping with rotary flutter; swims well; slow rolling walk; wary. *Ad W race (A.a. anser)* Head to breast buff-grey with indented lines on neck-sides; brown-grey above with pale bars, flanks and belly grey with blackish marks; bill orange with pink tinge behind white tip. *Juv/1st winter* Pattern on back and flanks less clear, no belly marks, legs dull pink; as ad in course of moult in Sep–Jan. *Ad E race (A.a. rubrirostris)* Slightly larger, paler; longer bill all pink but for white nail. VOICE Like farmyard goose: main flight-call loud, deep, sonorous, cackling *aahng-ung-ung*. HABITAT Boggy moorland lochs, heathery coastal islets in NBr (also feral on lakes, gravel pits); winters as Pink-footed, but more on flooded grassland. NEST Among heather or rushes near water, 4–6 eggs, mid Apr–May; 1 brood. FOOD Green plants in summer; grass, grain and roots in winter. RANGE Most breeders sedentary; winter visitor from esp Iceland, mid Oct–mid Apr; E race vagrant.

Bean Goose

B0 W2 S0 A0

Pink-footed Goose

B0 W5 S5 A5

Greylag Goose

B4 W5 S5 A5

Bean Goose

fabalis ad   *rossicus* ad   *fabalis* ad

fabalis ad

juv

Pink-footed Goose

juv   ad   ad   ad

Greylag Goose

anser ad

juv   *anser* ad   *rubirostris* ad

White-fronted Goose *Anser albifrons* 65–76 cm (26–30 in). Smaller/slimmer than Greylag (60), with squarer head, deep chest, longish pink or yellow bill, orange legs; grey-brown, ad with white face and black-barred belly; in flight, mainly dark (no contrasting forewings) and not unlike Bean Goose (60) when patterns of face and belly not visible, although head and neck shorter, wings longer/narrower. Actions as Greylag, but wing-beats faster, more agile when taking off or in flight, able to rise or turn more sharply than other grey geese; often large flocks, tending to bunch rather than straggle in lines. *Ad Eurasian race (A.a. albifrons)* White around base of bill (rarely extending to forecrown), bordered blackish; otherwise, grey-brown above with pale bars on back (less contrasting than on Bean); buff-brown chest in contrast to darker grey-brown flanks and belly with variable bold black bars or patches; bill pink, but tinged yellow behind white nail. *Juv/1st winter* Forehead blackish, no black bars below; browner and more mottled, with indistinct pale bars on back, and duller bill and legs, not unlike Greylag; as ad in course of moult in Nov–Mar. *Ad Greenland race (A.a. flavirostris)* Slightly larger and darker, more olive-brown than Eurasian race, with less white on forehead, less contrasting chest, usually more black patches below; bill longer, heavier, orange-yellow. *Juv/1st winter* Darker than juv Eurasian race, more olive-brown above; bill dull orange-yellow. VOICE Musical *kow-yow* very dog-like in flock, also loud buzzing and, in flight, high laughing *lyo-lyok*. HABITAT Wet grassland, saltmarshes, peat bogs and fields, roosting on estuaries, floods. FOOD Grasses, clover, grain, winter wheat, potatoes. RANGE Winter visitor from arctic Russia/Greenland: Eurasian race mainly Dec–mid Mar, esp England/Wales; Greenland race mainly mid Oct–Apr, esp Ir, also W Scotland/W Wales. COMPARE Lesser White-fronted Goose (258).

Snow Goose *Anser caerulescens* 64–79 cm (25–31 in). Medium to large, with stout bill, oval head: either all white with black wing-tips, or mainly blue-grey with white head. Actions as Greylag (60); agile on ground and in air; often with other geese. *Ad Lesser race (A.c. caerulescens)* Either all white except black primaries, blue-grey primary coverts and often orange-stained head; or ('Blue Goose') dusky blue-grey above and grey-brown below, with white head/upper neck, bold white-edged blackish elongated scapulars and tertials, and white undertail-coverts, axillaries and often belly; intermediates between these phases vary, but often much white below; bill always red with black cutting edges/white tip, legs red-pink. *Ad Greater race (A.c. atlanticus)* As white Lesser, but larger, stockier, with longer and heavier bill, thicker neck, longer legs. *Juv/1st winter (except blue Lesser)* Mainly grey-brown above, with paler grey-white forehead, cheeks and underparts; dark line through eyes, mottled back and coverts, patterned scapulars, black primaries; bill and legs dark grey; as ad in course of moult in Oct–Mar. *Juv/1st winter (blue Lesser)* Much as ad but head and neck slate-brown; browner above, with shorter and less contrasted scapulars and tertials, and paler below; head mottled white cNov–Feb. VOICE Harsh abrupt *kaah.* HABITAT Marshes, wet grassland, stubble, roosting on water. FOOD Grasses, winter wheat, water-plants, grain. RANGE Scarce migrant from arctic America/NW Greenland, mainly Oct–Mar, esp Ir/NBr, but position confused by escapes from captivity (wild birds often with Greenland White-fronted). NOTE **Ross's Goose** *A. rossii* sometimes escapes too: similar to white Snow, but smaller with rounder head, no black on tiny bill.

White-fronted Goose

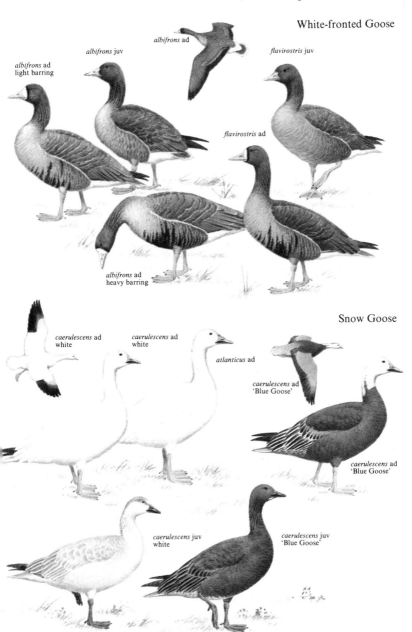

albifrons ad

albifrons juv

albifrons ad
light barring

flavirostris juv

flavirostris ad

albifrons ad
heavy barring

Snow Goose

caerulescens ad
white

caerulescens ad
white

atlanticus ad

caerulescens ad
'Blue Goose'

caerulescens ad
'Blue Goose'

caerulescens juv
white

caerulescens juv
'Blue Goose'

Canada Goose *Branta canadensis* 55–110 cm, but most in Br/Ir *c*90–100 cm (*c*36–40 in). Usually big and long-necked; grey-brown with black head/neck, whitish chest and white 'throat-strap'. Actions much as Greylag (60); dips head and up-ends; not shy. *Ad* Head/neck glossy black; buff-white tips on upperparts and flanks form bars. *Juv/1st winter* Head/neck duller brown-black, throat-strap tinged brown till early autumn, bars on upperparts/flanks less even; as ad in course of moult from autumn on. *Vagrant races* Probably *B.c. hutchinsii* (small, pale) and *B.c. parvipes* (medium, pale) and perhaps *B.c. minima* (small, dark) and *B.c. interior* (large, darkish): size, colour and proportions of bill, neck and legs vary between *c*10 N American races. VOICE Trumpeting flight-call *wah-onk* rises on 2nd syllable. HABITAT Lakes, gravel pits, rivers, marshes, farmland nearby; also certain estuaries. NEST On lake islets or marsh hummocks, 5–7 eggs, end Mar–May; 1 brood. FOOD Grass, water-plants, clover, cereals, grain. RANGE Introduced in 17th century; some moult-migration and local dispersal; small vagrants from N America with Greenland White-fronted or Barnacle Geese in Ir and W Scotland most winters.

Barnacle Goose *Branta leucopsis* 58–69 cm (23–27 in). Usually larger than Brent, with longer neck and small bill; black, grey and white, with creamy face and black crown, neck and breast; wings show grey in flight. Actions as other geese, but in general less wary; more terrestrial than Brent. *Ad* Face white or creamy, black from bill to or through eyes; crown to breast black, upperparts black to blue-grey with broad white-edged black bars, flanks delicately barred greyish-white. *Juv/1st winter* Face tinged grey, blacks browner, wings duller with buff bars, flanks pale grey-brown; more as ad in course of moult in *c*Oct–Mar, but wings with buff bars till 2nd autumn. VOICE Shrill fast barks like yapping dog; muffled growls when feeding. HABITAT Winters on coastal machair, pastures, marshes. FOOD Grass, clover, rush or sedge seeds. RANGE Winter

visitor from NE Greenland/Spitsbergen (few USSR), end Sep–mid May.

Brent Goose *Branta bernicla* 56–61 cm 22–24 in). Small, stocky, with short neck and legs, longish wings; dark, with black head to breast, whitish neck-patches, white stern accentuated by tiny black tail. Fast wing-beats; flocks fly in undulating lines; swims on sea, stern high, also up-ends; walks daintily; seldom with other geese. *Ad Dark-bellied race (B.b. bernicla)* Ragged white neck-patches; little contrast between black of head to breast and grey-black upperparts or slate-grey underbody, but whitish barring on flanks. *Ad Pale-bellied race (B.b. hrota)* Underbody much paler, upperparts browner. *Ad E Siberian/NW American race (B.b. nigricans)* Broader white neck-patches almost join; very dark with more contrasted whitish flanks. *Juv/1st winter* Head to breast browner, no contrast on flanks, no neck-patches at first, but pale lines on wings; 2 main races often similar below, but still distinct above; as ads with moult in Oct–Feb, but lines on wings till 2nd autumn. VOICE Guttural *krrook*, clamour in flocks. HABITAT Mudflats and sea, locally on adjacent grass/cereals. FOOD Eelgrass, green algae, salt-marsh plants. RANGE Winter visitor: Dark-bellied from USSR, esp Nov–Mar, E/SBr; Pale-bellied from Greenland/Spitsbergen, esp Oct–Apr, Ir and NE England; *nigricans* vagrant.

Canada Goose B5 W5 S5 A5

Barnacle Goose B0 W5 S5 A5

Brent Goose B0 W5 S5 A5

Canada Goose

parvipes ad

ad

ad

juv

hutchinsii ad

minima ad

minima ad

Barnacle Goose

ad

ad

ad

juv

Brent Goose

bernicla
1st winter

bernicla ad

bernicla ad

hrota juv

nigricans ad

hrota ad

Egyptian Goose *Alopochen aegyptiacus* 66–72 cm (*c*27 in). Stout, heavy-billed, long-legged sheldgoose; mainly rusty or olive-grey above, with paler head and underparts, chestnut 'goggles', collar and breast-patch, and bold white forewings above and below in flight. Flight fast and goose-like on broad wings; stands upright and spends much time on land, also perching on trees, but swims readily, stern high, and even dives; usually in pairs or family parties; often somewhat wary. *Ad* Proportions of red-brown and grey vary: darkest (esp in fresh plumage) show much chestnut at base of bill, round eyes, down hindneck, on collar and in patch on breast, with mantle and scapulars rusty-brown; palest (esp in worn plumage) have less or almost no chestnut on head, narrower collar and smaller or no breast-patch, and brown to olive-grey mantle and scapulars; rump and tail black; white wing-coverts (partly hidden at rest) contrast with black primaries and metallic-green or purple secondaries in flight; bill largely pink, legs pink to purplish-pink. *Juv/1st winter* Like dull ad without chestnut on head, neck and breast; wing-patches mainly pale grey-brown; bill and legs yellowish-grey; as ad with moult in Aug–Dec. VOICE Often silent; breeding ♂ loud hoarse wheezing or chuffing; ♀ cackles harshly; both hiss. HABITAT Lakes, pools and adjacent pastures, parks and wet open woodland. NEST In thick cover or in holes in ground or in trees, 8–9 eggs, late Mar–early May; 1 brood. FOOD Grass, plant leaves. RANGE Introduced from Africa in 18th century. COMPARE Ruddy Shelduck in flight (258).

Shelduck *Tadorna tadorna* 58–64 cm (*c*24 in). Long-headed, rather goose-like duck; mainly white with bold contrasting areas of black, dark green and chestnut. Flight slower and steadier than typical ducks, parties tend to form Vs or lines; walks and runs easily; spends much time on mud or sand, but swims well, though ads rarely dive; usually in pairs or parties. *Ad ♂* White with greenish-black head, chestnut body-band, black outer scapulars, primaries and tail-end, green-glossed

Egyptian Goose

ad

juv

grey ad

juv

red-brown ad

secondaries, chestnut tertials and blackish belly-stripe; bill pink-red, becoming bright red with prominent knob in spring, legs reddish-pink. *Ad* ♀ As ♂, but head duller with, when worn, some white round bill; chestnut belt paler and narrower; scapulars duller and belly-stripe narrower; bill duller pink with black tip and no knob. ♂ *eclipse* (variably in late Jun–early Dec) At extreme, head dull brown-black with hoary white face; chestnut on mantle paler, mottled blackish and white; underparts with only traces of chestnut and black; when flightless (for c1 month in Jul–mid Oct), looks still whiter without black flight-feathers. ♀ *eclipse* As ♂ eclipse, but head paler, face much whiter, and underparts white but for some tawny at sides of breast. *Juv* Crown, hindneck and upperparts dark grey-brown, contrasting with white face, spectacles and underparts; tail sooty-brown; forewings pale grey and all but outermost flight-feathers tipped white; bill and legs pinkish-white. *1st winter* Much as ads by Dec, but duller with more

broken patterns (esp ♀s), and juv wings retained till at least spring. VOICE Noisy in spring and summer: ♂ various melodious whistling calls; ♀ loud laughing *ak-ak-ak* and longer growling *aark-aark*. HABITAT Sandy shores, muddy estuaries, locally inland waters. NEST In rabbit burrows, other holes, thick cover, 8–10 eggs, May–Jun; 1 brood (many join into crèches). FOOD Mainly molluscs, crustaceans, insects. RANGE Many make moult-migration to NW Germany (also eg Somerset, Wash, Forth) for cJul–Nov, then return; some winter immigrants from esp Scandinavia.

Shelduck

Ruddy Duck *Oxyura jamaicensis* 36–43 cm
(c15½ in). Dumpy stifftail-duck, with
broad and slightly upcurved blue or grey
bill, contrasted 2-tone head, short neck,
short rounded wings; longish tail often
held upright; summer ♂ black, white and
chestnut; other plumages dark brown, off-
white and barred. Swims buoyantly, dives
or just sinks; gregarious; in courtship,
stretches up neck and tail, erects ear-tufts,
fans tail, shakes or rolls head, puffs up
neck and breast, slaps chest with bill;
seldom leaves water, and walks
awkwardly; flight rapid and whirring. ♂
summer Bright blue bill, glossy black cap,
white cheeks, and mainly rich chestnut
body with bold white undertail-coverts;
tail and wings brown with white central
underwings. ♀ *summer* Similar pattern,
but bill blue-grey, cap dark brown, cheeks
off-white divided by indistinct dark line,
upperparts brown tinged rufous, underparts barred buff and brown; more white
on underwings. ♂ *winter* Eclipse lasts
cAug–Mar; resembles ♀, but cap dull
black, cheeks still white, back often mixed
with chestnut. ♀ *winter* Back browner,
more barred, no rufous; cheeks greyer,
with ill-defined line. *Juv* As ♀, but duller,
greyer, scaled on breast and more clearly
barred on back, flanks, also undertail; as
♀ from moult in Aug–Oct. VOICE Courting
♂ low belch, grunt and non-vocal rattling
and slapping with bill; ♀ high squeak, hiss
and distinct bill-rattle. HABITAT Lakes,
gravel pits, with reedy edges; open
reservoirs in winter. NEST Platform in
emergent reeds, rushes, 6–10 eggs, mid
Apr–Sep; 1 brood. FOOD Insect larvae,
seeds of water plants. RANGE Introduced
from N America, breeding ferally since
1960; sedentary but for local seasonal
movements. NOTE Eurasian **White-headed
Duck** *O. leucocephala* does escape, could
occur wild: recognised by swollen bill-
base, no white under tail; ♂ mainly white
head, greyer back; ♀ stronger cheek-line.

Mandarin *Aix galericulata* 41–47 cm (c17
in). Large-headed perching-duck with
thick neck, longish tail and yellowish legs;
♂ flamboyant with multicoloured crest,

Ruddy Duck

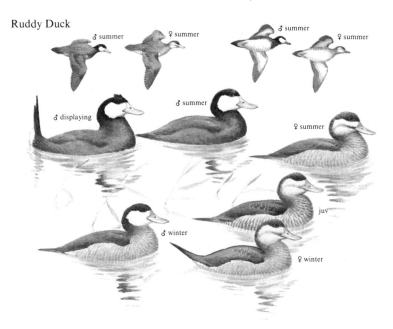

♂ summer   ♀ summer   ♂ summer   ♀ summer

♂ displaying   ♂ summer   ♀ summer

♂ winter   juv   ♀ winter

orange side-whiskers and wing-sails; ♀ crested grey head, white spectacles and cream-spotted below; in flight, primaries white-edged, secondaries white-tipped and speculum green. Flight fast, agile among trees; swims high on water, tail often raised, but seldom dives; in courtship, ♂ erects crest and sails, spreads whiskers, stretches neck up, shakes or jerks head, or flicks bill; walks easily, perches on branches; gregarious in autumn to winter. *Ad ♂* Bill red; exotic shape and plumage dominated by metallic sheens, cinnamon, orange-chestnut, white, black. *Ad ♀* Bill brown to pink; head mainly greyish, with white spectacles, white beside bill to throat; olive-brown above, breast/flanks greyer with oval creamy spots. *♂ eclipse* (cMay–Sep) Becomes much more as ♀, but bill dull red, spectacles less clear, no white beside bill, breast/flanks streaked buff. *♀ eclipse* As ♂ eclipse, but bill browner, head paler grey, crest shorter, upperbody duller. *Juv* As ♀ eclipse but more uniform above with indistinct head-markings, and streaked/spotted sepia below. VOICE Often

silent: courting ♂ whistles; ♀ loud sharp Coot-like *kek*, repeated plaintive *ak*. HABITAT Pools, lakes, slow rivers, edged by broadleaved woods. NEST In tree-holes, or rarely on ground in cover, 9–12 eggs, mid Apr–mid Jun; 1 brood. FOOD Acorns, chestnuts, beechmast, seeds, insects, snails. RANGE Introduced from E Asia, breeding ferally since c1930s; sedentary. NOTE Similar American **Wood Duck** *A. sponsa* often at large in Br: ♂ darker-headed, lacks sails and whiskers; ♀ whiter round eyes and on throat, darker and glossier above, bill-base U-shaped (not straight).

Mandarin

Wigeon *Anas penelope* 43–48 cm (*c*18 in). Short-necked dabbling-duck with small bill, steep forehead, pointed tail, narrow wings: ♂ has chestnut and cream head, mainly grey body, and white forewings; ♀ variably rufous or greyer, but bold white belly as ♂. Flight fast; often swims with neck retracted, up-ends infrequently; walks easily, feeds much on land; highly gregarious. *Ad ♂* Head chestnut with creamy-yellow forehead and crown; body grey with pinkish breast, white band of wing-coverts showing along sides, and white strip in front of black stern; in flight, white forewings and belly. *Ad ♀* Variably rufous or greyer, and broadly or narrowly barred paler on brown upperparts, but head always pink-brown spotted with black, breast more or less tinged pink, flanks cinnamon; in flight, white belly, blackish speculum edged with white, grey-brown forewings. *♂ eclipse* (Jun–Oct) As ad ♀, with similar variations, but crown and mantle darker, head, breast and flanks more rufous; white forewings still show. *♀ eclipse* (Jul–Nov) As ad ♀, but head and neck more spotted, and mantle, breast and flanks darker with fewer bars. *Juv ♂* Resembles ♀ eclipse, including colour variations, but upperparts blacker, belly sometimes mottled; forewings paler, greyer and often some white. *Juv ♀* As juv ♂, but head paler yellow-brown, mantle more uniform, forewings more as ad ♀. *1st winter* As ads with moult in Oct–Apr, but juv wings kept at least in part to 2nd autumn. VOICE ♂ loud whistle *whee-oo*; ♀ rhythmic purring growl. HABITAT Breeds by lochs, pools and rivers in moorland, marshes and wooded country with adjacent cover; winters along muddy coasts and on fresh water. NEST In thick cover, 7–9 eggs, May–Jun; 1 brood. FOOD Many water-plants, grasses; eelgrass on coast in winter. RANGE Breeders move only short distances; huge immigration from Iceland/N Europe/W Siberia, Sep–Mar. COMPARE American Wigeon (258).

Gadwall *Anas strepera* 48–54 cm (*c*20 in). Rather uniformly-coloured dabbling-duck with abrupt forehead, white

Wigeon

1st winter ♂

♀

♂

♂ eclipse

barred rufous ♀

♂

plain grey ♀

juv ♂

speculum and belly; ♂ greyish with black stern; ♀ greyer than ♀ Mallard (72) with smaller, orange-sided bill. Flight fast, pointed wings similar to Wigeon; floats high in water; in pairs or small parties. *Ad* ♂ Head and neck grey-brown peppered with black, darker at rear; otherwise dark grey, including tail and primaries, but for black stern, black crescents on breast and buff on scapulars; in flight black and white speculum, chestnut wing-coverts, white belly. *Ad* ♀ Head browner than ♂, spotting coarser; like other ♀ *Anas* but greyer with grey-brown tail; bill has well-defined orange-yellow sides, legs orange-yellow; in flight, white speculum as ♂ (sometimes much reduced), chestnut on coverts (sometimes absent), white belly. *♂ eclipse* (Jun–Aug) Much as ad ♀, including bill, but darker and less patterned above, more streaked on head, sometimes black spots on belly; wings still as ad ♂. *♀ eclipse* (Jun–Sep) As ad ♀, but darker above, more spotted on head, dusky spots on belly. *Juv* Like ad ♀, but more blackish above, underparts

strongly marked with brown; ♂ with more black and chestnut on wings than ♀. *1st winter* In Aug–Nov becomes as eclipse ♂♀, then ads, but juv wings and some juv plumage often retained to Mar or later. VOICE ♂ croaks and whistles; ♀ quacks and chatters. HABITAT Breeds by lakes and pools with extensive reeds; winters also on more open lakes, even estuaries. NEST In thick cover, 8–12 eggs, late Apr–end Jun; 1 brood. FOOD Water-plants. RANGE Most English birds introduced, sedentary; many Scottish winter in Ir; immigration from Iceland/N Europe, Aug–Apr.

Wigeon | B3 W6 S6 A6

Gadwall | B3 W4 S4 A4

Gadwall

♂

♀

♂

♀

juv ♂

1st year ♂

♂ eclipse

Teal *Anas crecca* 34–38 cm (*c*14 in).
Compact dabbling-duck with oval head,
short neck, narrow pointed wings, told by
small size alone from all regulars except
scarce summer Garganey (74); ♂ chestnut
and green head often simply looks darker
than body, white line above wings and
creamy stern-patches show best; ♀ dark,
mottled, with obscure face-pattern, dark
forewings, clear speculum, light patch at
tail-sides (*cf* Garganey). Flight fast,
swerving, wader-like, often low; shoots up
from water; swims daintily, rarely dives;
walks clumsily; often highly gregarious.
Ad ♂ Eurasian race (A.c. crecca) White
horizontal scapular line; in flight, green
and black speculum with broad buff-white
bar in front and faint whitish line behind.
Ad ♀ Some darker above, others paler or
more barred; breast mottled, breast-sides
with dark crescents, flanks streaked; bill
dark or olive-grey, edges yellowish dotted
with black; speculum as ♂ but bars thin,
white. *♂ eclipse* (*c*Jun–Oct) Like ad ♀, but
breast more spotted, breast-sides and
flanks with wavy bars, wings as ad ♂; bill
blackish, edges plain yellow to olive.
♀ eclipse (*c*Jul–Nov) As ♂ eclipse, but
breast-sides/flanks streaked, wings and
bill as ad ♀. *Juv ♂* Much as ♂ eclipse,
including wings, but spotted lower breast
and belly; bill mainly pinkish; much as ad
after moult Aug–Nov. *Juv ♀* As juv ♂, but
wings as ad ♀, pinkish bill dotted on lower
sides. *♂ American race = Green-winged
Teal (A.c.carolinensis)* Vertical white
crescent on breast-sides, no scapular line,
less cream outline to green eye-curves.
VOICE ♂ high, far-carrying, bell-like
whistle *preep* or *krit* and quiet piping
notes; ♀ as Mallard. HABITAT Breeds near
moorland pools and burns, also marshes,
reedy lakes; many winter on reservoirs,
also estuaries. NEST In thick cover, 8–11
eggs, mid Apr–early Jun; 1 brood. FOOD
Aquatic seeds, plants, invertebrates.
RANGE Often resident, but some go south
as far as Iberia; huge immigration from
Iceland/N Europe, Sep–Apr; American
race vagrant (total 160: Oct–Jun, wide-
scattered). COMPARE Blue-winged and
Baikal Teals (260).

Teal

Mallard *Anas platyrhynchos* 55–62 cm (*c*23 in). Very common bulky dabbling-duck with longish bill, head and neck; ♂ metallic green head, white neck-ring; ♀ mottled brown. Flight fast, with shallow beats; rises easily from water; walks well, body level; swims high with tail raised, up-ends, rarely dives; gregarious. *Ad ♂* Pattern unmistakable; note curled black central feathers on white tail; legs orange-red, bill yellow to olive; forewings greyish in flight, purple-blue speculum edged black and white. *Ad ♀* Buff variably patterned blackish; plain throat/foreneck, whitish tail; legs as ♂, bill dark with greenish to dull orange sides; forewings browner than ♂, speculum narrower. *♂ eclipse* (*c*Jun–Sep) As ad ♀ but darker, more uniform above, paler greyer face, brown-centred white tail, breast often tinged chestnut, wings as ad ♂; bill dull olive-yellow. *♀ eclipse* (*c*Jul–Oct) Little change: more uniform above, crown darker. *Juv ♂* Like ♂ eclipse, but underparts narrowly streaked, tail grey-brown marked with buff; bill red-brown slowly darkening, legs yellowish; much as ad after moult *c*Aug–Feb. *Juv ♀* As juv ♂, but back more marked buff above, wings as ad ♀; bill paler, often dotted along edge. VOICE ♂ weak nasal *raib*, also whistles, grunts; ♀ quacks, including laughing decrescendo series. HABITAT Any fresh or salt water; also fields. NEST In ground cover or tree-holes, may be 2 km from water, 9–12 eggs, Mar–mid Jul; 1 brood. FOOD Seeds, plants, invertebrates. RANGE Resident; also passage/winter visitor from N Europe, Sep–Apr, esp EBr. COMPARE Black Duck (258).

Teal		B4	Mallard		B6
		W5			W6
		S5			S6
		A5			A6

Mallard

♂
♀
♂ eclipse
♂
♀

Pintail *Anas acuta* 53–59 cm (*c*22 in) +
< 10 cm elongated tail of ♂. Slender
dabbling-duck with longish bill and neck,
and pointed tail; ♂ grey with chocolate
head and white neck; ♀ paler and greyer
than other *Anas*, with conspicuous eyes
and grey bill. Flight fast with rapid beats,
often in lines or Vs; floats high (neck
often straight and tail raised), up-ends;
walks gracefully; gregarious. *Ad* ♂ White
underparts with stripe extending up side
of chocolate head; back and flanks grey,
with black and cream scapulars; long
black central tail-feathers; stern black and
cream; in flight, bronze-green speculum
shows less than buff line in front and white
behind. *Ad* ♀ Pale, greyish; crescents on
flanks, bill blue-grey; in flight, obscure
speculum bordered with white at rear,
pointed tail mainly brown, underwings
darker than whitish belly. ♂ *eclipse* (Jul–
Sep) As ad ♀, but crown blacker, upperparts greyer and more uniform, flanks less
boldly marked, tail blacker and more
pointed, wings as ad ♂. ♀ *eclipse* (Aug–
Nov) As ad ♀ but paler above, upperparts

more narrowly marked, belly often more
spotted. *Juv* ♂ As ad ♀ but darker, back
and flanks browner barred with white,
belly heavily marked; wings as ad ♂, but
borders to speculum narrower. *Juv* ♀ As
juv ♂, but mantle unbarred, wings as ad
♀ with narrower border to speculum. *1st
winter* During Sep–Nov becomes like
eclipse ♂♀, then ads, but juv wings kept
and some juv plumage on upperparts and
belly. VOICE ♂ low whistle and long nasal
whee, ♀ quacks and growls, but both
usually silent in flight. HABITAT Breeds by
moorland pools, lochs with drier shores,
also in marshes in E Anglia; winters on
estuaries and fenland floods. NEST In short
cover, 7–9 eggs, late Apr–Jun; 1 brood.
FOOD Water-plants, invertebrates. RANGE
Some breeding sites irregular; many immigrants from Iceland/N Europe, Sep–Apr.

Garganey *Anas querquedula* 37–41 cm (*c*15
in). Small dabbling-duck with flattish
crown and slender neck; ♂ brown with
white supercilia, greyish flanks, drooping
scapulars, blue-grey forewings; ♀ like

Pintail

♂

♀

♂

♀

juv ♀

♂ eclipse

juv ♂

pale ♀ Teal (72), but more contrasted head, no pale patch at tail-sides. Flight fast and direct; swims low, dabbles but seldom up-ends; walks very awkwardly; in pairs or small parties, unobtrusive. *Ad ♂* Rich brown head with white curve from eyes to nape; upperparts black-brown mottled paler, with long scapulars striped with blue-grey, black and white; breast pink-brown with blackish markings, undertail white spotted with brown; flanks greyish in flight, forewings blue-grey, underwings white with dark leading edges, and sharp division between breast and white belly. *Ad ♀* Like ♀ Teal, but white throat, pale patch by base of bill and clearer supercilia contrasting with blackish eyestripes and line below eyes; speculum greyer with more white at front and esp rear; underwings as ♂. *♂ eclipse* (Jun–Feb) As ad ♀, but crown darker, sides of head more streaked, upperparts with narrower grey and buff feather-edges; wings as ad ♂. *♀ eclipse* (Jul–Feb) As ♂ eclipse but back-feathers all edged with buff, wings as ad ♀. *Juv ♂* As ad ♀, but

back-feathers edged with grey not buff; all underparts marked brown; wings as ad ♂ but forewings duller, white borders to speculum narrower. *Juv ♀* As juv ♂, but feather-edges buff and wings as ad ♀, though speculum dark grey, white borders narrower. *1st winter* Becomes like ads in winter quarters. VOICE ♂ dry crackling rattle, both settled and in flight; ♀ short quack. HABITAT Reedy meres, fens, water meadows. NEST In coarse grass, 8–11 eggs, end Apr–Jun; 1 brood. FOOD Invertebrates, water-plants. RANGE Summer visitor, Mar–Sep, wintering in Africa.

Pintail		B2 W4 S4 A4	Garganey		B2 W0 S4 A3

Garganey

♂   ♀

♂

♀

♂ eclipse

juv ♂

Shoveler *Anas clypeata* 47–53 cm (*c*20 in). Heavy-looking dabbling-duck with huge spatulate bill, flattened head and small pointed wings set far back in flight; ♂ white, chestnut and black with blue fore-wings (*cf* Garganey, 74); ♀ mottled brown with mainly dark belly, greyer forewings. Flight much as Wigeon (70), often on wing in spring; rises easily with wing-rattle; swims with front end low, dabbling bill in water or mud, also up-ends; pairs or small parties often swim in circles head to tail; pumps head up and down in threat; walks awkwardly; not shy. *Ad* ♂ Green-black head and chestnut underbody show against white breast, scapulars and rump-sides, black back and stern; blue forewings and green speculum divided by white bar. *Ad* ♀ Mottled brown with whitish tail and orange legs as ♀ Mallard (72), but pink-tinged feather-edges; wings much duller than ♂; bill grey-brown edged with orange-yellow, eyes brown to yellow. ♂ *eclipse* (*c*Jun–Aug) Resembles ad ♀, but much darker and more uniform above, crown black, breast and flanks

richer pink-buff, undertail-coverts clearly barred, forewings still blue as ad ♂; bill yellow-brown, eyes rich orange-yellow. ♂ *supplementary* (*c*Sep–Nov) With further moult, head black mottled with white (at peak forming crescent on forecheeks), breast and scapulars white with black crescents and bars, flanks chestnut heavily marked with black. ♀ *eclipse* (*c*Jul–Oct) Darker, less pink than ad ♀; head not as dark as ♂ eclipse, upperparts with broader pale fringes, breast/flanks dark brown edged buff. *Juv* As ♀ eclipse, but crown blacker, cheeks and underparts grey-brown or buff with finer markings, tail brown barred with buff; ♂ forewings grey-blue, ♀ faintly grey. *1st winter* During Aug–Apr, becomes as eclipse, then supplementary (♂) and finally ads. VOICE ♂ hoarse *took-took*; ♀ quacks. HABITAT Reedy meres with mud and weeds, marshy pools; open shallow lakes in winter. NEST In grass, rushes or heather, near water, 8–11 eggs, mid Apr–Jun; 1 brood. FOOD Small crustaceans, molluscs, insects, and seeds, water-plants. RANGE Most breeders

Shoveler

emigrate to Mediterranean area; winter
visitors from NE Europe/Iceland, Oct–
Apr. COMPARE Blue-winged Teal (260).

Red-crested Pochard *Netta rufina* 53–59
cm (*c*22 in). Plump diving-duck, with big
round head and longish neck; ♂ red bill,
golden-chestnut head, black, white and
brown body; ♀ brown with clear-cut pale
cheeks and throat (*cf* ♀ Common Scoter,
86). Flight strong with rapid wing-beats,
but rises awkwardly, pattering on surface;
swims high on water, often up-ends; walks
smoothly; wary. *Ad* ♂ Red bill, eyes and
legs; bushy golden crown, chestnut head,
glossy black neck and underparts, white
flank-patches; in flight broad white band
on hindwings, white shoulder-line, white
underwings. *Ad* ♀ Pale greyish cheeks/
throat contrast with dark cap/hindneck;
pale brown above and grey-brown below
with some barring; eyes brown (redder in
spring), bill dark with pink edges and
band near tip, legs pink; wing-band tinged
grey, underwings white as ♂. ♂ *eclipse*
(May–Oct) As ad ♀, but darker above,

mottled whitish on breast, with bushier
head; bill, eyes, legs and wings as ad ♂.
♀ *eclipse* (Jun–Oct) As ad ♀, but darker,
much white mottling on breast/belly. *Juv*
As ad ♀, but greyer above, mottled cheeks,
yellow-brown eyes, and duller bill. *1st
winter* ♂ After moult Aug–Nov, much as
ad, but belly duller and mottled, bill paler,
eyes duller. VOICE Migrants quiet. HABITAT
Reed-fringed lakes, brackish lagoons;
reservoirs on passage. FOOD Water-plants,
seeds. RANGE Scarce visitor from Continent, most Sep–Mar, but status confused
by escapes which have also nested in SBr.

Shoveler — B3 W5 S5 A5 | Red-crested Pochard — B0 W2 S2 A2

Red-crested Pochard

Pochard *Aythya ferina* 44–48 cm (*c*18 in). Stocky diving-duck with longish bill and forehead, high crown, and sloping back; ♂ chestnut, black and pale grey; ♀ rather yellow-brown with hoary face and greyish back; in flight, broad grey wing-stripe. Flight strong but looks heavy, rapid beats produce slight whistling sound; floats low with tail on surface; dives for food, often with jump, and occasionally up-ends; patters along surface to take off; often stands or sits on shore and walks quite easily; in scattered flocks. *Ad* ♂ Chestnut head, black breast and stern, pale grey back and flanks; eyes red, bill pale grey in middle, dark at ends. *Ad* ♀ Head and forebody yellow-brown with darker crown, hoary pattern round bill, cheeks and throat, often streak behind eyes, and whitish markings on breast; mantle, scapulars and flanks vermiculated grey-brown; eyes brown but reddish in spring, bill as ♂ but darker. ♂ *eclipse* (Jun–Sep) Like ad ♂, but head duller brown with dark crown, throat/neck mottled; breast blackish, speckled paler; back browner-grey. ♀ *eclipse* (Mar–Oct) As ad ♀, but back and scapulars more uniform and darker greyish-brown, flanks yellower-brown. *Juv* As ad ♀, but head and neck duller and greyer without pale streak behind eyes, upperparts also greyer (speckled white on ♂), breast and flanks dark grey variably marked with yellow-buff. *1st winter* ♂ starts to become like ad Sep–Dec, but variable amount of juv feathers remain, esp on underparts, at least until spring; ♀ retains more juv feathers throughout winter. VOICE Mostly silent, but ♂ soft wheeze in courtship, ♀ growl in flight. HABITAT Breeds by lakes and slow rivers with reeds; winters on open fresh water and estuaries. NEST In thick cover, 8–11 eggs, late Apr–early Jul; 1 brood. FOOD Water-plants, invetebrates. RANGE Disperses in winter, some emigrate; also many passage/winter visitors from N/Cent Europe, Sep–Apr.

Ferruginous Duck *Aythya nyroca* 39–43 cm (*c*16 in). Dainty diving-duck with high crown and white under tail; ♂ mainly

Pochard

♀ ♂

♂ eclipse

♀ ♂

♀ eclipse

juv ♂

chestnut with white eyes, ♀ duller and browner; in flight, broad white wing-stripe, white underwings and belly. Flight less heavy than other diving-ducks; floats buoyantly with tail more raised; takes off more easily; often skulks. *Ad ♂* Head, neck, breast and flanks rich chestnut, purplish on crown and hindneck, paler below esp towards rear flanks; collar and upperparts black or blackish; white under tail and belly; eyes white, bill grey, paler near black nail and on sides. *Ad ♀* Rather like ♂, but head and underparts browner and paler, some white mottling on throat, upperparts browner, often speckled with yellow-brown; in worn plumage, face paler, upperparts with more obvious buff edges; eyes brown, base and top of bill blacker. *♂ eclipse* (Jun–Sep) As ad ♂, but head and neck duller, crown and hindneck blacker, breast and flanks barred paler. *♀ eclipse* (Apr–Sep) As ad ♀, but head paler and browner, throat and foreneck more mottled white, belly mottled grey-brown. *Juv* As ad ♀, but head and neck paler (yellower on sides, greyer

on hindneck, more buff on throat) under-parts more mottled with buff, undertail with dark marks; eyes grey-brown, bill grey-black with paler base. *1st winter* Variable: some much like ad by end Nov, others still with much juv plumage in Mar; ♂ eyes pale grey, ♀ brown. VOICE Migrants silent. HABITAT Shallow fresh water with much vegetation. FOOD Water-plants, invertebrates. RANGE Scarce visitor from E/S Europe, mainly Sep–Apr, but pattern obscured by frequent escapes. NOTE *Aythya* hybrids, esp ♀s of Pochard × Ferruginous Duck, can be very similar.

Pochard		B3	Ferruginous Duck		B0
		W5			W1
		S5			S0
		A5			A0

Ferruginous Duck

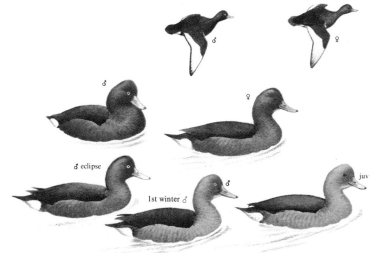

Tufted Duck *Aythya fuligula* 41–45 cm
(*c*17 in). Round-headed diving-duck with
distinctive drooping crest and short neck;
♂ black with white sides; ♀ mainly dark
brown with paler flanks; bold white wing-
bar and white underwings in flight. Flight
and actions as Pochard (78), but rises
more easily; swims with tail on surface,
dives with leap; comes ashore readily; in
scattered parties or flocks. *Ad* ♂ White
flanks and belly contrast with purple-
glossed head and otherwise black body;
eyes yellow, bill grey-blue (usually white
line behind broad black tip). *Ad* ♀ Shorter
crest than ♂; mostly dark brown, mantle
and breast with cinnamon feather-tips,
and often whitish speckling on scapulars;
flanks variably mottled whitish, belly
white; grey-brown mixed with white under
tail, but sometimes all white (*cf* Ferruginous); often white by bill-base ('Scaup-
faced'), but usually less than ♀ Scaup
and less well defined; eyes as ♂, bill darker
grey. ♂ *eclipse* (Jun–Sep) Like ad ♂, but
crest tatty, mantle/breast duller and
speckled white, flanks grey-brown barred

with blackish; may show whitish by bill.
♀ *eclipse* (Mar–Sep) As ad ♀, but browner
above, no more than white spot at bill-
base; flanks yellower without white
markings. *Juv* Generally greyer with buff
feather-edges, buff at base of bill, and
dark-blotched whitish undertail. *1st winter*
Head turns dark brown Aug–Nov, ♂
blacker, ♀ often with some white at base of
upper-bill; becomes much like ad by Apr,
sometimes by Dec. VOICE ♂ mostly silent,
but low whistle in courtship; ♀ growling
kurr-kurr. HABITAT Lakes and slow rivers
with reedy shores, often with islets;
winters on more open waters, occasionally sheltered estuaries. NEST Usually in
thick cover·near water, 8–11 eggs, mid
May–Jul; 1 brood. FOOD Invertebrates,
water-plants. RANGE Resident, but moves
from NBr to Ir; passage/winter visitor
from Iceland/N Europe, Sep–Apr.
COMPARE Ring-necked Duck (260).

Scaup *Aythya marila* 46–51 cm (*c*19 in).
Broad-bodied diving-duck with large bill
and crestless head higher at front and

Tufted Duck

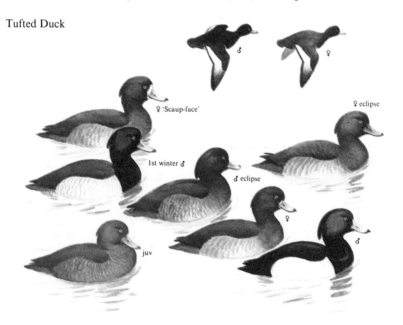

more sloping at back than Tufted; ♂
black at both ends, pale in middle; ♀
like ♀ Tufted but broad white face-band in
winter, whitish patch on ear-coverts in
summer; in flight, wing-bar and underwings as Tufted. Flight and actions as
Pochard (78), but seldom seen on land;
often in large but scattered flocks. *Ad* ♂
Back pale grey, head green-glossed; eyes
yellow, bill blue-grey with narrow black
nail. *Ad* ♀ Head dark brown with white
face, sometimes little whitish on hind-
cheeks; forebody paler with buff fringes;
back with grey tinge; flanks pale yellow-
brown and white; belly white, undertail
grey-brown and white; eyes yellow, bill
dark grey, darkest along ridge. ♂ *eclipse*
(Jun–Aug) Black areas duller than ad ♂,
with some whitish around bill, on hind-
cheeks and on breast; flanks marked
grey-brown. ♀ *eclipse* (Mar–Sep) As ad ♀,
but more uniform and yellower; less white
around bill and, except in fresh plumage,
increasingly clear whitish patch on hind-
cheeks. *Juv* Greyer than ad ♀, with white
often only on chin; belly mottled. *1st*

winter ♂ Starts to become like ad in Aug–
Oct, but plumage often still mixed in
Apr. *1st winter* ♀ Becomes like ♀ eclipse
by spring, but underparts as juv. VOICE
♂ mostly silent; ♀ growling *karr-karr*.
HABITAT Breeds by moorland lakes, pools,
rivers; winters along coasts, esp bays and
estuaries, and visits adjacent fresh water.
NEST As Tufted Duck, 8–11 eggs, May–
Jun; 1 brood. FOOD Invertebrates (esp
molluscs), water-plants. RANGE Passage/
winter from Iceland/N Europe, Oct–Mar;
few summer; nests sporadically NBr.

Tufted Duck		B4 W5 S5 A5	Scaup		B0 W4 S4 A4

Scaup

Eider *Somateria mollissima* 55–61 cm (*c*23 in). Bulky, short-necked, long-bodied sea-duck with long slope of bill and fore-head, eyes set far back, and diagnostic feathering to below nostrils; ♂ only duck with white upperparts and breast, black flanks and belly; ♀ cinnamon-buff mottled and barred with blackish. Flight strong and direct, often low over water in single file, but looks heavy on short, broad wings; take-off laboured; usually swims with head retracted and dives well, or dips head in shallows, occasionally up-ending; walks rather upright with slow rolling gait; regularly rests on rocks and sand-banks, esp in spring and autumn; often in scattered groups or large flocks; not shy. *Ad ♂* Mainly white except for black crown, flanks, belly, stern and all but front of wings; green patches on rear head, pink-tinged breast, white circles at sides of rump. *Ad ♀* Head and neck cinnamon-brown, streaked on crown and otherwise spotted black, with indistinct pale buff stripe from lores to behind eyes; rest of body barred cinnamon-buff and blackish,

becoming darker through wear; in flight, 2 white wing-bars border blackish (or sometimes purple-tinged) secondaries. ♂ *eclipse* (Jul–Nov) Flanks, belly and stern remain black to sooty-brown, and wing-coverts and back (but not mantle) white; other white areas become largely black-brown variably mottled with buff, much darker than ♀, and darkest on head but for often conspicuous mottled whitish stripe through eyes corresponding to ♀'s; mantle, scapulars and breast often show white feather-bases and some white feathers. ♀ *eclipse* (Aug–Mar) As ad ♀, but much darker; head sooty-brown with eye-stripes often more conspicuous; upperparts, breast and flanks with narrower pale bars, and rest of underparts dark brown almost unbarred. *Juv* As ad ♀, but upperparts almost uniform dull black on ♂, very dark brown on ♀, and underparts boldly marked with dense, narrow bars of buff and whitish; mottled whitish streak through eyes; cheeks and throat paler buff streaked with dark brown; usually no white wing-bars. *1st*

Eider

juv

juv ♀

early 1st year ♂

late 1st year ♂

2nd year ♂

year ♂ Very variable, but from Sep/Oct to spring head first grows blacker (but for more contrasted white eye-stripes), and then white feathers, often with blackish tips or mottling, develop on chest, sides (esp left) of breast, and mantle and lower scapulars, later particularly on head with mixture of green and black; but lower back, rest of underparts and wings remain as juv. *2nd year* ♂ From following Jul assumes eclipse as ad ♂ except for juv wings; then becomes like ad ♂, but white of head, neck, mantle and, to lesser extent, of foreneck, breast and patches at sides of rump mottled blackish and buff (this later often decreasing through abrasion), and forewings suffused sooty-brown. *1st year* ♀ As ad ♀ eclipse, but during Nov–Apr crown, nape and upperparts become still darker, cheeks and sides of neck still more heavily streaked blackish; wings as juv, usually without white bars. VOICE Very vocal, esp in spring and autumn flocks: ♂ various low but loud crooning, dove-like moans, as *coo-oh-wah* with 2nd syllable emphasised; ♀ repeated guttural *gok-gok-*

gok-gok ('like distant fishing vessel'). HABITAT Essentially marine, breeding on offshore islands, rocky coasts and by sand-flats and saltings, but also estuaries and sea lochs and, locally, several km inland by freshwater lakes and rivers; in winter often well out to sea, but also inshore, esp over mussel-beds and reefs. NEST Sometimes colonial; hollow lined with abundant down, in short turf or marram, or well-hidden in heather, bracken or rocks, 4–6 eggs, late Apr–end Jul; 1 brood. FOOD Largely molluscs, esp mussels; also many crabs, starfish, other invertebrates. RANGE Mainly sedentary or locally dispersive, but non-breeders wander south; some immigration from Netherlands, also Denmark, in winter. COMPARE King Eider, Steller's Eider (260).

Eider   B5 W5 S5 A5

♂   ♀

♀ eclipse   ♂ eclipse

♂

♀

Long-tailed Duck *Clangula hyemalis* 41–45 cm (*c*17 in) + 13 cm tail-streamers of ♂. Elegant sea-duck with short upturned bill, steep forehead, small head and triangular wings; only extensively white duck with all-dark wings; ♂ otherwise black-brown and white in summer, largely white with dark patches at other times; ♀ mainly dark brown above and white below. Flight distinctive, rapid and usually low in straggling lines or flocks, swinging from side to side showing alternate dark and white, with downcurved wings hardly brought above body on upstroke but coming unusually low on backward-flicking downstroke; swims buoyantly, long tail of ♂ often trailing on surface but raised to 45° or more when alert, and dives frequently, throwing head back and plunging forward with tail spread and wings often partly opened; lands breast first, without glide; seldom on land; often in restless flocks. Moults very complex, autumn + winter plumages corresponding to main plumage of other ducks. ♂ *autumn* (Sep–Nov) As ♂ winter, but head and neck white except for mottled grey-brown patch on lower cheeks and upper neck. ♂ *winter* (Nov–Apr) Head and neck white apart from pale grey area round eyes and blackish/chestnut patch below; white body and pale grey flanks contrast with black-brown breast-band joining in Y on back; wings uniform blackish above, but for chestnut secondaries, and mainly grey below; bill pink or orange-yellow with blue-grey nail and black base. ♂ *summer* (May–Jun) Head, neck and chest blackish-brown but for grey and white face-patch; mantle/scapulars black with chestnut and buff edges. ♂ *eclipse* (Jul–Sep) Much as ♂ summer, but duller and darker, no tail-streamers; new scapulars shorter, brown, narrowly edged buff; flanks browner. ♀ *autumn* (Nov–Dec/Feb) As ♀ winter but head/neck as ♀ eclipse. ♀ *winter* (Dec–Apr, although some remain as autumn) Head blackish but for grey-brown throat and central foreneck, buff sides of head with white round and back from eyes, and white lower neck; mantle, scapulars and wing-coverts dark brown with warm

Long-tailed Duck

brown edges, secondaries duller than ♂; underparts white but for brownish breast-band, flanks sometimes greyish; bill dark grey. ♀ *summer* (May–Jul/Aug) Head sooty-black but for mottled grey throat, dark grey sides of head in front of eyes, white round eyes to nape, and white neck-sides; upperparts as winter, but darker with narrower grey or buff feather-edges; underparts as winter, flanks sometimes greyer. ♀ *eclipse* (Aug–Nov) Head and neck white but for mottled blackish crown (sometimes also forehead) and cheek-patch, grey tinge to throat; otherwise as summer, but upperparts mottled brown, upper breast and flanks grey-brown. *Juv* Head mainly grey, darker on throat and hindneck, but for mottled blackish from forehead to nape and patch on rear and sides of neck, and white streak from eyes to nape; upperparts almost uniform dark grey-brown, with paler-edged scapulars; underparts whitish, with brown-grey across breast and paler on flanks. *1st winter* ♂ During Sep–Dec many develop new feathers as ♂ autumn then as

♂ winter on head, neck, upperparts and flanks, but very variable; some assume much white on head and neck, grey and white scapulars and occasionally tail-streamers, others stay as juv to spring; pink on bill from Oct. *1st summer* ♂ From Apr–May more like ♂ summer, but no dark breast-band; much as ad from Aug. *1st year* ♀ Much as ♀ autumn, or winter, then summer, but head-pattern less defined, mantle/scapulars edged with grey, underparts as juv. *2nd winter* ♀ As ♀ winter, but scapulars with broad white edges. VOICE ♂ noisy on sea and in flight, esp loud yodel *a-ahulee*; ♀ low quacks. HABITAT Essential marine; rare inland. FOOD Molluscs, crustaceans. RANGE Passage/winter visitor from parts uncertain of N Eurasia/Greenland; has nested NBr.

Long-tailed Duck

B0
W4
S4
A4

♀ winter

♂ winter

juv

1st winter ♂

♀ eclipse

1st summer ♂

♀ summer

1st winter ♀

Common Scoter *Melanitta nigra* 46–51 cm (*c*19 in). Squat sea-duck with deep-based bill, short neck, longish pointed tail and blackish legs; ♂ all black but for yellow on bill, ♀ brown with pale cheeks; in flight, undersides of primaries show paler. Flight strong with rapid whistling beats, usually low over sea in snaking lines or ragged bunches; swims buoyantly with tail often raised and dives for food; postures include stretching neck and raising tail, shaking head, fanning and raising tail vertically; seldom on land or even on sand-banks unless nesting or oiled and sick; walks upright and awkwardly; highly gregarious, ♂s often predominating in NBr (gathering here earlier also) and ♀s/imms farther south; shy. *Ad ♂* Body all glossy black; knobbed bill with orange-yellow ridge-patch. ♂ *eclipse* (*c*Apr–Nov) Only slightly duller, with mixture of old/new feathers. *Ad ♀* Defined buff-white cheeks/throat contrast with blackish crown, mainly dark brown body; fading and wear cause pale barring on body, greyish belly; small-knobbed bill green-black but often yellow line on ridge. *Juv* As ♀, but greyer-brown above and paler below; crown brown, breast and belly white; knobless bill olive with yellow-pink by nostrils. *1st year ♂* With moult from Nov, esp Apr–May, mottled black on head, upperparts, flanks, later breast and under tail; as ad ♂ by *c*Jun–Jul, but duller black with some brown; orange-yellow first shows on bill from *c*Jan. ♂ *American/E Asian race (M.n. americana)* Whole bill-base and flatter knob yellow. VOICE Whistling, piping: ♂ high-pitched, plaintive; ♀ hoarse or grating. HABITAT Nests by open moorland lochs, in Ir on large loughs with wooded islets; winters along sheltered coasts, but odd migrants well inland. NEST In cover near loch or on islet, 6–8 eggs, end May–mid Jul; 1 brood. FOOD Mussels, cockles, also crustaceans, fish eggs, worms, larvae. seeds. RANGE Summer visitor to nesting places, Apr–Sep; winter visitors from Iceland/N Europe, esp Sep–Apr, but non-breeders offshore all year; *americana* vagrant (2 records). COMPARE ♀s of Ruddy Duck (68), Red-crested Pochard (76).

Common Scoter

Velvet Scoter *Melanitta fusca* 53–59 cm (*c*22 in). Heavy-headed sea-duck with long swollen bill, thick neck, short pointed tail, white wing-patches and reddish legs; ♂ black with white eye-patches, ♀ brown with (usually) 2 pale head-patches; in flight, white secondaries (*cf* Goldeneye, 88; Merganser, 90). Actions as Common Scoter, but swims less buoyantly, red legs show when diving; rises from water less easily; rests more on sand-banks; swims in smaller parties, often in line; tamer. *Ad* ♂ Glossy black, white crescent by whitish eyes; bill with swollen black base, orange-yellow sides, redder nail. ♂ *eclipse* (Apr–Nov) Only slightly duller, with some browner feathers. *Ad* ♀ Dark brown in new plumage *c*Nov–Jan; with wear, some grey-buff barring above, much white mottling on belly, and 2 whitish patches on sides of head prominent till Oct. *Juv* As ♀, but greyer-brown above, paler and more barred below, with larger patches on head; juv ♂ darker mantle and contrasting grey-edged scapulars, juv ♀ more uniform above and whiter belly; legs greyish-pink to yellowish. *1st year* ♂ During moult beginning Nov–Jan, head blackens by *c*Mar, then scapulars, breast, flanks; but body still mottled brown in 1st summer and no white crescent by eyes; bill-sides paler from *c*Jan, yellow by spring. *1st winter* ♀ Head darker than body, no pale patches until worn. VOICE Rather silent: odd pipes or croaks from flocks. HABITAT Winters along open coasts and estuaries. FOOD Mussels, cockles, crabs, shrimps, starfish, worms. RANGE Winter visitor from N Europe, Oct–May; few all year. COMPARE Surf Scoter (262), esp ♀s.

Common Scoter		B3
		W4
		S5
		A5

Velvet Scoter		B0
		W4
		S4
		A4

Velvet Scoter

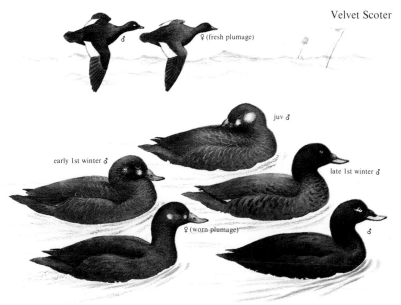

♂   ♀ (fresh plumage)

juv ♂

early 1st winter ♂

late 1st winter ♂

♀ (worn plumage)

♂

Goldeneye *Bucephala clangula* 40–48 cm (16–19 in). Stocky sea-duck with short bill and neck, high-peaked head and humped back; ♂ boldly pied, with white blob behind bill; smaller ♀ mottled grey, with chocolate head, whitish collar and wing-patches (showing at rest). Flight fast, often low, with rapid beats making singing sound (ad ♂ loudest); swims buoyantly, often on rough water with head held forward or sunk in shoulders (hiding collar and exaggerating humpback); dives tirelessly, sometimes several in unison; rises more directly from surface than diving-ducks; seldom on land, but walks easily, upright; restless, shy; singly or in parties, also big flocks. *Ad* ♂ Mainly black above and white below, but for green-glossed head, greyer tail, and white loral blob, scapular bands and square wing-patches; eyes yellow. *Ad* ♀ Chestnut head, white and greyish collar, blackish upperparts mottled with grey, greyish chest to flanks, white belly, broken white wing-patches; eyes yellow-white, bill yellow near tip. ♂ *eclipse* (Jul–Oct) As ad

♀, but larger, head darker with blackish lores, collar grey-brown, mantle and flanks browner, wings as ad ♂. ♀ *eclipse* (Jun–Nov) As ♂ eclipse, but head duller with no blackish, wings as ad ♀. *Juv* As ♀ eclipse, but head greyer-brown, upperparts and chest mainly brown; ♂ slightly larger, usually with bigger whitish patch on wing-coverts, yellower eyes. *1st year* With variable moults in cSep–Nov/Mar, head becomes redder-brown (♂ some black tinge), chest greyer-brown; by spring, some as ads but for juv wings, but often still many juv feathers and ♀ generally greyer fore-collar. VOICE Usually silent except in display, when ♂ loud *zeee-zeee* and soft rattle. HABITAT Coasts, estuaries, reservoirs, large rivers; breeds on wooded lakes and rivers. NEST In tree-holes or special nestboxes, 8–11 eggs, mid May–Jun; 1 brood. FOOD Molluscs, crustaceans, insects. RANGE Passage/winter visitor from N Europe, Oct–Apr; since 1970, small but increasing numbers breeding NBr. NOTE **Barrow's Goldeneye** *B. islandica*, of Iceland/N America, seen rarely Br, believed

Goldeneye

♂

♀

♀

1st winter ♂

♂

♂ eclipse

to be escapes: ♂ has oval, purplish head and white crescent (not blob), less white on scapulars; ♀ has richer chestnut head, ragged nape, more yellow on stubbier bill.

Smew *Mergus albellus* 36–43 cm (14–17 in). Compact sawbill-duck with small bill, steep forehead, slight crest, but more elongated with stiff straight neck in flight; ♂ looks mainly white on water, but pied in flight; smaller ♀ greyish with contrasting chestnut cap and white cheeks. Flight very fast and agile, taking off and swerving like Teal (72), groups in diagonals and Vs (not usually bunched); floats high, dives constantly; walks very upright; usually shy; singly or in small parties. *Ad ♂* White with black patches and lines, greyer stern; in flight, black back/wings with bold white pattern. *Ad ♀* Cap chestnut, lores blackish, mantle blackish-grey; white areas on wings smaller than ♂. *♂ eclipse* (mid Jun–Oct/Nov) As ad ♀, but larger, cap more orange-brown, no black on lores, mantle blackish with grey fringes, wings as ad ♂. *♀ eclipse* Head as ♂ eclipse; otherwise

much as ad ♀, but browner above. *Juv* As ♀ eclipse, but cap paler orange-buff, mantle still browner, median coverts more grey-brown than white; ♂ already larger. *1st winter ♂* With moults in *c*Sep–Mar, first more as ♂ eclipse, but still juv wings; by *c*Dec–Jan, cap and scapulars mixed with white, lores blackish, breast-sides with faint blackish lines. *1st winter ♀* Much as ♀ eclipse but for juv wings, then lores blacken. VOICE Usually silent in winter. HABITAT Reservoirs, lakes, also estuaries. FOOD Fish, also invertebrates. RANGE Winter visitor from N Europe, Nov–Apr.

Smew

late 1st winter ♂

Red-breasted Merganser *Mergus serrator*
♂ 56–61 cm (*c*23 in), ♀ 51–56 cm (*c*21 in).
Slender, rakish sawbill-duck with long
thin bill, thin neck and wispy double crest;
♂ dark-looking with bottle-green head,
tortoiseshell breast, grey flanks; ♀ has
brown cap/crest, dark mask, indistinct
whitish throat and rufous head/neck
shading into brown-grey upperparts; very
elongated cigar-shape in flight, with thin
neck held stiffly level, white on inner wings
with 1–2 black bands. Flight fast with
strong beats, often low over water but
sometimes quite high; take-off laboured;
less buoyant than other sawbills, often
swimming with to-and-fro head-motion;
dives constantly, or may just submerge
head; walks easily; usually in small parties,
also flocks. *Ad* ♂ Red bill, green-black
head, white lower neck, black-spotted
red-buff breast; otherwise black, white and
grey, boldly marked at breast-sides; inner
wings mostly white with black leading
edge and 2 bars. *Ad* ♀ Brown-red bill,
brown head with rufous cheeks and neck-
sides shading into ill-defined whitish
throat, mottled brown-grey upperparts,
greyer flanks; variable black by or around
eyes, white streak on lores; white on inner
wings confined to patch on rear half with
black bar across. ♂ *eclipse* (Jun–Nov) As
♀ eclipse, but mantle/scapulars blacker,
bill redder, wings as ad ♂. ♀ *eclipse* (Jul–
Dec) As ad ♀, but no black by eyes or
white on lores, crest shorter. *Juv* As ♀
eclipse, but crest still shorter, sides of head
more buff, mantle/scapulars greyer, bill
duller red-brown; ♂ already larger. *1st
winter* With moults in *c*Nov–Mar, ♂s
variously assume ad plumage, some
completely by spring but for juv wings;
♀s much as ad ♀, but usually no black by
eyes. VOICE In courtship, ♂ rattling purr,
♀ harsh *krrrr* or softer croak. HABITAT
Breeds on islets in sea-lochs, or by open or
forested lakes and rivers; winters mainly
along sheltered coasts/estuaries. NEST In
ground cover or holes, 8–10 eggs, May–
mid Jul; 1 brood. FOOD Fish, also invertebrates. RANGE Mainly resident, moving to
coasts in winter; also winter visitor from
Iceland/Scandinavia, Sep–May.

Red-breasted
Merganser

♂

♀

♂ eclipse

♂

♀

Goosander *Mergus merganser* ♂ 63–69 cm (*c*26 in), ♀ 57–62 cm (*c*23½ in). Larger and bulkier than Red-breasted Merganser, with compact shaggy nape; ♂ also much whiter; ♀ cleaner blue-grey above with sharply demarcated richer rufous head, white throat and whitish-grey lower neck; in flight, more white on inner wings (esp ♂) at most only part-broken by dark bar. Actions as Merganser; more wing-noise (humming whistle) in flight; floats higher. *Ad* ♂ Mainly white, tinged with pink or cream below, but for green-black head, black back, blackish outer wings, grey stern; bill bright red. *Ad* ♀ Mainly grey to blue-grey, but for crested rufous head, white throat and belly, blackish outer wings, white secondaries; bill dull red. ♂ *eclipse* (Jun–Nov) As ♀ eclipse, but mantle/scapulars blacker, flanks whiter, wings as ad ♂. ♀ *eclipse* As ad ♀, but crest shorter, crown browner, head paler, usually light streak from bill to eyes. *Juv* As ♀ eclipse, but bill yellow-brown, crest much shorter and thinner, head more grey-buff, white throat less defined (*cf*

Merganser), upperparts browner; ♂ already larger. *1st winter* ♂ Moults in same way as 1st winter ♂ Merganser. VOICE In courtship, ♂ twanging, croaking and bell-like notes, ♀ harsh *karr* and cackle. HABITAT Large lochs and rivers, esp in wooded areas; winters also on open lakes, reservoirs, sometimes estuaries. NEST In hollow trees, holes in rocks or banks, also among heather, 8–11 eggs, Apr–mid Jun; 1 brood. FOOD Fish. RANGE Resident; also winter visitor from N Europe, Oct–Apr.

COMPARE Hooded Merganser (262).

| Red-breasted Merganser | | B4 W5 S5 A5 | Goosander | | B4 W4 S4 A4 |

Goosander

KITES, HARRIERS, HAWKS, BUZZARDS,
EAGLES (Accipitridae)

Honey Buzzard *Pernis apivorus* 50–58 cm
(20–23 in). Slimmer than similar-sized
Buzzard (100), with slender bill, comparatively small Cuckoo-like head protruding
on thin neck; more pointed wings look
pinched in at body, and tail is usually at
least as long as width of wing, looking thin
when closed and slightly rounded at
corners; ad usually grey-brown above (but
some darker brown), and very variably
scallop-barred or mainly dark brown or
white below, with buzzard-like dark
carpal patches, but diagnostic pattern of
barring on flight-feathers and tail, latter
having broad band at tip and 2 narrower
bands at base; juv even more variable,
with less distinct barring, inc 4 tail-bands.
Flight strong with soft, deep, flexible
beats, often maintained for longer periods
than other raptors; glides with wings
angled and slightly arched (carpal joints
pressed forward, long 'hands' pointing
back slightly below level) and tail twisted

as rudder; soars with wings flat or just
upcurved and edges almost parallel at
right-angles to body; in courtship flights,
pair soars and undulates, ♂ dives and
swoops up or, most characteristically,
rises steeply, stalls, raises wings vertically
above back several times and quivers them,
then dives and repeats performance;
walks easily, even runs, on ground with
neck extended and body horizontal, and
uses feet for digging, but usually locates
wasp nests from tree perch or in flight; shy
and secretive; solitary, but flocks on
migration abroad. *Ad* Typically grey-
brown above with 3 bands on tail and
corresponding bands on trailing edge of
wings, bases of primaries and tips of
greater coverts, but ♂ usually greyer on
crown and head-sides, ♀ more brownish,
and some individuals rather darker on
upperparts; below, main bands on flight-
feathers and tail always clear, otherwise
typically whitish with variable dark
barring on body and wing-coverts and
distinct carpal patches, but dark birds
have more or less uniformly dark brown

Honey Buzzard

barred ad

dark ad

light ad

light juv

dark juv

underbody/wing-coverts and flight-feathers varying from whitish to dark grey on secondaries, pale birds have largely cream or white underbody/inner wing-coverts, and others are intermediate; cere dark blue-grey, eyes orange to red (♂) or yellow (♀). *Juv/1st winter* Typically dark brown above but for obscurely barred pale patch on primaries, thin whitish lines along tips of greater coverts and flight-feathers, whitish U on uppertail-coverts, and usually 4 indistinct blackish bars and whitish tip to tail, but pale birds also have white head with dark eye-patches, dark-mottled whitish forewings; typically dark rufous to blackish-brown below with dark grey tail and secondaries but whitish patch at base of primaries and often pale band along greater coverts, 4 indistinct tail-bars, 3-4 obscure bars and more extensive dark tips on wings (though no broad band like ad on trailing edge); pale birds have whitish underbody/coverts, often with brown streaks (not bars); cere yellow, eyes brown. *1st summer* With moult from early in year, becomes increasingly like ad, but

worn and faded juv flight-feathers retained till cJun–Aug. VOICE Much less noisy than Buzzard: main call piercing whistled *pew-ee-ew* or *pee-a*. HABITAT Old broadleaved woods, esp beech, but also mixed and coniferous; migrants often over open country. NEST High in trees, often on foundations of old Crow or Buzzard nests, 2 eggs, Jun–early Sep; 1 brood. FOOD Larvae, pupae, adults and honeycombs of wasps and bumble-bees, as well as ant pupae, mainly dug up with feet; also other insects and some voles, lizards, frogs, worms, eggs and young birds, even berries. RANGE Very scarce and local summer visitor, May–Sep, wintering in Africa: also scarce passage-migrant, probably from S Scandinavia, Apr–Nov, mainly May–Jun, Sep–Oct, very rare as far west as Ir.

Honey Buzzard

B1
W0
S2
A2

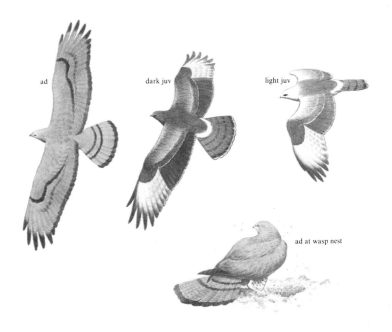

ad

dark juv

light juv

ad at wasp nest

Red Kite *Milvus milvus* 58–64 cm (*c*24 in).
Buzzard-sized, but slimmer, rakish, with
much longer, deeply forked tail (notched
even when spread) and long broadish
wings set well forward; very rufous with
pale head, black-cornered tail, blackish
flight-feathers and broad buff diagonal
across inner wings above, and large white
patch at base of primaries below. Flight
graceful, with slow deep flaps and up-and-
down body-movement; when gliding/
soaring, wings held forward, slightly
arched and kinked, and, like tail, constantly flexed and twisted independently;
in courtship, pair circles high on crossing
paths; takes prey on ground, where hops
awkwardly; perches on trees; shy; solitary.
Ad Mainly rufous-chestnut, browner
above, with whitish head, all streaked
blackish; tail bright rufous with black
corners; white patch beneath primaries
often not reaching rear of wing. *Juv* Head
less whitish, tail browner; above, wing-
diagonal broader/paler, also whitish line
along greater coverts, pale rufous tail-
coverts; below, clearly streaked buff-white,

with whitish patch on primaries almost to
rear edge. *1st year* Much as ad after moult
in *c*Oct–May, but wings/tail as juv. VOICE
Shrill mewing *weeoo*, rapidly repeated
weee-wee-wee. HABITAT Steep valleys with
mature woods, open ground. NEST High
in broadleaved trees, 2–3 eggs, Apr–mid
Jul; 1 brood. FOOD Small mammals, birds,
carrion. RANGE Widespread in Br to late
18th century, now rare; mainly sedentary,
but some wander end Jul–Apr; vagrants
from Continent, mostly Mar–Apr.
COMPARE Black Kite (264).

Marsh Harrier *Circus aeruginosus* 48–56
cm (19–22 in). Bulkiest, broadest-winged
of the harriers, which are rather slim,
elongated, ground-nesting hawks with long
wings, tails and legs, that hunt low over
reeds, heather or corn, gliding and soaring
with wings in shallow V. ♂ has dark back,
upperwing-coverts and underbody
contrasting with grey central wings and
tail; ♀/juv mainly dark but for variably
creamy head and (♀) buff shoulders and
breast. Flies with several heavy flaps, then

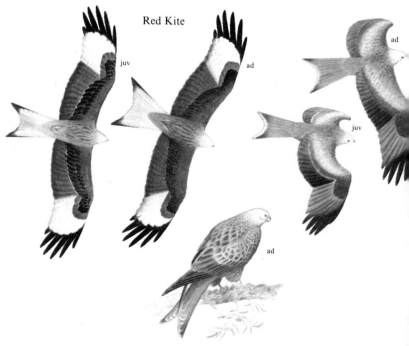

Red Kite

juv

ad

ad

juv

ad

a glide, usually low over reeds or water, but soars high; in courtship flight, ♂ dives with wings half-closed, shoots up again, loops-the-loop, or falls spinning; ♂ passes food to ♀ in air, ♀ turning on back with claws out; takes all prey on ground or water; perches low on posts, bushes, and often settles on ground, walking heavily; solitary, but ♂ sometimes polygamous. *Ad ♂* Streaky head, dark brown back and coverts (sometimes creamy shoulders), grey mid-wings and side-barred tail, black wing-tips, rarely whitish rump; below, streaky rufous body, pale grey tail, and variably whitish underwings with coverts rufous-buff to creamy-white and more or less dark trailing edges (old ♂s palest). *Ad ♀* Mainly chocolate-brown, but creamy head with dark eye-band, creamy-buff shoulders and breast-patch, and pale-based primaries below; tail tinged rufous, or variably grey on older ♀s. *Juv* As ad ♀, but largely lacks pale shoulders and breast, and sometimes all-dark but for slightly lighter tail and often paler-based primaries below. *Imm ♂* By 1st summer develops

streaked crown; by 2nd winter greyish mid-wings with black tips, brown-grey tail with some brown side-barring and broad band near end; in 2nd summer more streaked below. VOICE ♂ shrill *kee-oo* in courtship flight. HABITAT Extensive reed-beds, adjacent open country. NEST On or near ground or in shallows in reeds, 4–5 eggs, May–early Aug; 1 brood. FOOD Small mammals, birds, eggs, nestlings, carrion. RANGE Rare summer visitor, Apr–Sep, wintering south to Africa; scarce passage migrant from Continent, esp Sep–Nov, Mar–May; odd ones all year.

Marsh Harrier

all-dark juv

Hen Harrier *Circus cyaneus* 43–51 cm (17–20 in). Intermediate in bulk between Marsh (94) and Montagu's; ♂ grey and white, but for black wing-tips and dark trailing edges, with white rump; brown, white-rumped 'ring-tail' ♀/juv separated from ♀ Montagu's by head-pattern. Flight as Marsh Harrier, but wing-beats faster, glides usually shorter and sometimes on flat or bowed wings, though normally glides and always soars with wings in shallow V; ♂ courtship flights include steep dives, upward swoops, rolls, somersaults; similar food-pass; walks easily. *Ad* ♂ Grey above, but for white rump, black wing-tips, faint dark trailing edges (more obvious from below); mainly white below, with well-defined grey throat/chest. *Ad* ♀ Streaky owl-like head with barely darker crescent on rear cheeks separated by indistinct pale collar from ruff of dark streaks; otherwise dark brown above with white rump, dark-streaked buff below with broad bars on flight-feathers and tail. *Juv* Very like ad ♀, but underparts and wider fringes to upperwing-coverts more

rufous, secondaries and cheeks usually (sometimes much) darker. *1st summer/ 2nd winter* ♂ With moult in *c*May–Oct, gradually more as ad ♂, but browner-grey above and some rufous marks below. VOICE When breeding, ♂ dry cackling *chuk-uk-uk*, ♀ sharper higher *kek-ek-ek*; also whistled squealing *whit-tew* (esp ♀). HABITAT Moors, young conifer plantations; winter/passage also over downs, fields, dunes. NEST On ground in heather, rushes, conifers, 4–6 eggs, May–early Aug; 1 brood. FOOD Small birds, rodents. RANGE Mainly sedentary, but some emigrate; passage/winter visitor from Continent, mostly ring-tails, mainly Sep–Apr.

Montagu's Harrier *Circus pygargus* 39–46 cm (15½–18 in). Slimmer, with narrower wings, than Hen Harrier; ♂ looks dirtier, being darker grey, with black bar on upperwings, dark lines on underwings, rufous streaks on flanks, usually grey rump; ♀ separated from 'ring-tail' Hen Harrier by head-pattern, usually smaller white rump, but juv also unstreaked rufous

Hen Harrier

below. Actions as Hen Harrier, though wing-beats more leisurely and buoyant, glides more wavering with wings always in V, often deeper V when soaring. *Ad ♂* Grey above, but for black wing-tips and mid-wing bar, slight barring on outer tail, but rump sometimes whitish; white below, with dark grey throat/breast, rufous streaks on flanks/wing-coverts, 1–2 black bars and thin greyish trailing edge on secondaries, pale grey tail lightly barred. *Ad ♀* Dark crescent on rear cheeks (*cf* dark-cheeked juv Hen Harriers), white around eyes divided by faint dark streak, no pale collar; otherwise much as ♀ Hen Harrier. *Juv* Much as ad ♀, but mostly plain rufous below, with dark secondaries, and darker above, usually with pale nape-spot and thin pale line along greater coverts. *1st summer ♂* Brown-grey above with browner head, broad rufous streaks on grey-brown throat/chest and buff-white underbody, worn juv flight-feathers and outer tail. *2nd summer ♂* Much as ad ♂, but browner above (esp head), white marks on nape, less extensive grey below. *Melanistic form*

♂ all sooty-grey above and blackish below with paler tail; ♀ all dark chocolate but for banded tail (no white rump); both show whitish patch at base of primaries below. VOICE When breeding, staccato *yek-ek-ek* (♀ shriller), thin plaintive *psee-ee*. HABITAT Young conifer plantations, heaths, moors, dunes, reeds, corn. NEST On ground in dense cover, 4–5 eggs, mid May–late Aug; 1 brood. FOOD Small birds, rodents. RANGE Rare summer visitor, May–Sep, wintering in Africa; some passage Apr–May, Aug–Oct. COMPARE Pallid Harrier (264).

Montagu's Harrier

juv

melanistic ♂

melanistic ♀

Goshawk *Accipiter gentilis* 48–58 cm (19–23 in), ♂ much smaller than ♀. Like large ♀ Sparrowhawk (♂ not much bigger, but ♀ Buzzard-sized), with more protruding head, deeper chest, longer wings and wider-based, rounder-ended tail; grey-brown above, closely barred brown on white below, with paler-banded tail than Sparrowhawk, dark ear-coverts forming hood, and whiter supercilia and undertail-coverts (esp ♀); browner juv streaked and often orange-tinged below. Flight as Sparrowhawk, but stronger, heavier, with slower beats; glides on flat wings with tips somewhat pointed and trailing edges S-curved; often soars, with rounded wings held slightly forward and tail usually well spread (*cf* Sparrowhawk); courtship flights include soaring with white under-tail-coverts spread, interspersed with slow harrier-like beats, also plummeting dives and switchback of plunges and upward swoops; hunts by weaving with speed and agility among trees, or watching from perch, then dashes and glides at quarry; will chase birds into thick cover or from branch to branch; solitary. *Ad* ♂ Grey-brown above, with blackish crown above whitish supercilia and nape; tail grey-brown with *c*4 narrow dark bars and broader band behind thin white tip; whitish below, closely barred dark brown on body and underwings and banded on flight-feathers and greyish tail; eyes red-orange. *Ad* ♀ Browner above, with clearer white supercilia and undertail. *Juv* Brown above, tinged rufous or buff by pale fringes, with bolder tail-bands; whitish to rufous below with dark drop-like streaks, stronger-barred flight-feathers; eyes green-grey, turning yellow; much as ad from 2nd year. VOICE Shrill chattering *gek-gek-gek*, short plaintive scream *hee-aa*. HABITAT Lowland or upland woods, plantations. NEST In trees, 3–4 eggs, May–Jul; 1 brood. FOOD Birds, mammals. RANGE ?. Feral, nesting more since 1960s; wanderers may include Continental immigrants; 6 records of American race.

Sparrowhawk *Accipiter nisus* 28–38 cm (11–15 in), ♂ much smaller than ♀.

Goshawk

juv ♀

♀

♀

♂

juv ♂

Smallish, fierce-looking, with long square-ended tail, shortish broad wings usually looking much blunter than Kestrel or Merlin (104); grey (♂) or brown above with banded tail; whitish below, barred rufous-orange (♂) or brown, but for white undertail-coverts. Flight dashing burst of rapid beats, then short glide; soars with wings flat and slightly forward, tail often closed or only briefly fanned (cf Goshawk); courtship flights include soaring mixed with slow harrier-like wing-beats and shallow undulations, and ♂ also dives at perched ♀ or chases her through trees; hunts mainly by surprise, waiting on hidden perch, weaving through trees, or flying low along hedge and then flicking over to other side, also chases prey into thick cover; solitary. *Ad ♂* Slate-grey to paler blue-grey above with rufous cheeks; tail with 3-4 narrow dark brown bars and broader band behind thin white tip; whitish below, narrowly barred orange-red on body and underwings (often looking all-orange) and banded dark on flight-feathers and greyish tail; eyes yellow.

Ad ♀ Dark brown or grey-brown above, with whitish supercilia; barred brown below or rufous on flanks. *Juv* Brown above, tinged rufous by pale fringes; whitish to buff below with brown bars (more rufous and broken on breast of ♂); eyes green-grey, turning yellow; much as ads in 2nd year after moult in May-Aug. VOICE Shrill *kek-kek-kek*, plaintive *wee-oo*. HABITAT Woods (esp coniferous or mixed), farmland, also upland scrub, suburbs. NEST In trees, 5-6 eggs, May-Jul; 1 brood. FOOD Small birds. RANGE Sedentary; also passage/winter from Continent, Sep-Apr.

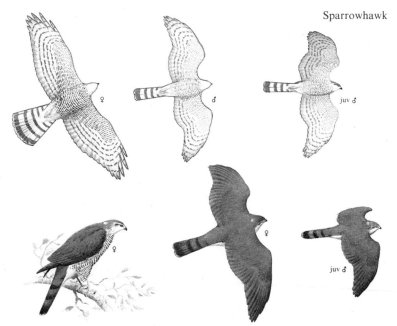

Sparrowhawk

Buzzard *Buteo buteo* 50–56 cm (20–22 in). Medium-sized and compact, with broad head and short neck (not projecting like Honey Buzzard, 92, or Golden Eagle, 102), fairly broad wings, and short tail (only $c\frac{3}{4}$ width of wing-base) rounded when spread but showing clear corners; varies from largely dark brown to mainly creamy-white, but in Br/Ir mostly dark with pale crescent on lower breast; lacks distinct tail-bands and wing-barring of Honey Buzzard and complete white tail-base of Rough-legged. Flight strong but slow, heavy-looking, with stiff, rather laboured and not very deep beats, mixed with easy glides; glides with wings flat or just upcurved, carpal joints pressed forward and trailing tips quite pointed; soars with whole wings raised and pressed forward, tips upcurved, and tail broadly fanned; sometimes hovers; in courtship, soars in circles, plunges and swoops up; perches prominently on trees, bushes, rocks, posts, telegraph poles; drops on to prey on ground, walks awkwardly; usually solitary, although sometimes several in air together. *Ad* Typically dark brown above, often with paler area at base of outer primaries (but may be mottled, streaked, blotched or largely creamy-white on head, body, wing-coverts and even extreme base of tail, *cf* Rough-legged Buzzard); typically dark brown below, often paler on throat, normally pale U on breast and pale bar on median coverts, always lighter flight-feathers with well-defined dark trailing edge and obscurely barred greyer tail with brown subterminal band (but sometimes much white below or showing distinct blackish carpal patches and dark flanks or belly, *cf* Rough-legged Buzzard). *Juv* Below, dark rear wing-edge and tail-band narrower, more obscure; as ad after 1st summer moult. VOICE Loud, drawn-out, plaintive, ringing *pee-yow*. HABITAT Moors, scrub, woods, cliffs, locally wooded heaths, farmland. NEST In trees or cliffs, 2–4 eggs, Apr–Jul; 1 brood. FOOD Rabbits, voles, also carrion, young birds, frogs, worms, insects. RANGE Mainly sedentary; some winter in Aug–Apr, irregular passage in Aug–Nov. Mar–Apr.

Buzzard

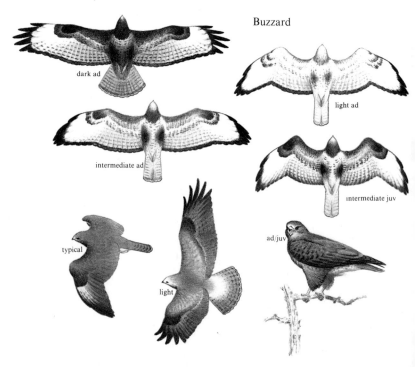

dark ad

light ad

intermediate ad

intermediate juv

typical

ad/juv

light

Rough-legged Buzzard *Buteo lagopus*
50–61 cm (20–24 in). Smaller head than
Buzzard, longer narrower wings, longer
tail (at least equalling width of wing-
base), feathered legs; tail white-based
with broad blackish subterminal band and
1–4 narrower bars on distal half (ad) or
just broader paler subterminal band (juv);
pale head and grey to whitish patch on
primaries above, esp juv (*cf* juv Golden
Eagle, 102, also with white-based tail),
and usually obvious dark carpal and belly
patches below. Actions as Buzzard, but
slower, more flexible beats; glides with
'arms' raised, 'hands' level. *Ad* Dark
above but for dark-streaked whitish head,
variable pale area on primaries, whitish
leading edge to wings, blackish-banded
white tail; below, throat/chest and wing-
coverts vary from mainly dark brown to
white more or less streaked brown, with
dark carpal patches, whitish U on breast
extending down to divide blackish patches
on sides of belly, whitish flight-feathers
with blackish tips and trailing edge and
variable dark barring on secondaries, tail-
pattern as from above. *Juv/1st winter*
Usually paler above, esp on head and
wing-coverts, with more distinct whitish
patch at base of primaries, but less white
at tail-base and paler broader subterminal
band; also paler below, sometimes largely
white but for blackish wing-tips, carpal
patches and usually all-dark belly, with
tail-end hardly contrasting. VOICE Thin
mournful mewing; migrants mostly silent.
HABITAT Open marshes, moors, hills,
heaths, dunes. FOOD Rabbits, voles, some
birds. RANGE Usually scarce winter visitor
from Scandinavia, Oct–Apr (Sep–May).

Buzzard		B5 W5 S5 A5	Rough-legged Buzzard		B0 W1 S2 A2

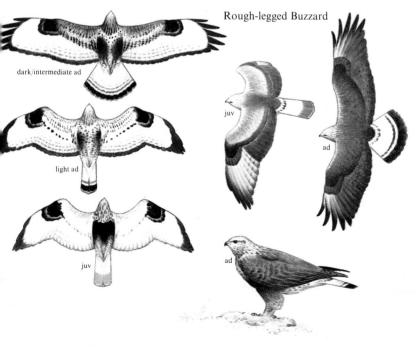

Rough-legged Buzzard

dark/intermediate ad

light ad

juv

juv

ad

ad

Golden Eagle *Aquila chrysaetos* 76–90 cm (30–35 in). Large, with protruding head, long wings bulging at secondaries but narrower by body, rounded tail as long as width of wing-base, feathered legs; often confused with much smaller Buzzard or Rough-legged Buzzard (100), but proportions of head, wings and tail quite different; ad mainly dark with golden head and often wing-coverts, imms with conspicuous white centre of wings and base of tail. Flight powerful with deep leisurely beats, long glides; soars with wings in shallow V and held slightly forward, primaries upcurved, tail spread; wings less raised when gliding; courtship flights include plunging and swooping up, rolling over; hunts fairly low, dropping on prey with half-closed wings; perches on crags, trees; solitary, but families together through autumn. *Ad* Dark brown to blackish (wearing much paler) with golden to buff crown/nape, often obvious grey to yellowish oblong on upperwing-coverts, and paler grey-brown flight-feathers and tail shading to broad blackish

tips. *Juv* Mainly blackish-brown, with rather paler crown/nape and 'trousers', often some whitish mottling (white feather-bases) on body, but esp bold white bases to flight-feathers (usually forming patch only on inner primaries above, but band along much of wing below) and whitish basal $\frac{1}{2}$–$\frac{2}{3}$ of tail. *1st–4th year* After slow moult in 1st summer, crown/nape dull tawny, body much as ad; but variable amount of white shows on wings and esp tail until at least well into 3rd summer. VOICE Usually silent; mewing *wee-o* (not unlike Buzzard), shrill yelping bark. HABITAT Hills, mountains, moorland crags; locally pine forests, sea-cliffs. NEST On cliffs or in trees, 2 eggs, mid Mar–Jul; 1 brood. FOOD Mammals, birds, carrion. RANGE Sedentary; formerly bred Ir, also NIr 1953–60. COMPARE White-tailed (264).

OSPREYS (Pandionidae)

Osprey *Pandion haliaetus* 51–59 cm (20–23 in). Moderate-sized raptor habitually near water, with smallish but well-

Golden Eagle

protruding and slightly crested head, long and narrow-ended angled wings, shortish tail; dark above, but much white on head and underparts, setting off blackish eye-bands, carpal patches and greater coverts, with narrowly barred tail and flight-feathers, pale-based black-tipped primaries. Flight powerful with shallow, flexible beats; soars and esp glides with wings bowed or kinked like large gull; courtship flights include plunges, upward swoops, and pauses on rapidly beating wings with slanted body; hunts by flapping and gliding *c*10–30 m over water, hovering at intervals with dangled legs, then diving down (feet forward at last moment), partly or wholly submerging but for upheld wings, but also dives from perch or plucks from surface; carries fish head first, usually with one foot behind the other; shakes wet off after rising and, having fed, often trails feet in water to clean them; perches on bare trees, posts, rocks; solitary. *Ad* Dark brown above, contrasting whitish rear-crown and nape; rusty-brown breast-band. *Juv* Paler above

through creamy feather-tips, crown/nape more streaked, breast-band less clear; much as ad through wear by 1st summer (when mostly stays in winter quarters). VOICE Shrill repeated whistling or yelping *cheep* or *chewk*, esp when breeding. HABITAT Lakes, large rivers, coasts. NEST Near tops of conifers with dead branches, 3 eggs, mid Apr–Jul; 1 brood. FOOD Fish averaging *c*300 g. RANGE Ceased to nest 1917–54, now scarce summer visitor, Apr–Sep, wintering in Africa north to Mediterranean; also on passage from Scandinavia, Apr–May, Aug–Oct.

Osprey

FALCONS (Falconidae)

Kestrel *Falco tinnunculus* 33–36 cm (*c*13½ in). Longish tail and long pointed wings; ♂ with blue-grey head and much of tail, black-spotted chestnut back; ♀/juv rufous above with blackish bars. Flight with fast shallow beats, occasional glides and twists; hunts by hovering head to wind, hanging almost motionless or with rapid shallow wing-beats, tail fanned, body sloping, then drops steeply to ground; also catches feeding or perched birds by sudden dashes; soars with wings and tail spread (*cf* Sparrowhawk, 98); perches on trees, poles, power lines, buildings, rocks; solitary. *Ad* ♂ Crown/hindneck blue-grey, mantle/wing-coverts black-spotted chestnut, wing-ends blackish, tail blue-grey with black band and white tip; buffish below, spotted black on breast and under-wings, faintly barred on flight-feathers. *Ad* ♀ Dark-barred rufous above (rump and often tail greyer) with blackish wing-ends, broader band behind white tail-tip; creamy-buff below, more streaked than ♂,

boldly spotted on underwings, barred on flight-feathers and tail; cere yellow. *Juv* As ad ♀, but more chestnut rump, and broader and paler streaks below, cere greenish; more like ads after body moult in Aug–Apr, but 2nd winter ♂ still with rufous crown, varying amount of grey and bars on tail, not fully ad until 3rd year. VOICE Shrill *kee-kee-kee*. HABITAT Open woods, farmland, parks, towns, cliffs, moors, marshes; often hovers over verges of motorways. NEST On ledge or in hole, esp cliff, old building, old Crow nest, hollow tree, or on ground, 4–6 eggs, Apr–mid Jul; 1 brood. FOOD Small mammals, birds, insects. RANGE Mainly sedentary, some move south to N Iberia; immigrants from Continent, Aug–May, esp in EBr.

Merlin *Falco columbarius* 27–32 cm (*c*10½–12½ in), ♂ thrush-sized, ♀ larger. Shortish tail and broad-based pointed wings; ♂ slate-blue above, ♀/juv dark brown with barred tail, all variously dark-streaked below, but moustaches obscure. Flight dashing and direct with fast win-

Kestrel

nowing beats, short glides, often low over ground (*cf* Sparrowhawk, 98); circles high over nesting area, but soars little, seldom hovers; hunts with shallow beats and undulating action through briefly closing wings, but when chasing prey follows every twist and turn; perches on rocks, hummocks, walls, fences, less on trees; solitary. *Ad ♂* Slate-blue above, palest on rump/tail but for broad black tip, with darker crown and wing-ends, rufous nape, rufous or greyish cheeks, obscure moustaches; buffish to rusty below with extensive blackish streaks, rufous-marked underwings, dark-barred flight-feathers, black-ended whitish tail. *Ad ♀* Largely dark brown above with cream-barred tail, whitish nape, streaky cheeks, greyer back/ rump and rusty fringes on mantle/scapulars; whitish to creamy below with heavy brown streaks, dark-barred flight-feathers and tail; cere yellow. *Juv* Very like ad ♀, though darker above, browner-white below with darker brown streaks, cere bluish to greenish; ♀s larger than ♂s, with darker cheeks, wider streaks; as ads from

1st summer/2nd winter after moults in Feb-Nov. VOICE Fast shrill chattering *kik-ik-ik* or *kee-kee-kee* near nest. HABITAT Moors, fells, bogs, rough ground above cliffs, coastal dunes; winters more widely in open country, marshes. NEST Scrape on ground, or sometimes in old Crow nests on cliffs or in trees, 3–5 eggs, May–Jul; 1 brood. FOOD Mainly small birds. RANGE Upland birds winter lower or go south, few to Iberia; passage/winter from Iceland/?N Europe, Aug–May.

COMPARE Other falcons (106, 264, 266).

Merlin

Hobby *Falco subbuteo* 30–36 cm (12–14 in), ♂ rather smaller than ♀. Smallish slender falcon with shortish tail and scythe-like wings (♀ broader-based), like huge Swift (184); dark slate above, heavily streaked below, with pointed black moustaches, cream throat and cheeks, rufous thighs and undertail (buff on juv). Flight dashing, with rapid stiff winnowing beats, short glides; soars with wings flat and tail spread, seldom hovers; courtship flights include spectacular plunging, spinning, rolling over, looping-the-loop; stoops on or outflies birds, but hawks insects (held in foot and eaten in flight) with slower flatter wing-beats and leisurely soaring; ♂ passes food to ♀ in air; perches mainly in trees; usually solitary. *Ad* Dark slate above, browner in worn plumage (esp ♀), with slightly paler tail, obscure buff-white nape-band; bold blackish moustaches against cream throat and neck-sides; cream to buff below streaked blackish, with rufous thighs/tail-coverts, dark-spotted wing-coverts, narrowly barred flight-feathers and tail, darker wing-tips;

cere yellow. *Juv* Blacker above with buff feather-edges, more heavily streaked below, with buff thighs/tail-coverts, cere grey-blue or greenish; as ad from 1st summer/2nd winter after moult in Mar–Sep. VOICE Clear plaintive *kew-kew-kew*, esp near nest with young. HABITAT Heaths/downs with pine clumps, farmland with old hedgerow trees, also wood-edges. NEST In old crow nests in trees, 3 eggs, Jun–Aug; 1 brood. FOOD Small birds (*eg* larks, martins, even Swifts), large insects. RANGE Summer visitor, late Apr–Sep, wintering in Africa; some on passage from Continent, Apr–Jun, Aug–Oct.

Peregrine *Falco peregrinus* 38–48 cm (15–19 in), ♂ smaller than ♀. Largish, compact, robust falcon with slightly tapered tail and pointed, broad-based wings; blue-slate above with paler rump, barred tail, broad moustaches, and mainly barred below, but juv dark brown above, streaked below. Flight powerful with stiff shallow winnowing beats, short or long glides, faster and with deeper beats when

Hobby

hunting; soars on more or less level wings, hangs on updraughts, but rarely hovers; courtship flights include spectacular plunging and shooting up, rolling over, figures-of-eight, talon-grappling; usually stoops on prey from height, very fast (c150–250 km/h) with wings nearly closed; ♂ passes food to ♀ in air; perches hunched on cliffs, rocks, also buildings, fences, trees; solitary. *Ad ♂* Blue-slate above, faintly barred blackish, with darker wing-ends, banded blackish and grey tail; blackish head and rounded moustaches against white throat and cheek-patches; cream to pink-buff below, flecked on chest and otherwise barred black, with paler flight-feathers and tail; legs and cere yellow. *Ad ♀* Darker above, nape sometimes buffish; often more heavily barred below, larger drop-like markings on chest. *Juv* Dark brown above with pale feather-edges, creamy forehead, buff nape, narrower moustaches, and cream to rufous-buff below with brown streaks (not bars), heavier on ♀; legs and cere blue-grey to greenish; as ads from 1st

summer/2nd winter after moult in Mar–Dec. VOICE Harsh staccato chattering *kak-kak-kak*, shrill whining *kee-errk*, creaking *wee-chew*, esp near nest. HABITAT Moorland, mountain and coastal cliffs, locally crags in wooded areas; juvs/immigrants winter also in open country, estuaries, marshes. NEST On cliff ledges, 3–4 eggs, Apr–Jul; 1 brood. FOOD Largely birds (pigeons, seabirds, grouse). RANGE Sedentary, but juvs disperse; also autumn/winter immigrants from Fenno-Scandia.

COMPARE Other falcons (104, 264, 266).

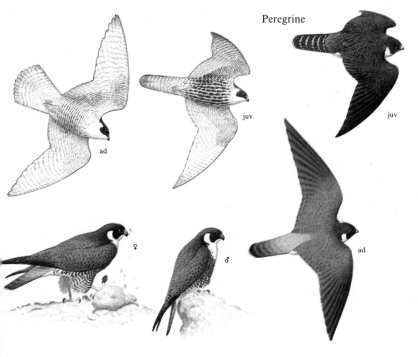

Peregrine

ad
juv
juv
♀
♂
ad

GROUSE (Tetraonidae)

Red Grouse *Lagopus lagopus* 33–39 cm (13–15½ in). Endemic Br/Ir race of N Eurasian Willow Grouse, common sight and sound of moors; plump, stout-billed, with small head, short rounded wings and tail, white-feathered legs; usually rufous or buff, barred black, looking all-dark at distance, with blackish wings (variably white on under-coverts) and tail (hidden at rest by long coverts), but much variation: some predominantly blackish or red (esp ♂s), or more spotted or barred whitish-buff (esp ♀s), while white marks of winter on belly/flanks may form patches (*cf* Ptarmigan). Flight fast, strong, with rapid beats and long glides on bowed wings after whirring take-off with noisy cackling, usually low over heather, often rocking from side to side; walks with roll, or runs, with rounded back; may settle in trees and ♂ will perch up on posts; shy, but often crouches until approached closely; gathers in family parties in autumn, then small flocks (often mainly

♀s/imm ♂s). *♂ summer* With moult in *c*Apr–Jun, rufous to tawny heavily barred black; red combs prominent. *♂ winter* With continuing moult in *c*Jul–Nov, darker rufous and chestnut more finely barred, variably tipped white on belly/flanks. *Ad ♀* Changes as ♂ (though summer moult in *c*Mar–May), but smaller, paler and more contrastingly barred and spotted: in winter more like summer ♂ (but tipped white below), in summer much yellower; combs less prominent. *Juv* Like small ♀ (winter above, summer below), but buffs duller, barring browner underneath, no combs; as ads after moult in *c*Jul–Nov. VOICE Rapid cackling *ko-ko-ko . . .*; crowing *raa ka-ka-ka . . . gobak-gobak-bak-bak-bak. . . .* HABITAT Drier heather moors, also peat-bogs, nearby stubble. NEST In heather, rushes, 5–9 eggs, Apr–Jun; 1 brood. FOOD Heather, also berries, insects. RANGE Sedentary; introduced Shetland, SWBr.

Ptarmigan *Lagopus mutus* 33–36 cm (*c*13½ in). Mountain grouse, slighter than Red,

Red Grouse

rufous ♂ / ♂ summer / juv / dark ♂ / ♀ summer

with daintier bill, shorter legs and narrower wings; grey, brown or buff, finely barred, with white wings and underbody, becoming all-white in winter but for black tail (obvious only in flight). Actions as Red Grouse, but flies spectacularly up and down steep slopes; walks agilely over rocks; often crouches, or ♂ may perch boldly; inquisitive but shy. ♂ *summer* With moult May–Jun, dark grey-brown, barred and speckled blackish, buff and white, but white wings, underbody and feathered legs; combs red. ♂ *autumn* With continuing moult in Jul–Sep, dark areas paler buff-grey with fine black barring; combs yellow-red, smaller. ♂ *winter* After further moult in cSep–Dec, more or less white but for black lores, black-sided tail; usually some coloured feathers. Ad ♀ Changes as ♂ (though moults faster, in May, Sep): in summer more sharply barred golden-buff and blackish, much less white below; by autumn as ♂ but yellower-grey, still some bold-barred golden feathers, and in winter rarely black on lores; combs smaller, orange-red when

breeding. *Juv* Like small autumn ♀, but wings and tail as upperparts (not white or black), no combs. *1st autumn* As autumn ads, but still many non-white juv wing-coverts, mottled primaries; as winter ad after moult in cSep–Dec, but often some primaries still mottled. VOICE ♂ hoarse crackling and ♀ higher yapping *kuk-uk-uk*, *aar-orr-kakarr*; song *er-ook-ka-ka-ka-ka . . . kwa-kwa-kwa*, belching then cackling, softer at end. HABITAT Stony mountains, esp above 700 m. NEST On ground, 4–9 eggs, mid May–mid Aug; 1 brood. FOOD Shoots, leaves, berries. RANGE Sedentary.

Ptarmigan

Black Grouse *Tetrao tetrix* ♂ 51–56 cm
(*c*21 in), ♀ 40–44 cm (*c*16½ in). Longer-
necked than Red Grouse (108), with tail
lyre-shaped (♂) or slightly forked (♀);
♂ glossy black with white wing-bar, undertail and underwings; ♀ mainly black-
barred rufous, with 2 narrow whitish
wing-bars, white on underwings. Flight as
Red Grouse, but sometimes much higher
with long glides over open moors and
valleys; tilts between trees like Capercaillie; walks sedately or runs; perches
on trees, walls, usually roosts on ground;
shy; often gregarious, sexes may segregate;
♂s display communally at regular leks (*cf*
Ruff, 134) with spread tail, drooped wings,
distended combs. *Ad* ♂ Mostly glossy
blue-black with contrasted white areas
and red combs (largest in spring), but in
Jun–Jul head and throat marked with
white and nape/neck (sometimes crown/
mantle) also barred rufous. *Ad* ♀ Mainly
rufous, barred glossy black above and
brown-black below; grey-white tips to
scapulars, belly, all tail-coverts. *Juv* Like
small dull ♀, often more buff and less

rufous (esp juv ♀) with duller, narrower
bars; buff-white shaft-streaks on scapulars
and wing-coverts. *1st year* ♂ Much as ad
♂ after moult in *c*Jul–Nov, but less glossy,
with various dark rufous bars or mottling
above and white marks on throat/breast,
tail less curved, small combs hidden.
VOICE At lek, ♂ hissing *chew-oosh* and
bubbling dove-like song ('rookooing'); ♀
loud barking *chuk-chuk* from perch, *kok-
ok* in flight. HABITAT Birch scrub, young
conifers, wood- and moor-edges, rushy
pastures. NEST In ground cover, 6–11 eggs,
May-Jul; 1 brood. FOOD Buds, shoots,
leaves, catkins, berries. RANGE Sedentary.

Capercaillie *Tetrao urogallus* ♂ 82–90 cm
(*c*34 in), ♀ 58–64 cm (*c*24 in). Very large
with heavy bill, longish neck, broad wings,
rounded tail; turkey-shaped ♂ dark with
yellow bill, white shoulder-patches/inner
underwings; ♀ mainly orange-buff boldly
barred blackish, but nearly plain rufous
chest, white on dark-mottled belly/flanks
and underwings. Flight powerful, tilting
from side to side among trees, sometimes

Black Grouse

♂ displaying

♂ Jun–Jul

♀

sustained and high; noisy flapping on take-off; walks sedately, but can run fast, esp ♀; much in trees, esp roosting and in winter, perching even on tops; shy, sometimes in parties, ad ♂s usually solitary; ♂ displays on tree, rock or ground, with neck and fanned tail erect, wings drooped, throat-feathers stuck out or whole neck bristled in ripples. *Ad ♂* Blue-slate with brown mantle and wings, green-glossed breast, white shoulder-patches, whitish markings on tail-coverts, tail and belly, red skin by eyes. *Ad ♀* Pale buff to orange-brown, boldly barred blackish, but orange-chestnut breast-patch, much white on flanks and belly; pale red skin by eyes. *Juv ♂* Like small ad ♀, but greyer above and on throat, still with dark bars; wing-coverts with buff-white shaft-streaks; breast rufous mottled dark brown, flanks rufous-buff, belly buff-white; tail barred/speckled whitish, buff, dark brown; no red by eyes. *Juv ♀* As juv ♂, but more rufous and bolder-marked above, throat black-spotted buff, flanks/belly barred dark

brown. *1st year ♂* As ad ♂ after moult in *c*Jun–Sep, but smaller with shorter bill and tail, duller head and breast. VOICE ♂ raucous retching or croaking, and 'song' of accelerating clicks, then pop like bottle cork, ending with rhythmic wheezing gurgle; ♀ soft whining bray, harsh cackling *kok-ok*, loud crooning. HABITAT Coniferous or mixed woods, esp pines on hillsides. NEST In ground cover, esp by trees, 5–11 eggs, end Apr–Jun; 1 brood. FOOD Plants, berries; conifer needles in winter. RANGE Extinct by 18th century, reintroduced in 19th; sedentary.

Black Grouse		B5	Capercaillie		B4
		W5			W4
		S5			S4
		A5			A4

Capercaillie

♀

♂

juv ♂

♀

♂ displaying

PARTRIDGES, PHEASANTS (Phasianidae)

Red-legged Partridge *Alectoris rufa* 33–36 cm (*c*13½ in). Larger, more upright than Grey Partridge, but with similar rufous tail; plain olive-brown to chestnut above, bold white supercilia and throat, black necklace, heavily barred 4-tone flanks, red bill and legs (but see juv). Actions similar; more often in open, tends to run rather than fly; coveys taking wing often scatter; often perches on fences, walls. *Ad* Supercilia and throat white, complete black necklace; flanks barred blue-grey, whitish, black, chestnut; belly orange-buff. *Juv* Faint supercilia and throat buff-white, sparse mottling instead of necklace, slight whitish and brown barring on orange-buff flanks, pale speckling and dark bars or blotches on mantle and esp scapulars/coverts; bill brown, legs pinkish; as ad after moult in Aug–Nov. VOICE Harsh *chuk chuk chukuk chukar*; song *kok-chak-chak* with rhythm of steam-engine. HABITAT Farmland, brecks, heaths, dunes, coastal shingle. NEST In ground cover, 10–16 eggs, end Apr–mid Jul; 2 clutches (1 incubated by ♂). FOOD Much as Grey Partridge. RANGE Introduced from SW Europe since *c*1770; sedentary.

Grey Partridge *Perdix perdix* 29–32 cm (*c*12 in). Rotund, chicken-like, with short rufous tail, rounded wings; pale-streaked above, with orange face, grey neck/breast, chestnut-barred flanks, variable inverted chestnut U on breast ('*montana*' variety has much more rufous below). Flight fast, whirring, low, with glides on bowed wings; neck stretched up when running for cover; crouches blob-like in large fields; rarely perches; shy; as other gamebirds, small young fly at only 2–3 weeks; autumn/winter coveys tend to keep together when flushed. *Ad* ♂ Face orange-chestnut; grey breast, greyish forecrown, neck, mantle (greyest *c*Apr–Jul); bold chestnut horseshoe; legs flesh-grey. *Ad* ♀ Face paler, neck/upperparts browner, breast buff-grey, horseshoe reduced to blotches or absent, lesser/median coverts barred; after moult in Mar–May, neck/chest with buff spots, breast/flanks barred also

pale and blackish. *Juv* Head/upperparts dark brown streaked pale, breast/flanks buff-brown streaked whiter, throat whitish, legs yellow; as ads after moult Aug–Jan. VOICE Slowing cackle *krikrikri-kri-kri kri*; song hoarse *kirrr-ik kirrr-ik* like rusty lock. HABITAT Farmland with hedges; also moors, dunes. NEST In thick cover, 9–20 eggs, mid Apr–mid Jul; 1 brood. FOOD Seeds, leaves, roots; some insects. RANGE Sedentary.

Quail *Coturnix coturnix* 17–18.5 cm (*c*7 in). Heard far more than seen; smallest gamebird, like part-grown juv partridge but longer thinner wings, more pointed brown tail; buff-barred blackish above with pale streaks, crown-stripe and supercilia, and sandy to rufous below, with black-edged pale streaks and blackish barring on flanks. Very secretive, flying only if nearly trodden on. *Ad* ♂ Variable blackish central throat-stripe and 2 bands curving up to cheeks. *Ad* ♀ No central stripe, 2 bands broken into spots, brown moustaches; breast-sides spotted blackish. *Juv* As ♀, but narrower streaks above, smaller breast-spots; as ads after moult in Aug–Oct. VOICE Double croak; song liquid *kwic-we-wic* by day or night, ventriloquial. HABITAT Corn, long grass. NEST In crops, 7–12 eggs, end May–mid Aug; 1–2 broods. FOOD Seeds, insects. RANGE Summer visitor, May–Oct, wintering in Africa/S Europe.

Red-legged Partridge		B6
		W6
		S6
		A6

Grey Partridge		B5
		W6
		S5
		A6

Quail		B3
		W0
		S3
		A3

Red-legged Partridge

ad
ad
juv

Grey Partridge

ad
♀ summer
♂ winter
juv
montana ♂

Quail

ad
♂
♀

Pheasant *Phasianus colchicus* ♂ 75–90 cm (30–35 in), ♀ 52–64 cm (20–25 in). Typical ♂ has green-black head, red facial skin, coppery body and barred tail, buff wing-coverts; ♀ brown and buff, with some chestnut, all marked black. Flight strong, direct, with rapid beats and long glides after whirring take-off and fast climb, usually to no great height; walks slowly or runs with long tail level or raised; roosts in trees; wary; small flocks in winter, sexes may segregate. *Ad* ♂ Mixture of several races, esp SW Asian *colchicus* (bronze-black crown, no collar, mainly coppery but wing-coverts and narrow-barred tail more buff) and E Asian *torquatus* (olive crown, white eyebrows and collar, mainly yellow-buff but coppery breast, greyish wing-coverts and rump, broad-barred tail); may be paler, more chestnut or greener above, or have white wing-coverts; melanistic form mainly glossy green above and glossy purple below. *Ad* ♀ Buff to pink-buff and brown, chestnut on mantle and chest, with dark marks; may be more rufous, or sandier. *Juv* Like small short-tailed ♀ but duller, usually paler, more spotted on head, more streaked buff above; much as ads by Sep–Nov. VOICE ♂ crowing *korrk-kok* and *kutuk . . . kutuk*; ♀ husky *kia kia* and purr. HABITAT Woods, fields, marshes, upland scrub. NEST In ground cover, 8–15 eggs, Apr–Jul; 1 brood. FOOD Seeds, berries, shoots, invertebrates. RANGE Introduced from Asia since 11th century; sedentary.

Golden Pheasant *Chrysolophus pictus* ♂ 89–109 cm (35–43 in), ♀ 61–71 cm (24–28 in). Smaller and slimmer than Pheasant, even longer tail; ♂ mainly yellow and red; ♀ buff, barred and speckled black, but more rufous tail, and yellowish bill, legs and facial skin (*cf* Lady Amherst's). High steps, springy jumps; flies little except to tree roost, wing-beats less noisy. *Ad* ♂ Barred 'cape', buff tail laced with black. *Ad* ♀ Crown cinnamon-barred black, otherwise buff and cinnamon marked with black, esp breast/flanks broadly barred. *Juv* As small short-tailed ♀ but markings fainter, esp on chest/flanks. *1st year* ♂ Partly as ad ♀ by Oct–Nov, but

much of head orange-yellow, rump/tail-coverts red. VOICE ♂ harsh crowing *chak* or *cha-chak*. HABITAT Dense conifers, mixed woods. NEST In ground cover, 5–12 eggs, Apr–May; 1 brood. FOOD As Pheasant. RANGE Introduced from SE Asia since end 19th century; sedentary.

Lady Amherst's Pheasant *Chrysolophus amherstiae* 115–150 cm (45–59 in), ♀ 58–68 cm (23–27 in). Bulkier than Golden, ♂ tail much longer, ♀ shorter; ♂ green-black and white, with some red and yellow; ♀ paler buff than ♀ Golden, with bolder barring, less marked throat and belly, and blue-grey bill, legs and facial skin. May inter-breed with Golden. *Ad* ♂ Black-scaled white 'cape', black-barred white and buff tail. *Ad* ♀ Forehead rufous, crown cinnamon-barred black; otherwise pale buff and cinnamon with clear black bars. *Juv* As small short-tailed ♀ but no rufous on forehead or black on crown, all barring duller. *1st year* ♂ Partly as ad ♂ after moult by Oct–Nov, with cape and tail shorter, head duller black, mantle and wings more as ♀, lower back and rump rufous-chestnut, long tail-coverts tipped orange-red, much whitish-buff below. VOICE ♂ sibilant crowing *ssu-ik-ik-ik*. HABITAT Woods with rhododen-drons, brambles. NEST In ground cover, 6–11 eggs, Apr–May; 1 brood. FOOD As Pheasant. RANGE Introduced from SE Asia since *c*1900; sedentary.

Pheasant — B6 W7 S6 A7

Golden Pheasant — B3 W4 S3 A4

Lady Amherst's Pheasant — B3 W3 S3 A3

Pheasant

melanistic ♀

colchicus ♂

♀

melanistic ♂

♀

torquatus ♂

Golden Pheasant

♂

♀

Lady Amherst's Pheasant

♂

♀

RAILS, GALLINULES, COOTS (Rallidae)

Water Rail *Rallus aquaticus* 27–29 cm
(*c*11 in). Like small Moorhen (118) with
long reddish bill; streaky brown above,
grey or buff below with boldly barred
flanks, whitish undertail marked buff and
black. Crepuscular, secretive; flutters
on short rounded wings with longish legs
dangling; swims short distances with jerky
Moorhen-like actions, but heard far more
than seen. *Ad* Chin white, face to breast
dark blue-grey, black flanks barred white;
legs pink-brown, sometimes greenish. *Juv*
Bill less red; throat whitish and face and
underparts buff, all mottled brown; flank-
barring dark brown and buff. *1st winter*
During Jul–Dec becomes more like ad, but
larger whitish chin, browner face, some
dark barring on brown-grey throat/breast.
VOICE 'Sharming' of grunts and squeals;
song measured hammering *kipp kipp kipp*.
HABITAT Dense reeds, sedges, osiers, in
lakes, rivers and fens; in winter also
reedy ditches, watercress beds. NEST In
reeds, sedges or grass tussocks, 6–11 eggs,
Apr–Jul; 2 broods. FOOD Mostly invertebrates, plants. RANGE Mainly sedentary;
winter visitor from Continent/Iceland,
Sep–early May (many in hard weather).

Spotted Crake *Porzana porzana* 22–24 cm
(*c*9 in). Smaller than Water Rail and with
shorter bill, tail and legs; upperparts and
less grey breast speckled with white, flanks
barred with brown, undertail buff, narrow
white line along outer primary. *♂ summer*
Lores blackish; spotting on rear of blue-
grey supercilia/throat, more over slate-
brown breast; bill yellow with red base
and olive tip, legs pale green. *♀ summer*
Supercilia and throat more spotted with
white than *♂*. *Ad winter* Head and breast
browner with more white spotting, lores
duller; ♀ usually browner than *♂*. *Juv* As ♀
winter, but breast more brown-buff with
few spots; bill dark with yellowish base.
VOICE *♂* Explosive whistling *hwet . . . hwet
. . . hwet* ('whiplash'); mainly at dusk and
in night. HABITAT Fens, bogs and thickly
overgrown lake-sides; passage-migrants
also in open marshes, ditches. NEST In
dense vegetation or in tussocks in shallow

water, 8–12 eggs, mid May–end Jul; 1–2
broods. FOOD Invertebrates, plants. RANGE
Breeding scattered and seldom proved,
but probably now annual, esp NBr; also
passage-migrant, Mar–May, Oct–Nov;
occasional in winter, most European birds
moving to Africa. COMPARE Sora, Little
and Baillon's Crakes (268).

Corncrake *Crex crex* 25–28 cm (*c*10½ in).
Terrestrial rail, like slender gamebird;
mainly yellow-buff, streaked above, with
chestnut wings and flank-bars. Crepuscular, often only heard; in some areas
seen flying low, walking in open or even
perching on walls; usually walks with
head and tail down. *♂ summer* Upperparts
yellow-buff variably tinged grey, with
black feather-centres; grey-blue supercilia
and grey tinge to throat-sides and breast.
♀ summer As *♂*, but with less grey. *Ad
winter* After rapid moult in Aug–Sep,
purer yellow-buff above, with narrower,
grey supercilia, less grey elsewhere; ♀ often
has only tinge of grey on supercilia, none
on breast. *Juv* As ad winter, but without
grey; flanks redder, less barred. VOICE *♂*
repeated, loud, rasping *krrx-krrx*. HABITAT
Mowing grass, rank clover, boggy
pastures, nettle-patches. NEST In hay,
nettles, 8–12 eggs,
mid May–Jul; 1–2
broods. FOOD
Invertebrates, plants.
RANGE Summer
visitor, mid Apr–
Sep, wintering in
Africa; on passage
mid Apr–May, Aug–
Oct; formerly
nested in most of Br.

Water Rail

ad

juv

1st winter

ad

Spotted Crake

ad

♀ winter

♂ summer

juv

Corncrake

♀ winter

♂ summer

ad

juv

Moorhen *Gallinula chloropus* 31–35 cm
(*c*13 in). Stocky waterbird with chicken-
like bill and long toes; mainly blackish and
slaty, but for white stripe along flanks,
white-sided undertail, and coloured bill
and legs. Low and brief flight looks
laboured with legs dangling or trailing
behind tail; swims buoyantly, jerking
head and often tail, and patters along
surface before taking off; rarely dives but
can stay submerged in cover with only
beak up; walks jauntily, with head up and
tail horizontal or cocked and nervously
flirted, but runs for cover with head down
and wings flapping; perches or clambers
in bushes; not usually gregarious; rather
wary. *Ad* Blackish-brown above and slaty
below, with ragged white streak along
flanks, bold white undertail divided by
black; red frontal shield and yellow-
tipped bill, and red-gartered, yellow-green
legs. *Juv* Pattern as ad, with similar
undertail, but head and underparts much
browner, with whitish throat and belly,
buffish flank-stripe; green-brown bill,
dull green legs. *1st winter* During Aug–
Jan head and neck become more like ad,
but still tinged brown and with whitish
throat; underparts slaty but variably
tipped buffish, flank-stripe thinner. *1st
summer* From Apr, like ad but head and
underparts brownish-slate. VOICE Deep,
throaty *curruc* of alarm; short, high
squawk *kik*, stammering *kikikikikik-kik-
kik-kik*. HABITAT Almost any fresh water
with emergent or adjacent cover, from
urban ponds and woodland streams to
lakes, rivers and marshes; also pastures
and hedges some distance away. NEST In
reeds, waterlogged branches, tussocks,
also under brambles or in hedges or trees,
5–11 eggs, mainly mid Mar–mid Aug; 2–3
broods. FOOD Water-plants, grass, seeds,
insects, worms, molluscs. RANGE Mainly
sedentary; but joined by winter visitors
from Low Countries/S Scandinavia, Sep–
Apr. COMPARE Imm with imm American
Purple Gallinule (268).

Coot *Fulica atra* 36–40 cm (*c*15 in). Rotund
and thickset bird of open water, slaty-
black, with glossy head and white frontal
shield and bill, and long, lobed toes. Flight
usually low, with large feet trailing like
long tail; swims high, with neck hunched,
back rounded, small head moving back
and forward, and dives often but briefly;
patters along to take off; splashes down
breast first with feet lowered; walks easily,
but usually stays near water; sometimes
roosts in bushes; quarrelsome, but highly
gregarious in winter, often with ducks. *Ad*
Jet-black head with white frontal shield
and bill; otherwise slate-black, greyer
below, with variably clear whitish-tipped
secondaries in flight; legs mainly green-
grey. *Juv* Brownish-black above and
brown-grey below, but much white on
face, neck, breast and belly; bill and small
frontal shield greyish. *1st year* During
Aug–Dec becomes more like ad, but
tinged with brown all over and often a few
white feathers on throat and neck. VOICE
Loud, piping squawk *kowk* or higher
tewk; various shrill, metallic, clipped or
explosive notes, and measured tapping
sounds. HABITAT Lakes, reservoirs and
slow rivers with extensive reeds and
sedges, and on adjacent water-meadows,
also tidal waters in Ir; in winter on any
large water body including bare reservoirs
and estuaries. NEST Built up from bottom
in reeds, sometimes in open, or in tussocks,
4–8 eggs, late Mar–end Jul; 2–3 broods.
FOOD Mainly water-plants, grass and
seeds, also insects, molluscs, leeches,
tadpoles, fish, eggs, young birds. RANGE
Mainly sedentary, but gathering on larger
waters in winter with many winter visitors
from Low Countries/E Europe, Oct–Apr.
NOTE **American Coot** *F. americana*,
recorded in Cork in 1981, has white under
tail, dusky band on bill, slight reddish
bump at top of smaller white shield.

Moorhen

ad

juv

ad

1st winter

1st summer

Coot

ad

juv

ad

1st year

OYSTERCATCHERS (Haematopodidae)

Oystercatcher *Haematopus ostralegus* 41–45 cm (*c*17 in). Bulky pied wader with stout orange-red bill, white wing-band. Flight strong with shallow beats; walks sedately, runs fast; perches on fences near nest; gregarious. *Ad summer* Glossy black; bill/eye-rings orange-red, bill-tip often yellower, legs pink, eyes red. *Ad winter* Duller black; white throat-band; bill orange, tip duskier; legs duller. *Juv* Throat-band indistinct, upperparts brownish with buff feather-edges; bill more pointed, darker; legs greyish, eyes brown, no eye-rings. *1st year* After moult Aug–Dec, as ad winter but browner above; bill orange with brownish tip, legs dark grey, eyes become redder, eye-rings yellowish; half-collar not lost until 2nd summer or older. VOICE Loud, shrill *peek* or *peek-kapeek*; in song, notes accelerate into trill. HABITAT Open shores; in NBr nests on river shingle, grass near lochs. NEST Scrape on shingle, sand, grass, crops, 3 eggs, Apr–Jul; 1 brood. FOOD Bivalve molluscs; worms inland. RANGE Inland only in summer; some emigrate as far as Iberia; also passage/winter visitor from Iceland/NW Europe, Jul–May.

STILTS, AVOCETS (Recurvirostridae)

Avocet *Recurvirostra avosetta* 41–45 cm (*c*17 in). Elegant white-and-black wader with long upturned bill, blue-grey legs. Flight fairly fast with legs projecting; walks gracefully with neck curved, often bobbing head when alert; feeds in shallows with side-to-side sweeps of bill, but in deeper water dips head or even up-ends; often in parties or small flocks. *Ad* Marked with black or brown-black; some ♀s have whitish mottling on forehead in winter; ♂ eyes redder-brown. *Juv* Cap brown with some buff flecks; other markings dark brown mottled with pale buff, extending to mantle; white tail-coverts and tail tipped with pale brown. *1st winter* As ad, but cap browner with white mottling at front; wings as juv through 1st summer. VOICE Liquid melodious *kleep* or *kloo-it*. HABITAT Breeds in shallow brackish

lagoons, also by estuaries; winters on estuaries and mud-flats. NEST Scrape by water, 3–4 eggs, mid Apr–early Jul; 1 brood. FOOD Insects, crustaceans, worms. RANGE Summer visitor, Apr–Sep, but most winterers of Br stock; also on passage from Continent, end Mar–Jun, Jul–Sep; recolonised in 1940s after century gap.

STONE-CURLEWS (Burhinidae)

Stone-curlew *Burhinus oedicnemus* 38–43 cm (*c*16 in). Ungainly-looking terrestrial wader, mainly brownish, with staring yellow eyes, yellow bill-base and legs and, in flight, 2 black-edged white wing-bars. Shy, active evening and night; slow wing-beats, glides, but high and erratic at dusk; walks with short steps, or runs furtively, hunched up, pausing at intervals; lies flat if alarmed; sociable. *Ad* Buff to grey-brown streaked blackish, belly and underwings white, undertail cinnamon; usually only wing-bar on greater coverts visible at rest. *Juv* Paler with narrower streaks; bar on lesser coverts less clear, on greater coverts thinner. VOICE Wailing *coor-ee*, shriller than Curlew (140); wild clamours during night. HABITAT Open stony, chalky or sandy country; increasingly, arable land and forestry rides. NEST Scrape on bare ground, 2 eggs, Apr–Jul; 2 broods. FOOD Insects, worms, young birds. RANGE Summer visitor, Mar–Oct, wintering in W/S Europe to Africa.

Oystercatcher   B5 W5 S5 A5

Avocet   B3 W3 S3 A3

Stone-curlew   B3 W0 S3 A3

Oystercatcher

1st year

ad winter

ad summer

juv

ad summer

Avocet

juv

ad

1st winter

ad

Stone-curlew

ad

juv

ad

122 Charadriidae

PLOVERS (Charadriidae)

Little Ringed Plover *Charadrius dubius*
14–16 cm (*c*6 in). Slighter than Ringed Plover, more 'tapered' rear, less rounded underbody; bill thinner, largely black; yellow eye-rings; longer dull pink or yellowish legs; black bands often narrower, white line above mask (ad); no real wing-bar. Actions as Ringed, but less gregarious. *Ad summer* Mask/breast-band black, ♀ often browner-black (esp behind eyes); bold eye-rings yellow. *Ad winter* Moults in Jul–Nov; mask/breast-band browner. *Juv* Whole cap brown, but pale buff forehead; eye-rings duller; upperparts scaled buff; breast-band brown, often incomplete. *1st winter* As ad winter, but (esp ♀) head-pattern less clear and brown breast-band narrower in centre; still some coverts with worn buff edges, eye-rings duller. VOICE High *pee-u*; grating *cree-a cree-a* in display flight. HABITAT Gravel pits, shingle by rivers and reservoirs, silt tips. NEST Scrape on ground, 4 eggs, Apr–Jul; 1–2 broods. FOOD Insects, also tiny molluscs. RANGE First nested in 1938 and now summer visitor, end Mar–Oct, wintering in Africa.

Ringed Plover *Charadrius hiaticula* 18–20 cm (*c*7½ in). Plump, with stubby bill and shortish legs showing orange to yellowish; white and black collars, pied head-pattern; broad white wing-bar and white-sided tail clear in flight. Flight fast, often low, with deliberate beats, gliding to land, then running with raised wings; runs like clockwork, pauses abruptly with head up, tilts body to pick up food; bobs head if uneasy; often in parties. *Ad summer* Mask/breast-band black (♂) or browner (♀); bill-base and legs orange, thin eye-rings orange (♂) or yellow-grey (♀). *Ad winter* From *c*Aug, mask/breast-band brownish (esp ♀), blacker again from *c*Jan; bill-base, eye-rings and legs duller (esp ♀). *Juv* Head-marks brown, but whitish forehead and stripe behind eyes (*cf* Little Ringed); breast-band brown, usually incomplete; upperparts scaled buff; bill blackish, legs dull yellowish. *1st winter* As ♀ winter from moult Aug–Jan, but some coverts with

worn buff edges; less colour on bill. VOICE Soft *poo-i*, more piping *queep*; trilling *kwitaleeyu* in display flight. HABITAT Shingle or sand by sea, locally inland; winters esp on mud-flats. NEST Scrape on ground, 3–4 eggs, Apr–Jul; 2–3 broods. FOOD Many invertebrates. RANGE Mainly resident; also passage/winter visitor from Scandinavia/Iceland/Greenland, Aug–May. COMPARE Semipalmated (274).

Kentish Plover *Charadrius alexandrinus*
15–17 cm (*c*6¼ in). Smaller, slighter and paler than Ringed; bill and longer legs blackish; patch at each side of breast; white forehead extends into supercilia; wing-bar thinner, white tail-sides wider. Actions as Ringed; runs very fast as if on wheels. ♂ *summer* Breast-patches and head-marks black, crown rufous. ♀ *summer* Crown, mask and breast-patches all tawny-brown. *Ad winter* As ♀ summer after moult Jul–Sep, but browner; ♂ has broader white supercilia and collar, may start to show some black from Nov–Dec. *Juv* Paler, with buff supercilia, mottled breast-patches, scaled upperparts. *1st winter* As ♀ winter but some coverts with worn buff edges; ♂ starts to show black like ad. VOICE Soft *wit-wit-wit*, rolling *chirrirrip*. HABITAT Mud, sand, shingle. FOOD Mainly insects. RANGE Scarce migrant, end Mar–May, Aug–Oct; few bred SEBr to 1956, 1 pair EBr in 1979. COMPARE Greater Sand Plover (274).

Little Ringed Plover — B3 W0 S3 A4

Ringed Plover — B5 W5 S5 A5

Kentish Plover — B0 W0 S2 A2

Little Ringed Plover

♂ summer

ad winter

ad

juv

1st winter

Ringed Plover

ad

juv

♂ summer

♀ winter

Kentish Plover

juv

♂ summer

♂ summer

♂ winter

♀ summer

Golden Plover *Pluvialis apricaria* 27–29 cm (*c* 11 in). Fairly large plover, with rather slender black bill, rounded head and green-grey or grey legs; upperparts speckled gold and black, underparts blackish in summer, whitish in winter; in flight, 'arm-pits' white, underwings whitish, wing-bar usually indistinct, no pale rump or visible tail-marks (*cf* Grey Plover). Flight fast with rapid beats; runs, pauses and tilts body like other plovers (*cf* Ringed Plover, 122); in breeding season often stands upright on moorland hummock; highly gregarious in winter. ♂ *summer S race (P.a. apricaria)* Breast and belly black, face dusky, indistinct whitish or yellowish border to underparts. ♀ *summer* Duller below, belly flecked with brown and whitish. ♂ *summer N race (P.a. altifrons)* Black face (to above bill) and underparts broadly bordered with white. ♀ *summer* More like S ♂, with black above bill indistinct, face dusky-brown flecked with yellow, white border much less distinct and more broken. *Ad winter* Underparts whitish, flecked gold on face

and breast; moult starts Jun–Jul, completed by Oct–Nov; summer plumage assumed Feb–May, often by mid March. *Juv* Like ad winter, but gold speckling paler, duller and more distinctly spotted; belly and flanks washed pale brown. *1st winter* Largely like ad from Sep–Nov, but more spotted scapulars and speckled flanks and belly often visible to Dec–Jan. *1st summer* Wing-coverts worn and greyish; summer plumage attained late (May), often incomplete. VOICE Liquid whistle *tlui*; in alarm when breeding, melancholy *tlee* or *tlee-oo*; in display-flight, mournful *tirr-pee-oo*. HABITAT Breeds on moors, bogs, upland pastures; winters on upland and lowland arable, pastures, much less on shores and mud-flats. NEST Scrape in heather or grass, often on bog hummocks, 3–4 eggs, Apr–Jun; 1 brood. FOOD Insects, worms, plants. RANGE Mainly resident, but breeding grounds deserted Sep–Feb, some cross Channel; many passage/winter visitors from Iceland/Fenno-Scandia, Aug–May; breeders mostly S type, late passage

Golden Plover

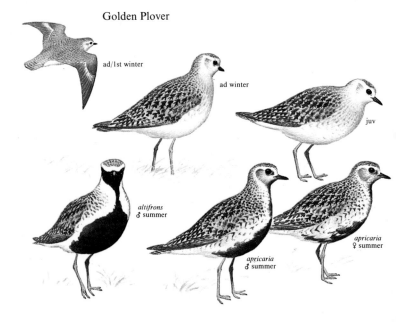

ad/1st winter

ad winter

juv

altifrons ♂ summer

apricaria ♂ summer

apricaria ♀ summer

includes N birds and few nest NBr.
COMPARE Lesser Golden Plover (274).

Grey Plover *Pluvialis squatarola* 28–31
cm (*c*11½ in). Stouter than Golden Plover
with thicker bill, larger eyes and longer
blackish-grey legs; in summer, speckled
with silver and grey above, all black
below but boldly bordered with white on
head, breast-sides and vent; in winter,
more uniform brownish-grey above and
whiter below than Golden, but juv shows
yellowish spotting above and streaks on
breast; in flight, easily distinguished by
black 'arm-pits', stronger wing-bar and
white rump. Behaviour much as Golden
Plover, but has more hunched, almost
dejected look at rest; wades much more
freely; usually in small parties, scattering
to feed. ♂ *summer* Face and underparts
black, rear belly and undertail white.
♀ *summer* Browner-black with whitish
mottling, undertail more barred brown.
Ad winter Brown-grey with whitish fringes
above, largely white below, but some
black often retained, at least to Oct-Dec;
moults to summer in Feb-May. *Juv* Grey-
brown above, spotted pale yellow and
cream, not unlike Golden; streaked buff-
brown on breast and flanks. *1st winter*
Upperparts more spotted than ad, median
coverts as juv until yellow wears away,
underparts largely white; juv plumage
moulted Sep-Jan. *1st summer* Much as ad
winter, little or no breeding plumage;
primaries moulted in May-Aug. VOICE
Plaintive whistle *tlee-oo-ee*. HABITAT Mud-
flats, sand beaches. RANGE Passage/winter
visitor from arctic USSR, end Jul-May;
some (esp 1st year) stay through summer.

Golden Plover		B5
		W6
		S6
		A6

Grey Plover		B0
		W5
		S5
		A5

Grey Plover

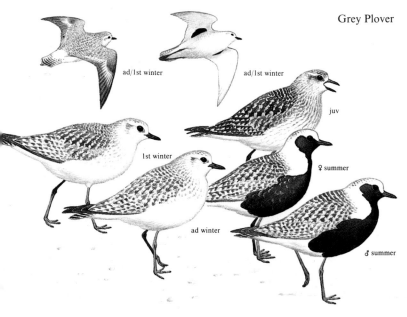

ad/1st winter

ad/1st winter

juv

1st winter

♀ summer

ad winter

♂ summer

Dotterel *Charadrius morinellus* 20–23 cm ($c8\frac{1}{2}$ in). Fat-bodied small-billed plover with upright stance, whitish supercilia and breast-line, dull yellow legs; shows grey, chestnut and black in summer, but much duller in winter; in flight, no real wing-bar but pale leading edge to primaries and white fringe to short tail. Runs, pauses and tilts like other plovers; in small parties on migration, and on breeding grounds ♀s group while ♂s incubate; can be remarkably tame. *Ad summer* Blackish crown and grey and brown upperparts contrast with broad white supercilia forming V on nape, and whitish throat; grey-brown upper breast separated from chestnut below by white line; belly black, vent/undertail white; ♂ usually duller than ♀, with streakier crown, less bold supercilia, browner back and chest, less black on belly. *Ad winter* Upperparts paler, throat streaked, breast browner, supercilia and breast-line dull whitish, belly white; moult in Jul–Nov finished in wintering areas; spring moult, Mar–Jun, finished on breeding grounds.

Juv Resembles ad winter, but upperparts darker brown with broader sandy-buff fringes, breast-line indistinct and breast brown-buff and streaked. *1st winter* Moults in Sep–Dec, then paler, more like ad winter, but retains juv wing-coverts. *1st summer* As ad summer, but some juv inner median coverts and very worn primaries. VOICE Soft *peep-peep* in flight, *titi-ri* in alarm. HABITAT Breeds on mountains at 800–1300 m among short cover and bare stony stretches; on passage in open upland country and often traditional sites on lowland fields, heaths, coastal marshes. NEST Scrape in sparse vegetation, 3 eggs, late May–mid/late Jul; 1 brood. FOOD Mainly flies, beetles and spiders. RANGE Summer visitor, May–Aug, wintering in N Africa; on passage (some from N Eurasia), Apr–May, Sep–Oct.

Lapwing *Vanellus vanellus* 29–32 cm ($c12$ in). Large plover with distinctive wispy crest; looks black-and-white at distance, but upperparts mainly green; in flight, boldly pied, with broad rounded wings

Dotterel

ad summer

juv

ad winter

♀ summer

dull ♂ summer

(but ♀'s less so than ♂'s). Flight often tumbling and erratic; distinctive flopping wing-beats; actions much as other plovers (*cf* Ringed Plover, 122), but does not run so fast or raise wings; outside breeding season, usually in large, loose parties that fly in straggling formations. ♂ *summer* Face, throat and breast black; sides and back of head white with black markings; upperparts mainly glossed bronzy-green, undertail cinnamon; tail white with black band, flight-feathers black with whitish tips to outer primaries, underwing-coverts white. ♀ *summer* As ♂, but crest shorter, black face and throat mixed with white, upperparts less glossy. *Ad winter* As ♂/♀ summer, but face less black (♂ more than ♀ in front of and below eyes), throat and foreneck white, some buff fringes above; moults in Aug–Nov and partially in Feb–May. *Juv* As ad winter, but crest very short; duller green above and paler with cream fringes, breast-band browner. *1st winter* After moult in Jul–Dec, difficult to distinguish from ads, but crest shorter (esp ♀), wing-coverts duller and some with buff

edges until these wear off. VOICE In flight shrill, nasal *pee-vit*; song *perr-yu-weet weet-weet . . . perr-yu-weet*, last part coinciding with headland plunge. HABITAT Open country from sea-level to 1000 m; uplands largely deserted after breeding, when flocks common on farmland and flat coasts. NEST Scrape in open, 3–4 eggs, mid Mar–early Jul; 1 brood. FOOD Invertebrates, some seeds, grasses. RANGE Some sedentary, others winter south to N Africa; also passage/winter visitor from N/E Europe, Jun–May, with strong onward movements in cold weather.

| Dotterel | B3 W0 S3 A3 | Lapwing | B6 W7 S7 A7 |

Lapwing

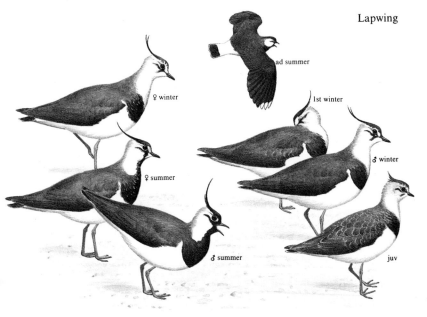

ad summer

♀ winter

1st winter

♀ summer

♂ winter

♂ summer

juv

TYPICAL WADERS (Scolopacidae)

Sanderling *Calidris alba* 19–22 cm (*c*8 in).
Just larger than Dunlin (132) and plumper,
with shortish straight black bill, black
legs, no hind toes, more 'bicycling' gait;
in summer mainly rufous above, in winter
pale grey and white with blackish 'shoulders'; bold white wing-bar in flight.
Dashes to and fro by waves on sandy
shores, legs moving so fast as to seem like
wheels, bill darting from side to side; also
feeds more sedately at pool edges;
gregarious. *Ad summer* Head/breast
rufous spotted with black, demarcated
from white belly; otherwise black above
fringed with rufous (♂) or greyish (♀), but
wing-coverts grey edged paler. *Ad winter*
After moult in Jul–Nov, white but for pale
grey crown, back and white-fringed
coverts, and blackish leading wing-edge.
Juv Crown streaked blackish; chequered
above with cream and white spots on
blackish; breast washed buff. *1st winter*
Much as ad after moult in Sep–Dec, but
worn brownish juv coverts/tertials with
traces of spots. VOICE High liquid *tyik-
tyik*, twittering in flock. HABITAT Esp
sandy shores, also mud-flats; scarce
inland. FOOD As Dunlin. RANGE Passage/
winter visitor from High Arctic, mid Jul–
early Jun (esp Oct–Mar).

Little Stint *Calidris minuta* 14–15.5 cm
(*c*5¾ in). Tiny, portly, with short fine
bill, black legs; in summer dark-mottled
rufous above, in winter grey-brown and
white, but juv has bright chestnut fringes
and whitish lines on blackish back. More
active than Dunlin (132); flight faster,
picks from surface, wades infrequently;
usually tame. *Ad summer* Blackish above
with bright rufous fringes; white below
but for brown-speckled rufous chest. *Ad
winter* After moult Aug–Dec, grey-brown
above with pale-fringed coverts, greyish
breast-sides (or gorget). *Juv* Black-brown
above with bright chestnut and whitish
fringes, latter forming clear Vs on back;
nape usually greyish; buff chest-band
mottled darker at sides; much as ad winter
after moult Sep–Dec but for browner
coverts, inner medians with rufous tips.

VOICE High *tit* or lower twitter; song
soft flat trill. HABITAT/FOOD Much as
Dunlin. RANGE On passage from NE
Europe/Siberia, late Jul–mid Oct, scarce
Apr–May, wintering in Africa (few north
to Br). COMPARE American stints (276).

Temminck's Stint *Calidris temminckii*
13.5–15 cm (*c*5½ in). Much plainer and
greyer and more attenuated than Little
Stint, with usually complete grey breast-
band, green-brown to yellowish legs and,
in flight shorter wing-bar and white (not
grey) sides to often fanned tail. Flight
more erratic and fluttering, often towers
when flushed. *Ad summer* Grey-brown
above marked blackish and dull rufous;
breast grey-brown with dusky streaks. *Ad
winter* After moult in Jul–Nov, plain dark
grey-brown above (but for white-fringed
coverts) and on breast (or only sides).
Juv Brown-grey above with fine dark
crescents and scaled buff; breast buff-
grey with contrasting white throat-patch;
much as ad after moult in Aug–Dec, but
worn brown juv inner medians tipped with
whitish-buff. VOICE Short high trill; song
ethereal trill, rising and falling. HABITAT
Muddy patches, often with cover, in
marshes, lakes, estuarine creeks. NEST
Scrape in short grass,
4 eggs, Jun–Jul; 1
brood. FOOD Mostly
insects. RANGE
Scarce passage-
migrant from N
Europe, May–mid
Jun, end Jul–Oct,
wintering Africa; has
nested NBr since
1969.

Sanderling	B0 W5 S5 A5
Little Stint	B0 W2 S3 A4
Temminck's Stint	B1 W0 S2 A2

Sanderling

ad winter

ad winter

♀ summer

♂ summer

juv

Little Stint

ad summer

ad winter

juv

juv

Temminck's Stint

ad summer

juv

ad summer

ad winter

Knot *Calidris canutus* 24–27 cm (*c*10 in).
Much bigger than Dunlin (132), rounded,
with shorter bill, neck and legs; mainly
chestnut in summer, and grey and white
in winter, with greenish legs; in flight
shows thin white wing-bar, and all-pale
rump. Actions as Dunlin but slower, more
deliberate; flight stronger, often in huge
dense flocks that carpet mudflats and fly
in even tighter ever-changing formations.
♂ *summer* Blackish above with chestnut
fringes, coverts grey edged white; rich
rufous head (crown streaked blackish) and
underparts. ♀ *summer* Fringes above much
greyer; underparts mixed with white,
belly whiter. *Ad winter* After moult Jul–
Oct, mainly grey above with thin white
fringes, whitish below with some streaks
on greyer breast. *Juv* Browner-grey above
with clear dark and creamy scaling;
strongly tinged pink-buff below. *1st winter*
Much as ad after moult Sep–Dec, but for
browner juv coverts with some scaling.
VOICE Low hoarse *knut*, twittering in
flock; higher, more whistled *kwit-it*, esp
in spring. HABITAT Mud/sand of estuaries;
scarce inland. FOOD As Dunlin. RANGE
Passage/winter visitor from High Arctic,
end Jul–May; few non-breeders summer.

Pectoral Sandpiper *Calidris melanotos*
17–21 cm (*c*7½ in). Size variable; elegant,
with short bill just decurved, small head,
longish neck often upstretched, yellow-
brown legs; dark above, usually 2 pale
lines at sides of mantle; well-streaked
breast ends sharply against white belly;
in flight, faint wing-bar, dark-centred
rump/tail. Flight sluggish; feeds slowly;
stands still in grass like snipe. *Ad summer*
Blackish above with chestnut and buff
fringes forming pale lines on mantle, but
coverts grey-brown with paler edges. *Ad
winter* After moult in Aug–Oct, greyer-
brown above with less contrasting, less
rufous fringes. *Juv* Much as ad summer
above, but brighter fringes and clearer
whitish lines on scapulars, buff-fringed
coverts; breast buff with finer streaking;
as ad winter after moult in Sep–Dec, but
darker juv inner medians with buff fringes.
VOICE Loud reedy *krreet*. HABITAT Marshy
places, wet meadows with short grass and

pools. FOOD Insects, crustaceans. RANGE
Visitor from N America, Aug–Oct (few
Apr–Jul, also Nov): 25–50+ per year.
COMPARE Sharp-tailed Sandpiper (278).

Purple Sandpiper *Calidris maritima* 20–22
cm (*c*8¼ in). Larger than Dunlin (132) and
much stockier, almost portly, with slightly
decurved bill, short legs; distinctively
sooty (purple gloss on back) with some
paler fringes (rufous in summer) but for
whitish throat, white marks on breast,
mainly white flanks and belly, weak wing-
bar with white patch near body, and dull
yellow legs and bill-base. Flight low,
direct; found on rocky shores, where
swims readily; tame; often with Turnstones. *Ad summer* Wide rufous and
whitish fringes above; blackish streaks
and spots on throat, breast, flanks. *Ad
winter* After moult in Aug–Nov, mainly
slate-grey and blackish; whitish fringes
on inner coverts, white throat and belly,
white mottling on lower breast and brown-
streaked flanks. *Juv* Narrow chestnut, buff
and whitish fringes above; like ad winter
below but breast spotted. *1st winter* As ad
winter after moult Sep–Dec, but for broad
whitish fringes to juv median coverts and
chestnut-tipped inners. VOICE Low *weet-
wit*; often silent.
HABITAT Rocky
coasts, also groynes.
FOOD Molluscs,
crustaceans. RANGE
Passage/winter
visitor from N
Europe/Arctic, end
Jul–May (esp Oct–
Apr); few summer;
nested NBr 1978–80.

Knot

ad winter

ad winter

♀ summer

juv

♂ summer

Pectoral Sandpiper

juv

ad summer

juv

ad winter

Purple Sandpiper

ad winter

juv

ad winter

ad summer

Curlew Sandpiper *Calidris ferruginea*
18–20 cm (*c*7½ in). Elegant and rather
upright, with longish legs, neck and thin
evenly curved bill; much chestnut-red in
summer, grey-brown and whitish in
winter, with white rump. Actions much as
Dunlin but wades more deeply; not shy;
usually singly or small parties. *Ad summer*
Dark brown above with broad chestnut-
red fringes, wing-coverts as winter; rump
slightly obscured by blackish bars; rich
chestnut-red below (♀ paler), variously
marked with brown and whitish (esp ♀),
and whitish around bill. *Ad winter* After
moult in Jul–Dec, brown-grey above with
dark streaks, but whitish fringes to coverts,
whitish supercilia; white below with thin
grey-brown streaks on chest. *Juv* Dusky
above with brownish coverts, all scaled
with broad pale buff fringes (some tinged
with chestnut); clean buff-white below,
barely streaked just on chest; as ad winter
after moult in Sep–Dec but for buff-edged
inner median and lesser coverts. VOICE Soft
whistling or twittering *chirrip* or *chirririp*.
HABITAT On passage much as Dunlin.

FOOD As Dunlin. RANGE Passage-migrant
from Siberia, mid Jul–mid Oct, also end
Apr–early Jun, wintering in Africa; much
commoner in some years; rare in winter.
COMPARE White-rumped Sandpiper (276).

Dunlin *Calidris alpina* 16.5–19 cm (*c*7 in).
Commonest shore-wader, rather hunched,
with shortish black legs, variably longish
bill slightly decurved at tip; in summer
black belly, in winter grey-brown above
and white below with streaked breast; in
flight, white wing-bar and rump-sides.
Flight fast, flocks wheeling in unison,
tilting to appear dark or white, and
changing shape from balls to lines or
towers; glides to land, then briefly holds
wings up, like many waders; usually walks
delicately with rounded back, head
lowered to peck at and probe mud or sand;
often wades or swims in shallows; stands
on one leg, facing into wind, bill buried in
feathers; small parties quite tame, large
flocks much less so; flocks feed close
together; mixes with other waders. *Ad
summer S race (C.a. schinzii)* Blackish

Curlew Sandpiper

juv

♀ summer

♂ summer

juv

ad winter

above with cinnamon and whitish fringes, wing-coverts as winter; nape of ♂ greyish contrasting with cap and mantle; breast buff-white with blackish streaks, small blackish belly-patch mixed with white. *N race (C.a. alpina)* As S race, but fringes on upperparts richer chestnut; grey nape of ♂ more contrasted; breast whiter, belly-patch larger and blacker. *NE Greenland race (C.a. arctica)* Paler above with buff and greyish fringes; faint breast-streaks, small belly-patch. *Ad winter* Brown-grey above, coverts greyer with whitish fringes, and white below with grey-brown breast-streaks; races indistinguishable, though those with short straight bills probably S ♂s and those with long curved bills probably N ♀s. *Juv* Blackish above with buff-white and chestnut fringes, but coverts browner with buff or chestnut fringes; as ad winter below, but blackish spots on flanks. *1st winter* As ad after moult in Aug–Nov, but brown inner median coverts with buff or chestnut fringes. VOICE Short, shrill, rasping *tree*, breeders also *wot-wot* and *kwoi-kwoi* when uneasy; song rich purring trill in flight or on ground. HABITAT Mud-flats, salt-marshes, sand or shingle coasts, also inland marshes, lake-edges; breeds on hummocky grass moors with peaty pools, lowland mosses, grassy saltmarshes. NEST In tussocks, 4 eggs, May–early Jul; 1 brood. FOOD Worms, small molluscs, crustaceans, insects. RANGE S race breeds Apr–Aug, some crossing Channel to winter; both races abundant passage/winter visitors from SE Greenland/Iceland/N Europe, mid Jul–May, also some *arctica* from NE Greenland.

Curlew Sandpiper B0 W0 S2 A3 / Dunlin B4 W7 S7 A7

Dunlin

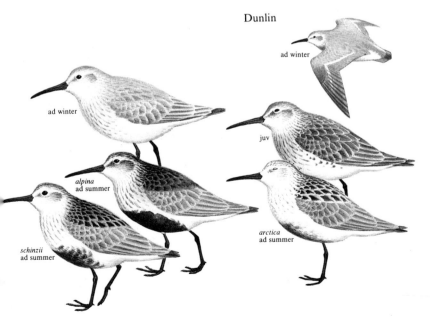

ad winter

ad winter

alpina ad summer

schinzii ad summer

juv

arctica ad summer

Ruff *Philomachus pugnax* ♂ 27–31 cm
(*c*11½ in), ♀ 22–25 cm (*c*9¼ in). Lumpy
wader, very variable in size, with small
head, longish neck and short, slightly
downcurved, mainly dark bill; legs range
from orange-red through yellow to green-
brown and grey; ♂ in summer has remarkable coloured head-tufts and ruff, which
give thick-necked appearance in flight;
other plumages less distinctive, but upperparts more or less scaly-looking, breast
plain buff (juv), greyish (ad winter) or
marked with sepia (♀ summer); in flight,
narrow white bar on rather long paddle-
shaped wings and obvious oval white
patch at sides of dark rump to tail. Flight
flicking, with erratic beats, sometimes
gliding; stands quite upright, but walks
deliberately with body rather horizontal,
searching in grass, probing in mud or
wading in shallows; often small flocks on
passage, also in ones and twos; many
autumn migrants in Br/Ir are juvs. ♂
summer During *c*Apr–Jul, head-tufts and
huge ruff in different combinations of
black, purple, chestnut, buff and white,
barred or plain; same colours extend to
much of upperparts, while sides of breast
and flanks sometimes correspond to ruff
but usually glossy purplish-black flecked
with white; contrasting white belly and
undertail-coverts; forecrown and lores
become bare, warty, and brown, yellow
or red. ♂ *moulting* Head-tufts and ruff
grown (Apr) and lost (Jun–Jul) rapidly;
without them, blackish above, variably
scaled and marked white, grey or rufous,
and lightly to heavily mottled blackish on
breast and flanks, contrasted with white
throat, foreneck and belly. ♀ *(Reeve)*
summer No tufts or ruff; head and hindneck variably streaked black; back black
or variably rufous, scaled with pale edges;
coverts grey-brown with paler tips; throat
white spotted dusky, breast and flanks
barred or mottled dark brown and scaled
with white, belly white. *Ad winter* More
uniform grey-brown above with some
scaly effect, esp on wing-coverts; sometimes white collar or pale head; white or
whitish below, with breast, sides of neck
and flanks greyish; legs and bill-base, as

Ruff

♂ summer

♂s DISPLAYING AT LEK

in summer, orange-red or pinkish, sometimes yellowish; sexes alike, but ♂s usually obviously larger. *Juv* Bold scaly pattern above of blackish-brown edged with warm buff; throat, foreneck, breast and flanks distinctively almost uniform buff; bill-base paler brown, legs yellow-brown or greenish, sometimes greyish; ♂ already larger than ♀. *1st winter* As ad winter after moult Aug–Oct, but still some juv feathers above; legs become browner or greener, and some have pink or orange tinge. *1st summer* Moults later than ads, usually retaining more winter feathers in spring; otherwise as ads but inner median coverts still often buff-fringed, primaries often very worn; ♂'s ruff usually smaller. VOICE Usually silent; occasionally low *chuk-uk* in flight. DISPLAY ♂s gather at special arenas, or leks, often on slight rise; each has small court, where scuttles about with head and neck horizontal, head-tufts raised, and wings spread, fluttering; periodically crouches with bill touching ground, ruff and tail spread, and shivers feathers; interspersed are short circular

flights and mainly mock fights; ♀s visit ♂s at leks for mating. HABITAT In Br breeds in grassy meadows after winter floods; passage/winter on marshes, sewage farms, mud edges of lakes and reservoirs, less often on side-creeks of estuaries. NEST Usually within *c*400 m of lek; hidden in sedges or grass, 4 eggs, May–mid Jun; 1 brood. FOOD Mainly insects, also worms, molluscs, crustaceans, seeds. RANGE Rare breeder, formerly much more widespread but ceased to nest regularly after 1871 (sporadically to 1922), then recolonised 1963; passage from Low Countries/Scandinavia, end Mar–early Jun and, esp, mid Jul–Oct; winters in Mediterranean/Africa (where many stay over 1st summer), but some now regularly in Br/Ir. COMPARE Juv with Buff-breasted Sandpiper (278).

juv

ad winter

juv

1st winter

♂ moulting

♀ summer

Jack Snipe *Lymnocryptes minimus* 18–20 cm (*c*7½ in). Small snipe with obviously short bill and silent escape flight – slower, more direct than Snipe (no real zigzag or towering), usually for short distance so that distinctive lack of white on more wedge-shaped tail hard to see. Often stays hidden until almost trodden on; not gregarious. *Ad/juv* Crown blackish in centre; upperparts glossed with purple and green, with brighter pale buff stripes than Snipe; neck and breast streaked rather than spotted with blackish, and flanks indistinctly mottled, not barred. VOICE Usually silent when flushed, sometimes a low, weak note. HABITAT Marshes, usually in thick, low cover. FOOD Insects, molluscs, worms, seeds. RANGE Passage/winter visitor from N Europe, Sep–May.

Snipe *Gallinago gallinago* 25–28 cm (*c*10½ in). Medium-sized with very long bill (6–7.5 cm), richly patterned in black, brown and rufous with cream stripes on head and back; white line along rear of secondaries and some white on edges of tail visible in flight. When flushed, usually calls and flies in low zigzag, then towers up and makes off with rapid beats, bill pointing down and body still tilting from side to side; often simply crouches and sometimes travels only short distance before landing, but flight seldom as weak and direct as Jack Snipe; largely crepuscular; often in small parties; secretive, seldom allows close approach. *Ad* Head striped, with buff down centre of crown; buff stripes down sides of mantle and scapulars; neck and breast buff with lines of dark brown spots and V-marks; flanks buffish barred dark brown; belly white. *Juv* Difficult to distinguish: buff stripes on back usually narrower and paler, sometimes almost white; light tips to wing-coverts lack ad's central blackish line. *Melanistic 'Sabine's Snipe'* (chiefly in Ir) Black and dark rufous above without buff stripes; neck, breast and flanks dull reddish-buff marked with sepia; belly sooty-brown. VOICE In flight, hoarse *scaap*; song quick, hollow *chip-per* constantly repeated; in display-dives, spread outer tail-feathers produce

throbbing *vuvuvuvuvu* (drumming). HABITAT Marshes, water-meadows. NEST In tussocks, 4 eggs, mainly Apr–Jul; 1 brood. FOOD Worms, insects, seeds. RANGE Mainly resident, some move to France; also passage/winter visitor from N Europe, Aug–Apr. COMPARE Great Snipe (278).

Woodcock *Scolopax rusticola* 32–36 cm (*c*13½ in). Heavy wader of open woodland; marbled red-brown with broad dark bars on back of head, finely barred below; shows rufous tail when flushed; in flight, ponderous with rather rounded wings, bill pointing down. Mainly nocturnal. When flushed, rises with swishing wings, dodging among tree-trunks; flight fast and straight or slow and wavering, but in roding display at dawn and dusk rather owl-like; walks with bill inclined down, tail sometimes cocked; solitary and shy. *Juv* Very like ad, but forehead more spotted, black bars on hindcrown duller and separated by narrower buff lines, barring on underparts narrower and paler. VOICE Generally silent except when roding: deep, grunting *kwar kwar* followed by thin, high-pitched *tsiwick*. HABITAT Woodland with ground cover, open rides and wet areas; also more open country. NEST Scrape under bracken, brambles, or tree, 4 eggs, early Mar–mid Jul; 1 brood. FOOD Worms, insect larvae. RANGE Mainly sedentary, few winter south to Iberia; also passage/winter visitor from Continent, mid Oct–Apr.

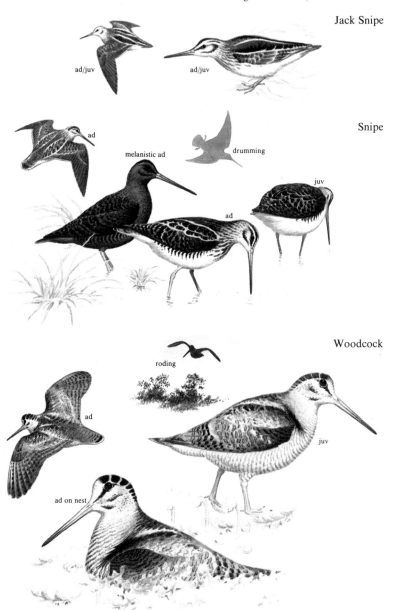

Jack Snipe

ad/juv

ad/juv

Snipe

ad

melanistic ad

drumming

juv

ad

Woodcock

roding

ad

juv

ad on nest

Black-tailed Godwit *Limosa limosa* 38–43 cm (*c*16 in). Large upstanding wader with long, almost straight bill (7.5–12.5 cm) and long legs trailing beyond black-banded white tail in flight; bold white wing-band; at rest, visible tibia half as long again as Bar-tailed; in summer, head and breast chestnut, flanks variably barred; in winter grey above and white below. Flight quite fast with rapid beats; walks rather gracefully, neck often at least partly upstretched; probes deeply in mud or sweeps bill in shallows, wading up to belly and even submerging head; gregarious. ♂ *summer Continental race (L.l. limosa)* Head and breast cinnamon-chestnut which seldom extends past breast, upper-parts marked dark-brown and red-buff, but wing-coverts grey-brown with whitish fringes. ♂ *summer Icelandic race (L.l. islandica)* Redder-chestnut clearly more extensive on breast/flanks; bill often obviously shorter. ♀ *summer* Races as ♂, but usually duller: crown browner, rest of head paler or brownish, upperparts with less red-buff; underparts paler with less red-buff, brownish-speckled and with fewer bars. *Ad winter* After moult in Jun–Oct, rather uniform grey-brown above with white edgings to wing-coverts; underparts white, face, neck, breast and flanks brownish. *Juv* More like ad summer than winter, with rufous tinge to neck and breast and pale pink-chestnut fringes on dark brown upperparts, but also red-buff edges to wing-coverts. *1st winter* After moult in Aug–Nov, as ad winter but some worn and faded buff-fringed wing-coverts remain. VOICE Loud clear *weeka-weeka-weeka* in flight; noisy when nesting, *krru-wit-tew* song in display-flight. HABITAT Breeds in water-meadows and adjacent crops, rough pastures, marshes and, in NBr, rushy bogs; winters on saltmarshes, sheltered estuaries. NEST Scrape in lush waterside vegetation, 4 eggs, mid Apr–mid Jun; 1 brood. FOOD Worms, molluscs, insects, seeds. RANGE Ceased to breed early 19th century, regular again since 1952, in nesting areas Mar–Jul; also passage/winter visitor from Iceland (esp Ir, N/WBr) and Continent

Black-tailed Godwit

ad winter

ad winter

limosa dull ♀ summer

limosa ♂ summer

islandica ♂ summer

juv

(esp SE/SBr), Jul–May; some non-breeders summer on coasts.

Bar-tailed Godwit *Limosa lapponica* 36–40 cm (*c*15 in). Less upstanding than Black-tailed, with more upturned bill about same length as Icelandic race (7–11 cm); shorter legs (with shorter visible tibia at rest) barely extend beyond barred tail in flight, when also shows whitish rump-triangle; no clear wing-bar; in summer, ♂ has whole underparts red-chestnut, ♀ much duller and browner; in winter, paler and less uniform than Black-tailed. Flight and behaviour as Black-tailed, but wing-action less loose; looks stockier and less graceful on ground, walks faster. ♂ *summer* Head, neck and all underparts red-chestnut, streaked dark brown on crown and nape, lightly marked on flanks and undertail; upperparts resemble Black-tailed. ♀ *summer* Much duller and browner than ♂, sometimes only little summer plumage: throat, breast and flanks at best pale pink-chestnut marked with brown; upperparts paler; bill usually longer. *Ad winter* After moult in Jul–Nov, obviously more streaked above than winter Black-tailed, also with more pale fringes; more white below, with faint streaks at sides of breast. *Juv* More brown and buff, and more streaked, than juv Black-tailed. *1st winter* After moult in Sep–Feb, as ad winter but some buff-fringed coverts remain. *1st summer* Often little summer plumage attained. VOICE Flight-call quick, low *kirrik kirrik*. HABITAT Mud-flats, sandy shores. FOOD Worms, molluscs. RANGE Passage/winter visitor, from NE Europe, Jul–May; few stay summer.

| Black-tailed Godwit | B3 W4 S5 A5 | Bar-tailed Godwit | B0 W5 S5 A5 |

Bar-tailed Godwit

ad winter

juv

ad winter

♂ summer

♀ summer

Whimbrel *Numenius phaeopus* 39–43 cm
(*c*16 in). Like small Curlew, with shorter
bill (7.5–10 cm) kinked down near tip,
striped crown, and whiter throat; darker
above, wings more uniform in flight;
Wing-beats faster; generally less wary.
Ad Eurasian race (N.p. phaeopus) Whitish
rump; upperparts indistinctly marked
buff. *Juv* Dark scapulars and wing-coverts
clearly notched and spotted buff. *1st
winter* Some faded spotting retained to at
least No. *N American race (N.p.
hudsonicus)* No white rump; browner
underwing. VOICE Tittering whistle
ti-ti-ti-ti-ti-ti-ti; song repeated *teeeu*
followed by very Curlew-like bubbling.
HABITAT Breeds on boggy moorland; on
passage, mud-flats, rocky shores, adjacent
fields. NEST Scrape on low hummocks,
4 eggs, mid May–early Jul; 1 brood. FOOD
Inland, insects, berries, molluscs; on coast,
crabs, molluscs. RANGE Summer visitor,
May–Aug, wintering mainly in Africa;
on passage, also from Iceland/N Europe,
mid Apr–mid Jun, Jul–Oct; American race
vagrant (2: May, Oct, Shetland/Kerry.)

Curlew *Numenius arquata* 51–61 cm (*c*22
in). Very large, streaky brown, with long
and evenly curved bill (♂ 9.5–14 cm, ♀ 14–
18.5 cm); whitish triangular rump. Flight
often leisurely, rather gull-like; walks
sedately; probes in mud or pricks from
surface; often in large flocks which fly
high in lines and bunches but scatter to
feed; usually extremely wary. *Ad* Scapulars
and coverts with indistinct pale markings.
Juv Upperparts warm brown (not grey-
brown like ad) with broad buff edges, and
scapulars and dark-centred wing-coverts
edged and notched buff; bill obviously
shorter at first. *1st winter* As ad, but to at
least Jan–Feb retains many juv scapulars
and inner median coverts which become
worn and heavily notched. VOICE Ringing
coour-lee; alarm fast *kvi-kvi-kvi*; song
of slow, then accelerating, liquid notes
and bubbling trill, in display-flight
shoots up, hangs poised, planes down on
bowed wings. HABITAT Breeds on moors,
upland pastures, locally lowland heaths,
water-meadows, mixed farmland, dunes;
winters mainly on mud-flats and adjacent

grassland. NEST Scrape on moss hummocks
or in tussocks, 4 eggs, mid Apr–end Jun;
1 brood. FOOD Inland, insects, worms,
plant material; on coast, worms, molluscs,
crabs. RANGE On nesting grounds Mar–
Aug, then moves to coasts, some to France
and Iberia; also passage/winter visitor
from N Europe, Jul–May.

Turnstone *Arenaria interpres* 22–24 cm
(*c*9 in). Portly, with stubby bill, orange
legs; pied plumage, chestnut back in
summer; unmistakable pattern in flight.
Tosses aside weeds and stones with bill.
♂ summer White head and underparts,
streaked on crown and patterned with
black on face and breast; mantle and
scapulars black-brown and orange-
chestnut. *♀ summer* Duller, with streaked
head, buffish on nape; mantle and breast-
pattern duller. *Ad winter* After moult in
Jul–Oct, head, upperparts and breast
blackish with some greyish fringes. *Juv*
Browner than ad winter, upperparts scaled
buff; legs duller than ad. *1st winter* After
moult in Aug–Nov, as ad winter, but may
show buff fringes on medians/scapulars.
1st summer After moult in Mar–Jun, some
♂s resemble ad ♀ summer, others and ♀s
assume little summer plumage. VOICE
Staccato *tukatuk*.
HABITAT Rocky/
stony coasts, also
sands, mud-flats.
FOOD Invertebrates,
carrion. RANGE
Passage/winter
visitor from N
Europe/NE America,
end Jul–May; some
in summer.

Whimbrel   B3
            W1
            S4
            A4

Curlew   B5
          W5
          S5
          A5

Turnstone   B0
             W5
             S6
             A6

Whimbrel

hudsonicus ad/juv

phaeopus ad/juv

juv

ad

juv

ad

Curlew

ad

juv

ad

Turnstone

♀ summer

♂ summer

ad winter

ad winter

juv

Spotted Redshank *Tringa erythropus* 29-32 cm (*c*12 in). Larger and more elegant than Redshank, with longer legs and longer finer bill; black, or grey and white (or mottled in moult), with long white patch on back and rump above barred tail (*cf* dowitchers, 278). Actions as Redshank; less noisy; wades in deeper water, often swims. *Ad summer* After moult Mar-May, mainly black, spotted above with white; ♀ has pale fringes on crown and underparts, more white under tail; bill-base dull red, legs dark brown-red. *Ad winter* With moult *c*Aug-Nov, mainly grey above, broadly fringed white on browner scapulars/wing-coverts; white supercilia; white below, grey wash on chest/flanks; legs orange-red. *Juv* Dark brown above spotted white, white below barred brown; much as ad winter by *c*Nov. VOICE Loud clear *tchu-it*. HABITAT/FOOD As Redshank. RANGE On passage between Fenno-Scandia and SW Europe/Africa, Jul-Oct, also Apr-Jun; increasingly in winter.

Redshank *Tringa totanus* 26-30 cm (*c*11 in). Red legs, longish straight red-based bill; brown or grey-brown and white with triangular white rump and white inner rear wings in flight. Nervous, noisy; flight fast, erratic, tilting, with jerky shallow beats; bobs if suspicious, stretching neck up and jerking tail down; when nesting, perches on posts, trees; gregarious. *Ad summer* After moult in Feb-Apr, brown above with some darker streaks and bars; white below, variably mottled/barred dark brown; legs orange-red. *Ad winter* With moult in Jul-Jan, more uniform grey-brown above; more white round eyes, finely streaked greyish throat/breast, less barred flanks. *Juv* Brown above with buff fringes; buff breast lightly streaked; legs orange-yellow. *1st winter* As ad after moult in Aug-Jan but for buff tips to inner median coverts. VOICE Musical whistle *tlu* or down-slurred *tlu-leu-leu*, taking wing with excited babble; alarm incessant *tewk*; song *teu* or *taweeo* increasing in speed. HABITAT Estuaries, saltings, marshes, muddy reservoirs; breeds in wet meadows, rushy fields, grassy moors. NEST In tussocks, 4 eggs, mid Apr-mid Jun;

1 brood. FOOD Crustaceans, molluscs, worms, insects. RANGE Resident, but moves to coasts in winter, some cross Channel; also passage/winter visitor from Iceland/N Europe, Jul-May.

Greenshank *Tringa nebularia* 29-32 cm (*c*12 in). Taller, lankier than Redshank, with longer and stouter slightly upturned bill, longer legs green (very rarely yellow); in flight, white wedge up back, and dark wings longer, narrower and more pointed than Redshank. Flight stronger, usually straighter; feeds by picking, probing, sweeping, and lunging; singly or parties. *Ad summer* After moult in Feb-May, blotched grey and black above, with head and breast heavily streaked/spotted blackish. *Ad winter* Pale greyish above, fringed white and sepia; wings darker; face whitish, neck and breast grey finely streaked. *Juv* Dark brown above, greyer on scapulars, with broad buff fringes; breast sparsely streaked. *1st winter* As ad with moult in Aug-Mar, but for some coverts buff-fringed and wearing to plain brown. VOICE Loud ringing *teu-teu-teu*, excited *chip*; song whistled *teu-i* repeated. HABITAT As Redshank; breeds on bare moors, open pine forest. NEST Open scrape, 4 eggs, May-mid Jun; 1 brood. FOOD As Redshank, also fish. RANGE Nesting areas Apr-Jul; passage/winter as Spotted Red-shank. COMPARE Marsh Sandpiper, Greater Yellowlegs (280).

Spotted Redshank
B0
W3
S4
A4

Redshank
B5
W5
S6
A6

Greenshank
B3
W3
S4
A5

Spotted Redshank

ad summer

ad winter

ad winter

juv

Redshank

juv

ad winter

ad summer

ad winter

Greenshank

ad winter

juv

ad summer

ad winter

144 Scolopacidae

Green Sandpiper *Tringa ochropus* 22–24
cm (*c*9 in). Larger, stouter than Wood
Sandpiper, with shorter legs, broader
wings; dark olive-brown upperparts and
breast-streaks, and dark underwings, give
all-black look in flight, but for white
belly, rump and banded tail. Shy, solitary; escape-flight similar to Snipe (136),
zigzagging low, then towering with
twisting jerky action; bobs head and tail,
but not constantly teetering like Common
Sandpiper. *Ad summer* By May, whitish
spots above (nearly worn away by Aug),
streaked head. *Ad winter* With moult
*c*Aug–Nov, more uniform above with
fewer indistinct buffish spots. *Juv* Paler
olive-brown with copious deep buff spots,
especially on tertials; much as ad by *c*Oct.
VOICE Ringing *weet tweet weet-weet*; more
rippling *tu-loo-ee*. HABITAT Mud gullies by
lakes, rivers, marshes. FOOD As Common
Sandpiper. RANGE On passage between
NE Europe and Mediterranean/Africa,
Jun–Nov, Mar–May; also winter; has bred
NBr. COMPARE Solitary Sandpiper (280).

Wood Sandpiper *Tringa glareola* 19–21 cm
(*c*8 in). Slender, with shorter bill,
longer (usually pale) legs, thinner wings
than Green Sandpiper; browner and more
spotted, with streakier head, clearer
supercilia, but less contrasting whitish
rump, more barred tail, pale underwings.
Escape-flight fast, erratic, with jerky
shallow beats, often rising high, but not
zigzagging or towering; less secretive;
gregarious; noisy. *Ad summer* By Apr,
dark brown above, barred and chequered
buff and white; breast whitish, streaked
and spotted dark brown. *Ad winter* With
moult Jul–Oct, more uniform, less
obviously spotted; breast grey-brown
obscurely streaked. *Juv* Warmer brown
above, copiously spotted rich buff; breast
grey-brown, mottled paler; much as ad by
*c*Oct. VOICE Shrill *chiff-iff-iff*; song *deedl-
eedl-eedl*. HABITAT Marshes; breeds near
lochs. NEST Scrape in grass or heather,
4 eggs, end May–early Jul; 1 brood. FOOD
As Common Sandpiper. RANGE On passage
between NE Europe and Africa, Jul–mid
Oct, also Apr–May; has bred NBr since
1959. COMPARE Lesser Yellowlegs (280).

Common Sandpiper *Actitis hypoleucos*
18.5–20.5 cm (*c*7¾ in). Compact, with
shortish pale-based bill and short grey-
green legs (rarely yellowish), but rear
body rather elongated and constantly
wagging or 'teetering'; olive-brown and
white, with white wedge behind rounded
brown breast-sides; in flight, brown rump
and white tail-sides, wing-bar and rear
edge to secondaries. Flight particularly
distinctive with wings stiffly flicked and
bowed in brief glides, low over water;
circles rapidly in courtship flight; singly
or small parties. *Ad summer* After moult in
Feb–May, bronzy-brown above with fine
dark marks; grey-olive chest-sides well-
streaked. *Ad winter* With moult in Jul–
Oct, more uniform olive-brown above,
wing-coverts obscurely barred (*cf* juv);
chest-sides thinly streaked. *Juv* Brown
above, barred darker and tipped buffish,
coverts and tertial-edges barred sepia
and buff; chest-sides mottled; much as ad
by *c*Nov. VOICE Shrill *tsee-wee-wee*; song
fast *titirri-tirri-tit* in flight or on ground.
HABITAT Lakes, reservoirs, marsh runnels,
estuaries; breeds by rocky streams, rivers,
lakes. NEST Scrape esp on banks near
water, 4 eggs, May–mid Jul; 1 brood.
FOOD Insects, also molluscs, crustaceans,
worms. RANGE Sum-
mer visitor Apr–
Aug, wintering
mainly in Africa; on
passage (inc from
Fenno-Scandia),
end Mar–May, Jul–
mid Oct; few winter.
COMPARE Spotted
Sandpiper (280).

ad summer

ad/juv   ad/juv

Green Sandpiper

ad winter   juv

ad summer

ad/juv   ad/juv

Wood Sandpiper

ad winter   juv

juv

ad/juv

Common Sandpiper

ad summer

ad winter

Red-necked Phalarope *Phalaropus lobatus*
17–19 cm (*c*7 in). Dainty, habitually
swimming wader with black, needle-like
bill, slate-grey legs; in summer, mainly
dark slate to brown above and white below
with orange on neck (♂ all duller than ♀);
in winter, grey and white with dark eye-
patches (*cf* Sanderling, 128); bold white
wing-bar and white sides to rump in
flight. Full flight fast but often flits
erratically over pools; runs quickly,
darting about, but much more often seen
swimming with Moorhen-like head-
bobbing, pecking from side to side, often
spinning round like top, even dipping head
or up-ending; floats buoyantly with neck
erect, back sloping down, tail level or
depressed; usually in ones and twos; very
tame. ♀ *summer* Slate-grey above, with
golden-buff lines on back; throat white,
and neck-patches orange-red mixing into
grey chest-band. ♂ *summer* Much duller
with brownish upperparts (mantle with
more buff streaking), ill-defined whitish
throat, less extensive orange on neck. *Ad
winter* After moult in Jul–Jan, sometimes
by Oct, pale blue-grey above, streaked
with white, and white face and underparts, but for darker wings, blackish
eye-patches and blue-grey breast-sides.
Juv Much darker than ad winter with
more extensive black-brown cap, upperparts dark brown with golden-buff lines;
lower throat, breast-sides and flanks all
suffused with pink-buff; legs blue-grey
to yellowish-pink, esp on toe-lobes. *1st
winter* More like ad winter, with some
grey above, but cap usually larger and
browner, upper mantle mottled black-
brown. *1st summer* Some assume summer
plumage, others remain in worn 1st
winter. VOICE Low *tyit*; *tchirrek* in alarm.
HABITAT Boggy edges of shallow pools,
waterlogged peat-cuttings, with bogbean,
sedges, and yellow iris; on passage mainly
at sea, rare inland. NEST In tussocks, 4 eggs,
Jun–mid Jul (♂ incubates); 1 brood. FOOD
Small insects, molluscs, crustaceans.
RANGE Rare summer visitor, May–Aug,
and scarce passage-migrant from Iceland/
Fenno-Scandia, Apr–Jun, mid Jul–Oct,
wintering at sea on tropics.

Red-necked Phalarope

♂ summer

ad winter

juv

juv

ad winter

♀ summer

Grey Phalarope *Phalaropus fulicarius*
19–21 cm (*c*8 in). Little larger/stockier
than Red-necked, with stouter broader
bill (often yellowish base), heavier head,
thicker neck, longer tail, shorter legs
(often yellowish toe-lobes); in summer,
chestnut-red below, with bold white sides
of head; in winter, as Red-necked but
upperparts more uniform and paler above,
wing-bar less contrasting. Swims with
back more level and tail higher than Red-
necked, giving more boat-shape, bill often
held more down-pointed; looks like tiny
gull on sea; often singly, sometimes in
flocks. ♀ *summer* Black-brown cap, white
cheeks, rich chestnut underparts; bill
yellow with black tip. ♂ *summer* Browner
cap and mantle streaked buff, cheeks
dingier, underparts duller, often some
white on belly; bill black with yellow base.
Ad winter After moult in Aug–Dec, much
as Red-necked, though paler grey, more
uniform and less streaked with whitish
above; bill black-brown, often yellowish
at base. *Juv* Black-brown above, streaked
with buff; white below, washed pink-buff

on face to chest; bill blackish, base
browner. *1st winter* More like ad winter,
but cap/mantle mixed grey and brown, and
with blackish juv wing-coverts and
tertials. *1st summer* Perhaps assumes only
partial summer plumage. VOICE Shrill
twit, higher-pitched than Red-necked.
HABITAT On passage at sea, rare inland.
FOOD Mostly invertebrates. RANGE
On passage between Iceland/Arctic and
seas off W Africa, late Sep–Nov (occasionally in hundreds); rare other months.

COMPARE Wilson's Phalarope (272).

Grey Phalarope

SKUAS (Stercorariidae)

Great Skua *Stercorarius skua* 56–61 cm
(*c*23 in). Big, stocky, with relatively
shorter, broader and less pointed wings
than other skuas, similar to large immature gull but for stout hook-tipped bill and
short tail with slightly projecting central
feathers; dark brown above, greyer-brown
to rufous below, streaked and mottled
rufous and buff, with bold white flash
across bases of primaries. Flight somewhat like large gull, often heavy, almost
laboured, but fast, dashing, hawk-like in
pursuit of birds; like other skuas, chases
terns and gulls in air, following every twist
and buffeting them until they are forced
down or drop/disgorge food, which it
snatches up, usually in flight; even tackles
Gannets, sometimes seizing wing or tail;
when nest is threatened by man or other
predator, makes awesome attacks, either
swooping from height or sailing in low,
shooting up at last moment and sometimes striking with foot; hovers to pick
up food from surface and will dive in;
settles on water more than other skuas
and, when nesting, habitually bathes in
lochs and pools; waddles on ground and
often stands on mounds on breeding
areas; raises wings in courtship, threat and
greeting; does not usually allow close
approach; often solitary when not nesting.
Ad summer Dark brown above with
obscure rufous streaks, much bolder
yellowish streaks on sides and back of
neck; grey-brown below, mottled rufous,
also streaked rufous and buff on darker
throat and on flanks; wing-flashes extensive. *Ad winter* After moult in *c*Jul–Feb,
lacks yellowish streaks around head.
Juv/1st year Darker and more uniform,
more blackish on head and upperparts
without yellowish streaks; wing-flashes
smaller. *2nd summer* More as ad, but still
somewhat darker and more uniform above
with thinner neck streaks, less marked
rufous all over. VOICE When nesting, loud
ha-ha-ha and gruff *kak-ak-ak*, or combined in attacking intruder. HABITAT
Breeds on moors near sea; otherwise
mostly pelagic. NEST Loosely colonial; on
ground, 2 eggs, mid May–mid Jul; 1

brood. FOOD Fish, birds, eggs, offal.
RANGE Summer visitor, end Mar–Sep,
wintering mainly in Atlantic west of
Europe, imms farther south; on passage
(inc some from Iceland) Mar–Apr, Aug–
Oct, esp off WIr; rare in winter and inland.

Pomarine Skua *Stercorarius pomarinus*
43–53 cm (*c*20 in). Smaller than Great
Skua, but larger, more thick-set and
stouter-billed than Arctic (150) with
similar slender and pointed wings angled
at carpal joint; central tail-feathers of ad
rounded and twisted, looking thick-ended
from side, and projecting 5–10 cm (unless
broken), but of juv straight and only
0.5–2 cm; light (most common) and dark
phases, with intermediates, much as
Arctic but 5–6 primaries white-shafted
with more white at bases. Flight heavier.
Light ad summer Contrasting dark rear
belly; often (esp ♀s) dark-barred chest and
flanks, white in tail-coverts. *Light ad
winter* With moult in Aug–Mar, cap and
upper back scaled pale, sides/back of neck
barred; underparts and tail-coverts
always as summer; tail 3–6 cm. *Juv* Varies
from all-dark to (usually) having underparts and esp all tail-coverts barred buff/
dark, underwing-coverts barred white/
blackish, upperparts scaled; rarely,
whitish dark-capped head, mostly whitish
underparts. *1st winter–4th summer* Gradually as ad; underwing barring lost last
(light birds). VOICE Migrants silent.
HABITAT Offshore and pelagic, also
coastal; occasionally on moors, inland
waters (mostly juvs). FOOD At sea, fish,
offal. RANGE Passage-migrant from arctic
Russia, Apr–early Dec (esp Aug–Nov),
wintering in tropical seas; rare in winter.

Great Skua

ad summer

ad summer

Pomarine Skua

light ad
summer

dark ad
summer

light
1st summer

light juv

light ad
winter

Arctic Skua *Stercorarius parasiticus*
38–48 cm (*c*18 in). Medium-sized, with
rakish shape, narrow pointed wings;
central tail-feathers of ad tapering and
pointed, projecting 6–10 cm, but of juv
blunter and only 1–2 cm; plumage varies
greatly from almost uniform dark brown
all over to dark above with light whitish
cheeks, hindneck and underparts but for
grey-brown breast-sides or pectoral band,
while imms variously barred; 3–4 primaries white-shafted, variable whitish bases
esp from below. Flight buoyant, graceful,
interspersed with glides, or dashing,
falcon-like when harrying terns and gulls
like Great Skua (148); will attack intruders
at nest or distract by fluttering on ground;
reluctant to settle on water; usually alone.
Dark ad All dark brown, usually more
greyish below, with blacker cap and, in
summer, yellowish streaks on cheeks/
neck. *Light ad summer* Cheeks/collar
typically yellow-white, underbody white
with grey-brown breast-sides, flanks,
undertail-coverts and often chest-band,
but many intermediate. *Light ad winter*
With moult in Aug–Dec, buff cheeks/neck
marked dark brown; chest to undertail-
coverts whitish barred black, belly mostly
white; scaled whitish above, uppertail-
coverts marked white. *Juv/1st winter* Very
variable: black above or variably barred
buff to white, head black to streaked
brown/buff; underparts including wing-
coverts all-dark, variably mottled, or
barred dark/white. *1st summer* (spent in
tropics) Much as juv after moult in Nov–
Mar (Jun), but crown darker, hindneck
streaked dark/yellowish; less barred
above, upperwing-coverts uniform. *2nd
year* Like ad winter but underwing-coverts
more as juv; some breeding plumage on
head/mantle in summer. *3rd–4th summer*
As ad, but light birds have some white
marks on mantle and all tail-coverts,
underbody with dark bars, underwing-
coverts as 2nd year. VOICE Miaowing
kay-yow, high pitched *took-took*; dry
tik-a-tik-tik when attacking intruder.
HABITAT/NEST As Great Skua, but locally
nests farther from sea; wanders inland
more (esp juvs). FOOD Fish, esp from gulls/
terns; also small mammals, birds, eggs,

insects, berries. RANGE Summer visitor,
end Apr–Sep, winters mainly in S Atlantic;
on passage inc some from N Europe/
Iceland, Apr–Nov; rare winter.

Long-tailed Skua *Stercorarius longicaudus*
38–56 cm (*c*21 in). Smaller, slimmer, with
finer bill than Arctic Skua; central tail-
feathers of ad flexible and tapering to long
point, projecting 13–25 cm (unless broken)
but of juv bluntly pointed and only
1.5–3 cm; ad summer pattern similar to
light Arctic, but almost grey above and on
underwings, with neater blacker cap,
yellower cheeks, white chest and dusky
rear belly (white in Greenland race
pallescens), while juv colder grey-brown
variably barred pale; only 2 primaries
white-shafted, little or no white at bases.
Flight more buoyant and tern-like; chases
terns/gulls less; swims more. *Ad winter*
With moult in Oct–Feb, face whitish,
mantle fringed pale, uppertail-coverts
boldly barred; white below but for dark
chest-band, barred flanks/undertail;
underwing stays uniform. *Juv* Ranges
from mainly grey-brown with faint pale
mottling/scaling, but pale patch on nape/
rear cheeks, to, more usually, neatly
barred upperparts and flanks, with dark
cap and largely whitish face/neck/breast/
central belly, but underwing- and all tail-
coverts usually boldly barred (*cf* Arctic).
1st year/2nd winter With moult in Oct–
Jun, as ad winter but underwings barred.
2nd summer Still many imm feathers.
VOICE Migrants silent. HABITAT As
Pomarine (148). FOOD Mainly fish at sea,
catching most itself. RANGE Scarce
passage-migrant from N Europe/? Greenland, May–Nov, wintering in S Atlantic.

Arctic Skua

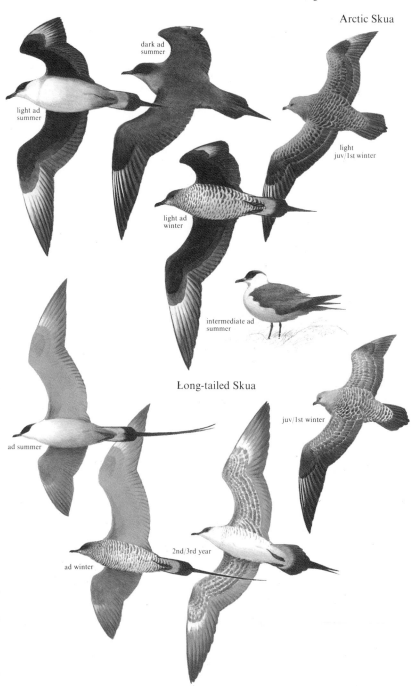

dark ad
summer

light ad
summer

light
juv/1st winter

light ad
winter

intermediate ad
summer

Long-tailed Skua

ad summer

juv/1st winter

ad winter

2nd/3rd year

GULLS (Laridae)

Mediterranean Gull *Larus melanocephalus*
37–40 cm (*c*15¼ in). Intermediate in size
between Black-headed (154) and Common
Gull (156), but stockier, chunky-headed,
with heavy droop-tipped bill, longer legs;
ad has blackish patch back from eyes, or
black head in summer, and pale grey and
white wings; 1st year head much as ad,
but wings like more contrasted 1st year
Common Gull with narrower tail-band.
Flight heavier than either, with stiffer
beats of less angled wings; struts, often
hunched; mixes (even breeds) with Black-
headed. *Ad* Only black streak at front of
white wing-tips; in *c*Feb–Oct, head black
with white eye-crescents, bill rich red
(sometimes dark-banded/yellow-tipped),
legs bright red; in *c*Aug–Mar, head white
with variable blackish patch back from
white-crescented eyes, bill/legs orange-red
to blackish (bill often yellowish at tip).
Juv Much brown on head, breast-sides
and scaly mantle, with narrow white eye-
crescents; wings with bands of brown,
pale grey and black; tail white, black band
near tip; bill/legs blackish. *1st winter*
After moult in *c*Jul–Oct, head and mantle
as ad winter; wings and tail still juv, but
faded; bill-base brown, pink or yellowish,
legs blackish or green-grey to orange-red.
1st summer After moult in Feb–Apr, head
variably black; wings and tail very faded,
but some new grey inner coverts; bill/
legs as 1st winter or red. *2nd year* Much as
ad winter/summer after moults in Jun–
Oct and Feb–Apr, but variable black
marks on outer 3–6 primaries, summer
hood sometimes white-flecked. VOICE
Mellow *kee-ow*. HABITAT Coastal lagoons,
marshes, estuaries, rare inland. FOOD Fish,
invertebrates. RANGE Scarce, all months:
most Jul–Nov, Mar–May; 6 nests 1968–80.

Little Gull *Larus minutus* 27–29 cm (*c*11
in). Smallest gull, dainty, with rather
rounded wings, more pointed on imm; ad
has blackish eye/ear-marks and grey
crown, or black head in summer, no black
on upperwings but dark underwings; 1st
year blackish cap, tail-band and bold W

Mediterranean Gull

ad winter

1st winter

juv

juv

2nd winter

ad summer

1st summer

across wings (*cf* Kittiwake, 162), white underwings; juv also blackish crown and mantle. Flight buoyant, tern-like; picks from surface. *Ad* Blackish underwings, white trailing edges above and below; in *c*Feb–Oct, whole head black, bill dark reddish, legs scarlet; in *c*Aug–Apr, head white with grey crown/nape and blackish eye/ear-marks, bill blackish, legs dull red. *Juv* Head white, with blackish eye/ear-marks, crown, nape, breast-sides and mantle; wings with broad blackish W from outer primaries across inner wings and rump, and faint bar on secondaries, underwings white; tail sometimes slightly notched, white with black band near tip, wider in middle; bill blackish, legs reddish-flesh. *1st winter* After moult in *c*Jul–Nov, much as juv with blackish crown and W, but nape, breast-sides and mantle grey. *1st summer* After moult in Feb–May, head with variable grey, brown or black hood, and whitish hindneck and often breast-sides; wings and tail as juv, but blackish bands faded to pale brown and often some (even all) new white tail-feathers; legs dull red. *2nd year* Much as ad winter/summer after moults in Jun–Oct and Feb–May, but variable blackish marks on outer 2-6 primaries; underwings grey or blackish, but smaller coverts paler; summer hood often white-flecked (rarely not developed), legs dull red. VOICE Low *kek-ek-ek* or higher *ka-ka-ka*. HABITAT Coasts, estuaries, inland lakes. FOOD As Mediterranean Gull, but many insects. RANGE Visitor all months: most Mar–May and esp Jul–Oct; 2 unsuccessful nests 1975–78. COMPARE Other dark-headed (154, 282) and W-winged gulls (162, 284).

Mediterranean Gull		B1 W2 S2 A2

Little Gull		B0 W2 S4 A4

Little Gull

2nd winter

juv

ad summer

ad winter

1st winter

juv

ad summer

1st summer

Sabine's Gull *Larus sabini* 32–34 cm (*c*13 in). Shape of small Kittiwake (162), with forked tail (not always apparent), and 3-coloured wing-pattern of white, black and grey (confusable with 1st year Kittiwake at long range); ad blackish nape and eye-marks, or grey hood and black collar in summer; juv has much grey-brown on head and breast-sides, scaled mantle and wing-coverts, tail-band. Flight buoyant, almost tern-like, feeding from surface; also runs on mud. *Ad* Grey mantle and inner wings, white tips and 'mirrors' on black primaries; underwings white with narrow black tips to primaries, faint bar on greater coverts; in *c*Mar–Oct, whole head grey with black collar; in *c*Sep–Mar, white with blackish eye-crescents and dark grey nape sometimes extending to cheeks, lower neck and rear crown; bill black with yellow tip, legs dark grey. *Juv* Grey-brown upper head and breast-sides, but white on face and around eyes; wings much as ad, but coverts, mantle and scapulars browner and scaled dark and whitish, only small white primary-tips, clearer dusky bar on

underwings; tail white with black band near tip, emphasising fork; bill black, legs pinkish-grey. *1st winter* After moult in Nov–Dec, head and grey mantle as ad winter; wings and tail still juv, but blacks faded, some new grey wing-coverts. *1st summer* Much as ad summer after complete moult in Feb–Apr, but partial grey hood on upper head only (often with blackish half-collar), small white primary-tips, sometimes some black on tail; less or no yellow on bill, legs pinkish-grey. VOICE Harsh, tern-like. HABITAT Mainly offshore, wind-blown to coasts and lagoons. FOOD Invertebrates and fish. RANGE On passage from Arctic, Aug–Nov, rare Dec–Jul, wintering in S Atlantic.

Black-headed Gull *Larus ridibundus* 35–38 cm (*c*14½ in). Most widespread small gull, with slim build, rounded head and tail, thin bill and narrow pointed wings, clearly smaller and slighter than Common Gull (156); outer wings always with dusky area below and white leading edge, both bolder on ad; ad has blackish eye/ear-

Sabine's Gull

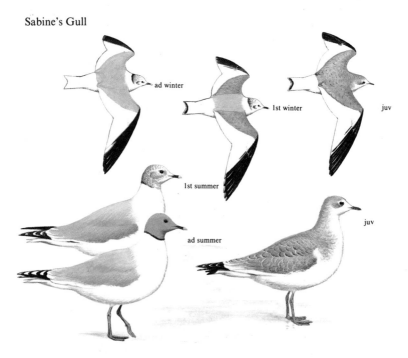

ad winter

1st winter

juv

1st summer

ad summer

juv

marks on white head, or brown forehood and white eye-rings in summer; 1st year shows brown carpal bar, blackish secondaries, tail-band; juv has much ginger above. Flight buoyant with fast beats; glides and soars, also hawks for insects; follows plough; swims, walks easily; perches anywhere; often tame; gregarious. *Ad* Black primary-tips; in *c*Mar–Oct, chocolate hood but white hindneck and eye-rings, bill and legs dark red; in *c*Aug–Mar, head white with blackish eye/ear-marks and 1–2 dusky bands running up from these, bill-base/legs dull red. *Juv* Much ginger on head, mantle and breast-sides; wings grey with brown carpal bar and white-tipped blackish trailing edge, and white panel on outer part; tail with black band near tip; bill-base and legs flesh-yellow. *1st winter* After moult in *c*Jul–Sep, head and body as ad winter; wings and tail juv, but dark areas faded and white tips worn. *1st summer* After moult Feb–Apr, variable brown hood (often flecked white); wings and tail juv, but very worn/faded; bill-

base/legs orange; usually as ad after moult in *c*Aug–Oct. VOICE Harsh angry *kwarr*, short *kuk*; noisy when nesting. HABITAT Breeds in gravel pits to moorland bogs, or coastal marshes and dunes; ubiquitous in winter, roosting on estuaries, lakes, and ranging far over surrounding fields and towns. NEST Colonial; in tussocks, or on flat ground, also in bushes over water, 2–3 eggs, mid Apr–Jul; 1 brood. FOOD Invertebrates, seeds, scraps. RANGE Resident, but much winter dispersal, a few moving south to Iberia; passage/winter visitor from Continent/Iceland, Aug–Apr.

| Sabine's Gull | B0 W0 S1 A3 | Black-headed Gull | B6 W7 S7 A7 |

Black-headed Gull

ad winter

ad winter

1st winter

juv

1st summer

ad summer

juv

156 Laridae

Common Gull *Larus canus* 38–43 cm (*c*16 in). Larger and wings less pointed than Black-headed (154), the other widespread smallish gull; ad pattern more as Herring but much smaller with slenderer yellow-green bill/legs, rounded head, thinner wings projecting more beyond tail at rest, daintier walk and easier flight; ad blue-grey and white, but for black outer primaries with white tips and bold 'mirrors'; 1st year has dense brownish streaking on crown, cheeks and breast-sides, brown carpal bar, blackish flight-feathers (but greyish inner primaries) and well-defined tail-band, black-tipped bill; juv also has scaly brown mantle. Actions much as other gulls, but drops molluscs as Herring Gull; flight buoyant, walks easily; favours fields and sheltered waters, rather than cliffs and sea. *Ad* Blue-grey mantle and wings, bold white trailing edges and tertial-crescents, white tips to black primaries and large 'mirrors' on 2 outermost, legs greenish-yellow; in *c*Aug–Mar, head white with dark streaks/eye-marks and white eye-crescents, breast-sides and flanks often with odd dark streaks, bill yellowish with darker base and faint band near tip; in *c*Mar–Oct, head and underparts white, bill yellow-green, red rings round brown eyes. *Juv* Crown, cheeks, lower nape, breast and flanks much more densely streaked/mottled than ad winter; mantle scaly buff; wings with bands of brown, grey-brown and blackish (less contrasted than imm Mediterranean Gull, 150, and underwings more dark-marked) and greyish showing on inner primaries between blackish outer wings and secondaries; tail white with clear blackish band near tip; bill blackish with usually paler base, legs flesh. *1st year* With moults in *c*Jul–Sep and Feb–Apr, mantle blue-grey, head and body progressively whiter and less streaked; wings and tail still as juv, but increasingly faded to pale brown and whitish; bill clearly black-tipped, legs sometimes tinged with yellow. *2nd year* With corresponding moults, becomes more as ad with mainly blue-grey wings and white tail, but black on outer wings extends to carpal joint, white tips and

'mirrors' smaller; head and flanks more streaked until summer; dark-tipped bill and legs grey-green to yellowish. VOICE Shrill *kee-ya*, trumpeting *hieeya*, higher and weaker than Herring Gull. HABITAT Breeds by lochs and on moors, shingle; winters on coasts, reservoirs, farmland. NEST On ground, 2–3 eggs, May–Jun; 1 brood. FOOD Mainly worms, insects, molluscs, fish. RANGE Resident, but much dispersal south; passage/winter visitor from Scandinavia/Baltic, Aug–Apr. COMPARE Ring-billed Gull (282).

Herring Gull *Larus argentatus* 53–59 cm (*c*22 in). Heavily built, with relatively short broad wings; ad all grey and white but for black outer primaries with white tips and 'mirrors'; see Lesser Black-backed (158) for imm plumage differences, and actions. Flight more graceful; carries molluscs/crabs aloft, dropping them to break them open. *Ad* Pale grey mantle/wings, bold white trailing edges, white tips to black primaries and 'mirrors' on 2 outermost; bill yellow with orange-red spot and whitish tip, eyes pale yellow with yellow or orange rings, legs pink to pale flesh (rarely yellow); in *c*Sep–Mar, whole head streaked brown; in *c*Feb–Sep, head white, white primary-tips smaller through wear. *Juv-3rd year* Plumage sequence much as Lesser Black-backed. VOICE As Lesser Black-backed, but less deep. HABITAT As Lesser Black-backed, but hardly breeding inland. NEST Colonial; on ground, cliffs or buildings, 2–3 eggs, end Apr–early Jul; 1 brood. FOOD As Lesser Black-backed. RANGE Mainly sedentary, some crossing Channel; passage/winter visitor from N Europe, Sep–Mar (Jul–Apr).

Common Gull

juv

1st winter

ad winter

ad summer

1st summer

juv

Herring Gull

ad winter

2nd winter

1st winter

juv

3rd summer

2nd summer

1st summer

yellow-legged ad winter

juv

ad summer

Lesser Black-backed Gull *Larus fuscus*
51–56 cm (*c*21 in). Barely slighter than
Herring Gull (156); *c* size of Great
Black-backed (162), with thinner bill,
smaller head, less bulky body; legs and
wings relatively longer than either, wings
narrower in flight and projecting more
beyond tail at rest. Ad has slate-grey
mantle and yellow legs, but note that N
race is as black as Great Black-backed
and some Herring Gulls have yellow legs.
Imm plumages (lasting over 3 years) are
harder to identify, but mantle colour
begins to show in 2nd winter. In general,
juv/1st year darker than Herring with
more coarsely streaked head and underparts, scalier mantle and inner wing-
coverts, blackish outer greater coverts,
almost entirely blackish outer wings, more
contrasting whitish rump and tail
emphasising blackish band near tip, and
black bill without pale base; separated
from Great Black-backed by much less
white head and chest, darker and more
scaly (not chequered) mantle, more clear-
cut tail-band, and smaller black bill

without whitish tip. Flight powerful with
leisurely beats; glides and soars; follows
boats; swims buoyantly, walks easily with
body horizontal; highly gregarious, often
standing or sitting with other large gulls
on sand-banks and shores or roosting on
water. *Ad W European race (L.f. graellsii)*
Slate-grey back and wings, bold white
trailing edges, white tips to black primaries
and 'mirrors' on 1–2 outermost; bill
yellow with red spot and whitish tip, eyes
yellow with red ring, legs creamy-yellow
or yellow; in *c*Aug–Mar, head streaked
brownish; in *c*Feb–Sep, head white, slate-
grey back becomes tinged with brown and
white primary-tips smaller through wear.
Ad N European race (L.f. fuscus) Similar,
but back blacker; head often whiter in
winter. *Juv* Head and underparts streaked
dark brown, with blackish eye/ear-patch,
and mottled blackish flanks; mantle and
inner wing-coverts dark brown scaled
paler, with blackish bar on outer greater
coverts; flight-feathers blackish; rump
and tail-base whitish, with contrasting
blackish band near tip; bill black, eyes

Lesser Black-backed Gull

juv

graellsii
1st summer

graellsii
3rd summer

graellsii
ad summer

graellsii
2nd summer

fuscus
2nd winter

fuscus
ad winter

brown, legs brownish-flesh. *1st year* Much as juv, but moults in Aug–Nov and Jan–Apr make head and underparts whiter, eye/ear-patch less clear, mantle less scaly; worn juv wings and tail paler brownish and more uniform. *2nd winter* After complete moult in May–Oct, head and underparts white with much dark streaking on crown, nape, breast-sides and flanks, and thicker area round eyes; mantle shows much dark grey, but inner wing-coverts still mainly pale-edged brown; outer wing-coverts and flight-feathers blackish; rump and tail mostly white with narrower blackish band near tip; bill usually pale brown or pinkish with dark patch near tip, eyes brown or greyish, legs pale creamy-flesh or tinged with yellow. *2nd summer* After moult in Jan–Apr, head/underparts whiter, mantle clearer slate-grey; wings/tail faded; eyes pale greyish, bill yellowish at base. *3rd year* After complete moult in Jun–Oct and partial in Jan–Apr, much as ad winter (streaky head) and then ad summer (white head), but some dark streaks on under-

parts, variable dark mottling and barring near tail-tip, dark mark near bill-tip; also inner wings mottled brown and outer part with more black, as well as smaller white primary-tips, all fading and wearing by summer. VOICE Noisiest when nesting; loud yelping *kyow-kyow-kyow*, shrill trumpeting *kyee kyee owkyowkyow-kyowkyow*, loud angry *kee-aa*, anxious *gag-gag-gag*. HABITAT Coasts, reservoirs, rubbish tips; breeds on dunes, shingle, cliffs, buildings, moors and bogs. NEST Colonial; on ground, cliffs or buildings, 2–3 eggs, May–Jul; 1 brood. FOOD Any animal food, garbage, plant material. RANGE Mainly summer visitor, mid Feb–Oct, wintering in Iberia/ NW Africa, but many all year; passage from Iceland, and N race from Scandinavia (esp EBr), mid Feb–May, Jul–Nov.

Lesser Black-backed Gull
B6
W5
S6
A6

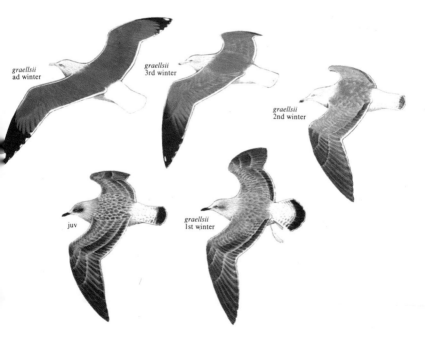

graellsii ad winter

graellsii 3rd winter

graellsii 2nd winter

juv

graellsii 1st winter

Iceland Gull *Larus glaucoides* 51–57 cm (*c*21 in). Near size of Herring Gull (156), but slimmer, gentler-looking and without any black on wings or tail; short thinnish bill less than half length of rounded head; legs also shorter than Glaucous and wings typically narrower and longer, projecting well beyond tail (by much more than bill-length), giving body elongated slender shape, but primaries often not fully grown in winter except in 1st year. Flight fast and buoyant. Plumages develop as Glaucous, but during *c*Apr–Aug eye-rings of ad usually red; 1st year often greyer-brown above, more neatly barred, with clearer whitish tail-end, and bill has only basal half dull grey-flesh shading into extensive black tip (may look all dark at distance); bill-pattern often still apparent in 2nd winter (but base now pale flesh), when some grey feathers may show on mantle/scapulars. VOICE As Herring but much shriller. HABITAT Much as Glaucous. FOOD Mostly fish. RANGE Scarce winter visitor from Greenland (not Iceland), Nov–Apr; rare other months.

Glaucous Gull *Larus hyperboreus* 58–69 cm (23–27 in). This and Iceland the only gulls without black on wings or tail at all ages. Size variable, from same as Great Black-backed (162) down to large Herring Gull (156); some little bigger than Iceland Gull, but still bulkier, with deeper chest, longer legs, long heavy bill over half length of fierce-looking, rather flat-crowned or angular head, and wings not projecting much beyond tail (never by more than bill-length); ad all white and pale grey with white wing-tips; 1st year rather, and 2nd year much, paler than other large gulls except Iceland, being more or less pale coffee-coloured to creamy-buff with fine barring, pale buff to whitish flight-feathers and no dark tail-band, also extensive pink on bill. Heavy flight and actions much as Great Black-backed. *Ad* White with pale grey mantle and wings, white trailing edges and tips; bill yellow with orange-red spot and whitish tip, eyes pale yellow with yellowish rings, legs pinkish; head and chest heavily streaked brownish in *c*Oct–Mar, white in *c*Feb–Sep. *1st winter* Head/

Iceland Gull

3rd year

1st winter

2nd year

ad winter

underparts rather uniform buff, often looking darker than wavy-barred mantle, wing-coverts and rump; flight-feathers buff with whitish tips, and pale buff tail mottled with whitish and brown; much variation all over in pattern and depth of colour, also fading in late winter; basal $\frac{2}{3}$ of bill bright pinkish to cream with well-defined black tip, eyes brown. *1st summer* After moult in Feb–Apr, more buff-white with fewer fainter markings; worn juv wings/tail faded paler; bill-base often yellow-flesh. *2nd year* With complete moult in Apr–Jan and partial in Jan–May, all pale buff-white, head/underparts variably streaked and mottled in winter, mantle/scapulars with fewer fainter bars and partly grey by summer, wings/tail faintly patterned and wearing almost uniform; bill yellow-flesh with less-defined dark end and pale tip, eyes lighten. *3rd year* Much as ad, but faint brownish mottling on underparts, mantle, rump and esp wing-coverts and tail; bill usually still marked blackish near tip and sometimes no red spot, eyes pale yellow.

VOICE Like hoarse Herring Gull. HABITAT Coasts, harbours, adjacent pastures, rubbish-tips, also inland waters. FOOD Carrion, fish, invertebrates. RANGE Winter visitor from Iceland/Arctic, Oct–Apr; occasionally other months; 1 paired with Herring Gull and bred in Shetland 1975–79. NOTE Confusion sometimes caused by pale leucistic or albinistic Herring and Great Black-backed Gulls, also moulting Herring Gulls missing outer primaries, pale imms with faded wings, and Glaucous × Herring hybrids: check bill-patterns (imms), plumage details, and shape.

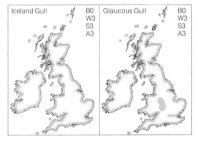

Iceland Gull	B0
	W3
	S3
	A3

Glaucous Gull	B0
	W3
	S3
	A3

aucous Gull

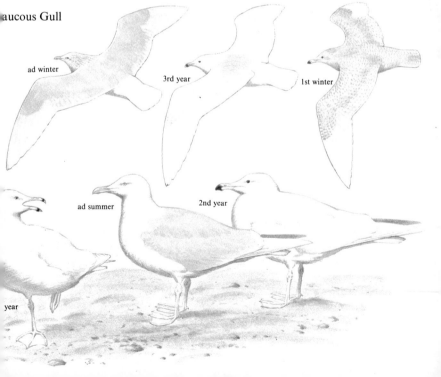

ad winter

3rd year

1st winter

ad summer

2nd year

year

Great Black-backed Gull *Larus marinus*
63–69 cm (*c*26 in). Bulky with heavy head
and stout bill, much larger than Lesser
Black-backed (158) and with relatively
shorter, broader wings and shorter legs;
ad has uniformly blackish back and wings,
otherwise mainly white, with flesh or
creamy-flesh legs; see Lesser Black-backed
for differences of juv/1st year. Actions
much as Lesser Black-backed, but flight
heavier, more ponderous; more predatory
and piratic; more often solitary. *Ad*
Blackish mantle and wings, white trailing
edges, white tips to black primaries joining
'mirrors' on 2 outermost in white patch;
underwings with dusky secondaries and
blackish tip; bill pale yellow with orange-
red spot, eyes pale yellow with red rings,
legs creamy-flesh; in *c*Sep–Mar, head
white with dark eye-mark, few streaks; in
*c*Feb–Sep, head white, black back tinged
brown, white primary-tips smaller with
wear. *Juv-3rd year* Plumage sequence
much as Lesser Black-backed; blackish on
mantle appears from 2nd/3rd year. VOICE
Stronger and deeper than Lesser Black-
backed, esp hoarse barking *yowk*,
trumpeting *ee-yowk-owk-owk*, guttural
uk-uk-uk. HABITAT Coasts, more locally
reservoirs; breeds rocky islands, headlands, locally on moors and lochs. NEST
Sometimes colonial; on ground ridges,
2–3 eggs, late Apr–Jun; 1 brood. FOOD As
Lesser Black-backed, but kills seabirds
and weak mammals. RANGE Mainly
resident, but some imms move south to
Iberia; also passage/winter visitor from
Iceland/N Europe, Aug–Apr. COMPARE
Great Black-headed Gull (282).

Kittiwake *Rissa tridactyla* 38–43 cm (*c*16
in). Near size of Common Gull (156), but
slighter, slimmer, with smaller head,
thinner pointed wings, very slightly forked
tail and short black legs; ad all grey and
white, but for black triangle of extreme
wing-tips; 1st year has blackish V on each
wing (not joining across rump in W as
Little Gull, 152), also tail-band, and often
half-collar on hindneck as juv. Flight
graceful with rapid beats, often in lines
over sea; feeds from surface in flight,
settles and dives, or plunges like tern;

coastal/pelagic; gregarious. *Ad* Darkish
grey and white, wings shading to white
trailing edges and line inside neat black
tips; bill greenish-yellow, eyes blackish
with orange-red rings, legs brown-black
to dark grey; during *c*Aug–Apr, rear head
grey as mantle, with blackish eye/ear-
marks; in *c*Feb–Oct, head all white. *Juv*
Head as ad winter, but nape only tinged
with grey, black half-collar on hindneck;
mantle and back grey as ad; wings
3-coloured with blackish outer forewings
joining diagonal carpal bar, coverts otherwise grey, and inner primaries and
secondaries whitish to white; tail white
with black tip, wider in middle and
emphasising slight fork; bill and legs
blackish. *1st winter* After moult in *c*Aug–
Oct, still as juv but back of head grey and
collar smaller or dark grey. *1st summer*
After moult in Feb–May, as 1st winter but
sometimes no ear-mark or collar; wings
and tail still juv, but blacks faded to pale
brown and partly worn away; bill
yellowish with darker tip. *2nd year* Much
as ad winter/summer after moults in Jun–
Oct and Feb–May, but sometimes traces
of imm plumage; bill often still partly
black. VOICE Noisy when nesting, esp
rhythmic nasal *kitti-week*. HABITAT Breeds
on sea-cliffs, locally on port buildings,
piers; nesting birds bathe regularly in
fresh water near shore; otherwise oceanic.
NEST Colonial; on ledges, 1–3 eggs, late
May–mid Aug; 1 brood. FOOD Fish,
marine invertebrates. RANGE At colonies
*c*Jan/Mar–Aug/Oct, otherwise ranging
across North Sea and Atlantic south to
NW Africa; also passage/weather movements from N Europe/Iceland, esp in
spring/autumn.

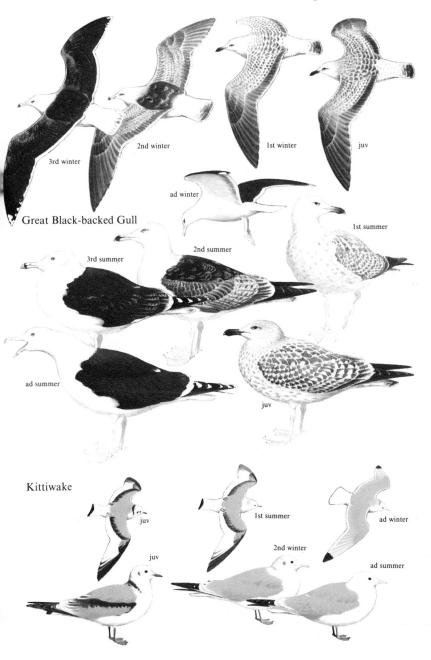

3rd winter

2nd winter

1st winter

juv

ad winter

Great Black-backed Gull

1st summer

3rd summer

2nd summer

ad summer

juv

Kittiwake

juv

1st summer

ad winter

juv

2nd winter

ad summer

TERNS (Sternidae)

Roseate Tern *Sterna dougallii* 32–40 cm (*c*15 in). Much paler pearl-grey above than Common or Arctic Tern (looking whiter at distance), with shortish wings, far longer tail. *Ad summer* Black cap; rosy wash on breast in spring; bill black with red base. *Ad winter* Moults Jul–Nov: head changes as Common; bill all-black. *Juv* As juv Common, but bill all-black, blackish cap more complete, upperparts paler with bolder scaling, narrow dusky inner forewing, greyish primaries, white trailing edge to whole wings, black legs. *1st winter* As ad winter, but wings/tail as juv. VOICE Soft *chuik*, musical *teeo*, rasping *aaak*. HABITAT Marine, nesting on islets and beaches. NEST Colonial; in rock hollows or under vegetation, 1–2 eggs, Jun–Jul; 1 brood. FOOD Fish. RANGE Summer visitor, end Apr–Sep, wintering off W Africa.

Arctic Tern *Sterna paradisaea* 30–39 cm (*c*15 in). Very like Common Tern, but shorter bill, neck and legs, longer tail (slightly longer than closed wings), no dark wedge on primaries above, all flight-feathers translucent from below, distinct calls. *Ad summer* Main plumage as Common, but underparts often greyer; bill all blood-red. *Ad winter* (unusual in Br/Ir as moult begins in Oct) Changes as Common but inner forewings less black. *Juv* Like juv Common, but forehead white, crown clear black, no buff or obvious brown on upperparts, dusky inner forewing less extensive, secondaries white, all flight-feathers translucent, primaries have only narrow black trailing edge. *1st and 2nd year* Changes (and occurrence) as Common, but distinguished by primary pattern of species. VOICE Resembles Common, but less slurred shorter *kee-yah*; and *prreeo*, piping *pee-pee-pee* and hard chattering all distinct. HABITAT Coastal. NEST As Common Tern, 1–3 eggs, mid May–Jul. FOOD Fish, invertebrates. RANGE Summer visitor, end Apr–mid Oct, wintering from S Africa to Antarctic; also passage from farther N/E, end Apr–Jun, and Jul–Oct.

Roseate Tern — ad summer, 1st summer, juv

Arctic Tern — ad summer, 1st summer, juv

Common Tern — ad summer, 1st summer, juv

Common Tern *Sterna hirundo* 20–36 cm (*c*14 in). Slender, with deeply forked tail. (but shorter than, or at most equal to, closed wings); blue-grey above, white or grey below; outer primaries form dusky wedge on upperwings, only inner primaries translucent from below (showing as light patch behind wing-angle). Flight buoyant with deliberate beats; fishes by diving, seldom swims; waddles gawkily. *Ad summer* Black cap; bill orange-red with black tip, legs red. *Ad winter* Begins moult in Jul–Aug: forehead becomes white, front crown streaked, inner forewing blackish, bill blackish with red base, legs duller. *Juv* Like ad winter, but basal half of bill pale flesh, legs orange, crown streaked blackish, forehead and mantle with gingery wash, upperparts barred brownish, bold blackish inner forewing, dark secondaries with white trailing edge, dusky opaque primaries, short tail. *1st winter* As dull ad winter, but wings/tail as juv. *1st summer* (rare in Br/Ir) As ad winter, but variable number of dusky juv flight-feathers, short tail. *2nd summer*

More like ad summer. VOICE Grating *keee-yah*, excited *kirri-kirri*, hard *kik-kik-kik*. HABITAT Coasts, lochs, rivers, gravel pits. NEST Colonial; open scrape, 2–4 eggs, May–Aug; 1 brood. FOOD Mainly fish. RANGE Summer visitor mid Apr–Oct, wintering off W Africa; also on passage from Continent, Apr–May, Jul–Oct.

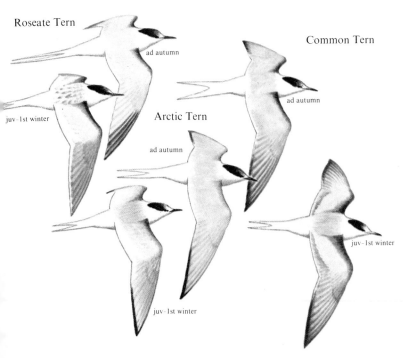

Roseate Tern

ad autumn

juv–1st winter

Arctic Tern

ad autumn

juv–1st winter

Common Tern

ad autumn

juv–1st winter

166 Sternidae

Sandwich Tern *Sterna sandvicensis* 38–43 cm (*c*16 in). Largest breeding tern; shaggy crest, long thin wings, forked tail, fine yellow tip (ad) to slender black bill, black legs; looks whiter than other terns except Roseate (164), with usually darkish wing-tips above. Flight stronger, less buoyant than smaller terns; hovers with straighter tail and plunges from greater heights. *Ad summer* Whitish-grey above, mainly white rump/tail; cap all-black to Jun. *Ad winter* With moult in Jun–Dec, forehead and then crown white, crown-sides and shaggy nape white-streaked blackish. *Juv* Cap black, heavily freckled first buff then whitish, almost no crest; wings/tail mainly greyish, rest of upperparts pale sandy-buff, wearing to white, all marked blackish with bars and clear Vs; bill all-dark. *1st year* As ad winter after moult beginning in Aug, but worn (darker) juv primaries in winter. *2nd summer* Often white forehead. VOICE Loud, shrill, grating *kier-rik*. HABITAT Sandy, shingly or rocky coasts; locally inland. NEST Colonial; scrape in open or grass, 1–2 eggs, mid May–Jul; 1 brood. FOOD Fish. RANGE Summer visitor, end Mar–Sep, wintering off W Africa; on passage mid Mar–May, Jul–mid Oct. COMPARE Gull-billed Tern (286).

Little Tern *Sterna albifrons* 23–26 cm (*c*9½ in). Tiny, squat, with narrow wings, short-forked tail, black-tipped yellow bill, orange legs; in summer, sharp white forehead, blackish outer forewings. Wing-beats much faster, more flickering than other terns; prolonged hovering before diving; less gregarious. *Ad summer* Blue-grey above; black eyestripes, crown and nape; bill-base yellow. *Ad winter* With moult from Aug, lores white, crown grey edged blackish from eyes round nape, lesser coverts dark grey, rump/central tail grey; outer primaries pale Nov–Jan; bill blackish. *Juv* Sandy-buff above, including forehead, but wearing to whitish, with black-streaked crown, brown U-bars on mantle and scapulars, but rump/tail and wings greyer, wings hoary-fringed blackish along whole leading edge; bill brown, legs brownish-yellow. *1st year* Generally much like ad winter after moult beginning in

Aug. VOICE Shrill *kitik*, harsher *kree-ik*, chattering *kirri-wirri*. HABITAT Sand or shingle coasts; scarce inland. NEST Loosely colonial; scrape on sand, shingle, mud, 2–3 eggs, mid May–Jul; 1 brood. FOOD Fish, crustaceans. RANGE Summer visitor, mid Apr–early Oct, wintering in Africa.

Black Tern *Chlidonias niger* 23–26 cm (*c*9½ in). Size of Little Tern, but bulkier; longer broader wings, barely forked tail; in summer blackish with white undertail-coverts, at other times white below with blackish patch at breast-sides, always pale grey underwings. Flight shallower than *Sterna* terns, beating to and fro, dipping to surface, not plunging in; rarely settles on water; singly or flocks. ♂ *summer* Black head, blackish underbody; bill black, legs red-brown. ♀ *summer* Greyer below, no contrast with pale wing-bend at rest. *Ad winter* With moult in Jun–Feb, black cap but white face, collar and underparts; all slaty-grey above. *Juv* Much as ad winter, but darker/browner above tipped pale; underwings whiter; bill-base and legs dark yellowish. *1st summer* Usually as ad winter. VOICE Squeaky *kik*. HABITAT Coasts, lakes; nests in flooded marshes. FOOD Insects. RANGE On variable passage from Continent, mid Apr–early Jun, Jul–Oct, wintering in Africa; nested SEBr to 19th century, irregularly since 1966, also Ir 1967, 1975. COMPARE Whiskered and White-winged Black Terns (286).

Sandwich Tern — B5 W0 S5 A5
Little Tern — B4 W0 S4 A4
Black Tern — B0 W0 S3 A3

Sandwich Tern

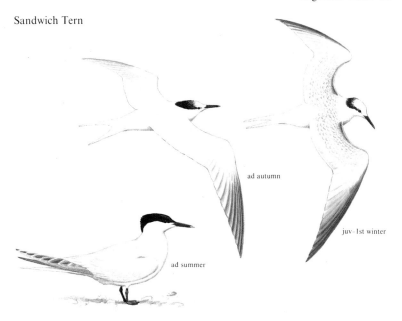

ad autumn

juv–1st winter

ad summer

Little Tern

ad summer

juv–1st winter

ad autumn

ad summer

Black Tern

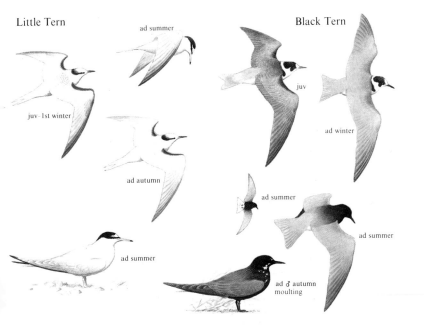

juv

ad winter

ad summer

ad summer

ad ♂ autumn
moulting

AUKS (Alcidae)

Guillemot *Uria aalge* 40–44 cm (*c*16½ in).
Commonest auk, slim, with slender
pointed bill, shortish rounded tail and, like
all auks, small narrow wings, short legs
set far back, and big feet; black or brown
above, white below, with white-tipped
secondaries forming wing-bar, whitish
underwing-coverts; note also 'bridled'
variety. Flight fast, direct, with whirring
beats, low over water; splashes in, breast
first; swims buoyantly, looking rather flat
with hunched neck; dives with flick of
legs and wings, and uses wings underwater; splashing take-off; at cliff-ledges,
brakes with feet out and lands with heavy
flutter; stands fairly upright, resting or
shuffling on tarsi, or waddling on feet
alone; also rests flat on rocks; highly
gregarious, parties often fly or swim in
lines. *Ad N race (U.a. aalge) summer* From
Dec–Mar onwards, black above with
deep chocolate head/neck; dark streaks
on flanks; bridled variety has white
spectacles. *Ad N race winter* With moult
in Jul–Oct, blackish crown, white throat/
cheeks divided by black line behind eyes,
sometimes whitish collar; bridled variety
still white round eyes. *Ad S race (U.a.
albionis)* As N race, but grey-brown
above, not black (many intermediate);
many fewer bridled farther south. *Juv
(both races)* As winter ad, but browner
above and scaled black, no dark streaks
on flanks; no flight- or tail-feathers till
moult in Aug–Sep. *1st winter* After moult,
hard to separate from ad winter except by
smaller bill, often whiter nape. *1st
summer* As ad summer after moult in Feb–
May, but worn juv wings pale brown,
throat often mottled white. VOICE Harsh
growls and trumpeting moans produce
enormous noise at colonies. HABITAT
Inshore and offshore waters, breeding on
cliffs. NEST Colonial; lays on bare ledges,
1 egg, May–Jul; 1 brood. FOOD Fish, also
crustaceans, molluscs, marine worms.
RANGE N race in NBr intergrades into S
race elsewhere; at colonies *c*Jan–Aug,
many then dispersing as far as Norway/
N Iberia; others arrive from N Europe.

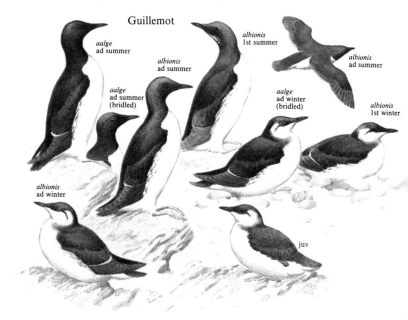

Guillemot

albionis 1st summer

aalge ad summer

albionis ad summer

albionis ad summer

aalge ad summer (bridled)

albionis ad summer

aalge ad winter (bridled)

albionis 1st winter

albionis ad winter

juv

Razorbill *Alca torda* 39–43 cm (*c*16 in). Size and pattern much as Guillemot, but with deep, laterally flattened bill crossed by white line when ad; heavier-headed and thicker-necked, with longer pointed tail; whitish line from bill to eyes, no flank-streaks, whiter underwing-coverts; looks blacker than browner Guillemots of S race in mixed colonies. Actions as Guillemot; longer tail often more cocked when swimming; usually much less numerous. *Ad summer* From *c*Mar, black above, chocolate throat/cheeks, line from bill to eyes white. *Ad winter* With moult in Aug–Oct, white throat and lower and rear cheeks, but brown round eyes, some mottling behind; line from bill to eyes faintly whitish. *Juv* Dark brown above, scaled black; whole head also brown (*cf* juv Guillemot) or sometimes mottled white on throat, and smaller all-dark bill, but still whitish line back to eyes; no flight or tail-feathers till autumn moult. *1st winter* As ad winter after moult in Jul–Oct, but for smaller, more pointed, all-dark bill and narrower white tips to secondaries.

1st summer As ad summer after early spring moult, but worn juv wings pale brown, throat sometimes mottled white. VOICE Deep or shrill growls and grunts. HABITAT As Guillemot. NEST Colonial; lays in crevices or under boulders, sometimes on sheltered ledges, 1 egg, May–Jul; 1 brood. FOOD As Guillemot. RANGE At colonies *c*Jan–Aug, many then dispersing as far as Scandinavia/NW Africa; others come into Br/Ir waters from N Europe and France.

COMPARE Brünnich's Guillemot (286).

Guillemot	B7 W6 S7 A7	Razorbill	B6 W6 S6 A6

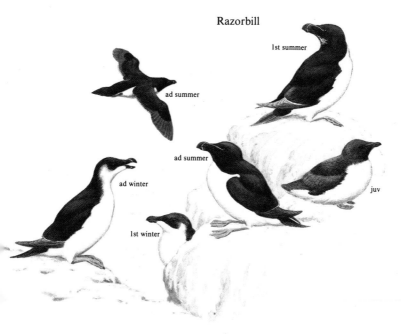

Razorbill

1st summer

ad summer

ad summer

ad winter

juv

1st winter

Black Guillemot *Cepphus grylle* 33–35 cm
($c13\frac{1}{2}$ in). Smaller than Guillemot (168),
with shorter bill, rich red legs and gape;
black with white wing-patch in summer,
ghostly white barred and mottled with
black above in winter. Actions much as
Guillemot, but walks more easily; solitary
or small parties. *Ad summer* From Feb or
Mar, all brown-black but for large white
patch on wing-coverts, black-edged white
underwings. *Ad winter* With moult in
Jul–Nov, first mainly black above and
mottled white below, then blackish and
white above and all-white below but for
blackish streaks on flanks, but still tail
black, and white patch on black wings.
Juv More uniform blackish-brown above,
mottled wing-patches; mostly speckled
below. *1st winter* Much as ad winter after
moult in Sep–Dec, but for mottled juv
wings, red-brown legs. *1st summer*
Browner than ad summer, mottled juv
wings; often flecked with white below.
VOICE Shrill whistling or whining *speeeeee*.
HABITAT Rocky coasts, staying inshore.
NEST Lays in holes or under boulders, 1–2

eggs, mid May–Aug; 1 brood. FOOD Fish,
crustaceans, molluscs, marine worms.
RANGE Mainly sedentary; some wander S
in winter, rarely even reaching Channel.

Little Auk *Alle alle* 20–22 cm ($c8$ in).
Starling-sized and chubby, with tiny bill
(*cf* juv Puffin) and rather long wings; black
above and white below, with white-tipped
secondaries forming thin wing-bar, white-
streaked scapulars, white spot over eyes,
dark underwings. More agile than Guillemot (168), taking off from water easily;
gregarious, though often seen singly in
Br/Ir. *Ad summer* Cheeks, throat and
breast chocolate. *Ad winter* Cheeks, throat
and breast white, variously mottled or
tinged blackish. *1st winter* As ad winter,
but esp wings browner, more often
speckled white across back of neck. VOICE
Migrants silent. HABITAT Offshore and
inshore waters. FOOD Planktonic
crustaceans. RANGE Winter visitor from
Arctic, mid Sep–mid Mar, esp Nov–Feb;
irregular except NBr, but sometimes in
numbers, occasionally blown inland.

Black Guillemot

ad summer

ad winter

1st winter

1st summer

ad summer

ad winter

1st winter

juv

Puffin *Fratercula arctica* 29–31 cm (*c*12 in). Big-headed and short-tailed with unmistakable colourful triangular bill when ad; smaller and fatter than Guillemot or Razorbill (168), with short red or yellow legs; likewise black above and white below, but with greyish clown-face, no wing-bar, dark underwings. Stands upright on feet; easy, rolling walk; breeding birds carry up to 10 fish cross-wise in bill; highly gregarious. *Ad summer* From *c*Mar, cheeks grey; bill blue-grey, yellow and bright red, with frilly yellow gape-edge; legs red. *Ad winter* After moult in Aug–Sep, cheeks darker, blackish in front of eyes; bill sheds horny plates at base, becoming smaller, grey-brown, yellow and orange; legs orange fading to yellow. *Juv/1st year* Smaller, but like dull ad winter, with darker cheeks, blacker lores, browner collar, pinkish legs turning yellow; much smaller bill looks all-dark, becoming as ad in 2nd year but still smaller. VOICE Deep groan *arr-ow-er* in burrow, more growling grunt in open. HABITAT Inshore and offshore waters, breeding on turfy slopes. NEST Colonial; lays in excavated or shearwater/rabbit burrows, or in crevices, 1 egg, May–Aug; 1 brood. FOOD As Black Guillemot, esp sand-eels when feeding young. RANGE At colonies *c*Mar–Aug, wintering mostly well out in North Sea/ Atlantic; some from Continent more in E/SBr waters.

Black Guillemot   B5 W5 S5 A5

Little Auk   B0 W3 S3 A4

Puffin   B7 W5 S7 A7

Little Auk

Puffin

ad winter

ad summer

ad winter

ad summer

ad summer

ad winter

juv/1st year

PIGEONS, DOVES (Columbidae)

Rock Dove *Columba livia* 31–35 cm (*c*13 in). Ancestor of widespread Feral Pigeon; plump, with shortish tail; blue-grey with pale back, 2 black wing-bars, white rump/ underwings/bill-base. Actions much as Woodpigeon; flight more dashing, often low; display-glides on V-wings; perches on rocks, buildings. *Ad* Blue-grey, with glossy purple-green neck, pale grey mantle/wing-coverts, white or whitish rump, white underwings. *Juv* Tinged brown, no gloss, greyer underwings. *Feral Pigeon* Some like Rock Dove but many variously blackish, white or brown. VOICE Crooning *oo-roo-coo*. HABITAT Sea-cliffs with caves, adjacent fields; Ferals much in towns, ruins, farms. NEST On ledges, 2 eggs, all year; 3–4 broods. FOOD Grain, seeds, crops, seaweed, molluscs. RANGE Mainly sedentary; any pure Rock Doves now confined to N/WBr, N/W/SIr coasts.

Stock Dove *Columba oenas* 31–35 cm (*c*13 in). Compact with shortish tail; grey-blue with blackish tips and rear edges to wings, short black bars on inner wings. Actions much as Woodpigeon, but flies with wings straighter, more flicking; usually in pairs or small parties. *Ad* Grey-blue head and rump, glossy green patch on sides of neck, purple tinge to breast. *Juv* Browner, no gloss on neck, duller breast; as ad after moult in May–Nov. VOICE Gruff repeated *coo-oh*. HABITAT Farmland, parks, wood-edges; also cliffs, ruins, dunes. NEST In holes in trees or buildings, rabbit burrows, 2 eggs, Mar–Oct; 2–3 broods. FOOD Much as Woodpigeon. RANGE Mainly sedentary, some move south; probably irregular immigrants from Continent in Oct–Apr.

Woodpigeon *Columba palumbus* 39–43 cm (*c*16 in). Small head, longish tail, deep chest; grey-brown, with white patches on dark-ended wings. Flight fast with quick beats of backswept wings, takes off with loud clatter; in display, flies up steeply, claps wings, glides down; walks with body level, head moving to and fro; perches mainly in trees; highly gregarious. *Ad* Grey-blue head and rump, green-

purple gloss and white patches on neck, purplish breast. *Juv* Dull grey head and rump, no gloss or white on neck, rusty breast; much as ad after moult in Jul–Oct. VOICE Hoarse, rhythmic *cooo-coo coo-coo cu*. HABITAT Suburbs to islands, esp farmland with woods. NEST In trees, bushes, on ground, 2 eggs, Apr–Nov; 2–3 broods. FOOD Cereals, clover, peas, nuts, roots, seeds, leaves, few invertebrates. RANGE Mainly sedentary, moving locally; some winter immigrants from Continent.

Collared Dove *Streptopelia decaocto* 29–32 cm (*c*12 in). Stockier than Turtle Dove (174), with longer tail, broader wings; pale brown and grey, breast pinkish; tail white-cornered above, widely white-ended below. Flight less tilting than Turtle Dove; sails round on spread wings, cocks tail on landing. *Ad* Black-and-white collar. *Juv* Greyer, scaled buff; no collar. VOICE Deep *coo-cooo cuk*, emphasis on 2nd syllable; harsh *kwurr* in flight. HABITAT Suburbs, villages, parks, farms. NEST Often in conifers, 2 eggs, Apr–Nov; 2–4 broods. FOOD Seeds, grain, scraps. RANGE Rapid spread after colonisation in 1955; sedentary, but surplus disperses; birds continue to arrive from Continent.

Rock Dove

Feral Pigeons

Stock Dove

Woodpigeon

Collared Dove

174 Columbidae/Cuculidae/Psittacidae

Turtle Dove *Streptopelia turtur* 26–29 cm
(*c*10¾ in). Small, slim pigeon, with longish
graduated tail; head and outer wing-
coverts grey, back and rump grey-brown,
scapulars and most wing-coverts black-
spotted rufous, breast pink, belly white,
and tail white-edged, white-ended below.
Flight fast with clipped action of backswept wings, tilting to side; in display,
climbs steeply with spread tail, glides down
in circle; perches much on bushes, wires;
in small parties in late summer. *Ad* Grey-
blue head, black-and-white patch on
neck-sides, rufous and grey on wings,
pinkish breast. *Juv* Grey-brown head, no
neck-patches, duller rufous and less grey
on wings, buff breast. VOICE Deep purring
rroorr repeated. HABITAT Bushy areas,
copses, wood-edges, young plantations.
NEST Typically in thorn bushes, 2 eggs,
mid May–mid Sep; 2 broods. FOOD Seeds.
RANGE Summer visitor, end Apr–Sep,
wintering in Africa; some on passage from
Continent, mid Apr–May, mid Aug–mid
Oct. COMPARE Rufous Turtle Dove (288).

CUCKOOS (Cuculidae)

Cuckoo *Cuculus canorus* 32–34 cm (*c*13 in).
Familiar summer sound, much less seen,
and often confused with hawk in flight;
slender, with pointed bill and wings, long
graduated tail; usually grey above and
barred below with white-spotted tail, but
many juvs and a few ♀s rufous and heavily
barred above. Flight direct, often fairly
low, with fast shallow beats below level of
back, gliding to perch on trees, bushes,
posts; droops wings and raises tail on
landing; waddles or hops on ground;
solitary; rather shy. *Ad ♂* Grey above and
on head to upper breast; white-barred
blackish below. *Ad ♀* Grey tinged brown;
browner barring on buff breast. *Juv* Either
dark grey-brown above, or rufous with
blackish bars, but always whitish fringes,
white nape-patch; buff-white below,
heavily barred blackish. *1st summer* As
ads after winter moult, but some greater
coverts and barred secondaries still juv; ♀
often has some rufous barring above and
on throat. *Hepatic ad ♀* Rare variety
resembles barred rufous juv, but rich

chestnut above, more rufous on throat/
breast. VOICE ♂ far-carrying *cuc-coo* or
cuc-cuc-coo; ♀ long bubbling chuckle;
both also hoarse *wha-wha-wha*. HABITAT
Woods, farmland, reedbeds, moors,
dunes. NEST Lays directly into nests of
other birds (esp pipits, Dunnock,
warblers, wagtails, Robin), each ♀ often
parasitising only 1 species; 6–18 eggs in
May–Jul; young Cuckoo ejects other eggs
or nestlings soon after hatching. FOOD
Mostly insects; ♀ eats 1 egg of foster
parent. RANGE Summer visitor, mid Apr–
Jul/Aug (juvs to Sep or later), wintering in
Africa. SEE Other cuckoos (290).

PARAKEETS (Psittacidae)

Ring-necked Parakeet *Psittacula krameri*
37–43 cm (*c*16 in). Very attenuated parrot
with largish head, narrow pointed wings,
and extremely long, thin, graduated tail;
mainly green with bluer-green tail. Flight
fast with shallow beats; clambers about on
branches and trunks, using bill as extra
foot; noisy, gregarious. *Ad ♂* Red bill;
black throat, thin pink collar, bluish
nape. *Ad ♀* Red bill; otherwise green. *Juv*
As ♀, but bill horn-coloured with dark tip.
VOICE Shrill screaming *keeo-keeo-keeo*.
HABITAT Open
woods, parks,
gardens, fields. NEST
In tree-holes, 2–6
eggs, Apr–Jul; 1
brood. FOOD Seeds,
nuts, fruit, berries,
scraps. RANGE Intro-
duced from Africa/
S Asia in 1960s,
now breeds ferally.

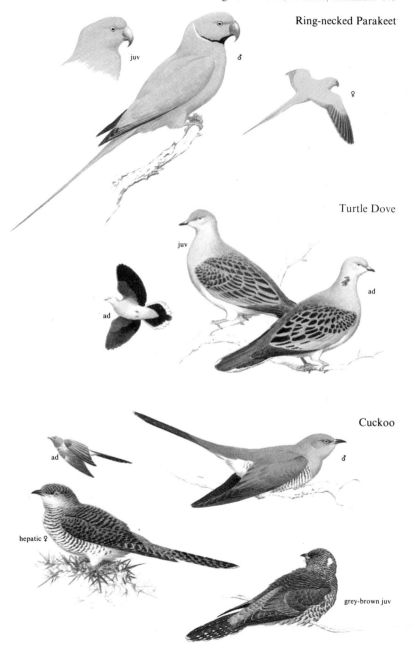

Ring-necked Parakeet

juv

♂

♀

Turtle Dove

juv

ad

ad

Cuckoo

ad

♂

hepatic ♀

grey-brown juv

BARN-OWLS (Tytonidae)

Barn Owl *Tyto alba* 33–36 cm (c13½ in).
Nocturnal and crepuscular; smallish black
eyes set in heart-shaped white face, longish
tapering wings, short tail; orange-buff
and white, looks ghostly pale in car lights.
Flight wavering; hunts by day when
feeding young and in winter; stands
upright on longish legs; swings lowered
head to and fro when agitated; roosts in
buildings, tree holes, rocks; solitary. *Ad
W European race (T.a. alba)* Orange-buff
above, mottled grey (esp ♀); white below,
often some buff tinge and fine dark spots
(esp ♀). *Juv* As ad, but cream down
adhering to crown, back, underparts. *Ad
dark-breasted Cent/E European race (T.a.
guttata)* Darker: greyer above and more
buff and spotted below; some intermediate. VOICE Shrill drawn-out shriek in
flight, short whistled hiss, also snore,
chirrup, sharp *ke-ak*. HABITAT Farms,
ruins, church towers, parks, timbered
hedges, cliffs, quarries, in open country.
NEST In roof-spaces, hollow trees, holes in
thatch or straw, rock crevices, 4–7 eggs,
Apr–Oct. FOOD Small mammals, also
birds, insects. RANGE Largely sedentary,
imms wander; dark-breasted race vagrant,
Aug–Apr, esp Oct–Dec, most SEBr.

OWLS (Strigidae)

Snowy Owl *Nyctea scandiaca* 53–66 cm
(21–26 in), ♀ larger than ♂. Diurnal; very
big, with round head, yellow eyes, broad
rounded wings and shaggy feet; white,
more or less marked with brown. Flight
powerful, fast, often low, with long glides;
kills birds on wing; perches slanted on
rocks, hummocks and posts; solitary. *Ad
♂* All white, but for scattered brown spots
and bars. *Ad ♀* Face, throat, underwings
and legs white, sometimes also central
breast, belly and rump; rest widely barred
brown. *Juv* Downy; mainly dark grey-
brown, speckled grey-white, but face,
wings and tail white marked with brown.
1st year ♂ As small ad ♀ after moult ends
Sep–Oct, but more heavily barred on nape
and belly, mottled on wings. *1st year ♀*
Much more heavily barred and mottled.

VOICE Rather silent; barking *ergh-ergh*
(♂♀), low deep hoot *hoorh* (♂), mew and
squeal (♀), when nesting. HABITAT Moorland with rocky outcrops, also coastal
flats in winter. NEST On open ground, 4–10
eggs, May–Jul. FOOD Birds, mammals (to
size of duck, rabbit), also beetles, fish.
RANGE Bred NBr 1967–75, then only ♀s
present; otherwise irregular visitor.

Little Owl *Athene noctua* 21–23 cm (c8½
in). Diurnal and crepuscular; squat, flat-
headed, with fierce yellow eyes set in
frowning face, short tail; brown dappled
with white. Flight fast, low, undulating
like woodpecker; perches upright on trees,
hedges, posts, wires, and rocks; bobs
when agitated; can run; roosts in holes or
dense cover; solitary. *Ad* Dusky-brown,
spotted and streaked with white; whitish
below, broadly streaked dark brown. *Juv*
Pattern similar, but downy; browns paler,
whites more buff, streaking narrower; as
ad after moult Aug–Nov. VOICE Plaintive
mewing *keeu*; yelps, barks and chatters
when nesting; song mellow whistle, often
in duet. HABITAT Farmland with old trees,
parks, also stony wastes, cliffs, suburbs.
NEST In holes in trees, barns, haystacks,
rabbit burrows, rocks, 3–5 eggs, Apr–mid
Jul; 1 brood. FOOD
Insects, small
mammals, also
birds, worms. RANGE
Introduced Br late
19th century, largely
sedentary, some
wander; rare
vagrant Ir. COMPARE
Scops and Teng-
malm's Owls (290).

Barn Owl | B4 W5 S4 A5

Snowy Owl | B0 W1 S1 A1

Little Owl | B5 W5 S5 A5

♀

♂

Snowy Owl

♂

Barn Owl

alba ad

guttata ad

alba ad

Little Owl

ad

Tawny Owl *Strix aluco* 36–40 cm (*c*15 in). Nocturnal, heard far more than seen; bulky, with big head, black eyes in rounded face, no ear-tufts, broad rounded wings; rufous (usually) to grey-brown, with whitish patches on scapulars. Flight slow with regular beats; may hunt by day in dark wood when feeding young, but mostly seen when disturbed from roost in hole or against trunk; often mobbed (as all owls) by chattering birds; solitary. *Ad* Red-brown, tawny or rarely greyish above, marbled and streaked; buff to whitish below with bold dark streaks. *Juv* Downy; brown to rufous above, grey-buff below, barred whitish and brown; moults from Jun–Jul, but often not as ad until Oct–Nov. VOICE Sharp *ke-wik*, juv shrill *tu-whit*; song prolonged, wavering *hoo-hoo . . . hoo . . . hoo-oo-oo-oo*. HABITAT Old woods, parks, suburbs. NEST In tree holes, chimneys, rocks, Magpie nests, rabbit holes, or on ground, 2–5 eggs, Mar–Jun; 1 brood. FOOD Small mammals, birds, also fish, frogs, insects. RANGE Sedentary.

Long-eared Owl *Asio otus* 34–37 cm (*c*14 in). Nocturnal, but also hunts by day; slender, with dark elongated cat-like face, orange eyes, V brows giving 'surprised' expression, ear-tufts (often invisible), broad longish wings, squared tail; grey-brown above, often looking uniformly darkish, and well streaked below; in flight, dark carpal patches (not obvious above), orange-buff patch on primaries, finely barred greyish secondaries and grey-buff tail (*cf* Short-eared). Flight deep jerky beats, then glide on straight, usually level wings; roosts upright by trunk, or on ground; sometimes small parties. *Ad* Grey-brown above, buff below, all dark-streaked. *Juv* Downy; brown and creamy-buff, all barred; moults from May–Jun but often not as ad until Nov. VOICE Squeals, screams, barks, also claps wings in display flight; juv mournful piping like unoiled gate; song (Jan–Apr) low, moaning, drawn-out *oo-oo-oo. . . .* HABITAT Woods, esp conifers, also moors, dunes, marshes. NEST In old nests (*eg* Magpie) or on ground, 3–6 eggs, Mar–Jun; 1 brood. FOOD Small mammals, birds, insects.

RANGE Sedentary, dispersal local; winter visitors from N Europe, Oct–mid May.

Short-eared Owl *Asio flammeus* 36–39 cm (*c*14¾ in). Diurnal; stocky, with whitish bulbous face, fiercely dark-ringed yellowish eyes, scarcely visible ear-tufts, long tapering wings and slightly wedge-shaped tail; tawny and buff above, looking blotched, and heavily streaked on throat and chest only; in flight, dark carpal patches above and below, pale buff to whitish on primaries, blotchy coverts and secondaries, pale trailing edges to wings, boldly V-barred buff tail (*cf* Long-eared). Flight more wavering than Long-eared, sometimes soaring high, and glides with wings held forward, often in shallow V; roosts in cover on ground; in parties in 'vole years' and on migration. *Ad* Blotched tawny, buff and brown; pale buff below, heavily streaked on forepart. *Juv* Downy; dark brown above, marked buff, and thinly streaked below; moults from Jun–Jul, but often not as ad until Oct. VOICE Shrill *kee-aw*, barking *kwowk*; in display flight, low *boo-boo-boo . . .*, claps wings. HABITAT Moors, marshes, dunes. NEST On ground, 4–7 eggs, end Mar–mid Jul; 1–2 broods. FOOD Small mammals, esp voles, also birds, insects.

RANGE Partial migrant, some moving SW, even to Iberia; many winter visitors from Iceland/N Europe, Sep–Jun.

COMPARE Other owls (176,290).

Tawny Owl — B6 W6 S6 A6

Long-eared Owl — B4 W5 S4 A5

Short-eared Owl — B4 W4 S4 A4

Tawny Owl

brown ad

grey ad

Long-eared Owl

Short-eared Owl

ad

ad

ad

ad

ad

NIGHTJARS (Caprimulgidae)

Nightjar *Caprimulgus europaeus* 25.5–28 cm ($c10\frac{1}{2}$ in). Nocturnal and crepuscular; tiny bill but huge gape, broad flat head, longish wings/tail; grey, camouflaged by brown, black, rufous and cream. Flight buoyant, erratic, with glides; by day on ground or lengthways on branch. *Ad ♂* White on wing-tips, tail-corners. *Ad ♀* No white. *Juv/1st winter* As ad ♀. VOICE ♂ shrill *coo-ic*, also claps wings; song loud churring, rising and falling, for up to 5 min. HABITAT Felled woods, tiny conifers, heaths, moors, dunes. NEST On bare ground, 2 eggs, end May–Aug; 2 broods. FOOD Insects, on wing. RANGE Summer visitor, May–Sep, wintering in Africa. COMPARE Common Nighthawk (290).

KINGFISHERS (Alcedinidae)

Kingfisher *Alcedo atthis* 15–16 cm ($c6\frac{1}{2}$ in). Stumpy with big head and dagger-like bill, short wings and tail; green-blue and chestnut, with brilliant blue mantle to tail, white throat and neck-patch. Flight fast, direct, whirring, low over water; perches or hovers, then plunges; if uneasy, bobs head, flicks tail. *Ad* Crown and moustache show blue bars; ♂ bill black or red at base, ♀ often more red or orange at base. *Juv/1st year* Duller, greener, esp crown, moustache; paler below, speckled pale on breast; bill black. VOICE Shrill *chee* or *chee-kee*; song whistled trill. HABITAT Rivers, streams, lakes. NEST In excavated tunnels in banks, 5–7 eggs, Apr–Aug; 2 broods. FOOD Fish, insects. RANGE Most sedentary; some move to coasts Aug–Mar. SEE Belted Kingfisher (290).

HOOPOES (Upupidae)

Hoopoe *Upupa epops* 27–29 cm ($c11$ in). Pink,brown, with boldly pied wings and tail, curved bill, and huge fan-like crest depressed into hammer-shape at rest. Flight lazy, jerky, big oval wings closed between beats; walks unobtrusively; perches on trees, walls. *Ad ♂* Throat/breast pinkish. *Ad ♀* Throat/breast usually

Kingfisher

Nightjar

browner with white tips; some inseparable. *Juv* Shorter bill and crest at first, then as dull ♀; as ad after moult Aug–Oct. VOICE Song low *poo-poo-poo*, far-carrying. HABITAT Wood-edges, parks, orchards, gardens. FOOD Insects. RANGE Scarce migrant, esp Mar–May, Aug–Oct, wintering in S Spain/Africa; rarely nests SBr.

WOODPECKERS (Picidae)

Wryneck *Jynx torquilla* 15–16 cm (*c*6½ in). More like bulky chat/warbler than woodpecker relative; grey-brown, mottled and barred. Flight jerky; perches, or clings to trunk; licks insects from bark or ground, where hops with tail raised. *Ad* Grey to brown marked with rufous and black; snaky stripe on back; buff below, barred, spotted and arrowed. *Juv* Paler above, less bold marks below; as ad after moult in Aug–Sep. VOICE Shrill *kyeu-kyeu-kyeu*, like far Hobby (106). HABITAT Open woods, orchards. NEST In tree holes, 7–10 eggs, May–Jul; 1–2 broods. FOOD Ants. RANGE Summer visitor, Apr–Sep, wintering south to Africa; once widespread in S/CentBr, now colonising NBr; on passage from N Europe esp end Aug–Oct.

Hoopoe

Wryneck

Green Woodpecker *Picus viridis* 30–33 cm (*c*12½ in). Robust tree-climber and wood-borer like all true woodpeckers, with strong bill, long sticky tongue, short spiky graduated tail, 2 toes forward and 2 back; dull green with red crown, black face, yellow rump, and paler grey-green below with barred yellowish underwings. Bounding flight, wings closed every 3–4 beats, sweeping up into trees; climbs or spirals up trunk with jerky hops, pressing tail (often very worn) against bark as prop, or along or under branch; hops upright on ground, alternately probing and looking round; solitary; wary. *Ad* ♂ Moustache-centres red. *Ad* ♀ Moustaches all black, belly often barred browner. *Juv* Greyer-green above with whitish spots and bars, and face and underparts streaked and barred with black; shorter, speckled moustaches (part red on ♂); as ads after moult Aug–Nov. VOICE Loud ringing laugh *keu-keu-keu*; rarely drums. HABITAT Farmland, orchards, copses, parks, commons, with old trees. NEST In excavated holes in trees, 5–7 eggs, end Apr–early Jul; 1 brood. FOOD Insects, esp wood-boring larvae, ants; some worms, few berries and seeds. RANGE Sedentary. COMPARE ♀ Golden Oriole (226).

Great Spotted Woodpecker *Dendrocopos major* 22–24 cm (*c*9 in). Smaller than Green Woodpecker and shorter-billed; boldly pied, with glossy black cap and back, big white or buff-tinged shoulder-patches, whitish sides of head and neck divided by black band joining moustache, whitish underparts and underwings but red under tail (*cf* Lesser Spotted). Behaviour as Green Woodpecker, but seldom on ground; wedges pine-cones in cracks to break out seeds; tamer, visits bird tables. *Ad* ♂ Small red patch on nape; buff-white below with red extending to lower belly. *Ad* ♀ As ♂, but no red on black nape. *Juv* Whole crown red; black moustache narrower, streaked with white; often few black streaks on shoulders and flanks; underparts paler and red area duller, less extensive; as ad after moult in Aug–Oct. VOICE Abrupt, explosive *tchick*; drums with bill on dead wood, Mar–May,

with loud hard vibration like creaking tree, lasting *c*1 sec. HABITAT Woods, copses, also gardens in winter. NEST In excavated holes in trees, 4–7 eggs, May–early Jul; 1 brood. FOOD Insects, esp wood-boring larvae; conifer seeds, nuts, berries, nestlings, eggs. RANGE Sedentary; some immigrants from Scandinavia, Sep–Apr, esp N/EBr Sep–Oct, rarely to Ir.

Lesser Spotted Woodpecker *Dendrocopos minor* 14–15.5 cm (*c*5¾ in). Sparrow-sized, with small pointed bill; crown red or whitish, no white shoulder-patches or red under tail, but wings and back barred black and white, flanks streaked blackish (*cf* Great Spotted). Actions as Green Woodpecker, but flight slower, more fluttering; mainly on high branches or twigs, rarely on ground; shy. *Ad* ♂ Crown red, mottled whitish. *Ad* ♀ Crown whitish to pale brown, sometimes flecked red; black of nape extends to rear crown. *Juv* Forecrown whitish, mottled black; rear part red on ♂, flecked red on ♀; flanks more spotted and streaked black; as ad after moult Jul–Oct. VOICE Shrill *pee-pee-pee-pee*, weaker, less ringing than Wryneck (180); also single *chik*, weaker than Great Spotted; drumming usually feebler, longer, *c*2 sec.

HABITAT Tall woods, parks, avenues, old orchards. NEST In excavated holes in branches, 4–6 eggs, end Apr–mid Jul; 1 brood. FOOD Wood-boring larvae. RANGE Sedentary.

Green Woodpecker

juv ♀

♂

ad

Great Spotted
Woodpecker

juv

♂

♀

Lesser Spotted
Woodpecker

♂

♀

♂

LARKS (Alaudidae)

Woodlark *Lullula arborea* 14.5–16 cm (*c*6 in). Stockier than Skylark with finer bill, more obscure crest, blunter wings; tail much shorter with brownish sides and white tips; bold whitish supercilia meet on nape, white-edged blackish mark at wing-bend; pinkish legs. Unobtrusive on ground; often lands in trees; flight undulating; usually singly or in family parties. *Ad* Streaked above and on breast; darker above and whiter below in summer through wear. *Juv* More spotted, with pale-edged, rounded feathers on upper-parts and breast; as ad after moult in end Jul–Sep. VOICE Liquid *toolooeet*; out-standing song of sweet, clear notes repeated in 3–5 sec phrases (esp rich *lu-lu-lu*) and sustained from tree, ground or in circling flight. HABITAT Heaths, brecks, felled woods (esp sandy soils), with scattered trees and bushes. FOOD Insects, seeds. NEST On ground, 3–4 eggs, Mar–Aug; 2 broods. RANGE Resident, decreased; some autumn/spring dispersal.

Skylark *Alauda arvensis* 17–18.5 cm (*c*7 in). Abundant aerial songster, often invisibly high, or streaky brown flutterer over fields, with longish tail (white-sided) and wings (rather pointed, with whitish trailing edges); bill stoutish, crest often prominent, supercilia obscure. Flight strong, slightly undulating; in song, climbs vertically, hangs poised for 2–5 mins, then sinks and finally drops; usually walks or runs crouched on bent legs, rather than hopping; perches on walls, fences, bushes, seldom trees; flocks in autumn and winter. *Ad* Brown above, streaked blackish; buff-white below with streaked breast; darker above and whiter below in summer through wear. *Juv* Scaled above with pale feather-edges, breast spotted rather than streaked, no crest; as ad after moult end Jul–Sep. VOICE Rippling *chirrup*; song loud, clear, sustained warbling in high flight, some-times on ground or on bushes. HABITAT Open fields, downs, moors, dunes, marshes, saltings. NEST On ground in grass or crops, often by tufts, 3–5 eggs,

Woodlark

Skylark

Apr–Aug; 2–3 broods. FOOD Seeds, weeds, worms, insects. RANGE Resident, but some cross Channel; many on passage/winter from N/Cent Europe, Sep–Apr.

Shore Lark *Eremophila alpestris* 16–17 cm (*c*6½ in). Rather uniform pink-brown above and whitish below; yellow and black of head partly obscured in winter; tail blackish with browner centre, thin white sides; bill stubby. Walks unobtrusively, runs, also hops; gregarious in winter, mixes with Snow Buntings. *Ad summer ♂* typically bold-patterned head with black 'horns', pink-brown nape; but some like ♀, duller blackish on head, with minute 'horns', nape only tinged pink-brown. *Ad winter* Black partly concealed by yellowish edgings; ♀ generally duller, less yellow-faced, browner-naped, more streaky above. *Juv* Darker above, spotted buff-white; no black/yellow. *1st winter* As dull winter ad; inseparable unless very little black on crown or pinkish on nape and both dark-streaked. VOICE Shrill, pipit-like *tseep*, wagtail-like *tsee-seep*; song

short warble from ground or in display flight. HABITAT Breeds on stony hills; winters on shingle, saltings, stubble. FOOD Seeds, insects, molluscs, crustaceans. RANGE Passage/winter visitor from Fenno-Scandia, Oct–Apr; bred NBr 1973, 1977.

COMPARE Pipits (188), vagrants (294).

Shore Lark

winter flock

juv

♂ summer

♀/dull ♂

SWIFTS (Apodidae)

Swift *Apus apus* 16–17 cm ($c6\frac{1}{2}$ in). Scythe-like wings and short forked tail (closes to point); sooty-brown with paler under-wings and obscure whitish throat; looks all-black at distance. Flies with rapid beats of stiff wings, and long glides, tilting from side to side, often high in air; screaming parties chase round roof-tops; never perches, but will cling under eaves to roost. *Juv* Hard to separate in flight, but browner, with whitish tips on forehead and wings, and larger, whiter throat-patch. VOICE Shrill, chattering scream. HABITAT Aerial; commonest over towns and water. NEST Colonial; in hole in eaves, thatch, church towers, cliffs, 2–3 eggs, May–mid Aug; 1 brood. FOOD Insects, on wing. RANGE Summer and passage visitor, end Apr–Aug; stragglers to Oct.

SWALLOWS, MARTINS (Hirundinidae)

Sand Martin *Riparia riparia* 11.5–12.5 cm ($c4\frac{3}{4}$ in). Slender, with barely-forked tail; brown and white with brown breast-band. Flight flitting, erratic, gliding less than Swallow, chiefly over water; perches on wires, bank vegetation; roosts gregariously in reedbeds. *Juv* As ad, but pale fringes on rump and wing-coverts, throat tinged buff. VOICE Hard, dry chirrup; song harsh twitter. HABITAT Rivers, lakes, sandpits. NEST Colonial; tunnel in sand or earth face, 4–5 eggs, May–Aug; 2 broods. FOOD Insects, on wing. RANGE Summer visitor, mid Mar–Oct; also on passage from Continent.

Swallow *Hirundo rustica* 16–22 cm ($c7\frac{1}{2}$ in). Long wings and (ad) tail-streamers; blue-black, chestnut and buff. Flight graceful, swooping, ever changing course, with regular beats and glides; perches and roosts as Sand Martin, also on and in buildings; autumn flocks common. *Ad* Metallic blue upperparts and breast-band, chestnut face, cream to buff belly, white tail-marks; longest tails on ♂, shortest on ♀, but much overlap. *Juv* Duller above; throat and smaller forehead-patch paler pink-buff; tail shorter than shortest ♀.

VOICE High *vit vit-vit-vit*; song of warbling twitters and trills. HABITAT Farms, suburbs; often over water. NEST Of mud, on ledges in sheds, porches etc., 4–6 eggs, May–Sep; 2–3 broods. FOOD Insects, on wing. RANGE Summer and passage visitor, end Mar–Oct; stragglers to Dec.

House Martin *Delichon urbica* 12–13 cm ($c5$ in). Compact, tail forked; blue-black and white with browner wings/tail, white rump. Flight slower, less swooping, often high; perches on roofs, wires; roosts in nest or trees; gregarious. *Ad* Metallic blue with white rump and underparts, buff-tinged through moult from Aug. *Juv* As ad in autumn, but bill-base yellowish, crown dull dark brown, tertials tipped white, white areas washed with brown-grey. VOICE Weak, hard *tchirrip*; infrequent twittering song. HABITAT Towns, villages, farms, bridges, cliffs; often over water. NEST Colonial; of mud, under house eaves, bridges, cliff over-hangs, 4–5 eggs, mid May–Sep, 2–3 broods. FOOD Insects, on wing. RANGE Summer and passage visitor, Apr–mid Oct; stragglers to Dec.

COMPARE Vagrant swifts, swallows (292).

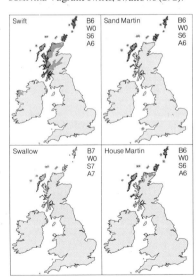

Swift

ad

juv

Sand Martin

juv

ad

juv

ad

Swallow

♂

♀

juv

House Martin

juv

ad

ad

PIPITS, WAGTAILS (Motacillidae)

Tree Pipit *Anthus trivialis* 14.5–16 cm (*c*6 in). Very like Meadow Pipit, also with white tail-sides, but plumper, more lightly streaked on yellower breast; legs pinkish with short hind-claws, bill stouter. Like all pipits, walks, runs, wags tail; terrestrial, but habitually also on trees; flight less jerky than Meadow; solitary. *Ad* Olive-brown above, streaked blackish; yellow-buff below, streaked on breast and flanks; in worn plumage, streaking bolder, under-parts less buff. *Juv* More buff-brown above with bolder streaks, less yellowish below, flanks plainer; as ad after moult in Jul–Sep. VOICE Hoarse *teez*, alarm *sip*; song loud Chaffinch-like notes ending in *seea-seea-seea* during 'parachuting' drop after upward flight (usually from tree). HABITAT Heaths, young plantations, clearings, bracken slopes, scrub with scattered trees. NEST In bank or tussock, 4–6 eggs, May–Jul; 1–2 broods. FOOD Insects. RANGE Summer visitor, Apr–Sep; on passage from N Europe esp Aug–Oct.

Meadow Pipit *Anthus pratensis* 14–15 cm (*c*5¾ in). Usually more olive above and paler below than Tree Pipit, with smaller but denser streaks on breast and flanks; tail-sides white; legs pink-brown with long hind-claws. Rises and falls jerkily in flight; mostly on ground, but also perches on trees; gregarious in autumn/winter. *Ad* Olive, green-brown or buff above, streaked blackish (except rump); whitish-grey to buff below; in worn plumage, darker above and paler below, with heavier streaking. *Juv* Darker above and yellower below, with clearer streaking; as ad after moult in Jul–Oct. VOICE Shrill hurried *eest-eest*, alarm *tissip* (*cf* Tree Pipit); song of accelerating calls, then whistling trill during 'parachuting' drop after upward flight (usually from ground). HABITAT Moors, marshes, rough pastures, dunes; winters in lowland marshes, fields, coasts. NEST In tussocks, 4–5 eggs, mid Apr–Jul; 2 broods. FOOD Insects, worms, some seeds. RANGE Leaves uplands Nov–Mar, some emigrating; on passage/winter from Iceland/N Europe, mid Aug–May.

Tree Pipit

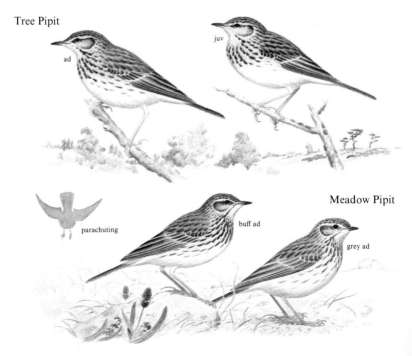

Meadow Pipit

Rock Pipit *Anthus spinoletta* 15–16.5 cm (*c*6¼ in). Larger, longer-billed, more obscurely streaked than Meadow Pipit, with dark legs, grey tail-sides (but see Water Pipits, below). Perches on rocks; in small parties in winter. *Ad (A.s.petrosus)* Dark olive-brown above; dingy buff below streaked grey-brown. *Juv* Much as ad, but chin and throat also speckled blackish. *Scandinavian race (A.s. littoralis)* Separable only in spring, when browner above with creamy supercilia, whiter below with pinkish throat/breast and rather fewer streaks. *Water Pipit of Continental mountains (A.s. spinoletta)* Warmer brown and whiter, with white tail-sides, bold supercilia; breast streaked in winter, but plain pinkish in summer when greyer above (esp head). *American race (A.s. rubescens)* As Water Pipit, but very buff below, usually with thinner blacker streaks all year. HABITAT Rocky shores; passage/winter also on flat coasts; Water Pipit winters by lakes, watercress beds. VOICE Strong *weest*, more penetrating than Meadow; song louder, more musical, with stronger trill. NEST In rock crevices, 4–5 eggs, mid Apr–Jul; 2 broods. FOOD Insects, worms, sandhoppers, molluscs. RANGE Resident, but with some dispersal; Scandinavian race (E/SBr) and Water Pipit (SBr) passage/winter Oct–Apr; American race vagrant.

COMPARE Vagrant pipits (296).

Tree Pipit	B6
	W0
	S6
	A6

Meadow Pipit	B7
	W7
	S7
	A7

Rock Pipit	B5
	W5
	S5
	A5

Rock Pipit

littoralis ad summer

rubescens ad winter

spinoletta ad winter

petrosus ad

spinoletta ad summer

Yellow Wagtail *Motacilla flava* 16–17 cm
(*c*6½ in). Slim, graceful, longish-tailed,
with yellow underparts, greenish back (*cf*
Grey Wagtail, 192). Chiefly on ground,
walking or running with wagging tail
and to-and-fro motion of head, darting
about and fluttering into air; perches on
fences, wires, bushes and trees, often
associates with cattle; flight markedly
undulating; gregarious when not nesting,
often roosting communally in reedbeds.
Several distinctive subspecies. ♂ *summer*
(*M.f. flavissima*, common race in Br)
Bright yellow forecrown, supercilia and
underparts; yellowish-green crown, cheeks
and mantle. ♂ *winter* With moult in Aug–
Sep, crown, cheeks and upperparts
browner, but rump still greenish; supercilia
and throat buff-yellow shading through
more buff chest to yellow belly, greener
flanks. ♀ *summer* Crown and upperparts
browner-green than ♂; supercilia and
underparts paler yellow with greener
markings on upper breast. ♀ *winter* As ♂
autumn, but crown and mantle still
browner, supercilia and throat whitish-
buff, upper breast buff, and belly paler
yellow. *Juv* Brown above with blackish
marks on sides of crown and creamy edges
to all feathers of wings and tail; supercilia buff, cheeks dark brown; throat pale
buff, surrounded by bib of blackish
markings; breast buff, shading to yellow-
buff belly. *1st winter* After moult in Jul–
Sep, as ♀ autumn, though mantle still
browner and belly even paler yellow;
whiter edges and tips to greater wing-
coverts. ♂ *summer Blue-headed (M.f.
flava)* Crown blue-grey, cheeks similar but
darker; supercilia and throat-sides white.
♂ *winter Blue-headed* Bluish-grey crown
duller, partly obscured by brown tips;
supercilia tinged creamy, ear-coverts
brown with whitish markings (thus, head-
pattern as summer but duller: same applies
to autumn heads of other races described
below); yellow underparts tinged buff on
breast, with dark brown feathers forming
obscure band. ♀ *Blue-headed* Crown and
cheeks brownish-grey, supercilia whitish,
throat buff-white or tinged yellow. ♂ *Grey-
headed (M.f. thunbergi)* Crown dark grey,

Yellow Wagtail

flavissima
♀ summer

flavissima
1st winter

flavissima
juv

flavissima
♀ summer

flavissima
♂ winter

flavissima
♂ summer

cheeks blackish; no supercilia, or at most white marks over and just behind eyes; chin and throat yellow. ♂ *Black-headed (M.f. feldegg)* Black head and yellow throat; no supercilia. ♀ *Black-headed* Crown and ear-coverts blackish, thus resembling ♂ Grey-headed, but often white on throat, sometimes slightly yellow supercilia. ♂ *Ashy-headed (M.f. cinereo-capilla)* As ♂ Blue-headed, but cheeks darker, supercilia ill-defined, white throat more extensive. ♂*Sykes's Wagtail (M.f. beema)* As ♂ Blue-headed, but crown much paler blue-grey, cheeks flecked white. ♂ *Eastern Blue-headed (M.f. simillima)* As ♂ Blue-headed, but crown marked with grey spots, supercilia broadening obviously behind eyes, cheeks plain blackish. ♂ *White-headed (M.f. leuco-cephala)* Crown, cheeks and chin all white, nape greyish. (♀s of all these races except Black-headed, described above, are usually indistinguishable from ♀ Blue-headed; ♂s showing the characters of the last four subspecies may be mutants rather than vagrants). VOICE Loud disyllabic

tswee-ip, harsh penetrating *tsee-tsreep*; irregular short warble incorporating calls, in flight or from perch. HABITAT Water meadows, rushy pastures, gravel pits, damp heaths, boggy moorland, also arable and hayfields near water. NEST On ground, by or under tussocks, 5–6 eggs, May–Jul; 1–2 broods. FOOD Insects, small molluscs. RANGE Summer visitor, Apr–mid Oct, wintering in Africa; casual breeding by other races (Blue-headed and birds resembling Sykes's, Ashy-headed, once White-headed); also on passage end Mar–Jun, Aug–mid Oct (Yellow, some Blue-headed, few Grey-headed esp E/SBr); other races vagrants/mutants (*eg* 12 records of Black-headed, though these may be only dark variant Grey-headed). COMPARE Other wagtails (192, 296).

Yellow Wagtail B5 W0 S5 A5

♂ SUMMER HEADS

thunbergi *beema* *cinereocapilla* *feldegg* *leucocephala* *simillima*

flava ♂ summer

feldegg ♀ summer

flava ♂ winter

flava ♀ summer

Grey Wagtail *Motacilla cinerea* 18.5–19.5 cm (*c*7½ in). Yellow below, often confused with Yellow Wagtail (190), but flanks whitish; grey crown/back with contrasting yellow-green rump; flesh (not black) legs; white-edged black tail 2.5 cm (1 in) longer. Behaviour as Yellow Wagtail, but wagging of longer tail more obvious; seen along streams, perching on rocks and overhanging trees; most singly or in family parties, but will roost gregariously, usually in waterside trees. ♂ *summer* Black throat, sometimes flecked whitish, separated from white-mottled grey cheeks by white stripe; supercilia also white; brightest yellow on breast and undertail-coverts. ♀ *summer* Throat white, or white mottled black and yellow; cheeks tinged green; breast paler. *Ad winter* Buff-white supercilia and throat; ♂ buff-yellow breast shading to yellow belly, ♀ buff-white shading to yellowish. *Juv* Grey-brown above (but 2 narrow buff bars on wings, pale buff-green rump) and mainly buff below, with grey-black marks at sides of throat and breast; undertail-coverts yellow, belly usually yellowish. *1st winter* After moult Jul–Sep, much as ♀ winter, but browner-grey above, more buff on breast. VOICE Clipped, high, metallic *tzitzi*; infrequent song louder, more trilling warble than Pied Wagtail. HABITAT Fast-flowing, rocky or gravelly streams; also lowland locks, weirs, locally lakes and slow rivers and, in winter, watercress beds. NEST On ledges or in holes of bridges, weirs, boathouses, old walls, usually over water, 4–6 eggs, Apr–Jul; 1–2 broods. FOOD Insects, also sandhoppers, molluscs. RANGE Resident, but some winter dispersal south and to lowlands; on passage Mar–Apr, Aug–Oct, inc some from Continent.

Pied Wagtail *Motacilla alba* 17–18.5 cm (*c*7 in). Black, white and grey, with long tail. Behaviour as Yellow Wagtail, but more catholic in habitat; roosts gregariously in reedbeds, bushes, trees, roofs of buildings, glasshouses, even towns. ♂ *summer* (*M.a. yarrellii*, common race in Br/Ir) Rear crown, upperparts, throat and breast solid black; forecrown,

Grey Wagtail

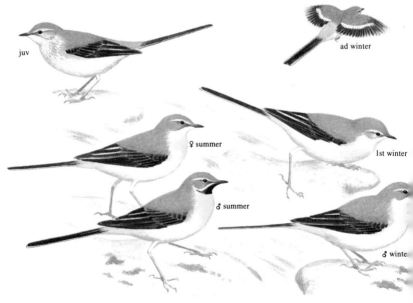

juv

ad winter

♀ summer

1st winter

♂ summer

♂ winter

sides of head, belly, tail-sides and 2 wing-bars all white. ♂ *winter* Throat white bordered with crescentic black bib, black of back (but not of rump) mixed with dark grey. ♀ *summer* As ♂ summer, but back blackish-grey to olive-grey, black of crown and breast less extensive. ♀ *winter* As ♂ winter, but black of back mixed with more grey. *Juv* Brown-grey above, grey-buff below, with buff sides of head and throat, blackish rump and 'double' breast-band. *1st winter* After moult in Aug–Oct, not always separable from ♀ winter, but usually has back dark olive-grey with no black, hindcrown black mixed with olive-grey. *1st summer* Some ♀s still show no black on olive-grey back. ♂ *summer White Wagtail* (*M.a. alba*, race of rest of Europe) Back and rump pure pale grey, usually demarcated sharply from black nape. ♀ *summer White Wagtail* As ♂, but back duller grey shading into black of crown. *Ad/1st winter White Wagtail* Forehead and crown often grey with little or no white and black (except some ad ♂s); further distinguished by greyer mantle

and grey rump from 1st winter Pied (back olive-grey, rump blackish). VOICE Shrill *tchizzik*; infrequent song simple twitter of slurred calls and warbles. HABITAT Farms, any open country, gardens, towns, often but not necessarily near water. NEST In recesses in walls, sheds, thatch, ivy, banks, rocks, or under stones, clods or plants, 5–6 eggs, Apr–Jul; 2–3 broods. FOOD Insects, some molluscs, seeds. RANGE Resident, but many move south in Oct–Mar, some emigrate; White Wagtails on passage from Iceland/N Europe, end Mar–May, Aug–Oct, seen most on W/N coasts.

Pied Wagtail

yarrellii ad winter

yarrellii 1st winter

yarrellii ♂ winter

yarrellii ♀ summer

yarrellii ♂ summer

yarrellii juv

alba ♀ winter

alba ♀ summer

alba ♂ summer

WAXWINGS (Bombycillidae)

Waxwing *Bombycilla garrulus* 17–18.5 cm (*c*7 in). Mainly pink-brown to chestnut, with bold crest, black bib and mask, grey rump, short yellow-ended tail, and white, yellow and waxy red wing-marks. Flight strong, undulating, on triangular wings like Starling (234) but under-coverts whitish; feeds acrobatically; gregarious, tame. *Ad ♂* Sharp black bib; bright yellow and white V-tips to primaries; bold waxy tips to secondaries; broad yellow tail-band. *Ad ♀* Bib smaller, fading into sooty-grey; V-tips tend to be duller and less complete, waxy tips smaller, tail-band paler and narrower. *Juv* Duller, browner, with short crest, no black bib, buff streaks on underparts, only outer edge of primaries tipped pale yellow. *1st winter* After moult in Aug–Nov, more as ads, but browner wings, primaries as juv; waxy tips small or missing, tail-band duller and narrower (esp ♀). VOICE Weak, high trill *zhreer*. HABITAT Scattered trees, gardens, wherever berries. FOOD Berries, hips, buds. RANGE Scarce passage/winter visitor from N Europe, Oct–Apr; periodically widespread in larger numbers.

WRENS (Troglodytidae)

Wren *Troglodytes troglodytes* 9–10 cm (*c*3¾ in). Tiny and stumpy, with short cocked tail, slightly curved bill; rufous and buff, barred darker, with pale supercilia. Flight whirring, usually not far; busily seeks food in tangled cover, crevices, leaf litter; hops crouched with flicking tail; not gregarious, but sometimes 20 or more in roosts. *Ad/1st year* Crown unmarked, throat faintly mottled; undertail spotted white. *Juv* Very like ad, but more mottled on crown and throat, supercilia fainter; undertail not spotted. *Island races* Of 4 distinct forms on St Kilda, Outer Hebrides, Fair Isle and Shetland, first (*T.t. hirtensis*) is esp pale, more grey-brown, and last (*T.t. zetlandicus*) is esp dark; these also larger, longer-billed. VOICE Hard ticking, harsh churring; explosive song of loud notes with trill near end of each phrase. HABITAT

Gardens, woods, farmland, scrub, reeds, broken cliffs. NEST Domed, in hedges, ivy, crevices, 5–6 eggs, Apr–mid Aug; 2 broods. FOOD Esp insects. RANGE Sedentary, some local dispersal; migrants from Continent, end Sep–mid Apr, esp EBr.

DIPPERS (Cinclidae)

Dipper *Cinclus cinclus* 17–18.5 cm (*c*7 in). Plump and short-tailed, aquatic; blackish with bold white gorget. Flight fast, mainly low over water; runs, walks, hops on rocks, bobbing, curtseying, jerking tail; walks or plunges into streams, swimming on or under water or walking on bottom; solitary. *Ad Br race (C.c. gularis)* Blackish, with chocolate head, white round eyes, white gorget, chestnut belly-band. *Juv* Slate-grey above, wings scaled whitish; dingy white below, marked with grey. *1st winter* As ad after moult in Jul–Sep, but wings and belly with whitish feather-tips. *Ir race (C.c. hibernicus)* Blacker above; chestnut band duller, narrower. *N European race (C.c. cinclus)* As Br race above; no chestnut below. VOICE Loud *zit-zit*, metallic *clink*; song broken mixture of clear, grating and warbling notes. HABITAT Swift streams and rivers, edges of upland lakes. NEST Domed, on ledges or in crevices by water, 4–6 eggs, Mar–Jun; 2 broods. FOOD Invertebrates. RANGE Sedentary; also vagrants from N Europe, Oct–Apr, coastal EBr.

Waxwing B0 W2 S2 A3

Dipper B5 W5 S5 A5

Wren B8 W8 S8 A8

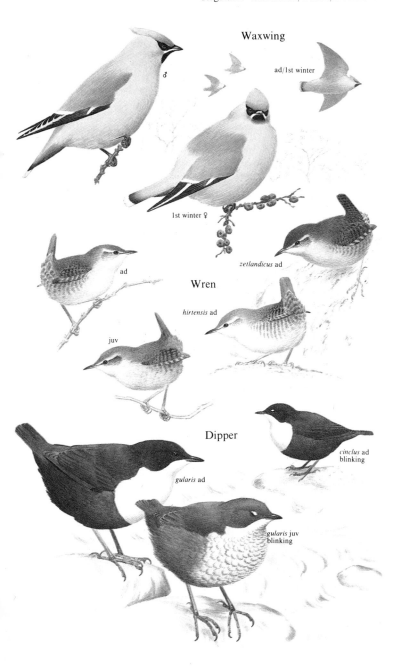

Waxwing

ad/1st winter

♂

1st winter ♀

zetlandicus ad

Wren

ad

hirtensis ad

juv

Dipper

cinclus ad
blinking

gularis ad

gularis juv
blinking

ACCENTORS (Prunellidae)

Dunnock *Prunella modularis* 14–15 cm
($c5\frac{3}{4}$ in). Unobtrusive, drab, sparrow-like,
but with dark slender bill, grey head and
breast, and streaked flanks. Flight low
and undulating, seldom far; mostly on
ground, hopping slowly or shuffling, often
flicking wings; also inside hedges, now
and then on top; special wing-waving
display in parties, but mainly solitary. *Ad*
Head and breast grey, but crown and ear-
coverts browner; mantle, wings and flanks
rufous streaked with black; eyes red-
brown. *Juv* Head browner, upperparts
less rufous, throat whitish, breast and
flanks buff with dark streaks; as ad after
moult in Aug–Oct. VOICE Shrill, piping
tseek; song high, clear, hurried warble
with broken phrases, like squeaky trolley.
HABITAT Gardens, hedges, open woods,
moorland scrub. NEST In bushes, young
conifers, tangled cover, 4–5 eggs, mid
Apr–Jul; 2–3 broods. FOOD Insects, seeds.
RANGE Sedentary; some immigrants from
N Europe, end Sep–mid May, esp coastal
EBr. COMPARE Alpine Accentor (296).

CHATS, THRUSHES (Turdidae)

Robin *Erithacus rubecula* 13.5–14.5 cm
($c5\frac{1}{2}$ in). Fat and neckless; orange-breasted
when ad, juv spotted. Flight flitting and
jerky, usually low, not far; darts from
perch to ground and back; hops crouched,
pausing upright with drooped wings, head
often on side; bobs head, flicks wings and
tail; quite tame, but skulking when in
summer moult; pugnacious, solitary. *Ad*
Face and breast red-orange, edged with
grey; upperparts olive-brown, belly white.
Juv Spotted buff; tail brown (*cf* juv Nightingale, Redstart, 198); as ad after moult in
Jun–Sep. VOICE Repeated *tic tic-tic*, thin
tseee, soft *tsip*; song of prolonged notes,
short warbles and trills, thinner and more
melancholy in autumn. HABITAT Gardens,
hedges, woods. NEST In banks or any
crevice or ledge, 5–7 eggs, mid Mar–
mid Jul; 2–3 broods. FOOD Insects, worms,
berries. RANGE Mainly sedentary, some
move SW as far as Iberia; immigrants
from Continent, end Sep–Apr, esp EBr.

Bluethroat *Luscinia svecica* 13.5–14.5 cm
($c5\frac{1}{2}$ in). Like slim dark Robin with whitish supercilia, rufous-based tail; blue
varies with age/sex, throat often whitish
above dark breast-band. Skulking; flight
Robin-like, into cover at ground-level,
spreading tail; creeps mouse-like, but
also in open with Robin-like gait and
bobbing, upright stance with tail cocked
or moved sideways and often spread. ♂
Red-spotted (L.s. svecica) Chestnut-
centred blue gorget edged below by bands
of black and chestnut; in autumn, upper
throat black, some buff and white tips.
♂ *White-spotted (L.s. cyanecula)* Smaller
spot in centre of gorget white (rarely all
blue); in autumn, this often mottled
chestnut. *Ad ♀ (both races)* Buff-white
moustaches and throat, latter edged
blackish with some blue and ill-defined
chestnut; sometimes rufous spot, rarely
blue on sides of throat in summer (even
almost as much blue as ad ♂, but not
glossy and centre of throat whitish, not
blue). *1st winter ♂* As ad ♀, but breast
and esp sides of throat often bluer; outer
greater coverts tipped with red-buff. *1st
winter ♀* Duller, no blue, little chestnut.
VOICE Sharp *tac tac*, plaintive *hweet*.
HABITAT Migrants in coastal scrub, root
crops. FOOD Insects,
some seeds, berries.
RANGE Scarce mi-
grant from N (Red-
spotted) Cent
Europe (White-),
end Aug–mid Oct,
few Mar–May;
nested NBr 1968,
2 singing ♂s 1980.

Dunnock

ad

juv

Robin

ad

juv

Bluethroat

svecica
♂ summer

cyanecula
♂ summer

ad/1st winter

1st winter ♀

svecica
♂ winter

juv

svecica
1st winter ♂

ad ♀

Nightingale *Luscinia megarhynchos* 16–17 cm (*c*6½ in). Heard far more than seen; sturdy, with longish rounded tail; rufous and buff-white. Actions as Robin (196), but very skulking, on or near ground with tail cocked, often crown-feathers raised; solitary. *Ad* Red-brown above, all but central tail-feathers richer chestnut (more obvious when spread in flight or display); whitish around eyes; underparts buff-brown, whiter on throat and belly. *Juv* Spotted as juv Robin, but larger, with chestnut tail. *1st winter* After moult in Jul–Sep, as ad, but buff spots at tips of greater coverts and tertials. VOICE Hard *tak tak*, Chaffinch-like *hweet*, grating *kurrr*; rich song, by day or night in Apr–Jun, with repetitions of clear notes, esp slow sad *peeoo* in crescendo, fast deep *chook*, and hard trill. HABITAT Broad-leaved woods, copses, damp thickets. NEST On ground or low in tangled cover, 4–5 eggs, May–Jun; 1 brood. FOOD Insects, worms, berries. RANGE Summer/passage visitor, Apr–Sep, wintering in Africa. COMPARE Thrush Nightingale (298).

Black Redstart *Phoenicurus ochruros* 14–15 cm (*c*5¾ in). Tail as Redstart; bulkier, darker, no orange/buff below in W European stock. Actions as Redstart, but much more on ground, even running; favours cliffs, tall buildings. *Ad ♂* Mainly black with white wing-patches; after moult in Aug–Sep, black obscured by grey tips which wear off during winter. *Ad ♀/1st winter ♂♀* Dark grey-brown, no wing-patches. *Juv* Much as ♀, but browner, less grey, and speckled darker, esp on paler breast and flanks (far less spotted than juv Redstart). *1st summer ♂* Some as ♀; others with blackish throat and breast, sometimes small white patches on brown wings. VOICE Short *tsip*, stuttering *tititic*; song fast warble with scratchy 'gravelly' hiss. HABITAT Breeds in towns, power stations, cliffs; winters on cliffs, rocks, coastal ruins and dumps, stony downs. NEST In crevices or on ledges, 4–6 eggs, mid Apr–mid Jul; 2 broods. FOOD Insects, also crustaceans, berries. RANGE Breeding areas Apr–Sep; on passage from Cent Europe, Mar–May, Sep–Nov; few winter.

Nightingale

Black Redstart

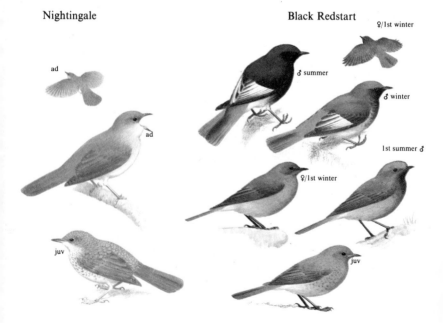

♀/1st winter

ad

ad

juv

♂ summer

♂ winter

1st summer ♂

♀/1st winter

juv

Redstart *Phoenicurus phoenicurus* 13.5–14.5 cm (*c*5½ in). Slim; orange-red tail constantly shivered, not flicked; paler below than above, showing orange-buff. Flight/actions recall Robin (196), but seldom on ground, usually in trees where flits about and flutters into air; solitary. *Ad* ♂ Grey upperparts, black face, white forehead, orange breast and flanks; after moult in Jul–Sep, colours obscured by brown and whitish tips which wear off during winter. *Ad* ♀/*1st year* ♀ Brown-grey above; orange-buff breast and flanks, dulled with whitish tips in winter; pale throat and eye-rings (rarely ad ♀ much as 1st year ♂). *Juv* Spotted as juv Robin, but with red tail. *1st winter* ♂ After moult in Jul–Sep, as ad ♂ but browner above, white forehead virtually hidden, black throat heavily mottled off-white. *1st summer* ♂ Usually browner above than ad ♂; throat more mixed with white. VOICE Plaintive *hweet* like Chiffchaff, or *hweet tuc-tuc*; brief song clear Robin-like warble that disappointingly peters out into feeble tinny jangle. HABITAT Old woods, parks, orchards, heaths with old trees; on passage by coasts. NEST In crevices or on ledges of trees, walls or quarries, 5–7 eggs, May–mid Jul; 1–2 broods. FOOD Insects, berries. RANGE Summer visitor, Apr–Sep, wintering in Africa; on passage from Germany/Scandinavia, end Mar–mid Jun, Jul–Oct, esp E/S coasts.

Redstart

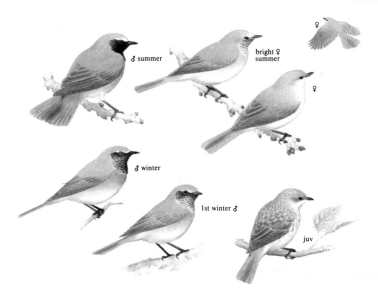

♂ summer

bright ♀ summer

♀

♀

♂ winter

1st winter ♂

juv

Whinchat *Saxicola rubetra* 12–13 cm (*c*5 in). Compact but longish-winged, with short squared tail; warm buff breast, white or whitish supercilia, white sides to tail-base (ads also white wing-mark). Perches prominently on tall plants, bushes, trees, wires or fences, bobbing and flicking wings and tail, flying low and jerkily from perch to perch; hops on ground; surprisingly active at dusk; solitary, or family parties in summer. ♂ *summer* Streaky brown and blackish above, bright buff below, with bold white supercilia and line down throat-sides (showing up blackish cheeks), also white wing-band and well-defined tail-patches. ♀ *summer* Duller, with less distinct buffish-white supercilia and throat-sides, brown cheeks; paler below, often with odd spots; less white on wings, less sharply defined tail-patches. *Ad winter* After moult in Jul–Sep, creamy supercilia and throat-sides, redder-brown cheeks, often dark flecks on breast; ♂ more white on wings, clearer tail-patches. *Juv* More rufous above with pale shaft-streaks, duller buff below with dark mottling on throat/breast; supercilia ill-defined, no contrast between throat-sides and centre, no white on wings. *1st winter* As ad after moult in Jun–Sep, but usually much less white on wings. *1st summer* ♂ Contrast between black inner and worn brown outer greater coverts. VOICE Scolding *tic-tic* or *tu-tic-tic*, short churring rattle; song short warble, variably like Stone-chat or Redstart (198), but sweeter and more broken like Robin (196). HABITAT Commons, rough pastures, railway banks, downs, water meadows, young conifers, bracken slopes. NEST In grass tussocks, or under thicker cover, 5–6 eggs, mid May–Jul; 1–2 broods. FOOD Insects. RANGE Summer visitor, Apr–Sep, wintering in Africa; also on passage from Scandinavia, Apr–May, mid Jul–early Oct, esp E/SBr.

Stonechat *Saxicola torquata* 12–13 cm (*c*5 in). Dumpier than Whinchat, with shorter wings, perching even more upright; breast reddish, head dark with no supercilia (but see E races) or tail-patches; ♂ white on neck, wings, rump.

Whinchat

♂ winter

juv

♂ summer

♀ summer

♂ summer

1st winter

Actions as Whinchat; bobs and flicks
constantly. ♂ *summer W European race
(S.t. hibernans)* Black head, throat and
back; bold white neck-patches and wing-
marks, whitish rump streaked with black;
reddish-orange breast. ♂ *winter* After
moult in Aug–Sep, black upperparts
streaked with rufous, white patches
reduced, black throat mottled buff, breast
duller reddish. *Ad* ♀ Like duller, browner
winter ♂: no white on rump, less on wings;
neck-patches/dark throat obscured in
winter. *Juv* As ♀ but streaked pale buff as
well as rufous above; grey-buff throat and
rufous-buff breast speckled with black.
1st year ♂ As ad after moult in Aug–Sep,
but slight contrast between black inner
and worn dark grey-brown outer greater
coverts; worn juv flight-feathers pale
brown by spring. *E Eurasian races (S.t.
maura/stejnegeri)* Large orange or white
rump; ♂ has buff (not rufous) streaks
above, often bolder white patches, sandy
below, blacker (not buffish) axillaries;
♀/imm plain buff throat, light wing-panel,
with pale supercilia and sandy-buff
colours not unlike Whinchat. VOICE Hard
tsak-tsak (clinking stones) or *weet-tsak-
tsak* (*cf* Wheatear, 202); song lively
repetition of sharp and deeper notes, not
unlike Dunnock (196), often in dancing
flight. HABITAT Heaths, commons, moors,
young conifers, coasts, esp where gorse.
NEST In gorse or at end of tunnel in thick
cover, 5–6 eggs, Apr–early Aug; 2–3
broods. FOOD Insects, worms, some seeds.
RANGE Often resident, but many from
N/uplands move south in autumn, some
as far as Iberia; E races vagrant (46: Sep–
May, esp Oct–Nov EBr).

Stonechat

Wheatear *Oenanthe oenanthe* 14–15.5 cm (*c*5¾ in). White rear with black inverted T on shortish tail; dapper, erect, in open country and short grass; variously grey or brown, and buff below, with white or pale supercilia, more or less contrasting dark wings. Restless, flying low, pausing on rock or ground; bobs up and down, flicks wings, wags and flirts tail, then moves with long hops or flutters up to catch insects; when nesting, often hovers; perches on walls, fences, wires, bushes, less on trees; solitary. ♂ *summer Eurasian race (O.o. oenanthe)* Grey upperparts, white supercilia, blackish mask and wings, sandy-buff breast and white belly. ♂ *winter* With moult in Jul–Aug, brownish-grey above and deep to creamy-buff below (very variable), with whitish to buff fringes on all wing-feathers, but still blackish mask and white supercilia. *Ad* ♀ Duller, with dark brown mask, creamy supercilia; grey-brown above and variably buff below in summer, brown to rufous above in winter with buff-edged wings. *Juv* Spotted light and dark above, and mottled brown on creamy-buff throat/breast; much as ♀ winter after moult in Aug–Sep. *1st summer* ♂ Much as ad ♂, though often browner-grey above, but worn wings clearly paler brown than mask. *Greenland race (O.o. leucorrhoa)* Larger, longer-winged, more erect; spring ♂ much browner-grey above, more wholly rufous-buff below. VOICE Harsh *chak-chak* or *weet-chak-chak* (*cf* Stonechat, 196); song short warble mixed with harsh creaky notes and finch-like whistles, often in dancing flight. HABITAT Mountains, rocky moors, upland pastures, downs, brecks, dunes, shingle. NEST Deep in hole in rocks, walls, rabbit burrows, or *eg* under corrugated iron, 5–6 eggs, late Apr–Jul; 1–2 broods. FOOD Insects. RANGE Summer visitor, Mar–Sep, wintering in Africa; also on passage from N Europe/Iceland/Greenland, Mar–early Jun, end Jul–Oct. COMPARE Vagrant wheatears (298, 300).

Fieldfare *Turdus pilaris* 24–27 cm (*c*10 in). Large thrush, with longish wings and tail; build and white underwings like Mistle

Wheatear

leucorrhoa
♂ summer

juv

♂ summer

♂ summer

♀ summer

1st summer ♂

♂ winter

♀ winter/1st winter

Thrush (206), but head and rump grey, back chestnut, tail black, supercilia whitish, breast rusty-yellow streaked with black, white flanks more spotted. Flight leisurely, less undulating than Mistle Thrush; perches in open on bushes/trees, but wary; runs or hops on ground, pausing erect with wings drooping; highly gregarious in winter, congregating on berried hedges or scattered over fields, flying up into trees when disturbed (often all facing same way). *Ad ♂* Large blackish centres to crown-feathers; crown/nape and rump otherwise blue-grey tinged with brown, mantle rich chestnut, breast rufous-buff; becomes greyer and paler in summer by abrasion, with bolder markings. *Ad ♀* Smaller blackish marks on crown; otherwise browner-grey, duller chestnut, paler buff, with browner flank-marks, though head and rump rather greyer in summer. *Juv* Much duller and browner with whitish streaks above, rounder blackish spots below. *1st winter* Much as ad after moult in Aug–Sep, but often keeps juv outer greater coverts (dull brown with whitish tips or streaks) in contrast to new chestnut inners. VOICE Harsh chatter *chak-chak-chak*, soft drawn-out *seeh*; weak song of harsh and squeaky sounds mixed with flutier notes. HABITAT Breeds in wood-edges, often near water; winters in fields with berried hedges. NEST Mainly in trees, 4–6 eggs, May–Jul; 1–2 broods. FOOD Slugs, worms, insects, berries, fallen apples, grain. RANGE Mainly passage/winter visitor from Fenno-Scandia/N Russia, Sep–Apr, esp Nov–Mar; occasionally seen in summer and odd pairs have bred most years since 1967.

Wheatear   B6 W0 S6 A6   Fieldfare   B1 W8 S8 A8

Fieldfare

juv

ad

♀ winter

♂ summer

Ring Ouzel *Turdus torquatus* 23–25 cm
(*c*9½ in). Near size of Blackbird, wings/
tail longer; blackish to brown with white
or more obscure crescent on breast, pale
scaling and wing-panel, yellowish bill
(yellower in summer, yellowest on ad ♂).
Actions as Blackbird, but hill-dweller,
with more dashing flight; perches on
boulders, trees, but shy, dodging behind
rocks. ♂ *summer* Sooty-brown with bold
white gorget, greyish wing-panel; sometimes traces of pale scaling, esp below. ♂
winter Blacker after moult in Jul–Sep,
but scaled greyish above (least on head) and
whitish below; gorget dulled by brown-
grey fringes. *Ad* ♀ Browner, more scaled,
with narrower gorget dulled by brown
tips and often obscure in autumn. *Juv*
Much browner, no gorget, creamier wing-
panel; whitish shaft-streaks on mantle,
scapulars, coverts; spotted and barred
creamy-buff and dark brown below, throat
buff mottled darker (*cf* more rufous juv
Blackbird). *1st winter* Much as ads after
moult in Aug–Sep, though gorget usually
duller on ♂, barely visible on ♀; juv outer

greater coverts browner with broader
whitish (♂) or creamy (♀) edges. VOICE
Loud hollow rattling scold or chatter
chaka-chaka, piping *pee-u*; far-carrying
song of 2–4 shrill piping notes *pee-pirri-
pee*, then chuckle. HABITAT Steep moorland with rocky outcrops, scrubby slopes;
on passage, lowland hedges, bushes. NEST
Usually in tufts on rock-faces or steep
banks, 4–5 eggs, mid Apr–Jul; 2 broods.
FOOD Insects, worms, snails, berries.
RANGE Summer visitor, Apr–Sep,
wintering in S Europe/N Africa; some on
passage from Scandinavia, Mar–May,
end Aug–Nov, esp EBr; rare in winter.

Blackbird *Turdus merula* 24–27 cm (*c*10
in). Stocky; black, or shades of brown
and mottled rufous, with yellow to brown
bill; white-patched and even all-white
birds not rare. Flight often low, flicking,
with glides, looking weak and undulating,
but can be high, strong, direct; raises
fanned tail and droops wings on landing;
hops or runs on ground, pausing less erect
than Song Thrush (206), head on one side,

Ring Ouzel

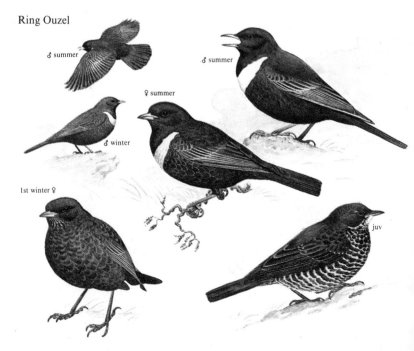

♂ summer

♂ summer

♀ summer

♂ winter

1st winter ♀

juv

often with tail up; tends to skulk in or near cover, but readily perches high; shy or tame; gregarious only on migration or at roosts. *Ad ♂* Glossy black, with browner wings in summer; bill and eye-rings orange-yellow. *Ad ♀* Dark grey-brown to black-brown above, tinged with olive, and variable below: throat greyish with blackish to rufous streaks, breast grey-brown to rufous with dark mottling, belly pale brown to slate with pale fringes (generally browner, less rufous and more dully mottled in summer); bill dark flesh-brown to yellowish. *Juv* More rufous than ad ♀, with rufous shaft-streaks above, more extensive mottling below; ♂ darker, more blackish-brown above (esp wings/tail). *1st year ♂* After moult in Aug–Oct, brown-black above (not tinged olive as ♀) with browner wings; juv outer greater coverts paler than others, with pale tips; brown-grey to brown-black below, less uniform than ad, throat/breast sometimes as ♀; bill blackish, turning yellow in cDec–Apr. *1st year ♀* As ad ♀ but for paler juv outer greater coverts. VOICE Scolding

chik-chik-chik, deeper *chook-chook-chook* (often extended into hysterical screeching alarm-chatter with repeated *chewee*), thin *tsee*; song languid clear fluty warble, ending in low squawky chuckle. HABITAT Gardens, hedges, woods, scrub, from town centres to upland brambles. NEST In hedges, trees, banks, walls, sheds or on ground under cover, 3–5 eggs, Mar–Aug; 3–5 broods. FOOD Worms, insects, snails, berries, seeds, fruit. RANGE Often sedentary, but many move south in autumn; also abundant passage/winter visitor from Continent, end Sep–May.

Ring Ouzel | B5 W0 S5 A5 | Blackbird | B8 W8 S8 A8

Blackbird

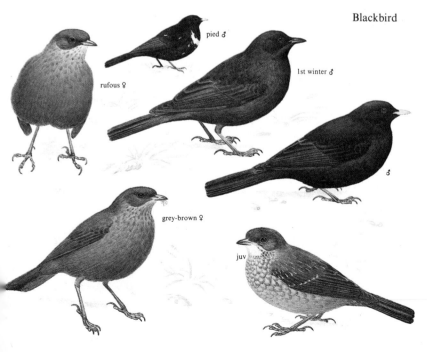

rufous ♀

pied ♂

1st winter ♂

♂

grey-brown ♀

juv

206 Turdidae

Song Thrush *Turdus philomelos* 22–24 cm
(*c*9 in). Compact; warm brown above, well
spotted below with yellow-buff underwings, no bold supercilia or whitish on
tail. Flight fast, direct; hops/runs, then
pauses rather upright, often with head to
one side; feeds in open or undergrowth;
smashes snails on stones; often sings
hidden; solitary except as migrant. *Ad*
Uniform above, with 2 faint wing-bars;
breast and flanks buff, throat and belly
whiter, with blackish spots/arrows.
(Hebridean race *T.p. hebridensis* darker
above, spots denser; migrants from Continent can look greyer.) *Juv* Buff streaks
above; largely buff below, spots smaller;
much as ad after moult in Jul–Sep. VOICE
Flight-call thin *tsip*; alarm loud *tchuk*
extended into chatter like Blackbird (204);
song loud, clear, with varied phrases, each
uttered 2–4 times. HABITAT Gardens, thick
hedges, woods, rough ground with cover.
NEST In hedges, trees, ivy, sheds, banks,
heather, 3–5 eggs, Mar–Aug; 2+ broods.
FOOD Worms, snails, slugs, insects,
berries. RANGE Mainly sedentary, some
winter SW to Iberia; passage/winter from
Cent/N Europe, Sep–Apr, esp E/SEBr.

Redwing *Turdus iliacus* 20–22 cm (*c*8¼ in).
Smaller, darker than Song Thrush, with
bold supercilia; streaked below, reddish
flanks/underwings. Far more gregarious
in winter; shyer. *Ad* At most, pale-edged
tips to greater coverts/tertials; streaked
and rich reddish below. *Juv* Like juv Song
(streaked above, spotted below), but for
whitish supercilia, pale chestnut-tinged
underwings. *1st winter* As ad after moult
in Aug–Sep, but triangular whitish tips to
outer greater coverts and some tertials.
VOICE Flight-call soft *tseeip*, drawn-out,
more penetrating than Song Thrush;
chattering *chittuck*, soft *chup*;
monotonous song of 3–6 fluty notes
ending in short, reedy warble; winter
flocks have babbling subsong. HABITAT
Breeds in woods, shrubberies, scrub;
winters in fields, open woods. NEST In
rhododendrons, bushes, trees, stumps,
banks, 5–6 eggs, May–Jul; 2 broods. FOOD
As Song Thrush; fewer berries. RANGE
Winter visitor from Iceland/N Europe,

Sep–Apr; few breed NBr, esp since *c*1953.

Mistle Thrush *Turdus viscivorus* 26–28 cm
(*c*10½ in). Bigger, deeper-chested than
Song Thrush, with longer wings and tail;
greyer, less uniform above with paler
rump, and whitish tail-corners; more
boldly spotted below, underwings white
(*cf* Fieldfare, 202). Distinctive flight with
marked wing-closure, often high; stands
upright with tail down, wings drooped;
not found in undergrowth; sings from
treetops; small flocks from late summer;
pugnacious, but shy. *Ad* Grey-brown
above, pale edges to back, rump, coverts;
breast and flanks light buff, throat and
belly whiter, with bold blackish spots/
wedges. *Juv* Spotted and streaked whitish
above, flecked dark; throat unmarked,
breast spots smaller; as ad after moult in
Jun–Sep, but often deeper buff below, odd
scapulars pale-streaked, greater coverts
whiter-edged. VOICE Rasping chatter like
wooden rattle, Redwing-like *seeip*, hard
tuc-tuc-tuc; song like Blackbird (204), but
less mellow, louder, faster with shorter
pauses between phrases. HABITAT Woods,
avenues, parks, orchards, conifers, upland
scrub; winters in fields, moors. NEST
Usually in trees, 3–5 eggs, Mar–Jun;
2 broods. FOOD
Berries, fruit, slugs,
worms, insects,
nestlings. RANGE
Fairly sedentary;
migrants from Con-
tinent, Sep–Apr.

COMPARE Other
thrushes (202, 204,
302, 304).

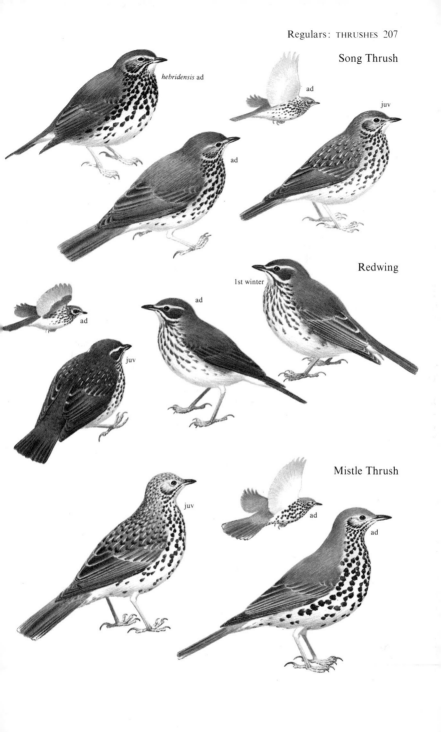

Song Thrush

hebridensis ad

ad

juv

ad

Redwing

1st winter

ad

ad

juv

Mistle Thrush

juv

ad

ad

WARBLERS (Sylviidae)

Cetti's Warbler *Cettia cetti* 13.5–14.5 cm (*c*5½ in). Robust, with short rounded wings and longish rounded tail; dark rufous and greyish, like small Nightingale (198), but tail less chestnut than back, and short white supercilia. Skulks, emerging briefly with flicking or cocked tail (showing barred under-coverts). *Ad* Chestnut above, less on head, wings, tail; whitish below shading to grey and brown at sides. *Juv* Less rufous above, less white below; as ad after moult in Jul–Aug. VOICE Repeated *chee*; song remarkably loud and abrupt *chee cheweechoo-weechoo-weechoo-wee*. HABITAT Waterside tangles, reeds. NEST Low in thick cover, 3–5 eggs, May–Jul; 1–2 broods. FOOD Insects, snails, seeds. RANGE Resident since 1972.

Grasshopper Warbler *Locustella naevia* 12–13 cm (*c*5 in). Streaky above but only faint supercilia (*cf* Sedge Warbler); rounded tail and usually pinkish legs. Cocks tail on alighting (showing streaky under-coverts); skulks, but often sings openly; creeps or runs in undergrowth. *Ad* Olive- to yellow-brown above with dark streaks (faint on rump); buff-white below, few streaks. *Juv* Redder-brown above, darker buff below; as ad after moult in Aug–Oct. VOICE Sharp *tchick*; song (day or night) sustained churring like fishing-reel or cricket, ventriloquial with turning head. HABITAT Wet or dry: rank fens, marshes, scrub, moors, plantations. NEST Low in thick cover, 5–6 eggs, May–Jul; 1–2 broods. FOOD Insects. RANGE Summer visitor, Apr–Oct, wintering Africa.

Savi's Warbler *Locustella luscinioides* 13.5–14.5 cm (*c*5½ in). Unstreaked, like large Reed Warbler (210) but with broad, very rounded tail; redder-brown above, more rufous-buff below, with purple-brown legs. Actions as Grasshopper Warbler, inc tail-cocking, but less secretive. *Ad* Dark red-brown above; whitish below shading to red-buff at sides. *Juv* Still darker red-brown above. VOICE Sharp *tswit*; song as Grasshopper Warbler, but lower-pitched, more buzzing,

often briefer. HABITAT Reed swamps with scattered bushes. NEST Low in reeds or sedges, 4–6 eggs, mid May–Jul; 1–2 broods. FOOD Insects. RANGE Summer visitor, Apr–Aug, wintering in Africa.

Sedge Warbler *Acrocephalus schoeno-baenus* 12–13 cm (*c*5 in). Bold cream supercilia, rather streaky upperparts but plain tawny rump; pointed, graduated tail. Flight jerky, usually low with tail fanned and depressed, but also short vertical song-flight; creeps in tangles, sidles up stems, but also perches in open. *Ad* Brown above with blackish streaks, thickest on crown; rump yellow-brown; white below shading to buff and tawny at sides. *Juv* Yellower above, esp rump, often ill-defined creamy crown-stripe; breast brown-speckled; some of these characters persist after moult in Jul–Sep. VOICE Sharp *tuc* extended to stutter; song fast vigorous mix of musical and harsh phrases with mimicry. HABITAT Tangled growth, mainly by water. NEST In rank cover, 5–6 eggs, May–Aug; 1–2 broods. FOOD Insects, berries. RANGE Summer visitor, mid Apr–Sep (mid Oct), wintering in Africa.

COMPARE Vagrant warblers (esp 306, 308),

| Cetti's Warbler | B3 W3 S3 A3 | Grasshopper Warbler | B5 W0 S5 A5 |
| Savi's Warbler | B2 W0 S2 A2 | Sedge Warbler | B6 W0 S6 A7 |

Cetti's Warbler

ad

ad

Grasshopper Warbler

ad

ad

juv

Savi's Warbler

ad

ad

Sedge Warbler

ad

ad (worn plumage)

juv

Marsh Warbler *Acrocephalus palustris*
12–13 cm (*c*5 in). But for song, very like
far commoner Reed Warbler, but with
flatter crown, plumper belly and longer
wings reaching tip of tail-coverts; ad lacks
rufous tinge, more uniformly pale below;
whiter eye-rings and front of supercilia,
pinkish legs. Less skulking than Reed,
perching higher in open trees. *Ad* Olive-
brown with yellower rump, wearing to
paler/greyer with browner rump by end of
summer; white and pale yellow-buff
below. *Juv/1st winter* Rusty-tinged,
inseparable in field from Reed. VOICE Song
rich, varied, mimetic, esp Greenfinch-like
nasal *tswee* and trills. HABITAT Osiers,
bushy areas by rivers. NEST With 'basket
handles' in nettles, meadowsweet, willow-
herb, willow, 4–5 eggs, Jun–mid Jul;
1 brood. FOOD Insects, berries. RANGE
Summer visitor, end May–Aug (Oct),
wintering in E Africa.

Reed Warbler *Acrocephalus scirpaceus*
12–13 cm (*c*5 in). Longish bill, rounded
tail and wings not reaching tip of tail-
coverts; warm brown with rufous-tinged
rump, deep buff flanks; faint supercilia
and grey-brown legs. Flight jerky, low,
tail spread and depressed; skulks, sidles
up reed stems with one foot above other.
Ad Warm olive-brown with rusty rump,
wearing to greyer, less rufous, by end
summer; white and buff below, darkest on
flanks. *Juv* Rustier-brown and deeper buff;
as unworn ad after moult in Jul–Sep.
VOICE Song like Sedge Warbler (206), but
harsher, grumpier, inc *jag-jag-jag kerr-
kerr-kerr*. HABITAT Reeds, osiers. NEST
Woven round reeds, other plants, twigs,
3–5 eggs, late May–Aug; 1–2 broods.
FOOD Insects, berries. RANGE Summer
visitor, mid Apr–Sep (Oct), wintering in
Africa. COMPARE Vagrants (esp 308).

Icterine Warbler *Hippolais icterina* 13–14
cm (*c*5¼ in). Large bill, squared tail, wings
reaching tip of tail-coverts (folded
primaries $c\frac{1}{3}$ of wing); pale yellow to
whitish below, yellow supercilia, bluish
legs; wing-patches on spring ad and
autumn imm (*cf* Melodious). Flight
strong; stance rather upright; takes

berries with upward tug. *Ad* Olive-green
and lemon-yellow (few browner or greyer
above, whitish below); yellow wing-
patches lost by late summer. *Juv* Brown
and pale yellow; yellow-buff wing-
patches. *1st winter* After moult Aug–Oct,
more as ad of brown/grey type with
whitish-yellow underparts; wings as juv.
VOICE Short *teck*, churr. HABITAT Trees,
tall bushes. FOOD Insects, berries. RANGE
Scarce migrant from E/N Europe, Aug–
Oct, few Apr–Jul, wintering in E Africa.

Melodious Warbler *Hippolais polyglotta*
12–13 cm (*c*5 in). Very like Icterine, but
smaller, with plumper belly, shorter tail,
wings not reaching tip of tail-coverts
(folded primaries $c\frac{1}{4}$ of wing); yellow to
creamy below, shorter supercilia, grey
legs (seldom bluish); wing-patches rare
and in spring only. Flight more fluttery.
Ad Green-brown and rich yellow (few
grey-brown and cream). *Juv* Brown and
creamy. *1st winter* After moult in Aug–
Oct browner above than ad, pale yellow
or creamy below. VOICE Sharp *tic*, chatter
like sparrow. HABITAT/FOOD As Icterine.
RANGE Scarce migrant from SW Europe,
Aug–Oct (May–Jul), wintering W Africa.
COMPARE Garden (214), Willow etc. (216).

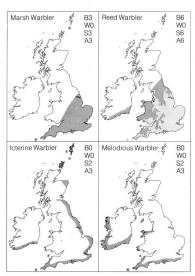

Marsh Warbler

ad

Reed Warbler

ad

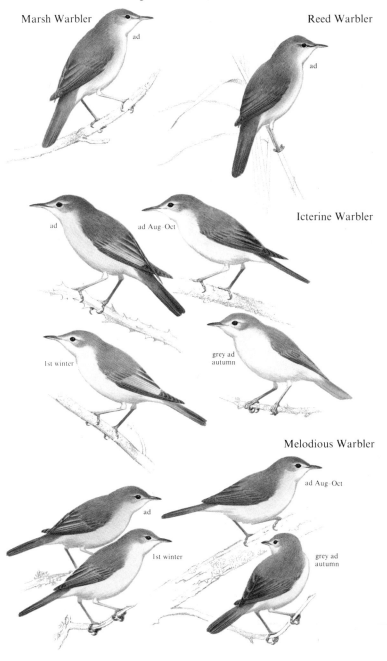

Icterine Warbler

ad

ad Aug-Oct

1st winter

grey ad
autumn

Melodious Warbler

ad Aug-Oct

ad

1st winter

grey ad
autumn

Dartford Warbler *Sylvia undata* 12–13.5 cm (*c*5 in). Tiny body with short wings, and often-cocked tail half total length; brown to dark grey above and more or less pinkish-brown below. Flight weak, undulating, with whirring wings and bobbing tail, usually low and brief before diving into cover; secretive, but will sit on bush-tops, esp in calm weather; flicks and fans tail; in small parties in autumn/ winter. ♂ *summer* Dark brown above with slate-grey head, rufous and greyish fringes to wing-feathers; dark brownish-pink below with small white spots on throat, white central belly. ♂ *winter* After moult in Aug–Nov, head browner, wing-feathers less clearly fringed, underparts with more whitish tips and fringes. *Ad* ♀ Not so dark brown above with browner-grey head; much paler pink–buff below. *Juv* Duller sooty-brown above than ad ♀, brownish-buff below with darker breast-sides/flanks, less rufous wing-fringes; as ads after moult in Aug–Nov. VOICE Buzzing *chirr*, hard *tik* or combined *chirr-ik-tik*; song short metallic warble mixed with mellower notes. HABITAT Heaths with gorse and rank heather. NEST In gorse or heather, 3–4 eggs, mid Apr–Jul; 2 broods. FOOD Insects, other invertebrates. RANGE Resident; some wander in autumn/winter.

Lesser Whitethroat *Sylvia curruca* 13–14 cm (5¼ in). More compact, shorter-tailed than Whitethroat; greyer above, with dark mask, no chestnut in wings, dark grey legs, very different song. Much more skulking except when young fledged; more in trees. *Ad* Grey-brown above with greyer rump, grey cap and dark grey lores/ear coverts; pinkish breast and pink-buff flanks, whitening by *c*May–Jun; some white on tail-sides. *Juv* Cap grey-brown like back, throat off-white, breast and flanks buffish, tail-sides only brownish-white. *1st winter* Much as ad after moult in Jun–Aug but for juv tail without pure white. VOICE Hard *tak tak*, hoarse *charr*; far-carrying song rapid rattle on 1 note, preceded by short fast warble audible only at close range. HABITAT Thick hedges, thorn scrub, young conifers. NEST In hedges or bushes, 4–6 eggs, May–early

Aug; 1–2 broods. FOOD Insects; berries in autumn. RANGE Summer visitor, end Apr–Sep, wintering in NE Africa/SW Asia; on passage mid Apr–Jun, mid Aug–Oct (Nov), inc few from Scandinavia.

Whitethroat *Sylvia communis* 13–15 cm (*c*5½ in). Slim, with longish white-sided tail; white throat, rufous on wings, pale brown legs. Flight undulating, jerky, usually low, diving into cover; restless, sometimes skulking, but may perch prominently; solitary or in family parties. *Ad* Brown to grey-brown above, breast/ flanks tinged buff to pink; crown greyer and breast pinker in summer, when some ♂s separable by almost pure grey crown, pure white throat and tail-sides, pinkish breast, grey-tipped lesser coverts and rufous eyes (♀s may show some of these). *Juv* Brown above, buffish below, with dull white throat and belly, less rufous wing-coverts, pale brown tail-sides. *1st winter* As dull ad after moult in Jul–Sep, but no pink, still juv pale brown tail-sides. VOICE Sharp *tak tak*, harsh scolding *charr* and quieter *weet weet wit-wit-wit*; song short scratchy warble, often in brief dancing flight. HABITAT Hedges, commons, scrub wood-edges, young conifers. NEST In low cover, 4–5 eggs, May–mid Aug; 1–2 broods. FOOD Insects, berries. RANGE Summer visitor, mid Apr–Sep, wintering in Africa; passage Apr–May, Aug–Oct, inc some from Scandinavia.

Dartford Warbler — B3 W3 S3 A4

Lesser Whitethroat — B5 W0 S5 A6

Whitethroat — B7 W0 S7 A7

Dartford Warbler

♂ summer

♀

♂ winter

♂

juv

Lesser Whitethroat

ad

ad (worn plumage)

juv

Whitethroat

♂ song-flight

♂ summer

1st winter

♀/dull ♂

juv

Barred Warbler *Sylvia nisoria* 14.5–16 cm (*c*6 in). Robust warbler with stout bill and legs, steep forehead, and longish, squared tail; grey, whitish and barred (ad) or grey-brown and buff (imm), with narrow white tail-sides and whitish tips to flight-feathers and wing-coverts. Flight heavy, undulating; restless, skulking; often raises crown, flicks tail. *Ad summer* Grey/grey-brown above with white/whitish tips on wings; white below, barred with grey crescents except on mid breast and belly; fierce yellow eyes (♂s often – but not reliably – greyer, more barred, with whiter tail-sides, brighter eyes). *Ad winter* After moult in Jul–Aug, browner above, only sides of breast and flanks barred. *1st winter* Brown to grey-brown above with broad whitish to pale buff tips on wings; buffish below with little barring (often only on undertail-coverts); eyes grey-brown, rarely yellowish by mid Sep. VOICE Harsh chatter, tacking, churring. HABITAT Migrants in coastal trees, bushes, crops. FOOD Insects, berries. RANGE Migrant from E Europe (most 1st winter), Aug–mid Oct, wintering in Africa; very rare in spring. COMPARE Imm with imm Orphean (310).

Garden Warbler *Sylvia borin* 13.5–14.5 cm (*c*5½ in). Plump, with stubby bill, rounded head, shortish tail; brown and buff, rather featureless but for obscure line over eyes and grey-tinged neck, yet shape and soft shades distinctive. Actions as Blackcap; more skulking. *Ad* Brown and buff, with buff-white throat and belly; in worn plumage, greyer-brown above and paler below, with whiter throat, olive-grey flanks; after moult in Jul–Sep, more olive-brown above, flanks olive-buff. *Juv* Tinged rusty above, darker buff below; as ad in fresh plumage after moult in Jul–Sep. VOICE *Tac tac* and grating churr, much as Blackcap; song mellow warble, usually faster, quieter, more even and prolonged than Blackcap. HABITAT As Blackcap, but also scrub, young plantations. NEST Low in brambles, nettles, small conifers, 4–5 eggs, May–mid Jul; 1–2 broods. FOOD As Blackcap. RANGE Summer visitor, mid Apr–mid Sep, wintering in Africa; on passage from

Continent, mid Apr–mid Jun, end Jul–Oct (Nov), esp E/SBr. COMPARE Brown Icterine and Melodious Warblers (210).

Blackcap *Sylvia atricapilla* 13.5–14.5 cm (*c*5½ in). Slim, with thinnish bill, longish tail; brown and grey, with distinctive black or rufous cap to eye-level. Flight jerky, undulating, tree to tree; restless, often skulking; in parties on migration. *Ad ♂* Cap glossy black; grey-brown above, greyer in worn plumage; nape, cheeks, throat and breast grey. *Ad ♀* Cap red-brown; olive-brown above, browner and paler when worn; cheeks, throat, breast and flanks grey-brown. *Juv* Cap black-brown (♂) or yellow-brown (♀); otherwise as ad ♀, but tinged rusty above, breast and flanks darker and duller. *1st winter ♂* As ad ♂ after moult in Jul–Sep, but black cap mixed with brown; old juv greater coverts edged with brown in contrast to other new grey-edged coverts. VOICE Hard *tacc tacc* and churr; song short, rich and varied warble with clear phrasing, but subdued versions very like Garden Warbler. HABITAT Broadleaved/mixed woods with undergrowth, to gardens. NEST In hedges, evergreens, ivy, brambles, 4–5 eggs, May–Jul; 1–2 broods. FOOD Insects, berries in autumn. RANGE Summer visitor Apr–Sep, wintering in Africa, W/S Europe; on passage end Mar–mid Jun, mid Aug–Oct, esp E/SBr; some winter. COMPARE Orphean, Sardinian Warblers (310).

Barred Warbler
B0 W0 S0 A3

Garden Warbler
B6 W0 S6 A6

Blackcap
B6 W4 S6 A6

Barred Warbler

1st winter

ad

Garden Warbler

ad

juv

Blackcap

♂

1st winter ♂

♀

juv ♀

Wood Warbler *Phylloscopus sibilatrix*
12–13 cm (*c*5 in). Larger than Willow
Warbler, with longer wings, shorter tail;
yellow-green above, yellow supercilia,
throat and chest, contrasting white belly.
Less restlessly active; droops rather than
flicks wings; more arboreal. *Ad* Bright
yellow-green and yellow, wearing greyer-
green and dull yellow by *c*Jun; after body
moult in Jul–Sep, brownish-green and
paler yellow, with worn brown flight-
feathers and tail. *Juv/1st winter* As ad
autumn, but duller greyer-green, new
flight-feathers/tail with yellow-green
fringes. VOICE Plaintive piping *piur*; song
accelerating *stip-stip* . . . ending in
shivering trill *shreeee*, also repeated
mournful *pwee*. HABITAT Woods, upland
scrub, with sparse undergrowth. NEST
Domed, on ground in thin cover, 5–7 eggs,
mid May–Jul; 1–2 broods. FOOD Insects.
RANGE Summer visitor, mid Apr–Aug,
wintering in Africa; scarce on passage
from Continent, Apr–Jun, Aug–Sep.

Chiffchaff *Phylloscopus collybita* 10.5–
11.5 cm (*c*4¼ in). Dumpier than Willow,
rounder head, shorter wing-point of
folded primaries; typically dingier above,
less yellow below, clearer eye-rings, dark
grey-brown legs (sometimes pale).
Constantly flicks wings, wags tail. *Ad W
race (P.c. collybita)* Olive-brown and
buff, wearing to browner and whiter by
*c*Jun till moult in Jul–Sep. *Juv* Browner
also below; as ad after moult Aug–Sep.
N Eurasian races (P.c. abietinus/tristis)
Increasingly grey and whitish towards E,
sometimes pale wing-bar. VOICE Emphatic
hweet (N races *tseep/tseeoo*); song
staccato mix of *tip*, *tap* and *titti* (= *chiffchaff*), interspersed with low *chrr-chrr*.
HABITAT Open woods with undergrowth;
on passage in scrub, gardens, reeds. NEST
Domed, off ground in tangle, 6 eggs, May–
Jul; 1–2 broods. FOOD Insects. RANGE
Summer visitor, mid Mar–Oct, wintering
in Mediterranean/Africa; also on passage
from Continent, inc N races, and some
winter. COMPARE Greenish Warbler (312).

Willow Warbler *Phylloscopus trochilus*
10.5–11.5 cm (*c*4¼ in). Far the commonest

leaf-warbler; small, neat, green-brown
above, yellow below, pale supercilia, pale
brown legs (sometimes dark). Flits restlessly, flicking wings and tail; flycatches,
hovers. *Ad W race (P.t. trochilus)* Olive-
green/brown, streaky yellowish below,
wearing to browner and whiter by *c*Jun
till moult in Jul–Aug. *Juv* Brown above,
buff below (*cf* Chiffchaff); much as ad
after moult in Jul–Aug, but more evenly
yellow below. *E European race (P.t.
acredula)* Sometimes grey-brown and
whitish (*cf* Chiffchaff). VOICE Plaintive
disyllabic *hoo-eet*; short rippling song
starts quietly, grows louder, falls away in
terminal flourish *swee-sweetew*. HABITAT
Copses, bushes, scrub. NEST Domed, on or
near ground in cover, 6–7 eggs, May–Jul;
1–2 broods. FOOD Insects. RANGE Summer
visitor, Apr–Sep, wintering in Africa; also
passage end Mar–Nov, inc E race.

Yellow-browed Warbler *Phylloscopus
inornatus* 9.5–10.5 cm (*c*4 in). Tiny; green
and whitish with 2 creamy wing-bars, bold
supercilia (few also faint crown-stripe).
Ad = 1st winter. VOICE Shrill sharp *swee*
or *sweeoo*. HABITAT Trees, scrub. FOOD
Insects. RANGE From Asia, Sep–Oct (end
Aug–Dec). COMPARE Pallas's (312).

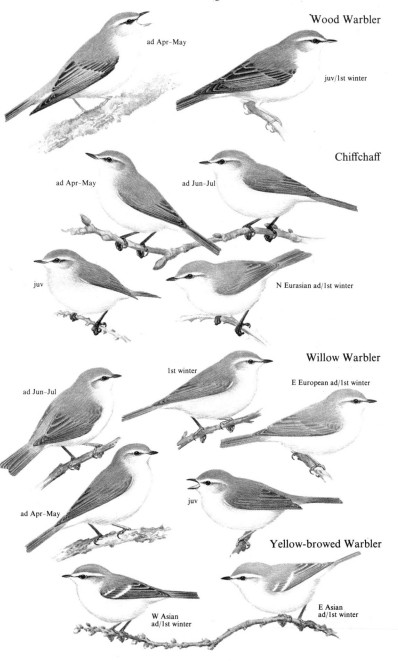

Wood Warbler

ad Apr–May

juv/1st winter

Chiffchaff

ad Apr–May

ad Jun–Jul

juv

N Eurasian ad/1st winter

Willow Warbler

1st winter

E European ad/1st winter

ad Jun–Jul

ad Apr–May

juv

Yellow-browed Warbler

W Asian
ad/1st winter

E Asian
ad/1st winter

FLYCATCHERS (Muscicapidae)

Spotted Flycatcher *Muscicapa striata*
13.5–14.5 cm ($c5\frac{1}{2}$ in). Like all flycatchers,
has flat broad-based bill, large dark eyes,
longish wings, squared tail and short legs;
grey-brown and whitish, looking rather
featureless but for dark streaks on head
and breast; told by stance and behaviour.
Perches upright on bare twigs or fences
and sallies after insects, twisting, turning,
often low over ground, then back to same
or nearby perch; usually seen well below
tree canopy, $c1$–5 m up, flicking or
drooping wings, wagging tail; solitary. *Ad*
Brown to grey-brown above, with crown
streaked blackish, coverts and tertials
edged buff to whitish; whitish below but
for brown breast-streaks. *Juv* Scaled above
by dark edges to pale buff spots; breast
spotted with brown rather than streaked.
1st winter As ad after moult in Jul–Sep,
but new plumage browner; broader pale
edges to tertials; still buffish spots at tips
of greater coverts. VOICE Thin scratchy
tzee (*cf* Robin, 196), extended into *tzee-
tzucc* of alarm; song $c6$ faint squeaky
notes, well separated. HABITAT Wood-
edges, parks to suburban gardens,
avenues, quarries. NEST On ledges or in
open cavities of trees, ivy, creepers, walls
rocks, 4–5 eggs, end May–mid Aug; 1–2
broods. FOOD Insects. RANGE Summer
visitor, end Apr–Sep, wintering in Africa;
on passage from Continent, end Apr–early
Jun, Aug–mid Oct, esp EBr.

Red-breasted Flycatcher *Ficedula parva*
11–12 cm ($c4\frac{1}{2}$ in). Small; grey-brown and
buff with bold white patches at base of
blackish tail (only ad ♂ has red throat).
Secretive, restless, keeping to cover
and often feeding more like warbler;
frequently cocks tail. *Ad ♂* Grey to grey-
brown head, pale eye-rings, orange-red
throat; brighter in spring than autumn.
Ad ♀ Head browner, still with pale eye-
rings; whole underparts creamy-buff. *1st
winter* As ad ♀, but buffish spots on tips of
coverts/tertials; ♂ rarely tinged orange
on throat (usually not until 1st summer
or even 2nd autumn). VOICE Low rattle,
chic, sad *hwee*. HABITAT Migrants in

coastal trees, scrub. FOOD Insects. RANGE
Scarce migrant from E Europe, mid Aug–
Nov, rare Apr–Jul, wintering in SE Asia.

Pied Flycatcher *Ficedula hypoleuca* 12–13
cm ($c5$ in). Smaller and plumper than
Spotted Flycatcher; boldly pied, or brown
and whitish, with white wing-patches.
Changes perch frequently, often dropping
to ground, also takes prey from bark and
leaves by clinging briefly to trunk or
hovering; flicks wings and tail often. ♂
summer Jet-black above, with white forehead, wing-patches, tail-sides, underparts;
rarely grey-brown instead of black, but
still with white forehead, blacker tail. *Ad*
♀ Olive-brown and whitish, no white on
forehead; less white on wings and more
buff below in autumn. ♂ *winter* Inseparable
from ♀ after moult in Jul–Aug, unless
some white on forehead or blackish on
coverts, rump or tail. *Juv* Scaled/spotted
as juv Spotted Flycatcher, but white in
wings and tail. *1st winter* As ad after moult,
but few median coverts often still have
pale spots. VOICE Sharp *whit*, short *tic*,
often combined; song deliberate repeated
zee-chi, then liquid jangle. HABITAT Old
open woods, parks. NEST In holes in trees,
walls, boxes, 5–8 eggs, May–Jul; 1 brood.
FOOD Insects. RANGE
Summer visitor,
mid Apr–Aug,
wintering in Africa;
on passage from
N/E Europe, mid
Aug–mid Oct, fewer
Apr–mid Jun, esp
EBr. COMPARE Col-
lared Flycatcher
(312).

Spotted Flycatcher

ad

1st winter

juv

♀/1st winter

♂

1st summer ♂

Red-breasted Flycatcher

1st winter

♀

♀

♂ summer

Pied Flycatcher

well-marked ♂ winter

juv

♀

KINGLETS (Sylviidae)

Goldcrest *Regulus regulus* 8.5–9 cm (*c*3½ in). This and next are smallest European birds, small-billed, short-tailed, with black-edged yellow/orange crowns, 2 white bars and dark band on wings; Goldcrest otherwise dull green and whitish, with 'surprised' pale area around large-looking eyes. Flits restlessly from tree to tree; usually in canopy with flicking wings; winter flocks mix with tits; unobtrusive but not shy. *Ad ♂* Crown yellow and orange. *Ad ♀* Crown yellow. *Juv* Browner above, no yellow crown, but black mottling at edges; as ad after moult in Jul–Sep. VOICE Persistent high *zi-zi-zi*; song repeated *zeeda* ending in flourish *zeeda-zeeda-zeeda-sissi-peeso*. HABITAT Woods, gardens, esp in conifers; locally in bushes. NEST Esp in conifer or ivy, 7–8 eggs, mid Apr–Aug; 2 broods. FOOD Spiders, insects. RANGE Mainly sedentary, but some move south; on passage/wintering from Continent, end Sep–Apr, esp E/SBr.

Firecrest *Regulus ignicapillus* 8.5–9 cm (*c*3½ in). Brighter green and whiter than Goldcrest, with white supercilia and black eye-stripes, bronzy by shoulders. Actions similar; often in low cover. *Ad ♂* Crown yellow and orange. *Ad ♀* Crown yellow. *Juv* As juv Goldcrest, but whitish supercilia, dark eye-stripes. VOICE Lower stronger *zit-zit-zit*; song crescendo extension of calls, often with terminal flourish. HABITAT Esp mixed woods; also bushes, scrub in winter. NEST Usually in conifers, 7–11 eggs, mid May–mid Aug; 1–2 broods. FOOD As Goldcrest. RANGE Scarce breeder since *c*1961; on passage/wintering from Continent, mid Sep–Apr.

REEDLINGS (Timaliidae)

Bearded Tit *Panurus biarmicus* 16–17 cm (*c*6½ in). Tit-like reed-bird with long tail; tawny, marked with black and whitish. Flight weak, whirring, with 'loose' twisting tail, usually low over reeds; gregarious. *Ad ♂* Grey head, black moustaches, pink-grey breast, black under tail; bill orange. *Ad ♀* Tawny head, greyer

breast; bill brown and yellow. *Juv* As ♀ but black on mid-back and tail-sides; ♂ black lores and yellow bill, ♀ usually blackish bill; as ads from moult in Jul–Oct. VOICE Twanging *ping ping*; ticks, churrs. HABITAT Big reedbeds. NEST Low in reeds, 5–7 eggs, Apr–Aug; 2–3 broods. FOOD Insects, reed seeds. RANGE Sedentary, but spreads in *c*Jul–Apr, inc Dutch birds.

LONG-TAILED TITS (Aegithalidae)

Long-tailed Tit *Aegithalos caudatus* 13.5–14.5 cm (*c*5½ in). Tiny bill and body, very long narrow tail; blackish and dull white, pink scapulars, rump and belly. Flight weak, undulating; restless, acrobatic; gregarious. *Ad Br/Ir race (A.c. rosaceus)* Dark head-bands, whitish wing-patches, much pink. *Juv* Tail shorter; browner, with dark cheeks, whitish scapulars, little pink; as ad after moult in Aug–Sep. *Ad N/E European race (A.c. caudatus)* White head, whiter wing-patch, less pink. VOICE Low *tupp*, persistent *zee-zee-zee*, rippling *tsirrp*. HABITAT Wood-edges, thick hedges, bushy places. NEST Oval ball esp in thorny bushes or high tree-forks, 7–12 eggs, Apr–Jun; 1 brood. FOOD Insects, seeds. RANGE Mainly sedentary; N/E race rare vagrant.

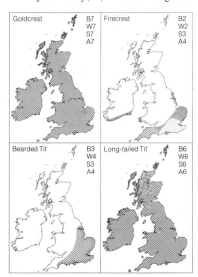

Goldcrest — B7 W7 S7 A7

Firecrest — B2 W2 S3 A4

Bearded Tit — B3 W4 S3 A4

Long-tailed Tit — B6 W6 S6 A6

Goldcrest

juv

♀

♂

Firecrest

♀

♂

juv

Bearded Tit

♀

♀

♂

juv ♀

juv ♂

juv

Long-tailed Tit

ad

caudatus ad

TITS (Paridae)

Marsh Tit *Parus palustris* 11–12 cm (*c*4½ in). Like all tits, stubby-billed, thick-necked, acrobatic, social; looks sleek, round-headed; brown and buff-white with glossy black cap, whitish cheeks, neat bib, pale flanks, no wing-panel (*cf* Willow Tit). Actions as Blue Tit (224); less in canopy or parties. Cap glossy, bib flecked with white, warm brown above, uniformly buffish below; abrasion by summer makes brown darker, bib blacker. *Juv* Cap dull sooty, bib browner, greyer-brown above, paler below, like juv Willow Tit; as ad after moult in Aug–Sep. VOICE Loud *pitcheu*, often with short nasal *tchay-tchay . . .*; scolding *chika-ke-ke-ke*, thin *zee-zee-zee*; song clear *chip c*7 times or extension of *pitcheu* note. HABITAT Dry or damp scrubby broadleaved woods, copses (not marshes). NEST In holes in trees, stumps, walls or ground, 6–8 eggs, Apr–Jun; 1 brood. FOOD Insects, seeds, berries. RANGE Sedentary.

Willow Tit *Parus montanus* 11–12 cm (*c*4½ in). Very like Marsh Tit, but bigger longer head, more bull-neck, dull sooty-black cap, larger whitish cheeks, more diffuse black bib, darker flanks and pale panel on wings. *Ad Br race (P.m. klein-schmidti)* Pale wing-panels and deep buff flanks most obvious after moult in Aug–Sep, less so by summer through abrasion. *Juv* Inseparable from juv Marsh Tit. *Ad N European race (P.m. borealis)* Larger, cheeks whiter, upperparts greyer, wing-panels grey-white. VOICE Buzzing *erz-erz-erz*; high thin *zi-zi-zi* or *chi-chi*, often followed by loud, long, harsh *tchay tchay . . . (cf* Marsh Tit); song clear sad *piu piu piu*, not unlike Wood Warbler (216), or short warbling trill. HABITAT Overlaps Marsh Tit, but esp in elder and damp birch/alder woods, also conifers; in winter, also hedges, scrub. NEST Excavates holes in rotten stumps, 6–9 eggs, Apr–Jun; 1 brood. FOOD As Marsh Tit. RANGE Sedentary; N European race rare vagrant.

Coal Tit *Parus ater* 10.5–11.5 cm (*c*4½ in). Smallest tit, with big head and stumpy tail; olive-grey and buff, with crown and extensive bib black, cheeks and large nape-patch white or yellowish, 2 white wing-bars. Actions as Blue Tit (224); on trunks rather like Treecreeper (226); unobtrusive. *Ad Br race (P.a. britannicus)* Cheeks and nape white; after moult in Aug–Sep, crown glossy, bib flecked white, upperparts olive-grey, flanks buff; by summer, abrasion makes crown duller, bib blacker, upperparts greyer, wing-bars thinner, flanks paler. *Ad Ir race (P.a. hibernicus)* Cheeks and nape yellower, esp in winter; upperparts olive-buff, flanks yellower-buff. *Juv (both races)* Browner above, yellower below; crown and small bib sooty-brown; cheeks, nape, wing-bars yellowish. *Continental race (P.a. ater)* Cheeks and nape purer white, upperparts slate-grey. *1st winter (all races)* As ads after moult in Jul–Sep, but buff-edged greyish juv outer greater coverts contrast with other new grey-edged blackish coverts. VOICE Piping *tseu*; thin *zee-zee-zee* call and *titsissi-sissi-sissi-sissiwee* song resemble Goldcrest (220), but usual song sweet piping *weecho-weecho-weecho (cf* Great Tit, 226). HABITAT Woods, gardens, esp conifers, highland scrub. NEST In holes in ground, tree-roots, low stumps, rocks, walls, 7–11 eggs, Apr–early Jul; 1–2 broods. FOOD Insects, seeds, nuts, fat. RANGE Sedentary; immigration from Continent as Blue Tit, but much more irregular and usually few.

Marsh Tit

ad

juv

Willow Tit

ad Sep-Mar

borealis ad

ad Apr-Aug

Coal Tit

britannicus ad

hibernicus
ad winter

juv

224 Paridae

Crested Tit *Parus cristatus* 11–12 cm (*c*4½ in). Brown and whitish, with pointed crest speckled with black and white; otherwise dingy white head but for black bib, thin collar and curve behind eyes. Actions as Blue Tit; fluttering display flight round tree-tops; moves rather like Treecreeper (224) on trunks. *Ad* Crest up to 2 cm long from moult in Aug–Oct, but dull white fringes gradually abraded, so shorter and blacker by summer; throat and collar black. *Juv* Crest shorter, more rounded, duller; bib browner and flecked white, no collar; as ad after moult in Aug–Sep. VOICE Deep purring trill, repeated loudly as song *chirr chirr chirr-r-r*; thin *zee-zee-zee* as other tits. HABITAT Old pine forest with stumps and heather, or pines mixed with birch/alder. NEST Excavates holes in rotten wood, 5–7 eggs, mid Apr–mid Jun; 1 brood. FOOD Insects, pine seeds, berries. RANGE Sedentary.

Blue Tit *Parus caeruleus* 11–12 cm (*c*4½ in). Blue and yellow, with green back, white cheeks and wing-bar; but juv more green and yellow. Flight looks weak, fluttery, often tree to tree, but higher and undulating across fields; in display slow, moth-like and floating; hops on ground or branches, hangs acrobatically from twigs; uses foot to hold down food that needs breaking; winter parties mix with other tits; common at bird-tables. *Ad* Blue crown, wings and tail, also black bib, brighter in summer (esp ♂); white crown-border and cheeks contrast with black eye-stripes and dark blue collar and nape with whitish spot; otherwise green above, yellow below with dark belly-mark. *Juv* Much duller, esp head with greenish-brown crown and hindneck, whites replaced by yellow, no clear bib; back more olive, wings and tail greener-blue. *1st winter* As ad after moult in Aug–Sep, but dull blue-green juv primary-coverts contrast other new bright blue coverts. VOICE Varied, esp quick *tsee-tsee-tsee-tsit*, scolding churr; song 2–3 *tsee* notes, then fast trill. HABITAT Woods, orchards, gardens, parks, hedges; even reeds in winter. NEST In holes , eg in trees or walls, 7–16 eggs, mid Apr–Jul; 1 brood.

FOOD Insects, also seeds, nuts, fruit. RANGE Sedentary, or moving locally; variable immigration from Continent, end Sep–Apr, esp SEBr.

Great Tit *Parus major* 13.5–14.5 cm (*c*5½ in). Larger than other tits; black head with white cheeks and yellowish spot on nape, black band on yellow underparts, green and blue-grey upperparts with white wing-bar, white-sided tail; but juv more brown and yellow. Actions as Blue Tit, but flight heavier, more undulating. *Ad* ♂ Band on underparts black, broad, widest on belly; crown and throat shiny blue-black, duller in summer; wings blue-grey. *Ad* ♀ Band sooty, usually narrower or even may be broken, mixed with white on belly; throat dull blackish; most wing-fringes greener-grey. *Juv* Much duller, esp head; blacks all sooty-brown, cheeks yellowish, upperparts browner, underparts duller. *1st winter* As ads after moult in Jul–Sep, but on ♂ dull green-grey juv primary-coverts contrast with other new blue-grey coverts. VOICE Very varied inc Chaffinch-like *zink zink*, hard scolding; song loud, ringing or rasping *teecha-teecha-teecha* and variations. HABITAT Much as Blue Tit; less ubiquitous in winter. NEST As Blue Tit, but larger holes, less in walls, 5–12 eggs, mid Apr–Jul; usually 1 brood. FOOD Insects, also slugs, snails, worms, seeds, fruit. RANGE Sedentary, or moving locally; immigration as Blue Tit, but irregular.

Crested Tit

ad Sep–Mar

ad Apr–Aug

juv

ad Sep–Mar

ad Apr–Aug

Blue Tit

juv

Great Tit

♀

♂

juv

NUTHATCHES (Sittidae)

Nuthatch *Sitta europaea* 13.5–14.5 cm
(*c*5½ in). Sleek, short-tailed, with sharp
bill and woodpecker-like actions; blue-
grey and buff, with black mask, white
throat, whitish tail-corners. Flight
undulating, mainly from tree to tree;
moves in jerks up, down and sideways on
trunk, not using tail as prop; breaks open
wedged nuts by heavy blows (loud tapping
noise); hops on ground; wary, restless;
often in pairs, joins tit flocks. *Ad ♂* Flanks
chestnut, demarcated from buff breast/
belly. *Ad ♀* Flanks paler rufous-buff,
shading into breast/belly. *Juv* Upperparts
tinged with brown, mask brown-black,
flanks duller than ♀; as ad after moult in
Jul–Aug. VOICE Ringing *chwit chwit*; song
shriller, rapid *twee-twee-twee . . .* or fast
trill. HABITAT Woods, parks, gardens,
with old trees. NEST In holes in trees or
walls, reduces entrance size with mud,
6–9 eggs, Apr–Jun; 1 brood. FOOD Nuts,
large seeds, insects. RANGE Sedentary;
some wander, mainly locally.

TREECREEPERS (Certhiidae)

Treecreeper *Certhia familiaris* 12–13 cm
(*c*5 in). Mouse-like trunk-climber with
thin curved bill and stiff pointed tail;
streaky brown (blending with bark), with
whitish supercilia, dark-edged buff wing-
bar, white underparts. Climbs jerkily in
spirals round trunk or along underside of
branch, with feet apart, tail pressed on
bark, then drops with tit-like flight to foot
of next tree; solitary, or in families, but
joins tit flocks. *Ad Br/Ir race (C.f.
britannica)* Brown streaked buff and dark,
with rufous rump; underparts white
(often dirty from rubbing on trees), but
flanks pale buff. *Juv* Colder brown above
and spotted buff, rump paler red-brown;
dull white to buff below, flecked brown on
breast and flanks; as ad after moult in
Aug–Oct. *Ad N race (C.f. familiaris)*
Paler above, flanks nearly white. VOICE
Shrill *tseu*, softer *tsit*; song thin, high *tsee-
tsee-tsee-tissi-sissi-tsee* (*cf* Goldcrest,
220). HABITAT Woods, parks, gardens.
NEST Behind bark or ivy, or in cracks,

Treecreeper

Nuthatch

juv

♂

♀

ad

juv

5–6 eggs, mid Apr–Jun; 1–2 broods. FOOD Insects. RANGE Mainly sedentary; N race vagrant, EBr. COMPARE Short-toed (314).

ORIOLES (Oriolidae)

Golden Oriole *Oriolus oriolus* 23–25 cm (*c*9½ in). Usually heard more than seen; yellow and black, or yellow-green/grey/ brown, with pink-red bill (ad). Flies in long undulations, ending in upward sweep into tree; secretive, arboreal, rarely on ground; solitary, or in family parties. *Ad* ♂ Rich yellow but for black lores, mainly black wings and tail. *Ad* ♀ Yellow-green and greyish, streaked dark brown below, with browner wings and tail (old ♀s very like ♂, but greyish lores). *Juv* As ad ♀, but speckled yellow above, less streaked below; bill brown. *1st year* As ad ♀, but ♂ often yellower, with blacker tail, weaker streaking; ♀ duller green, with greener tail, stronger streaking; 1st autumn ♂♀ also have brown bills, usually yellow-tipped median coverts. VOICE Harsh Jay-like notes, but song unmistakable: loud, melodious, fluty whistle *weela-whee-oh*. HABITAT Broadleaved/ mixed woods, parks. NEST In tree-forks, 3–5 eggs, end May–Jul; 1 brood. FOOD Insects, berries, fruit. RANGE Rare summer/passage visitor, Apr–Jul (few Aug–Nov), wintering in Africa. COMPARE ♀ with Green Woodpecker (182).

Nuthatch | B5 W5 S5 A5

Treecreeper | B6 W6 S6 A6

Golden Oriole | B2 W0 S2 A1

Golden Oriole

♀

♂

1st year ♂

old ♀

♀

juv

SHRIKES (Laniidae)

Red-backed Shrike *Lanius collurio* 16–18
cm (*c*6¾ in). Slim, with hook-tipped bill,
longish tail, pointed wings; chestnut or
red-brown back, no white on scapulars,
wings or rump. Flight strong, undulating,
with glides, often low from bush to bush
ending in upward sweep; also hovers but
mostly darts down on prey from lookout
perch; often fans and waves tail; carries
prey in bill or feet, may impale it on thorns
in 'larder'; solitary. *Ad ♂* Grey crown and
rump, chestnut wings and back, black
mask, white-sided black tail; pink-white
below. *Ad ♀* Rufous above, with browner
crown/rump, rufous ear-coverts, whitish
supercilia and lores, white-sided brown
tail, and whitish below barred with dark
crescents (crown rarely grey with blackish
mask/tail, so resembling ♂, but still some
barring below). *Juv* Rufous above and
creamy below, all barred with blackish.
1st winter As ♀ after moult in Jul–Sep, but
crown and rump redder, upperparts still
barred with blackish. VOICE Harsh *chack*
or *chee-uk*; song prolonged warble mixed
with mimicry and harsh calls. HABITAT
Bushy heaths with gorse. NEST In thorny
bushes or tangles, 3–6 eggs, mid May–
Jul; 1 brood. FOOD Big insects, small birds.
RANGE Scarce summer-visitor, May–Sep,
wintering in E Africa; much decreased,
but now colonising NBr; passage from
Continent, May–Jun, Aug–Oct. COMPARE
Isabelline and Woodchat Shrikes (314).

Great Grey Shrike *Lanius excubitor* 23–25
cm (*c*9½ in). Large with longish bill and
tail, but short rounded wings; grey/black/
white with grey forehead, and white
supercilia and scapulars. Actions as Red-
backed but perches more on tree-tops,
telegraph wires. *Ad* Grey above and white
below, with white line over black mask,
white on scapulars, white bar on black
wings, white sides to black tail; some ♀s
show faint brown crescents on breast. *Juv*
Brown-grey above and brownish-white
below with much faint barring; supercilia
very small, mask and wings browner. *1st
winter* After moult in Jul–Dec, as ♀ with
faint wavy bars on breast, but greater

coverts dull black-brown tipped with
whitish. VOICE Harsh *shek shek*. HABITAT
Winters among scattered trees/bushes.
FOOD Small birds, voles, big insects.
RANGE Winter visitor from N Europe,
Oct–Apr. COMPARE Lesser Grey (314).

CROWS (Corvidae)

Jay *Garrulus glandarius* 33–36 cm (*c*13½
in). Thickset, with stout bill and rounded
wings; brownish-pink with streaked
erectile crown, black moustache, white
throat, blue and white on wings, white
rump usually seen contrasting with black
tail when flying among trees. Flight
laboured, with quick jerky beats; hops
clumsily both on branches and ground,
jerking tail; like all crows, buries excess
food, esp acorns in autumn; usually in
pairs or noisy groups; very wary. *Ad*
Whitish crown streaked with black; body
soft brownish-pink. *Juv* Crown streaks
smaller, body redder-brown above and
red-buff below; as ad after autumn moult.
VOICE Harsh *kaaa*, barking *kah*, drawn-
out mew; sub-song mixture of weak
gurgling and harsh notes. HABITAT Woods,
plantations, parks; visits hedges, orchards,
gardens. NEST In trees, tall bushes, 5–6
eggs, end Apr–mid
Jul; 1 brood. FOOD
Acorns, nuts, fruit,
berries, peas, eggs,
nestlings, voles,
snails, worms,
insects. RANGE
Sedentary; irregular
migrants from Con-
tinent, Oct–Apr,
E/SBr.

Red-backed Shrike B2
W0
S3
A4

Great Grey Shrike B0
W2
S2
A3

Jay B6
W6
S6
A6

Red-backed Shrike

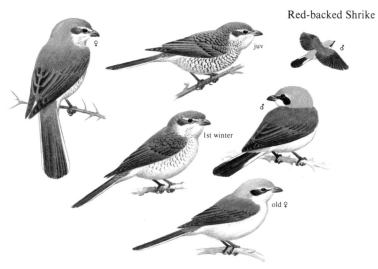

♀

juv

♂

1st winter

♂

old ♀

Great Grey Shrike

barred ♀

ad

ad

Jay

ad

ad

juv

Magpie *Pica pica* 42–50 cm (*c*18 in). Long wedge-shaped tail; pied plumage with contrasted white scapulars, flanks, belly and, in flight, broken panels near tips of rounded wings. Flight looks weak with fast beats, long glides; walks with tail up or moves with sidling hops; perches in open in trees or tall hedges; wary; often in pairs or parties, at times larger flocks, esp at roosts. *Ad* Tail half total length; black parts show metallic sheens at close range (head, breast and back blue-purple, wings blue and green, tail bronze-green to red-purple); whites pure white, but rump varies from whitish to black-brown. *Juv* Tail much shorter at first; blacks of body dull sooty, rump dark, wings/tail less glossed, whites tinged buff; as ad from moult in Aug–Sep, but tail averages 2–3 cm shorter (much overlap). VOICE Rapid, harsh, rattling *chaka-chaka-chaka*; more musical chattering and piping in spring. HABITAT Grassland with tall hedges, wood-edges, parks, moorland fringes, coastal scrub. NEST Domed, in trees or thorn bushes, 5–7 eggs, Apr–Jun; 1 brood. FOOD Insects, slugs, worms, nestlings, eggs, rodents, carrion, grain, berries, fruit. RANGE Sedentary; some winter dispersal.

Chough *Pyrrhocorax pyrrhocorax* 36–41 cm (*c*15½ in). Glossy black, with curved red bill, red legs; in flight, broad wings with tips usually well spread/upcurved, and squared tail. Flight strong, buoyant, acrobatic, but splayed wings give ragged look; soars, glides, dives with wings almost closed; walks, runs, hops; perches on rocks and cliffs, but rarely in trees; wary; in pairs, parties or flocks, mixing with Jackdaws. *Ad* Glossy blue-black, with greener wings and tail. *Juv* Duller, tinged with brown, hardly glossy on body; bill pinkish-yellow, turning redder. *1st year* As ad from moult Aug–Sep, but wings and tail less glossy, wearing brown by 1st summer. VOICE Drawn-out explosive *kee-ah*, higher pitched and clearer than Jackdaw; also softer *chuff*, deeper gull-like *kaa* and *kwuk-uk-uk*. HABITAT Coastal cliffs, inland crags and quarries, adjacent pastures and rough grazing. NEST In cliff crevices, sea caves or old mineshafts, 3–5

eggs, Apr–Jun; 1 brood. FOOD Insects, worms, slugs, grain. RANGE Sedentary.

Jackdaw *Corvus monedula* 32–34 cm (*c*13 in). Small, compact, short-billed; dark with grey nape, contrasting glossy black cap and throat; in flight, rather narrow wings with tips little spread, rounded tail. Flight hurried, pigeon-like, with faster beats than larger crows (230); glides and dives; walks jauntily; perches on trees, buildings, cliffs; bold, inquisitive; gregarious, also mixes with Rooks. *Ad Br/Ir/W European race (C.m. spermologus)* Back and wings glossy black, nape ash-grey, underparts tinged with grey; eyes pearl-grey. *Juv* Browner, less glossy, with black-brown crown and back, brown nape, paler brown underparts; eyes brown. *1st year* As ad from moult in Aug–Sep, but wings and tail browner, less glossy, wearing browner still by 1st summer; eyes dull whitish. *Ad Scandinavian race (C.m. monedula)* Nape often paler silver-grey, and whitish at base of neck, but many inseparable. VOICE Shrill *kya* or *keeaw*; short, high *chak*, often repeated. HABITAT Farmland, old woods, parks, towns, ruins, quarries, cliffs. NEST In cavity in trees, buildings or rocks, 4–6 eggs, mid Apr–Jun; 1 brood. FOOD Insects, slugs, worms, nestlings, eggs, mice, frogs, grain, berries, fruit. RANGE Largely sedentary; immigrants from Continent (inc Scandinavia), Oct–Apr.

Magpie

ad

juv

ad

Chough

ad

juv

ad

Jackdaw

monedula ad

ad

ad

juv

232 Corvidae

Rook *Corvus frugilegus* 44–47 cm (*c*18 in). Glossy black, with rather slender pointed bill; ad has bare whitish face, often swollen with pouched food; peaked head, loose thigh feathers ('baggy trousers') and, in flight, long 'hands' backswept as Raven but rounded tail (*cf* Carrion Crow). Flies with rapid, rather flexible beats; also glides, and autumn flocks tumble, roll and dive; waddles on ground, and hops; not shy; gregarious, mixing with Jackdaws. *Ad* Black, glossed purple (esp head) and green; nostrils/chin/lores bare. *Juv* Duller and browner, esp above; head fully feathered. *1st year* As ad from moult in Jul–Aug, but wings and tail increasingly dull brown; chin and lores bare from Jan–Feb, nostrils from Apr–May. VOICE Very varied: esp cawing *kaah* or drawn-out *kaa-aah*, higher and less raucous than Carrion Crow, not in series but often in chorus. HABITAT Mainly lowland arable and pasture with trees, also parks, open downs. NEST Colonial; in tree-tops, 4–6 eggs, mid Mar–mid Jun; 1 brood. FOOD Corn, roots, potatoes, berries, worms, insects, molluscs. RANGE Largely sedentary; immigrants from Continent, end Sep–Apr, mainly EBr.

Carrion/Hooded Crow *Corvus corone* 45–49 cm (*c*18½ in). All-black (Carrion) or black and grey (Hooded), intermediate where ranges meet; Carrion separated from imm Rook by stouter, more rounded bill, rounder cap, neater thighs and, in flight, shorter head, shorter straighter 'hands' and squarer tail (*cf* also Raven). Flight slower, more deliberate than Rook, not normally soaring like Raven; drops hard-shelled prey from height to break it open; sedate walk, sidling hops; perches anywhere; wary; often solitary, but also in parties/flocks. *Ad Carrion (C.c. corone)* Black, glossed green (esp on head) and purple. *Juv* Browner, hardly glossed (very like juv Rook). *Ad Hooded (C.c. cornix)* Back, breast, belly and also lesser/median underwing-coverts grey with fine streaks. *Juv* Browner-grey with dark speckles above, browner wings/tail. *1st year (both races)* As ads after moult in Jul–Aug, but wings/tail duller, browner. *Intermediate Carrion*

x *Hooded* Very variable: usually at least some grey, esp below. VOICE Loud, harsh, croaking *kraa*, repeated 3–4 times; also higher *keerk*, plaintive *honk* like old motor-horn. HABITAT Farmland, woods, town parks, lakes, moors, hills, cliffs, open shores. NEST In trees, hillside bushes, or on rock ledges, buildings, telegraph poles, 4–6 eggs, Apr–Jun; 1 brood. FOOD Carrion, small mammals, birds, eggs, frogs, crabs, molluscs, insects, worms, grain, fruit. RANGE Largely sedentary; immigrants (both races) from Continent, Oct–Apr, esp EBr.

Raven *Corvus corax* 60–67 cm (*c*25 in). Largest crow; black, with heavy bill, shaggy throat and, in flight, well projecting head, long thin 'hands' backswept, wedge-shaped tail (*cf* Carrion Crow). Flight powerful, with slow beats, often high up; glides, soars, tumbles, dives with wings closed; gait as Carrion Crow; often in pairs; flocks at food/roosts. *Ad* Black, glossed green or purple. *Juv* Browner, far less glossy. *1st year* As ad, but wings and tail increasingly dull brown. VOICE Deep *prruk prruk*; other croaks, grunts. HABITAT Coast and inlands crags, woody glens. NEST On rock-ledges or in trees, 4–6 eggs, mid Feb–May; 1 brood. FOOD Carrion, sheep placentae, dead fish, injured mammals and birds, eggs, frogs, snails, beetles, some grain. RANGE Mainly sedentary, but some winter dispersal.

Rook

Carrion/Hooded Crow

Raven

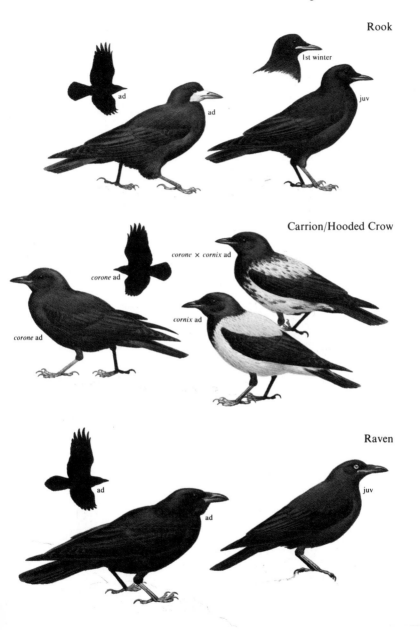

ad

ad

1st winter

juv

corone × cornix ad

corone ad

cornix ad

corone ad

ad

ad

juv

STARLINGS (Sturnidae)

Starling *Sturnus vulgaris* 20.5–22.5 cm
(*c*8½ in). Abundant and familiar, with
longish pointed bill, flat forehead, short
tail, triangular wings in flight; mainly
blackish, glossed green/purple, variously
pale-spotted, with buff-edged wings (but
see juv). Flight direct with rapid beats,
glides; hawks insects; singing ♂ droops
and flutters wings; bustles jerkily or runs
on ground, probing by opening bill;
boisterous, noisy, quarrelsome; highly
gregarious; huge winter roosts in reeds,
conifers, cities. ♂ *summer* No spots; bill
yellow with bluish-grey base, eyes dark
brown. ♂ *winter* After moult in Jun–Sep,
finely spotted buff above and white below;
bill mainly brown. ♀ *summer* Some spots;
bill yellow with pinkish base, eyes usually
brown with thin whitish circle. ♀ *winter* As
♂ winter, but larger, rounder spots; eyes
as ♀ summer. *Juv* Grey-brown, with dark
lores, whitish throat and belly-streaks,
buff fringes on brown wings/tail; bill
brown. *1st winter* Much as ad ♀ after

moult in Jul–Oct (when strikingly patchy);
♂♀ eyes differ as ads. VOICE Grating
tcheerr, whistled *tsoo-ee*, clicking, harsh
scream; all but last in rambling gurgling
song with much mimicry (*eg* Curlew,
telephone). HABITAT Urban areas, farmland, cliffs; also breeds in woods. NEST In
any holes, or in ivy, 4–7 eggs, Apr–mid
Jul; 1–2 broods. FOOD Insects, worms,
seeds, berries, fruit, cereals. RANGE Mainly
sedentary; abundant passage/winter
visitor from N/NE Europe, Oct–Apr.
COMPARE Rose-coloured Starling (316).

SPARROWS (Passeridae)

House Sparrow *Passer domesticus* 14–15.5
cm (*c*5¾ in). Brown and buff-white with
black-streaked mantle, ♂ also has grey
crown and blackish throat; often dingier
in towns. Flight direct or undulating,
with hurried beats; hops with flicking tail
or stands erect; cheeky, but wary;
gregarious. *Ad ♂* Chestnut and whitish,
with grey crown and rump, black throat/
chest, short white wing-bar; black bill in

Starling

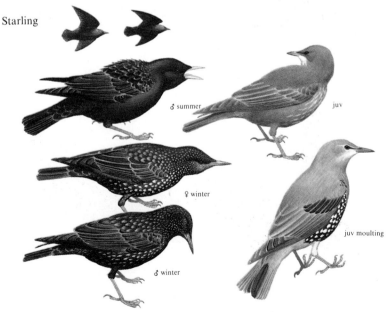

♂ summer

juv

♀ winter

♂ winter

juv moulting

summer, brown and yellowish in winter (when upperparts duller, bib mixed with whitish). *Ad* ♀ Buff streak behind eyes, 2 faint buff wing-bars; bill as ♂ winter. *Juv* As ♀, but crown and rump mottled dark, mantle and wings paler, throat whiter (if dusky central patch, usually ♂), bill yellow with blackish base; as ads after moult in Jun–Oct. VOICE Chirps and twitters, esp *chee-ip* and *chreek* in flocks; chirruping song. HABITAT Houses, farms. NEST Colonial; in holes, or in foliage, 3–6 eggs, Apr–Aug; 1–4 broods. FOOD Seeds, scraps, insects. RANGE Most sedentary. COMPARE Spanish Sparrow (316).

Tree Sparrow *Passer montanus* 13.5–14.5 cm (*c*5½ in). ♂♀ alike with chestnut crown, neat bib and cheek-spot, partial white collar, yellow-brown rump, 2 thin wing-bars. Shy; mixes in winter with House Sparrows and finches. *Ad* Bib/cheek-spot black, wing-bars white; bill black in summer, base yellowish in winter. *Juv* Crown duller, bib/cheek-spot dark grey, wing-bars buff, bill as ad winter; as ad

after moult in Aug–Oct. VOICE In flight *tek tek*; chirps higher-pitched than House Sparrow, esp fast *chip chip chip*. HABITAT Pollard willows, old trees, ruins, cliffs. NEST Colonial; mostly in holes, 4–6 eggs, mid Apr–Jul; 2–3 broods. FOOD Seeds, insects. RANGE Mainly sedentary; immigrants from N Europe, Sep–Apr.

Starling	B8
	W8
	S8
	A8

House Sparrow	B7
	W8
	S7
	A8

Tree Sparrow	B6
	W6
	S6
	A6

House Sparrow

♂ summer

♂ winter

♀

juv ♂

Tree Sparrow

ad

juv

FINCHES (Fringillidae)

Chaffinch *Fringilla coelebs* 14.5–16 cm
(*c*6 in). Commonest finch, with thick
pointed bill, slightly peaked head, shallow-
forked tail; white shoulder-patch and
wing-bar, white tail-sides, yellow-green
rump. Flight undulating, as all finches,
closing wings every few beats; hops
jerkily or walks with short steps; gregarious in autumn/winter. ♂ *summer* Abrasion
makes forehead black, crown/nape grey-
blue, mantle chestnut, cheeks and breast
pinkish; bill blue-grey. ♂ *winter* After
moult in Aug–Sep, crown/nape grey-blue
washed rufous-buff, mantle, cheeks and
breast duller; bill whitish-brown with dark
tip. *Ad* ♀ Yellow-brown above with greyer
central crown/nape (esp summer) and
brown-grey cheeks and underparts, often
tinged pink on breast; bill brown. *Juv* As
♀ winter, but white nape-spot, paler buff
face and breast, smaller brownish-green
rump, ♂ mantle chestnut-tinged; moults
in Jul–Sep. VOICE Loud metallic *pink-pink*,
low *chip* in flight; spring ♂ clear *wheet*,
rattling song *chip-chip-chip-chwee-chwee-
tissi-chooeeo* ('cricketer running to wicket,
bowling'). HABITAT Woods, hedges,
orchards, gardens; winters in farmland.
NEST In bushes, trees, 4–5 eggs, mid Apr–
Jul; 1 brood. FOOD Seeds, fruit, insects.
RANGE Resident; passage/winter visitor
from esp N Europe, end Sep–Apr.

Brambling *Fringilla montifringilla* 14–15
cm (*c*5¾ in). Shape as Chaffinch, but tail
slightly shorter and more forked; less
white in wings and tail, orange-buff
shoulders and breast, narrow white rump
(*cf* Bullfinch), yellow on axillaries. Flight
more erratic than Chaffinch. ♂ *summer*
Abrasion makes head/mantle black, breast
and shoulders pale orange; bill blue-
black. ♂ *winter* After moult in Aug–Sep,
head and mantle mottled buff, nape and
neck-sides greyish, breast and shoulders
rich orange-buff; bill yellow with black
tip. *Ad* ♀ Browner-black head and mantle
mottled buff, greyer nape and cheeks,
duller breast and esp shoulders; bill varies
as ♂. *Juv* As ♀, but rump and belly tinged
with yellow. *1st winter* ♂ As ad after moult

in Aug–Sep, but primary coverts and outer
greaters paler grey-brown (not black),
lesser coverts pale rufous (not orange) and
often spotted black. VOICE Hoarse *tsweek*,
hard Chaffinch-like *chik* in flight; spring
♂ prolonged *dzwee* like Greenfinch (238).
HABITAT Winters in beech woods, farmland; breeds in birch/conifer woods.
FOOD Beechmast, seeds, berries. RANGE
Passage/winter visitor from N Europe, end
Sep–May; has nested NBr, may colonise.

Bullfinch *Pyrrhula pyrrhula* 14–15 cm
(*c*5¾ in). Portly and neckless, with short
deep bill joining curve of large head,
shortish rounded wings, and squared tail;
black cap, wings and tail, whitish wing-
patch, bold white rump. Flight slow and
bouncing; secretive; in pairs or families.
Ad ♂ *Br/Ir race (P.p. pileata)* Blue-grey
above, pink-red below. *Ad* ♀ Dark grey-
buff above with greyer hindneck, paler
below, tinged with pink. *Juv* Head and
back brown, rump tinged buff, underparts
yellow-buff; much as ads after moult in
Aug–Oct. *N Eurasian race (P.p. pyrrhula)*
Larger; ♂ paler grey, brighter pink; ♀
much greyer above. VOICE Low *deeu*;
sub-song broken creaky warble. HABITAT
Woods, bushes, orchards. NEST In bushes
or brambles, 4–6
eggs, May–Aug; 2
broods. FOOD Seeds,
berries, buds, also
insects. RANGE
Largely sedentary;
N race scarce
migrant, end Mar–
early May, esp end
Oct–Nov, mainly
NBr.

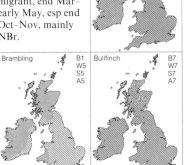

Chaffinch B8 W8 S8 A8

Brambling B1 W5 S5 A5

Bullfinch B7 W7 S7 A7

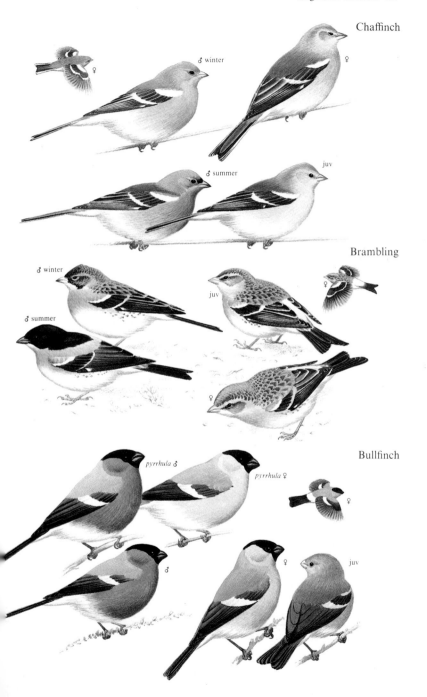

Chaffinch

♂ winter

♀

♂ summer

juv

Brambling

♂ winter

juv

♂ summer

♀

Bullfinch

pyrrhula ♂

pyrrhula ♀

♀

♂

♀

juv

Greenfinch *Carduelis chloris* 14–15 cm
(*c*5¾ in). Thickset, with stout pale bill and
short well-forked tail; green to streaky
brown, rump yellow-green (not juv),
yellow patches on primaries and sides of
tail-base. Actions much as Chaffinch
(236); ♂ makes butterfly-like display-
flights round tree-tops in spring. ♂ *summer*
By abrasion, olive-green above and bright
yellow-green below, with greyish greater
coverts/inner secondaries. ♂ *winter* After
moult *c*Jun–Aug, grey-brown above with
greyer cheeks/flanks, all tinged green;
still yellow-green below but tinged grey.
Ad ♀ Grey-brown above with faint
streaks, greyer below tinged yellow,
whiter belly, all slightly more green-
yellow in summer; less yellow on wings
and tail than ♂. *Juv* Dark-streaked brown
above, inc rump, and yellow-grey below
streaked brown; ♂♀ wings/tail differ as
ads; as ads after moult in Jul–Sep if no
brown juv greater coverts. VOICE Trill in
flight, *chup* or *teu* repeated, uneasy *tsooeet*;
in spring ♂ drawn-out nasal *tsweee*, mixed
with twittering song. HABITAT Gardens,
parks, hedges, wood-edges; winters in
farmland. NEST In bushes, trees, 4–6 eggs,
mid Apr–Aug; 2–3 broods. FOOD Seeds,
berries, buds, also insects. RANGE Mainly
resident, but some go as far as Iberia;
winter visitor from Continent, Oct–Apr.

Goldfinch *Carduelis carduelis* 11.5–12.5
cm (*c*4¾ in). Dainty, with pointed whitish
bill, well-forked tail; red, white and
black head (not juv), yellow wing-band,
white tips on black wings/tail. Flight
dancing; perches high or flits about on
thistles, often hanging head down; flocks
seldom mix with other finches. *Ad* Head
coloured; tawny above and buff breast in
winter, greyer-brown and whitish with
whiter nape-spot and less white on wing/
tail-tips in summer; ♂ red extends farther
back above and below eyes, ♀ lesser
coverts have much broader greyer tips.
Juv Mostly grey-buff, paler below, with
faint dark spots and streaks; much as ads
after moult in Aug–Sep. VOICE Liquid
twittering *tswitt-witt-witt*, clear high
whistled *pee-u*; song fast twittering trill.
HABITAT Gardens, parks, wood-edges;

feeds on weedy ground. NEST In trees, tall
bushes, 5–6 eggs, May–Aug; 2–3 broods.
FOOD Seeds, insects. RANGE Many go south
to Iberia/NW Africa, Sep–Apr.

Siskin *Carduelis spinus* 11.5–12.5 cm
(*c*4¾ in). Dumpy with sharply pointed bill
and short well-forked tail; yellow-green
to green-grey above and yellowish to
white below, all variably streaked, with
yellow wing-bars and sides to tail-base.
Flight fast, undulating; mainly in trees,
flits restlessly, hangs acrobatically;
gregarious with Redpolls; ♂ makes
butterfly-like display-flights in spring.
Ad ♂ Yellow-green above, faintly streaked
except on yellower rump, and grey-yellow
below, streaked black on whiter flanks;
crown and bib black, mottled with grey in
winter. *Ad* ♀ Greyer above, whiter below,
more heavily streaked (also rump); no
black on head. *Juv* More streaked than ♀
and browner above, rump greyish; as ads
from *c*Aug, but ♂ more streaked above and
♀ browner. VOICE Shrill clear *tsu*, wheezier
tsu-eet and hard twitter, often combined;
song warbling twitter ending in discordant
bleating note. HABITAT Breeds in
coniferous/mixed woods; winters in birch/
alder thickets. NEST High in conifers, 4–5
eggs, end Apr–mid
Jul; 2 broods. FOOD
Tree seeds. RANGE
Mainly sedentary,
some dispersal south;
passage/winter
visitor from N/E
Europe, mid Sep–
mid May. COMPARE
Serin (316).

♂ summer ♂ winter ♀

Greenfinch

juv ♂ ♀

Goldfinch

ad juv ad

Siskin

♀ ♀ juv ♂

Linnet *Carduelis cannabina* 13–14 cm ($c5\frac{1}{4}$ in). Small finch with pointed bill, long wings and longish forked tail; streaky brown with streaked buff throat, white in wings and tail, dark bill in winter; ♂ also shows grey, chestnut, and red or pink. Flight undulating and flitting; hops on ground; perches on low bushes and fences; gregarious. ♂ *summer* Abrasion makes head greyer, mantle plain chestnut, throat whiter, forehead and breast red. ♂ *winter* After moult in Aug–Oct, dark streaks and buff fringes obscure colours. *Ad* ♀ Duller, no pink/red, less chestnut, more heavily streaked. *Juv* As ♀, but narrower streaks, throat nearly plain buffish; juv ♂ more chestnut-buff above; as ads with moult in Jul–Sep. VOICE Flight-note rapid *chichichichit*, call *tsooeet*; song musical twitter of fluty and twangy notes. HABITAT Commons with gorse, thorn bushes, young plantations, hedges, dunes; winters in stubble, fallow marshes. NEST In bushes or in cover on ground, 4–6 eggs, mid Apr–mid Sep; 2–3 broods. FOOD Seeds, also insects. RANGE Partial migrant, some going to S France/Spain, others coming from N Europe, Sep–Apr.

Twite *Carduelis flavirostris* 13–14 cm ($c5\frac{1}{4}$ in). Suggests small ♀ Linnet and looks longer-tailed; darker, tawnier above, with plain warm buff throat, less white in wings and tail, yellow bill in winter; ♂ pink rump. *Ad* ♂ Streaked blackish above and dark rufous on breast/flanks; in summer, stronger streaking, pink rump, greyish hindneck, buff throat, yellow-grey bill; in winter, paler above, buff-pink rump, rufous-buff throat, less streaked below, yellow bill. *Ad* ♀ As ♂, but rump streaky, usually no pink. *Juv* Slightly greyer head, rustier mantle, no pink rump, dirty buff throat, paler and more streaked below, with bill cream-yellow; as ads after moult in Jul–Sep. VOICE Flight-note and song Linnet-like, but harder, more metallic; *chweek* call nasal, twanging. HABITAT Moors, upland pastures, rocky ground near sea; winters on shores, saltmarshes, coastal fields. NEST In heather, banks, walls, bushes, on ground, 5–6 eggs, May–mid Aug; 1–2 broods. FOOD Seeds, also

insects. RANGE Some resident, but others move south on coasts, even cross Channel; few come from Norway, Oct–Apr.

Redpoll *Carduelis flammea* 11.5–13 cm ($c4\frac{3}{4}$–5 in). Dumpy finch with short tail; red forehead, black chin, yellowish bill, pale rump, 2 buff wing-bars; streaked tawny, buff or greyish upperparts/flanks; ♂ rump and breast pink. Actions as Siskin (238); similar circling song-flight, acrobatic feeding. *Ad* ♂ *Br/Ir race (C.f. cabaret)* Tawny above, with variably pink rump, cheeks, throat, breast and upper flanks, all much brighter in summer. ♀/*1st year* ♂ Little or no pink, streakier below. *Juv* No red on crown, less black on chin, much streakier; moults in Jul–Sep. *N race = Mealy Redpoll (C.f. flammea)* Larger, paler, greyer above with whiter wing-bars and rump (may be almost plain pink on ♂). Greenland race *(C.f. rostrata)* More as Br/Ir race, but bulkier, bill heavier, 'striped' flanks. VOICE Metallic flight-note used as song with rolling trill *rrrr*, *chee-chee-chee*; call plaintive *tsooeet*. HABITAT Birches, alders, willows, conifers, in woods, parks, gardens; rocky ground on passage. NEST In bushes or trees, 4–6 eggs, May–mid Aug; 1–2 broods. FOOD Seeds, also insects.
RANGE Partial migrant, many wintering in Low Countries/Germany; immigrants from N Europe/Greenland, Oct–May. COMPARE Arctic Redpoll (316).

		Linnet
B7		
W6		
S7		
A7		

Twite		Redpoll	
B5		B6	
W5		W6	
S5		S6	
A5		A6	

Redpoll

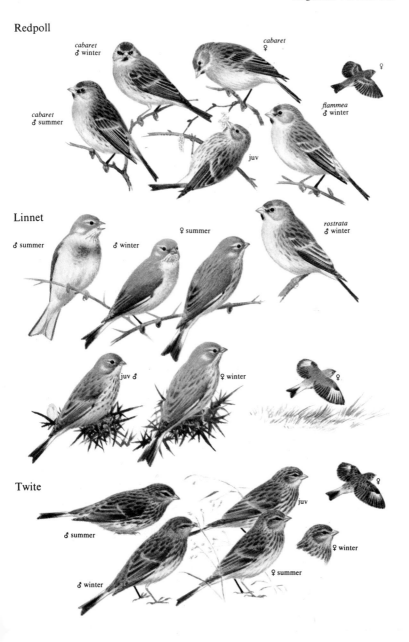

cabaret
♂ winter

cabaret
♀

♀

cabaret
♂ summer

flammea
♂ winter

juv

Linnet

♂ summer

♂ winter

♀ summer

rostrata
♂ winter

juv ♂

♀ winter

♀

Twite

♂ summer

juv

♀

♂ winter

♀ winter

♀ summer

Crossbill *Loxia curvirostra* 16–17 cm (*c*6½ in). Thickset, big-headed finch with long wings, short forked tail and elongated mandibles crossed at tip (lower turned to left or right); crimson, orange, yellow-green or streaky greenish-grey according to sex/age, all with dark wings and tail. Flight fast, undulating, usually at tree-top level; clambers or sidles on branches like parrot, even using bill as support; hangs down to wrench off conifer cones, holds them with foot while extracting seeds with tongue (dropped cones have character-istically split scales); except for drinking, seldom on ground, hopping awkwardly, but migrants will hang from thistles; gregarious; tame. *Ad ♂* Crimson of varying richness, often mixed with orange: brightest on crown, rump and underparts; more vivid in summer. *Ad ♀* Generally yellow-green with grey tinge, but some more golden or even with few orange-red feathers; throat greyer, breast and flanks mottled brown. *Juv* Green-grey heavily streaked blackish; mandibles not crossed for 1–2 weeks after fledging. *1st year ♂*

With moult in May–Nov, greenish-gold to orange, mixed with red and yellow-green: some like ad ♂ but for green-fringed juv wings and tail, others have orange only on crown and rump like bright ♀. *1st year ♀* As ad ♀, but wing-coverts buff-tipped. VOICE Metallic *jip jip*, more explosive than Greenfinch (238); song 5–10 calls trilled together, then series of high clearer *jee* or *terjee*, ending with warble like Redstart (198). HABITAT Conifers, esp woods or clumps, but also in parks/gardens after invasions. NEST High in conifers, 3–4 eggs, Feb–Jun; 1–2 broods. FOOD Conifer seeds, also berries, thistles, insects. RANGE Fluctuating, and boosted by periodical invasions from Continent, end Jun–Sep; has bred in most counties. COMPARE Other Crossbills, Pine Grosbeak (318).

Scottish Crossbill *Loxia scotica* 16–17.5 cm (*c*6⅝ in). Differs from Crossbill only in deeper, blunter-tipped bill; plumages and habits similar. VOICE Similar; also stronger *joop*. HABITAT Caledonian pine forest.

Crossbill

♂

♀

♀

juv

1st year ♀

1st year ♂

FOOD Pine seeds. RANGE Endemic resident.

Hawfinch *Coccothraustes coccothraustes*
16–17 cm (*c*6½ in). Stout, bull-necked, with
long wings, short squarish tail, and huge
bill on big head; rich brown mantle, grey
hindneck, white wing-patches, black bib;
identified in flight by call, shape, trans-
parent band on primaries and white-
tipped tail. Flight fast, undulating, high;
perches in tree-tops; rather upright on
ground, with strong hops or gawky
waddle; solitary or parties; very shy. *Ad
♂* Hindcrown and rump rufous, underparts mainly pink-brown, much black
round bill-base, flight-feathers predominantly glossy black; bill blue in summer,
yellowish in winter. *Ad ♀* Head, rump and
underparts greyer-brown, less black on
face, flight-feathers predominantly grey,
bill alters as ♂. *Juv* Brown above, buff
below, all mottled/barred blackish, with
green-brown head, yellowish throat,
horn-yellow bill; ♂♀ wings differ as ads,
juv ♂ also black line round bill-base and
♀ whiter underparts; as ads after moult in

Aug–Sep. VOICE Explosive clicking *pzik*
or *pzik-ik*, thin whistling *tzeeip*; song
halting *teek teek tur-whee-whee*. HABITAT
Broadleaved woods,
orchards, parks.
NEST In trees, 3–6
eggs, end Apr–Jun;
1 brood. FOOD
Kernels, seeds,
berries; insects in
summer. RANGE
Resident, but
wanders (? also from
Continent), Oct–Jun.

Scottish Crossbill

Hawfinch

♂ winter

♂ summer

♂

juv ♂

♀ summer

BUNTINGS (Emberizidae)

Lapland Bunting *Calcarius lapponicus*
14–16 cm (c6 in). Bulkier, longer-winged,
shorter-tailed than similar Reed Bunting
(248); in autumn/winter has yellowish bill,
pale crown-stripe, black-cornered ear-
coverts, thin moustaches, obscurely
marked breast, chestnut greater coverts
between thin whitish bars (instead of
rufous shoulders), less white tail-sides and
often at least hint of rufous nape; ♂ has
black, white and chestnut head in summer.
Flight fast, undulating, often high; much
on ground, creeps or runs crouched, also
hops; shy; gregarious in winter with other
buntings, finches, larks. ♂ *summer* Black
head and throat, chestnut nape; upper-
parts/flanks streaked black and chestnut.
♂ *winter* After moult in Aug, black and
chestnut largely hidden by brown and
buff-white tips, head-sides sandy-buff
with black ear-corners and faint
moustaches, upperparts/flanks duller.
♀ *summer* Browner crown, buff supercilia
reaching bill, blackish face/cheeks/throat

mixed with whitish and pale brown, pale
chestnut nape streaked black, flank-
streaks narrower and more chestnut. ♀
winter As ♂ winter, but nape streaked
black/buff so chestnut barely visible, ear-
corners and chest-marks browner-black,
less black on crown and flanks. *Juv*
Mainly buff, paler below, streaked
blackish; chestnut on wings as ads. *1st
winter* ♂ As ♂ winter after moult in Aug–
Sep, but obscure chestnut nape spotted
black. *1st winter* ♀ As ♀ winter, but ear-
corners and moustaches browner, chest-
marks streakier. VOICE Dry rippled *trrrr*,
soft *chew*. HABITAT Coastal fields, saltmarshes; nests on hummocky moors. FOOD
Seeds; insects in summer. RANGE Passage/
winter visitor from Greenland/?N Europe,
end Aug–May; has nested since 1977.
COMPARE Rustic and Little Buntings (326).

Snow Bunting *Plectrophenax nivalis* 16–17
cm (c6½ in). Largish and stocky, with long
wings reaching well down tail; whitish
below, white in wings, white tail-sides,
variously tawny on head and breast, but

Lapland Bunting

♀ winter

♂ winter

♂ summer

summer ♂ black and white. Flight fast, undulating, flock dropping like flickering snowflakes, then skimming ground; much on ground, runs, also hops; perches on rocks, also posts, wires; gregarious in winter. ♂ *summer* White head (often with rufous speckles), rump (sometimes black streaks), secondaries, most wing-coverts; black bill, back, primaries, central tail. ♂ *winter* After moult in Aug–Sep, tawny-buff crown, cheeks, breast-sides (or even across chest); black mantle obscured by tawny to whitish-buff; brownish-yellow bill. ♀ *summer* Rufous and greyish head, grey-black mantle/rump and whitish; much less white on browner wings with dark marks on secondaries, usually blackish-based coverts; bill as ♂. ♀ *winter* As ♂ winter, but dull buff above, crown/nape and rump speckled black, wings as ♀ summer. *Juv* Grey-buff above streaked black, throat grey, breast/flanks buff marked darker; wings only little white on secondaries, covert-tips. *1st winter* ♂ As ♂ winter after moult in Aug–Sep, but darker tawny above, speckled

black on nape, wings as juv but median coverts white; as ad by summer but for black flecks on nape, mainly black rump. *1st winter* ♀ As ♀ winter but wings less white, often black-speckled breast-band. VOICE Rippled *tirrirri-ripp*; loud *peeu* as Little Ringed Plover; song high musical *titti-turee-turee*. HABITAT Breeds on bare mountains; winters on coasts, adjacent pastures, also moors. NEST In crevices, 4–6 eggs, end May–early Aug; 1–2 broods. FOOD Seeds, moss, invertebrates. RANGE Passage/winter visitor from Greenland/Scandinavia, mid Sep–mid Apr; few nest.

Snow Bunting

♀ winter

♂ winter

♀ summer

1st winter ♂

♂ summer

♂ winter

juv

Yellowhammer *Emberiza citrinella* 16–17 cm (*c*6½ in). Slim, with longish wings, longish cleft tail; yellow on head/underparts, streaky chestnut upperparts, plain chestnut rump, white on tail-sides. Flight undulating or direct; much on ground, mainly hops; perches prominently, often flicking tail; gregarious in winter with other buntings and finches. *♂ summer* Mainly yellow head and underparts, variably streaked with olive on sides of head and with blackish on chestnut flanks (some much brighter, with more yellow than others); usually chestnut moustache; often pale chestnut band across breast. *♂ winter* After moult in Aug–Oct, head and throat more streaked brownish-green (but still much yellow), chest greener, breast-sides and flanks duller chestnut and more streaked, wings with yellowish fringes. *Ad ♀* Duller than ♂ winter, much less yellow and more dark grey-brown on crown and throat, more rufous breast and flanks with heavier streaking, paler yellow belly; rather brighter and more clearly streaked in summer. *Juv* Much duller than

ad ♀: heavily streaked head, browner and streakier rump, bolder and blacker streaks on browner breast and flanks; ♂ shows dull yellowish on central crown, throat and belly, ♀ more greyish. *1st winter ♂* After moult in Jul–Oct, much as ad ♀, but yellows brighter, breast and flanks more chestnut. *1st winter ♀* Crown/nape yellow-brown with blackish streaks, throat/breast more buff, belly paler. VOICE Sharp *twik* or *twitik*, hoarse *chiff*; song tinkling series of high notes, ending usually with prolonged wheezy *chwee* ('little-bit-of-bread-and-no-cheese'). HABITAT Arable .with hedges, bushy areas, young conifers, scrub, bracken slopes; often stubble and stackyards in winter. NEST On or near ground in banks, hedge-bases, brambles, 3–5 eggs, mid Apr–Aug; 2–3 broods. FOOD Seeds, grain, shoots, berries; insects in summer. RANGE Largely sedentary; apparently some immigrants from N Europe, Sep–May.

COMPARE ♀/imm Yellow and Cirl with vagrant buntings showing yellow (326, 328).

Yellowhammer

♂ summer

juv

♀

♂ winter

♀

Cirl Bunting *Emberiza cirlus* 15.5–16.5 cm (*c*6¼ in). Slightly smaller and more compact than Yellowhammer, with shorter, more rounded wings; most plumages rather similar except for olive-grey to grey-brown (not chestnut) rump, but ♂ has black, olive and yellow head-pattern. Flight weaker than Yellowhammer, more undulating; less gregarious. ♂ *summer* Black throat and eyestripes bordered with yellow bands; olive-grey crown streaked black; grey-green chest-band with chestnut at sides; chestnut mantle/scapulars, olive-grey rump and shoulders. ♂ *winter* After moult in Aug–Oct, black and chestnut partly obscured by buffish tips, chest-band greyer. *Ad* ♀ Much duller than ♂: less chestnut above, crown and rump browner, supercilia and dark-speckled throat yellow-buff, chest and flanks buff and well-streaked, only chestnut tinge at breast-sides, belly pale yellow; in summer, yellow-buff and chestnut brighter, less marked below, and greyer crown, rump and breast. *Juv* Buff above, yellow-grey below, all streaked

blackish, with vague supercilia, buff-tipped blackish (not grey-green) lesser coverts; as winter ads with moult in Aug–Oct. VOICE Thin *sip* or *sissi-sissi-sip* in flight, churring alarm; rattling song like fast Lesser Whitethroat (212). HABITAT Bushy chalk/limestone slopes, pastures with timbered hedgerows, scrubby coastal cliff-tops, parkland and gardens near sea, esp with elms. NEST In hawthorn, gorse, brambles, yew, or in banks, 3–4 eggs, mid May–Aug; 2–3 broods. FOOD Much as Yellowhammer. RANGE Largely sedentary, much decreased in numbers and range.

| Yellowhammer | B7 W7 S7 A7 | Cirl Bunting | B3 W4 S3 A4 |

Cirl Bunting

♂ summer

♀

♀/juv

juv

Ortolan Bunting *Emberiza hortulana* 15.5–
16.5 cm (*c*6¼ in). Slim, long-winged; ads
greenish head, yellowish throat, chestnut-
buff underparts and yellow-brown rump;
juvs streaked; always reddish bill/legs,
pale eye-rings, white on tail-sides. Actions
as Yellowhammer (246); shyer. *♂ summer*
Head and chest grey-olive but for yellow
throat, cheek-stripe. *♂ winter* After moult
in Jul–Aug, yellow more buffish, crown
streaked, chest mottled dark (even
spotted, then inseparable from ♀ unless
olive band clear). *Ad ♀* Very like *♂* winter,
but head browner, chest grey-buff (not
olive) with dark marks. *Juv* Streaked
black and buffish; paler throat and cheeks.
1st winter More as ad ♀ after moult in
Aug–Oct, but crown browner, throat
paler, chest greyer-buff with heavier
streaks. VOICE Soft *tlip*, harder *twik*,
whistled *cheu*. HABITAT Migrants in
coastal scrub, fields. FOOD Seeds, insects.
RANGE Scarce migrant from Continent,
Aug–Nov (esp Sep), rare end Apr–Jun,
wintering in Mediterranean/E Africa.
COMPARE Cretzschmar's Bunting (326).

Reed Bunting *Emberiza schoeniclus* 14–16
cm (*c*6 in). Rather rounded wings, longish
tail; buff to rufous with blackish streaks
and moustaches, buff supercilia, brownish
cheeks, grey-brown rump, rufous
shoulders, white on tail-sides; summer *♂*
has black and white head. Flight jerky,
often low; hops, creeps or runs on ground;
perches on reeds or bushes, flicks wings,
opens tail; mixes with other buntings,
finches, pipits. *♂ summer* Black head,
white collar and cheek-stripe; white
below, flanks streaked. *♂ winter* After
moult in Aug–Nov, head-pattern obscured
by rufous-buff tips, whitish collar and
blackish throat just visible. *Ad ♀* No white
collar (greyish when very worn in
summer); buff below (whiter in summer),
streaked also on breast. *Juv* As ♀, but
paler, less rufous, with bolder streaks,
yellower-buff below. *1st winter ♂* More as
♂ winter after moult in Aug–Sep, but black
throat largely obscured, less collar,
supercilia often buff. VOICE Shrill *tsee-u*,
metallic *chink*; dreary song 2–5 wheezy
notes then *zizzizik*. HABITAT Marshes,

young conifers, gorse, hedges, coastal
bushes; often winters in farmland. NEST
On or near ground in tussocks, bushes,
4–5 eggs, end Apr–mid Aug; 2–3 broods.
FOOD Seeds, insects. RANGE Sedentary but
leaves uplands in winter; also passage/
winter visitor from Continent, end Sep–
May. COMPARE Little and Pallas's Reed
Buntings (326, 328).

Corn Bunting *Miliaria calandra* 17–18.5
cm (*c*7 in). Big, thickset, with heavy head
and shortish tail; streaky brown, yellowish
bill, no white on tail. Flight sparrow-like;
perches on wires, bushes; singing *♂* often
flutters off with legs dangling; hops on
ground; gregarious in winter. *Ad summer*
Grey-brown above, streaked blackish;
whitish-buff below finely streaked from
throat-sides to flanks, variably across
breast. *Ad winter* After moult in Sep–Nov,
more buff; more streaked below. *Juv*
Paler buff with bolder streaks above,
wings fringed pale buff (not rufous),
throat-sides/flanks less streaked; as ad
after moult Sep–Oct. VOICE Harsh *chip*,
scolding *zeep*; sharp *kwit* or *kwit-it* in
flocks; stuttering song speeds into harsh
trill like jangling keys. HABITAT Downs,
extensive arable with low hedges, coastal
scrub. NEST On
ground in cover, 3–5
eggs, end May–Aug;
1–3 broods. FOOD
Seeds, berries,
insects. RANGE
Sedentary; appar-
ently some
immigrants from
Continent, Sep–
May.

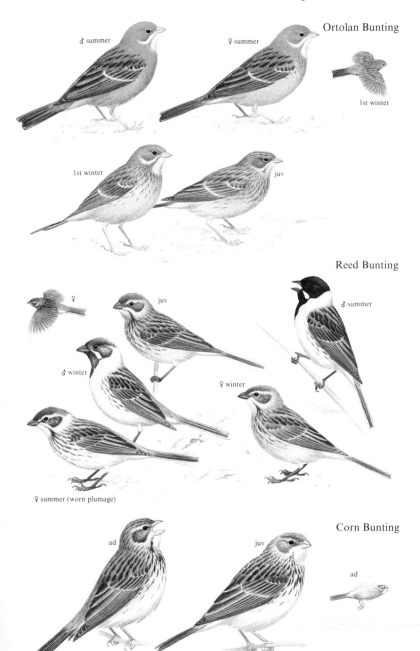

Ortolan Bunting

♂ summer

♀ summer

1st winter

1st winter

juv

Reed Bunting

♀

juv

♂ summer

♂ winter

♀ winter

♀ summer (worn plumage)

Corn Bunting

ad

juv

ad

DIVERS (Gaviidae)

White-billed Diver *Gavia adamsii* 75-90 cm (*c*32 in). Very like Great Northern Diver (42), separated by colour/shape of bill, angular outline of uptilted head, pattern of upperparts, and white-shafted primaries. *Ad summer* Bill whitish-yellow with straight culmen and up-angled lower mandible; fewer/wider streaks on collars than Great Northern, larger checks on upperparts. *Ad winter* Bill often darkish towards base, but outer culmen pale; face-sides lighter than Great Northern, and whitish round eyes like Red-throated (42). *Juv* Bill much as Great Northern, but paler (esp outer culmen); head and neck paler, upperparts greyer-brown with clearer scaling than juv Great Northern. RANGE 74: Oct-Jun, mainly coastal N/EBr, 2 Ir. (Arctic Russia, Asia, NW America.)

GREBES (Podicipedidae)

Pied-billed Grebe *Podilymbus podiceps* 31-38 cm (*c*13½ in). Shape like large Little Grebe (46), but stout chicken-like bill, larger head, longer neck. *Ad summer* Black-banded white bill, white eye-rings, black forehead and throat. *Ad winter* Bill yellow-brown, foreneck grey-brown, throat whitish; white stern conspicuous. *Juv* Bill darker yellow-brown than ad winter, with pinker lower mandible; head stripy, no eye-ring; lower foreneck rufous, breast and flanks greyer than ad winter; white stern as ad. *1st winter* After moult by Dec, much as ad winter, but eye-rings dull green, bill greyish. VOICE Spring 'song' loud, slurred, gulping *cow-cow-cow* speeding up and rising in pitch before ending in wail. HABITAT Shallow waters with emergent cover. FOOD Invertebrates, fish. RANGE 7: all months (some for long periods), most E/SBr. (N/S America.)

ALBATROSSES (Diomedeidae)

Black-browed Albatross *Diomedea melanophris* 75-90 cm (*c*33 in), wingspan 215-245 cm (*c*7½ ft). Huge, stout-bodied, with heavy bill, short tail, long narrow

Pied-billed Grebe

White-billed Diver

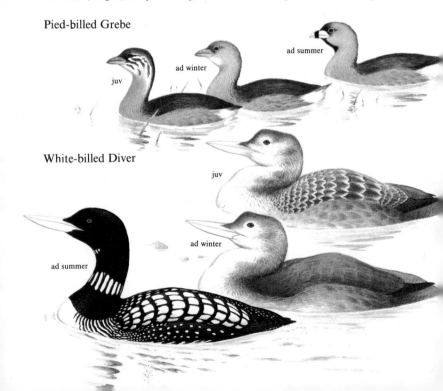

wings; 1 of several species in Atlantic, so important to note bill colour/shape, whether grey on head, form of any eye-patches, back colour, underwing pattern, and build. *Ad* Bill yellow with black basal line, head white with frowning eye-patches; back blackish; broad, ill-defined blackish margins to white underwings, wider in front. Gliding flight, heavy head, thick neck and humped shape similar to outsize Fulmar (48). *Juv/imm* As ad, but bill grey-black, later yellow with dark tip; top of head and neck grey at first, then only lower neck; underwings show little white, then increasing central stripe. VOICE Silent at sea. HABITAT Oceanic. FOOD Squids, jellyfish, offal. RANGE 23 (also 17 not identified to species): Feb–Dec, esp Mar–Oct, mostly coastal SW/NWIr, E/SBr, but 2 inland; single summering ads on Bass Rock (1967–79) and Hermaness, Shetland (since 1974). (S Oceans.)

FRIGATEBIRDS (Fregatidae)

Magnificent Frigatebird *Fregata magnifi-*

cens 95–110 cm (*c*40 in), wingspan 215–245 cm (*c*7½ ft). Black or pied, rakishly elongated with hook-tipped bill, narrow pointed wings and forked tail; 4 frigate-bird species in Atlantic often inseparable, but points to note include bill and leg colour, shape of any white areas, whether white tinged rusty (juvs), colour of throat (♀s), and any paler collar, wing-band or breast-patch on the black. All soar and sail, sometimes flap with deep beats; never settle on sea. *Ad* ♂ Glossy black with red throat-pouch (barely visible unless inflated in display); bill grey to dark horn, legs black. *Ad* ♀ Blackish with white anvil-shape below and narrow collar, pale band on wings; bill blue-grey, legs red. *Juv/imm* As ♀, but head and underbody white (at first with broken brownish breast-band), then becoming mottled. VOICE Silent at sea. HABITAT Aerial, oceanic. FOOD Fish, squids, offal, snatched from surface or other birds. RANGE 1: Jul, Argyll; 2 others in Aug (Aberdeen, Cork) not identified to species. (Tropical Atlantic, E Pacific.)

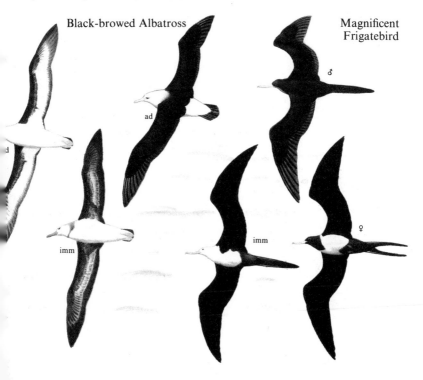

Black-browed Albatross

Magnificent Frigatebird

ad

♂

d

imm

imm

♀

PETRELS, SHEARWATERS (Procellariidae)

Bulwer's Petrel *Bulweria bulwerii* 25–28 cm (*c*10½ in). Rather small, all-dark petrel with stubby bill, long narrow backswept wings, and long tail actually wedge-shaped but looking round-ended at distance or from side; lacks white rump of still smaller storm-petrels (52, and below), and shape and flight different from them and from also mainly dark, but larger, longer-billed and shorter-tailed Sooty and Balearic Shearwaters (50, 52). Flight fast with swooping careening action and erratic twisting glides, and beats slower and deeper than shearwaters. *Ad/juv* Sooty-brown, duller below, but for paler band on upperwings, grey chin; legs pinkish. VOICE Silent at sea. HABITAT Oceanic. FOOD Plankton. RANGE 4: Feb, May, Aug, Yorks/Cork. (Cent Atlantic, Pacific.)

Little Shearwater *Puffinus assimilis* 25–30 cm (*c*11 in). Small, compact shearwater, ⅓ smaller than normal-sized Manx Shearwater (52) (but Manx runts may be hardly any bigger); similarly black above and white below, but shorter wings, smaller bill, whitish round eyes. Flight distinct from other shearwaters (50, 52), with far more flapping and, even when banking/gliding (mainly in stronger winds), frequently interspersed with rapid beats; fluttering action and short wings recall Puffin (170); feeds while swimming and by plunging, as Manx. *Ad/juv Madeira/Canaries race (P.a. baroli)* Black above and mainly white below, with more restricted black cap than Manx (cheeks in front of/around eyes mottled grey, like sides of neck and breast, and looking whitish at distance); undertail-coverts white, extending almost to end of tail; legs blue (not pinkish as Manx). *Cape Verdes race (P.a. boydi)* Browner above; less whitish in front of eyes; undertail-coverts largely brown, so tail looks dark. VOICE Silent at sea. HABITAT Oceanic. FOOD Fish, cephalopods. RANGE 58: Apr–Oct (esp Aug–Oct), most SW/NWIr, also W/EBr; only Madeira/Canaries race certainly identified (Cent Atlantic, S oceans.)

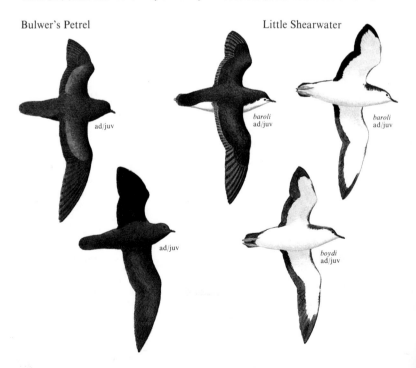

Bulwer's Petrel

ad/juv

ad/juv

Little Shearwater

baroli ad/juv

baroli ad/juv

boydi ad/juv

STORM-PETRELS (Hydrobatidae)

Wilson's Petrel *Oceanites oceanicus* 17–18 cm (*c*7 in). Small, black with white rump, very like Storm Petrel (52), but with long spindly legs usually projecting well beyond short square tail, broader and more rounded wings uniformly dark underneath. Flight less bat-like than Storm Petrel with stronger fluttering, longer glides, more rolling from side to side; similarly patters on sea, but also regularly 'hops', with wings level or slightly raised and tail fanned, stretching legs forward to dip toes and then pushing back with them as it rises; even 'stands' on water, facing into wind with rigid wings and webbed feet acting as anchors; flight sometimes rather more wader-like, with flicking action and feet retracted, or martin-like, darting around and up into air; follows ships, sometimes settles on sea. *Ad/juv* Sooty-black, but for white rump curving down to lower flanks and, in new plumage, whitish line on upperwings; yellow on webs of feet rarely visible. VOICE Silent at sea. HABITAT Oceanic. FOOD Fish offal, plankton. RANGE 8: Aug–Oct, esp SWBr/ Ir. (S oceans, migrating to N Atlantic.)

Madeiran Petrel *Oceanodroma castro* 18–20 cm (*c*7½ in). Very like Leach's Petrel (52), but bolder and laterally more extensive white rump, less marked band on upperwings, larger bill, much less forked tail (often looking square). Flight intermediate between rapid and erratic bounding of Leach's and fluttering of Storm: typically steady with fast shallow beats, and glides on bowed (not angled) wings; at least sometimes also proceeds in regular horizontal zigzags, beating to left and then right. *Ad/juv* Black-brown with all-white rump more evenly curved than Leach's above tail and more clearly extending to lower flanks; wing-band slightly browner and less distinct (but whiter and bolder on juv in new plumage). VOICE Silent at sea. HABITAT Oceanic. FOOD Plankton, tiny fish, offal scraps. RANGE 2: Oct–Nov, Hants/Mayo (E/Cent Atlantic, Pacific.)

Wilson's Petrel

Madeiran Petrel

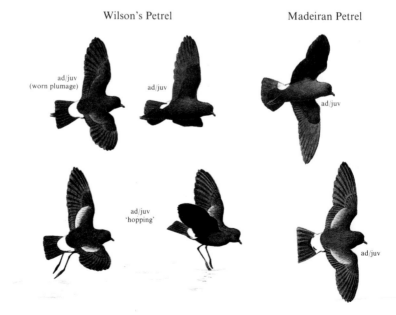

ad/juv
(worn plumage)

ad/juv

ad/juv

ad/juv
'hopping'

ad/juv

BITTERNS, HERONS (Ardeidae)

American Bittern *Botaurus lentiginosus*
60–70 cm (*c*26 in). Smaller, browner than
Bittern (56) (*cf* also imm Night Heron),
with much less bold markings above, warm
brown crown, creamy supercilia, blackish
flight-feathers, usually black stripe on
sides of neck. Faster beats of narrower,
less rounded wings; feeds more in open.
Ad Clear black neck-stripe (longer on ♂).
Juv No neck-stripe until moult in Aug–
Nov. VOICE Throaty *ok-ok-ok-ok*.
HABITAT Marshes, meadows. FOOD Frogs,
fish, insects. RANGE 55: Sep–Mar (esp
Oct–Nov), most Ir, S/WBr. (N America.)

Little Bittern *Ixobrychus minutus* 33–38
cm (*c*14 in). Tiny; black and buff, or
streaky, with pale wing-panel. Flight
rapid, with shallow beats, dropping into
cover with glide, bank and pitch; walks
crouched, climbs reeds, very skulking;
camouflage posture as Bittern (56). *Ad* ♂
Black and pale buff, hardly streaked, with
large rounded patch on inner wings. *Ad* ♀
Pattern as ♂, but duller, variously tinged
rufous: upperparts much browner with
narrow buff streaks, underparts striped
brown; wing-patches brown-buff with
rusty carpal. *Juv* More boldly streaked
buff above and brown below; crown also
streaky and wing-patches mottled brown;
some redder above. *1st year* As ads after
moult in Nov–Jan, but wing-patches darker, more spotted; ♂ also browner flight-
feathers and more streaked below. VOICE
Flight-call *kwer* or *ker-ack*; ♂ in spring
muffled croaking bark at 2 sec intervals.
HABITAT Reeds in swamps, lakes, rivers.
FOOD Fish, frogs, insects. RANGE 280 + :
most Apr–Jun, also Jul–Sep, esp S/EBr,
few Ir/NBr. (Eurasia, Africa, Australia.)

Night Heron *Nycticorax nycticorax* 58–65
cm (*c*24 in). Stocky, with stout bill,
shortish legs; ad black, grey and white, but
juv not unlike Bittern (56). Crepuscular;
flight rapid on short rounded wings, only
toes projecting beyond tail; clambers
bittern-like in reeds. *Ad* Black above, grey
wings/tail; white nape-plumes, forehead,
and below; legs briefly red in spring.

Juv Dark brown above, boldly spotted
whitish-buff; grey-buff below, streaked
dark brown. *Imm* From *c*Jan, becomes dark
brown above, spotted only on worn wings
until *c*May, and whiter below with brown
streaks; more as ad from 2nd autumn, but
greys/blacks tinged brown, no plumes till
2nd summer. VOICE Raven-like croak.
HABITAT Roosts by day in trees; feeds in
shallows. FOOD Frogs, fish, insects. RANGE
278: all months (esp Apr–Jun), most
S/EBr. (S Eurasia, Africa, N/S America.)

Squacco Heron *Ardeola ralloides* 43–48 cm
(*c*18 in). Small, thick-necked, with striped
mane; brown or buff at rest, but on take-
off white wings, rump and tail alter whole
appearance. Flight faster, more fluttery
than other small herons; rather skulking.
Ad summer Mostly yellow-buff and pink-
buff with black and cream mane; long
scapulars cover white areas at rest; bill
with black tip, green or blue base. *Ad
winter* Browner above, shorter mane
blackish and buff; breast streaked grey-
brown; bill-base yellower. *Juv* As ad
winter, but darker, more streaked; wings
mottled brown, exposed by short scapulars. *1st winter* More as ad winter after
moult in Jul–Dec, but tinged rusty above;
still mottled juv wings. VOICE Harsh *karr*.
HABITAT Rank marshes. FOOD Insects,
frogs, fish. RANGE 116: most May–Oct,
esp SBr. (S Europe, SW Asia, Africa.)

Cattle Egret *Bubulcus ibis* 48–53 cm (*c*20
in). Short-necked, with heavy jowl;
mainly white, with pale bill. Wing-beats
faster, shallower than other small herons;
walks less gracefully with swaying motion,
neck hunched or straight; often with
cattle; not shy. *Ad summer* Long feathers
of crown, breast and mantle pink-buff;
bill and legs briefly red. *Ad winter* Crown
paler; only ♂ has mantle and chest
feathers slightly elongated, tinged cream-
buff; bill yellow, legs dark green and
yellowish. *Juv* Crown white, then just
tinged buff, legs blackish-green; as ♀
winter after moult in Sep–Dec. VOICE
Usually silent. HABITAT Grassland, drier
marshes. FOOD Mainly insects. RANGE 26:
Mar–May, Jul–Jan, esp S/W/EBr, 3 Ir.
(Cosmopolitan, inc S Europe.)

American Bittern

ad

ad

juv

Night Heron

Little Bittern

juv

juv

1st year Feb-May

♀

♂

ad

Squacco Heron

ad spring

ad

juv/1st winter

Cattle Egret

ad winter

ad summer

juv

Little Egret *Egretta garzetta* 53–58 cm (*c*22 in). White, with thin neck; long bill and legs black, but feet yellow. Leisurely flight on rounded wings; darts about in shallows. *Ad summer* 2 long head-plumes; elongated aigrettes on mantle and scapulars. *Ad winter* No head-plumes; fewer, shorter aigrettes. *Juv* No aigrettes or long breast-feathers; these appear rudimentarily during moult in Aug–Nov. VOICE Usually silent. HABITAT Lakes, marshes, estuaries. FOOD Largely fish, insects, frogs. RANGE 260: all months, esp Apr–Jul, most coastal S/SEBr, SIr, few NBr. (S Eurasia, Africa, Australia.)

Great White Egret *Egretta alba* 85–100 cm (*c*37 in). Slim, white, with long, angular, sinuous neck, at least partly yellow bill and long blackish legs variously yellow at tops; note possibility of albino Grey Heron (56). Flight more buoyant than Grey Heron, slower than Little Egret; walks sedately. *Ad summer* Elongated scapular aigrettes, loose feathering on chest; bill black with yellow base, lower legs black. *Ad winter* No aigrettes; bill yellow, lower legs blackish-green. *Juv* As ad winter, but no loose chest-feathering until moult in Aug–Nov; lower legs browner. VOICE Usually silent. HABITAT/ FOOD As Little Egret. RANGE 21: Apr–Oct (esp May–Jun), most coastal S/EBr. (Cosmopolitan, inc SE Europe.)

Purple Heron *Ardea purpurea* 75–85 cm (*c*31 in). Slighter, much darker than Grey Heron (56), with thin head, snaky neck. Flight less ponderous, body lifting on downstroke, with drooping neck-bulge, narrower wings, larger feet; skulks. *Ad* Red-buff, chestnut, dark grey and black; ♂ purple gloss on mantle, chestnut (♀ buff) tips to long scapulars. *Juv* Browner above, buffish below, brown streaking; crown mainly chestnut. *Imm* Some longer scapulars and breast-feathers appear in Nov–Apr; more like ad from 2nd autumn, but duller, some chestnut on crown, less black on belly. VOICE Higher *frarnk* than Grey Heron. HABITAT Wetlands with dense reeds. FOOD As Little Egret. RANGE 378: Feb–Nov, esp S/SEBr. (S Eurasia, Africa.)

STORKS (Ciconiidae)

Black Stork *Ciconia nigra* 90–100 cm (*c*38 in). Form as White Stork, but mainly dark. Wing-beats faster; shy. *Ad* Glossy black with white lower underparts; bill and legs scarlet in summer, dark red in winter. *Juv* Browner, less glossy; head to breast dark grey-brown, specked paler; bill and legs grey-green; moults in Feb–Oct. VOICE Silent. HABITAT Marshes with cover. FOOD Fish, frogs, insects. RANGE 46: May–Aug (Mar–Nov), most E/SBr, few NBr. (SW/E Europe, Asia, S Africa.)

White Stork *Ciconia ciconia* 95–105 cm (*c*40 in). Large with long neck, red bill and legs; white with black flight-feathers. Flies with neck extended, slow beats; glides, soars; neck stretched in walking, hunched at rest. *Ad* Black areas glossy; bill and legs bright red. *Juv* Blacks browner, less glossy; bill brown-red with blackish tip, legs dull red; moult in Dec–Aug. VOICE Silent. HABITAT Open grass-land, marshes. FOOD Insects, frogs, small mammals. RANGE 269: all months, esp Apr–Jun, well scattered but most E/SBr. (Cent/S Europe, SW Asia, NW Africa.)

IBISES, SPOONBILLS (Threskiornithidae)

Glossy Ibis *Plegadis falcinellus* 50–65 cm (*c*22 in). All-dark, with decurved bill, long neck and legs. Flies with fast beats, glides, looking elongated, flattened; walks sedately with neck in extended curve. *Ad summer* May appear black, but mainly deep chestnut (inc shoulders); purple gloss on upperparts, green on wings. *Ad winter* Head and neck blackish streaked with white, mantle blacker, underparts browner. *Juv* Duller, mainly brown, little gloss; face and foreneck variously white, spotted white, or brown. *Imm* After moult in Aug–Oct, head and neck streaked as ad winter; no chestnut shoulders before 2nd winter. VOICE Harsh croak; usually silent. HABITAT Marshes, mud-flats. FOOD Mainly insects, leeches, molluscs. RANGE Many in past, but only 23 since 1958: all months, esp Aug–Dec, May, widely scattered; some probably escapes, inc 2 in Kent for several years. (Cosmopolitan, inc SE Europe.)

Little Egret

ad summer

juv

Great White Egret

ad summer

juv

Purple Heron

ad

juv

ad

Black Stork

ad

ad

juv

White Stork

ad

juv

ad

Glossy Ibis

ad

juv

ad winter

SWANS, GEESE, DUCKS (Anatidae)

Lesser White-fronted Goose *Anser erythropus* 53–66 cm (21–26 in). Some overlap in size with White-fronted (62), but daintier, neater, with small rounded head and shorter neck, longer folded wings projecting well beyond tail, small bright pink bill, swollen yellow eye-rings; darker above, white on face up to fore-crown over eyes and usually less black barring below (ad). Actions as Greylag (60); flight even more agile than White-fronted; walks/feeds noticeably faster; seen with White-fronted or Bean Geese. *Ad* Extensive white round base of bill on to forecrown; dusky brown above with dull pale bars, paler below with usually few black blotches on belly; bill bright pink with white nail, eye-rings and legs orange-yellow. *Juv/1st winter* Forehead blackish with no white, no black bars below, back almost uniform; bill, eye-rings and legs duller; as ad with moult in Nov–Mar. VOICE As White-fronted, but higher, squeakier. HABITAT Wet grassland.

FOOD Grass. RANGE 107: esp Dec–Mar, most Glos, EBr, SW Scot. (N Eurasia.)

Red-breasted Goose *Branta ruficollis* 51–58 cm (20–23 in). Thick-necked with tiny bill; mainly black with bold white flanks and face-spot, russet cheeks and foreneck outlined in white. Flight agile and walks/ feeds fast and daintily; mainly with White-fronted. *Ad* Blacks, whites and russets clearly defined. *Juv/1st winter* Blacks browner, whites less well defined, russets dingier, and browner cheek-patch smaller or even missing; as ad in course of winter moult. VOICE Shrill staccato screech *kee-kwa.* HABITAT Wet grassland. FOOD Grass. RANGE 25: Oct–Mar, esp SBr; some may be escapes. (W Siberia.)

Ruddy Shelduck *Tadorna ferruginea* 61–67 cm (*c*25 in). Thickset, goose-like duck with small blackish bill, dark legs (*cf* Egyptian Goose, 66); orange-brown with paler head, black wing-tips and tail; in flight, striking white forewings, green speculum. Actions as Shelduck (66), but flight

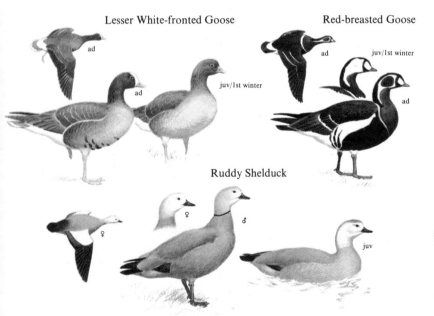

Lesser White-fronted Goose

Red-breasted Goose

ad

ad

juv/1st winter

ad

juv/1st winter

ad

Ruddy Shelduck

♀

♀

♂

juv

heavier; swims stern-high; walks easily, grazing like goose. *Ad* ♂ Head yellow-buff, face creamier; black collar (reduced or lost during moult in *c*Jul–Oct); body orange-brown, wing-coverts white or tinged pink/cream. *Ad* ♀ Head whiter, no collar. *Juv* As ad ♀, but head pale grey, crown browner (juv ♀ often whiter face); upperparts duller and browner; as ads after moult in Jul–Nov, but ♂ lacks collar until *c*Feb, greater coverts grey till 2nd winter. VOICE Loud nasal honking. HABITAT Lagoons, wet pastures. FOOD Grass, water-plants, invertebrates. RANGE Many: most/?all in last 50 years probably escapes. (NW Africa, S Eurasia.)

American Wigeon *Anas americana* 44–50 cm (*c*18½ in). Shape and actions as Wigeon (70), only ♂ distinctive; head greyish, paler than rufous body (reverse of Wigeon ♂, but not always of ♀); white (not grey) axillaries hard to see; ♀ tertials may be more contrasted. *Ad* ♂ White crown, speckled grey head, green patches; body pink-brown, forewings white. *Ad* ♀ Greyish head, spotted sepia, reddish body, some whitish on forewings. *Juv* Head more streaked than ♀; as ads by *c*Nov–Mar, but ♂ wings not white till 2nd winter. VOICE ♂ 2–3 soft whistles *whee-whee-whee*. HABITAT/FOOD As Wigeon. RANGE 110: Oct–Apr, widely scattered. (N America.)

Black Duck *Anas rubripes* 53–61 cm (*c*22 in). Shape and actions as Mallard (72); ♂♀ both resemble very dark sooty-brown ♀ Mallard, but with contrasting pale head and white underwings; no white on tail or at front of purple-blue speculum (and less at rear). *Ad* ♂ Body sooty-black, and head mainly pale buff finely streaked sepia; bill yellow to olive-yellow, legs orange-red. *Ad* ♀ Body almost as dark, but head greyer and more coarsely streaked; bill dull olive-green, legs orange-brown. *Juv* As ad ♀, but browner below, streaked with buff; bill and legs of juv ♀ dusky-olive; as ads by *c*Dec. VOICE/HABITAT/FOOD As Mallard. RANGE 11: all months, esp Oct–Mar, most SBr/SEIr; ♀ hybridised with ♂Mallard, Scilly, 1977–80. (N America.)

American Wigeon

Black Duck

Baikal Teal *Anas formosa* 39–43 cm (*c*16 in). Larger and bulkier than other teals, with high forehead, slender bill. *Ad ♂* Black stripe down cream cheeks, white stripes at front and rear of body. *Ad ♀* Brighter than other ♀ teals, esp contrasted nead with dark-ringed white spot by base of bill, broken supercilia, dark vertical line below eyes sometimes extended into 'bridle' at side of throat; rufous band in front of speculum. *Juv* Much as ad ♀, but line below eye more smudged, wing-band almost white; as ads by late winter. VOICE ♂ deep chuckling *wot-wot* or *proop*; ♀ quacks. HABITAT Lakes, marshes, sometimes on sea. FOOD Seeds, invertebrates. RANGE 3: Sep–Apr, NBr/Ir (others considered to be escapes). (Cent/E Siberia).

Blue-winged Teal *Anas discors* 36–40 cm (*c*15 in). Shape and actions as Garganey (74); forewings pale blue. *Ad ♂* Grey head glossed with magenta, white face-crescent and pied stern; bright blue forewings, white band, green speculum. *Ad ♀* Dark crown/eye-stripes, pale supercilia and patch by base of bill (*cf* Baikal Teal); whitish under tail; forewings nearly as bright as ♂, but band and speculum much duller. *Juv* Much as ad ♀, but ♂♀ wings differ as ads; as ad by *c*Dec–Mar. VOICE Usually silent: ♂ faint *peep*, ♀ soft quack. HABITAT Marshes, lakes, pools. FOOD Plants, invertebrates. RANGE 95: all months, esp Apr–May, Sep–Oct, widescattered. (N America.)

Ring-necked Duck *Aythya collaris* 40–46 cm (*c*17 in). Like Tufted Duck (80) but flatter forehead, peaked rear crown, no crest, grey (not white) wing-band. *Ad ♂* 2 white bands on grey bill, grey flanks with white peak at front. *Ad ♀* Pale band near bill-tip, white spectacles, variably whitish by bill-base. Swims higher than Tufted; often in shallows, dabbling or up-ending. *Juv* Duller brown above than ad ♀, with ill-defined head/bill markings, and more mottled below; ♂ chest blackish by *c*Sep–Oct, as ad by *c*Apr. VOICE Usually silent; ♀ soft growl in flight. HABITAT Marsh pools, shallow-edged lakes. FOOD Much as

Baikal Teal

Blue-winged Teal

Ring-necked Duck

Tufted. RANGE 128: all months, esp Nov–May, wide-scattered. (N America.)

King Eider *Somateria spectabilis* 53–59 cm (*c*22 in). On average, smaller than Eider (82) and shorter-billed, rounder-headed and neater; ♀/imms distinguished by pointed extension of frontal feathering to above nostrils and well beyond lores. Mixes with Eiders; flight lighter with slightly faster beats. *Ad ♂* Black back; looks white from front with orange bill/shield and pale mauve-grey crown/nape, and black from rear but for white patches at stern and on forewings in flight. *Eclipse ♂* Dull black with paler chest; shield smaller, duller. *Ad ♀* Paler than Eider, more rusty-buff; bolder-spotted scapulars, paler throat, more crescentic flank-marks; sometimes pale round eyes and at corner of bill; expression 'self-satisfied'. *Juv* More like juv Eider, with heavily streaked head, less rusty colour, more barred below, but head/underparts paler; 2 years to ad plumages, with much variation as Eider, but ♂s show grey on

crown and black on scapulars in 1st summer, bill much as ad in 2nd winter. VOICE Mostly silent. HABITAT/FOOD Much as Eider. RANGE 159: all months, esp Oct–Jun, most NBr. (Circumpolar Arctic.)

Steller's Eider *Polysticta stelleri* 43–48 cm (*c*18 in). Much smaller than Eider (82), more like dabbling-duck; squarer head, long triangular bill, longish tail; white underwings, speculum much like Mallard, (72). Flight lighter than other eiders, narrower wings making singing noise like weak Goldeneye (88). *Ad ♂* Mainly white head and orange-buff underparts. *Ad ♀* Rich dark red-brown with paler cheeks, chest and esp eye-rings. *Eclipse ♂* Like ad ♀ but hint of ♂ pattern on foreparts; white forewing. *Juv* Like ad ♀, but greyer above fringed buff, paler below; speculum with less white, little blue in ♂ and none in ♀; 2 years to ad plumages. VOICE Vagrants usually silent. HABITAT/FOOD Much as Eider. RANGE 13: all months because of long stays, most NBr. (Arctic Russia east to NW Canada.)

King Eider

Steller's Eider

Harlequin *Histrionicus histrionicus* 41–45 cm (*c*17 in). Small dark sea-duck with short bluish bill, high forehead, pointed tail; plain-winged ♀/imm confusable with imm Long-tailed Duck (84), though more uniformly dark with usually 3 light head-patches, but even harlequin-patterned ♂ mainly blackish at distance. Flight fast, swinging from side to side; swims buoy-antly with jerking head, tail often cocked (or slowly raised and lowered); dives in rough water, also plunges in from wing; rarely with other ducks. *Ad* ♂ Dark grey-blue with bizarre black-edged white marks on head, breast, scapulars, wings and stern, and rufous crown-bands, chestnut flanks. *Ad* ♀ Dark slate to sooty-brown with white circle behind eyes, 2 patches in front (latter mottled brown when new, merge as whitish face/throat when worn); belly only mottled whitish. *Juv* As ♀, but paler, more olive-brown above; colours variably like ads on head and later upper-parts/flanks during Sep–May, but ♂ still duller in 1st summer with smaller white patches, mottled belly, plain juv wings.

VOICE Usually silent; ♂ piping whistle, ♀ harsh *ek-ek-ek*. HABITAT Surf off rocks. FOOD Molluscs, crustaceans. RANGE 9: esp Dec–Feb (1 pair Jan–May), NBr. (Ice-land, Greenland, N America, NE Asia.)

Surf Scoter *Melanitta perspicillata* 51–56 cm (*c*21 in). Resembles Velvet Scoter (86), but Eider-like profile with deeper, less knobbed bill (♂'s multicoloured), more white/whitish on flatter head, frontal feathers to near nostrils; no white in wings, underwings dark. *Ad* ♂ Dull black but for red-orange and white bill with large black patch near base, white tri-angles on forehead and nape (latter lost during eclipse). *Ad* ♀ Sooty-brown with 2 whitish patches on head-sides (as ♀ Velvet Scoter), clearer in worn plumage and mottled brown after moult in *c*Aug–Nov; also variably distinct whitish nape-patch. *Juv* As ♀, but greyer-brown, with less clear buffish patches on head-sides, no white on nape, mottled whitish or almost white belly; variably as ads, but still mottled belly, after moult in *c*Nov–May; ♂ then

Harlequin

Surf Scoter

white on nape but not forehead, bill as ad from cMar. HABITAT/FOOD As Velvet Scoter. RANGE 166: all months (esp Sep–Apr), most NBr, few Ir/SEBr. (N America.)

Bufflehead *Bucephala albeola* 33–38 cm (c14 in). Like tiny Teal-sized Goldeneye (88) with small bill, puffy head, dark eyes; ♂ has large white bonnet on glossy head, ♀/imm white oblong on rear cheeks and only small white wing-patch in flight. Restless; springs easily from water; no wing-noise in flight. Ad ♂ Black and much white, as ♂ Goldeneye, but head glossed green, purple and bronze, with wide white wedge from below eyes over hindcrown; outer scapulars more evenly white, stern mostly grey. Ad ♀ Darker above but whiter chest than ♀ Goldeneye; white patch on slaty head. Juv Much as ♀; ♂ pale greyish uppertail-coverts from Aug–Sep, white mottling on scapulars/flanks from Oct–Nov and some ad plumage in Mar–Jun, rarely full but for juv wings. HABITAT/FOOD As Goldeneye. RANGE 6: Jan–Mar (Jun), NW/SW/EBr. (N America.)

Hooded Merganser *Mergus cucullatus* 42–48 cm (c17½ in). Smaller, shorter-bodied than Red-breasted Merganser (90), with shorter thin bill and larger head, ♂ mainly black and white with erectile fan crest, ♀/imm darker than Red-breasted (esp bill, head, neck, upperparts) with bushy crest; both much less white (mainly striped) on inner wings. Flight faster, more agile; walks more easily, with body horizontal; secretive; rarely with other ducks. Ad ♂ Head and back black with huge white patch behind eyes (forming black-edged rounded cockade when oblong crest raised); breast white with 2 black sidebands, vermiculated flanks buff shading to rufous; bill black. Ad ♀ Head dark grey-brown with tawny crest, whitish throat; blackish above, greyish and buff below with white belly; bill black, edged orange. Juv As ♀ but browner above, crest shorter, still less white on wings, bill grey with pinkish edges; partial ad plumage in 1st year. HABITAT Shallow wooded lakes, marsh pools. FOOD Fish, invertebrates. RANGE 5: Dec–Jan, most Ir. (N America.)

Bufflehead

Hooded Merganser

KITES, HARRIERS, ETC (Accipitridae)

Black Kite *Milvus migrans* 53–59 cm (*c*22 in). More compact than Red Kite (94) with shorter, less forked tail (often straight-ended when spread) and relatively broader wings similarly bowed forward; darker, browner, with dark-streaked greyish head, duller pale panel on upper wing-coverts, less contrasting underwing-patches (clearer on juv) and brown tail. Flight as Red Kite, but less graceful; likewise glides on slightly arched wings (*cf* dark Marsh Harrier, 94). *Ad* Grey-brown to rufous below, with indistinct paler area at base of primaries. *Juv* Head paler, with darker ear-coverts; upperwing panel more obvious; brighter and cream-streaked below, with paler belly and tail-base (latter can look reddish against light like dull Red Kite), clearer whitish area at base of primaries; as ad after 1st summer moult. HABITAT Open country, by water. FOOD Carrion, rodents, insects, frogs, birds. RANGE 43: esp Apr–Jun, also Jul–Nov, most SE/NEBr. (Eurasia, Africa.)

White-tailed Eagle *Haliaeetus albicilla* 69–91 cm (27–36 in). Bulky with huge bill (*cf* Golden, 102); in flight, head and short wedge-shaped tail protrude equally from long, broad, rectangular wings, giving 'flying door' appearance; ad pale head and white tail, juv mainly dark. Flight rather clumsy with shallow beats, but soars effortlessly with wings almost flat; often hunts low over ground or water; snatches prey from surface or plunges in; perches on rocks, trees or hunched motionless on ground. *Ad* Brown, scaled paler, with yellow bill, buffish head, dark flight-feathers, white tail; wing-coverts/body wear lighter. *Juv* Dark brown, mottled rufous, with grey-black bill, rustier breast and patch on mid wings above, whitish marks on 'armpits' and greater coverts below, variably whitish-centred tail-feathers; mottled whitish above and below from 1st summer/2nd winter; all brown with yellow bill and mottled tail from *c*4th year (not full ad until *c*8th). HABITAT Rocky coasts, estuaries. FOOD Fish, birds, mammals, carrion.

RANGE Bred to *c*1916 (esp NBr, Ir); then vagrant, most Oct–Apr E/SBr; attempted reintroductions Fair Isle (1968), Rhum (since 1975). (N Eurasia to Greenland.)

Pallid Harrier *Circus macrourus* 41–48 cm (16–19 in), ♂ smaller than ♀. Shape as Montagu's (96), but ♂ slimmer, much paler, wing-tips black-wedged; ♀/juv separated from Montagu's by head-pattern. ♂ flight more buoyant, almost tern-like. *Ad* ♂ Pale grey above, white below; narrow black wedge on primaries. *Ad* ♀/juv Very like Montagu's (juv likewise plain below), but clear black eye-stripes, whitish collar behind dark crescent on ear-coverts, emphasised on juv by dark neck-patches. HABITAT Grass-lands. FOOD Voles, birds. RANGE 3: Apr–May, Oct, NE/SBr. (E Europe, SW Asia.)

FALCONS (Falconidae)

Gyrfalcon *Falco rusticolus* 50–62 cm (20–24 in). Larger/stouter than Peregrine (106) with longer broader tail, broader-based and blunter wings; varies from dark grey-brown heavily spotted/barred or streaked below, through range of dark/light grey and whitish intermediates with heavy pale scaling above and variable dark markings below, to largely white. Flight slower than Peregrine with shallower beats; glides and soars on level or slightly bowed wings; hunts low over ground, also stoops like Peregrine. *Darkest ad* Dark grey-brown above, with dark-streaked creamy forehead and often nape, obscure moustaches; below, densely spotted and barred body/wing-coverts contrast with lightly marked flight-feathers/tail, pale area at base of dark-tipped primaries. *Whitest ad* All white but for dark wing-tips and scattered blackish Vs, spots or bars above, sometimes also on flanks. *Juvs* As ads, but marks mainly streaks, cere/legs blue-grey to greenish (not yellow); darkest are heavily streaked below, clearer moustaches; whitest with brownish streaks, sparser below. HABITAT Rocky coasts, fells, open country. FOOD Birds, mammals. RANGE Many (61 since 1958): Sep–May, scattered, esp N/SWBr (most white). (Circumpolar Arctic.)

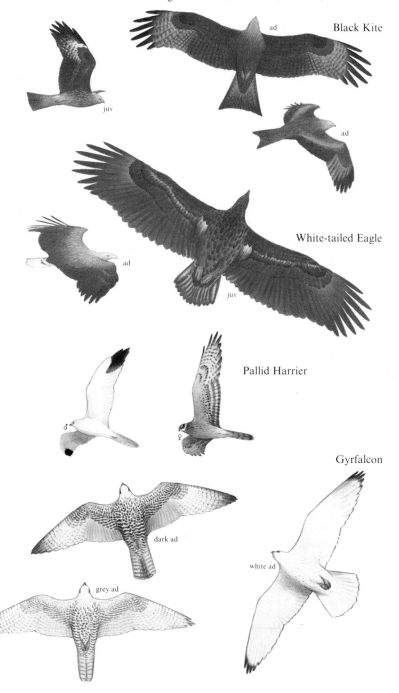

Black Kite

juv

ad

ad

White-tailed Eagle

ad

juv

Pallid Harrier

♂

♀

Gyrfalcon

dark ad

white ad

grey ad

Lesser Kestrel *Falco naumanni* 29–32 cm (c12 in). Very like Kestrel (104), but slimmer with narrower wings, thinner and often wedge-tipped tail; ♂ bluer head and tail, also wing-coverts, whiter below, no moustaches, unspotted back, but ♀ much as ♀ Kestrel; claws pale brown to whitish (not black). Flight looser, shallower, more winnowing; hovers much less, hawks insects far more. *Ad ♂* Crown/hindneck and tail grey-blue, mantle/wing-coverts plain chestnut but outer coverts grey-blue; cream to pink-buff below, plain or lightly spotted, but underwings white, sometimes spotted, with darker tips and trailing edges. *Ad ♀* As ♀ Kestrel, but narrower bars above, obscurer moustaches, paler and less spotted below. *Juv* As ad ♀; less yellow on bill. *1st year ♂* As ad ♂ with moult in Oct–May, but still worn juv flight-feathers and odd spots/bars above. HABITAT Open country. FOOD Insects. RANGE 18: Feb–May, Jul–Nov, most S/EBr. (S Europe, Asia, NW Africa.)

American Kestrel *Falco sparverius* 23–28 cm (9–11 in). Smaller than Merlin (104), with relatively longer tail, shorter thinner wings; 3 black strips on white and buff sides of slate-capped head with rufous central crown; otherwise rufous above barred black, but ♂ plain tail with black band, grey-blue wings. Flight fast, graceful; habitually hovers, soars (showing translucent spots along tips of flight-feathers); perches on trees, wires, buildings, often jerking tail. *Ad ♂* Narrowly barred above, tail with black band, white tip and barred white edges; wing-coverts grey-blue, spotted black; breast/flanks pink-buff, lightly spotted. *Ad ♀* Head duller, whole upperparts browner-rufous and more barred; underparts buff, streaked rufous. *Juvs* Much as ads, but far paler yellowish legs/cere; ♂ browner crown-patch, more barred tail, streaked breast; moults Sep–Oct, but worn juv tail until 1st summer. HABITAT Open country. FOOD Insects, mice, birds. RANGE 2: May–Jun, Shetland/Cornwall. (N/S America.)

Red-footed Falcon *Falco vespertinus* 28–31 cm (c11½ in). Shape as small Hobby (106),

with broader-based wings, longer tail; ♂ dark grey with chestnut 'trousers', red legs; ♀ grey and barred above, with rufous-buff crown/underparts. Flight as Hobby, but faster beats; glides, soars, hawks insects, hovers; perches on trees, wires, bushes, ground; often crepuscular. *Ad ♂* Dark grey, with paler flight-feathers and underbody, chestnut thighs/undertail-coverts; legs/cere/eye-rings red. *Ad ♀* Grey above, barred blackish, inc tail, but head/underparts rufous-buff with cream throat, blackish eye-patches/moustaches; flight-feathers dark above, barred below; legs/cere/eye-rings orange. *Juv* Browner than ♀ above with rufous fringes, streaked crown, whitish half-collar, stronger moustaches; below, creamier and more streaked, broad dark trailing edge to wings; legs/cere/eye-rings yellow. *1st summer ♂* Grey above with rufous nape, worn brown juv flight-feathers and barred tail-sides; variably rufous to grey below; flight-feathers pied in moult in 2nd autumn. HABITAT Open country, trees. FOOD Insects. RANGE 327: mainly Apr–Oct (esp May–Jun), mostly S/EBr. (E Europe, Asia.)

Eleonora's Falcon *Falco eleonorae* 35–41 cm (c15 in). Slim, like large Hobby (106) with even longer narrower wings, longer tail (both less clear on juv); all blackish-grey (cf ♂ Red-footed), or rufous-buff below with heavy streaks whitish throat (cf Hobby), always underwing-coverts darker than flight-feathers. Flight fast, agile, or with flatter, slower beats; soars, stoops as Peregrine (106), hawks insects as Hobby; perches on rocks, trees. *Dark ad* Blackish-slate above (♀ browner), dark grey-brown below with paler-based flight-feathers/tail; cere bluish-yellow (♂) or blue (♀), legs yellow. *Pale ad* Differs mainly in rufous underbody streaked blackish, with cream throat/lower cheeks, black moustaches. *Juvs* Browner than ads, scaled cream/rufous above, tail barred, cere blue, legs greenish; dark form also barred flanks/undertail-coverts; pale form brownish below with broader streaks, white tail-coverts. HABITAT Usually sea-cliffs. FOOD Insects, birds. RANGE 1: Aug, Merseyside. (Mediterranean, NW Africa.)

Lesser Kestrel

American Kestrel

Red-footed Falcon

Eleonora's Falcon

RAILS, CRAKES, GALLINULES (Rallidae)

Sora *Porzana carolina* 20–23 cm (*c*8½ in). Resembles Spotted Crake (116), but has longer neck, shorter wings, yellow bill (no red) with long nostrils; black centre to plain tawny crown, more uniform chest and wing-coverts, whiter long undertail-coverts; ad also has black face/throat, white speck behind eyes; juv black lores, plain buff supercilia and whitish throat. More erect than Spotted Crake; feeds more in open. ♂ *summer* Bold black face/throat; usually only greater coverts speckled. ♂ *winter* After moult in Jul–Sep, black throat mottled grey, grey chest with white fringes (not spots). *Ad* ♀ Usually black more restricted and grey supercilia extending across forehead, wing-coverts more speckled. *Juv* Buff supercilia and underparts, whitish throat and belly, flanks less strongly barred; as ad winter after variable moult in *c*Aug–Feb, but black throat narrower and more mottled (esp ♀), less grey below, bill greener as juv. VOICE Sharp *keek*. HABITAT/FOOD As Spotted Crake, but winters more in salt-marshes. RANGE 6: Sep–Nov, Apr; only 1 since 1920 (Scilly 1973). (N America.)

Little Crake *Porzana parva* 18–20 cm (*c*7½ in). Slender, with longer neck, wings, tail and legs than Baillon's; olive-brown above with indistinct whitish streaks and mostly uniform wing-coverts, grey or buff below with boldly barred undertail but only faint narrow flank-bars, red-based bill, usually green legs. *Ad* ♂ Face and underparts slate-grey, faint white bars on lower flanks; bill pale green with red base. *Ad* ♀ Face pale grey, throat whitish, underparts creamy-buff, faint white bars on greyish flanks; bill as ♂. *Juv* Face creamy-white, underparts creamy-buff, variably barred grey and buff on chest (or chest-sides) and flanks; scapulars and wing-coverts more marked white than ad; bill olive with pinkish gape; much as ads after variable moult in *c*Sep–Jan, but ♂ browner on flanks/belly, ♀ paler buff on belly. VOICE Sharp explosive squawks; ♂ song repeated barking *kwek* dropping into

Sora   Little Crake

juv

juv

ad

♀ winter

♂ summer

guttural ending, ♀ shriller and accelerating into trill. HABITAT/FOOD Much as Spotted Crake (116). RANGE 94: all months, esp Mar–May, Aug–Nov, most E/SBr, also SWIr, NBr. (Cent/E Europe, W Asia.)

Baillon's Crake *Porzana pusilla* 17–18.5 cm (*c*7 in). Rounded, with short neck, wings, tail and legs; ♂♀ resemble ♂ Little Crake, but more rufous above with many small white spots/streaks outlined in black (also on wing-coverts), flanks boldly barred as undertail, bill plain green, legs usually brownish to green-grey. Flight weaker, more fluttering than other crakes. *Ad* Face and underparts slate-blue, black and white bars on lower flanks/belly, bill dark green; ♀ throat often paler grey in summer and whitish in winter (when ♂ paler grey), sometimes brown streak behind eyes. *Juv* Face rufous-buff; chest and upper flanks barred brown and whitish-buff, lower flanks blackish and white; bill olive-brown; much as ads after variable moult in *c*Sep–Jan. VOICE Resembles Little Crake, but song repeated rasping or creaking *trrrrr-trrrrr*. HABITAT/FOOD As Little Crake. RANGE Many before 1900, even nested; only 5 Br since 1958: Feb, May–Jun. (Eurasia, Africa, Australasia.)

American Purple Gallinule *Porphyrula martinica* 31–35 cm (*c*13 in). Size/actions as Moorhen (118), but deeper bill, longer neck and legs; ad purple-blue and green, juv sandier below than juv Moorhen; no dark centre to white undertail, or white/buff line on flanks. *Ad* Head/underparts purple-blue, mantle/wings bronze-green, with some light blue on hindneck and wings; bill red with yellow tip, shield blue-white, legs yellow. *Juv* Olive-brown above but green-tinged mantle/wings, and pale buff to cream below; bill greenish with red-brown base, shield grey-brown, legs green-brown to yellowish; as ad after variable moult in *c*Sep–Mar. HABITAT/FOOD Much as Moorhen. RANGE 1: Nov, Scilly. (Americas north to S Carolina.) NOTE Old World **Purple Gallinule** *Porphyrio porphyrio* sometimes escapes, but far larger with heavy red bill and legs.

Baillon's Crake　　　　　　　　　　　American Purple Gallinule

juv

♂ summer

juv–1st winter

ad

CRANES (Gruidae)

Crane *Grus grus* 106–118 cm (*c*44 in). Tall, stately, with shortish bill, long neck and legs, long tertials drooping over tail; grey (browner-grey with wear) but for black and white head with obscure bare red patch, blackish flight-feathers and 'tail' (imm all brownish). Flight strong, with slow beats of rectangular wings, neck/legs extended; soars like eagle; flocks fly in Vs or lines; sedate walk with long strides, body level, neck curved; often stands more upright; shy. *Ad* Head/upper neck black with white curve, red crown-patch. *Juv/1st winter* Brown to rufous head and mottling on darker body; shorter 'tail'. VOICE Short rolling *krroo*; juvs pipe. HABITAT Marshes, fields. FOOD Esp plant material. RANGE 775+ since 1958 (500+ in 1963, SBr), all months, esp Mar–Jun, Aug–Nov, widely scattered; bred Br/?Ir until *c*1600. (N/Cent Eurasia.) NOTE **Sandhill Crane** *G. canadensis* has occurred (1905, 1981); other species escape, esp Sarus *G. antigone* and Demoiselle *Anthropoides virgo*.

BUSTARDS (Otididae)

Little Bustard *Tetrax tetrax* 41–45 cm (*c*17 in). Compact, duck-sized, with shortish neck; sandy-brown above, finely marked with black; in flight, rounded wings mainly white with black tips and primary-coverts (like giant Snow Bunting). Flight fast, often high, with shallow beats of bowed wings, also gliding grouse-like with occasional flicks; ♂'s wings whistle; walks, runs, crouches in cover with neck extended; rises sharply with wing-rattle; shy/skulking. ♂ *summer* Slate-blue cheeks/throat; black neck with 2 white bands. ♂ *winter* Fine wavy black bars above; head/neck buff, streaked and barred black; breast/belly white, few black spots on flanks. *Ad* ♀ As ♂ winter, but coarse bars above, inc secondaries; more buff and barred on breast/flanks. *Juv/1st winter* As ♀, but black of wings mottled buff, more black marks on secondaries; after moult in Mar–Apr, 1st summer ♂ much as winter ♂. VOICE Grunt when flushed. HABITAT Grassland, crops. FOOD

Crane   Little Bustard

ad

juv/1st winter

ad

♀

♂ summer

♀

Plants, invertebrates. RANGE *c*100 (only 10 since 1958): all months, esp Oct–Jan, esp E/SBr. (S Europe, W Asia, NW Africa.)

Houbara Bustard *Chlamydotis undulata* 51–56 cm (*c*25 in). Goose-sized; longish neck, long tail, long rather narrow and pointed wings with little white (like huge Stone-curlew); sandy-buff, above, finely marked with black; grey foreneck, long black and white tufts on neck-sides. Flight low; slow, rather flicked wing-beats; walks sedately, or runs with short steps and body horizontal. *Ad ♂* Black-tipped white crest, whitish nape, fine buff and black tips on grey throat. *Ad ♀* Shorter mainly black crest, buff nape, stronger tips on throat. *1st winter* Much as ad ♀, but imm ♀ has tail barred brown (not slate), no crest; both ♂♀ tend to show brown on white tail-tips, rufous tinge at base of black on outer primaries, white mottling at tips. HABITAT Deserts, steppes; vagrants in fields. FOOD Seeds, plants, invertebrates. RANGE 5: Oct–Dec, EBr (last Suffolk 1962). (Asia, N Africa.)

Great Bustard *Otis tarda* ♂ 95–105 cm (*c*40 in), ♀ 75–85 cm (*c*31½ in). Swan- to goose-sized, turkey-shaped, stout, deep-chested, with long thick neck, longish tail, and very long white and black spread-tipped wings, but ♀ slighter; rufous above boldly marked with black, white below, head grey. Flight powerful with slow, shallow beats of bowed wings; very shy. ♂ *summer* Head grey, throat and long side-whiskers white, chest rufous marked with black. ♂ *winter* Head and throat grey, short side-whiskers whitish, only sides of chest rufous and black. ♀ *summer* Head grey, very short side-whiskers, foreneck tinged buff; more dark marks on white of wings than ♂. ♀ *winter* Rufous and black bars on crown, no side-whiskers, foreneck grey. *1st year* Much as small winter ♀, but narrow pointed outer primaries with buff tips, mottling on secondaries and greater coverts. HABITAT Grassland, crops. FOOD Plants, insects, voles. RANGE 10 since 1958: Jan–May, Aug, esp EBr; bred Br to 19th century; recent attempt at reintroduction (Wilts). (Cent/S Eurasia.)

Houbara Bustard

Great Bustard

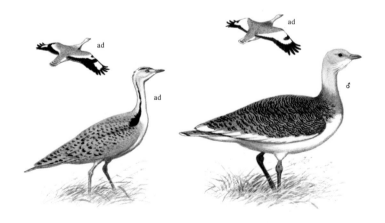

STILTS, AVOCETS (Recurvirostridae)

Black-winged Stilt *Himantopus himantopus*
36–40 cm (*c*15 in). Slender, long-necked,
with needle-bill, thin triangular wings,
extraordinarily long pink legs; white,
with dark back and wings. Flight direct,
usually low, with neck normally drawn in,
legs trailing; often glides, esp before
alighting when legs dangle as rudders or
brakes; walks delicately with long strides,
neck hunched or extended, and wades
deeply; bends legs to pick up food and
even more to spring into air; bobs head to
and fro when suspicious; often rests on
one leg. *Ad ♂* Mantle glossy black; crown/
nape black or mainly white in summer,
grey-brown in winter. *Ad ♀* Mantle dark
brown against glossy black wings; crown/
nape usually mottled dusky. *Juv* All upperparts marked with buff, flight-feathers
mostly white-tipped; legs pink-grey. *1st
winter* After moult in Jul–Feb, as ad ♀,
but flight-feathers white-tipped (sometimes also 1st summer), wing-coverts buff-
fringed. VOICE Shrill *kyik-kyik-kyik*.
HABITAT Wet marshes, lagoons. FOOD
Insects. RANGE 163: Apr–Feb, esp Apr–
Jun, Aug–Sep, most SBr; 2 pairs bred
in Notts in 1945. (S Eurasia, Africa,
Australasia, N/S America.)

COURSERS, PRATINCOLES (Glareolidae)

Cream-coloured Courser *Cursorius cursor*
22–24 cm (*c*9 in). Slim, plover-like, with
short decurved dark bill, long creamy legs,
short tail, surprisingly large wings; mainly
sandy, but white supercilia and black eye-
stripes meeting on nape, black underwings and outer upperwings, white-tipped
secondaries and tail. Flight direct, fast;
runs fast with pauses, crouches to hide.
Ad Uniform sandy above, breast greyer;
head-marks white and black, grey on rear
crown. *Juv* More buff, barred brown above,
spotted on breast; head-marks cream and
brownish; legs greyer. *1st winter* More as
ad after moult in May–Nov, but still juv
buff-tipped primaries, usually some juv
coverts. VOICE Harsh *praak-praak*.
HABITAT Deserts; vagrants in dunes, fields.
FOOD Insects. RANGE 32: Sep–Dec, esp
Oct, widely scattered. (SW Asia, Africa.)

Collared Pratincole *Glareola pratincola*
24–27 cm (*c*10 in). Rather tern-like wader
with long pointed wings, deep-forked tail,
short legs, stubby bill and red gape-patch;
brown above, with white rump, white-
tipped secondaries, chestnut underwings
(not easy to see). Flight buoyant, erratic,
tern-like, hawking insects; walks or runs
like plover; often crepuscular. *Ad summer*
Uniform brown above, black line round
creamy throat; ♂ lores black, ♀ olive-
brown. *Ad winter* Streaked head with ill-
defined border of streaks round throat.
Juv Mottled buff and blackish above,
heavily streaked head and throat-border,
shorter tail; much as ad after moult in
Aug–Nov, but buff-tipped inner secondaries. VOICE Tern-like *kik* or *kirrikik
kit-ik*. HABITAT Dry mud, grass, esp near
water. FOOD Insects. RANGE 61 + of 88
pratincoles: most May–Jul (Feb–Nov),
scattered. (S Europe, SW Asia, Africa.)

Black-winged Pratincole *Glareola nordmanni* 24–27 cm (*c*10 in). As Collared, but
darker above (little contrast between
coverts and flight-feathers), secondaries
not white-tipped, underwings black, less
red on gape. Plumage sequence similar;
black lores in spring, far more on ♂.
RANGE 16 + (see above): Aug–Sep (May–
Sep), esp SBr. (S Russia, W Asia.)

TYPICAL WADERS (Scolopacidae)

Wilson's Phalarope *Phalaropus tricolor*
22–26 cm (*c*9½ in), ♂ smaller than ♀.
Larger than other phalaropes (146), with
longer needle-bill, longer black (summer)
or yellowish legs; very pale in winter, no
wing-bar but white rump; dark and chestnut down neck-sides on to back in summer.
Often runs; swims less. *♂ summer* Brown
or grey-brown above; dark brown eye-
stripes and dull cinnamon on neck and
back. *♀ summer* Blue-grey above; black
eye-stripes extend into chestnut on back.
Ad winter Pale grey above. *1st winter* By
end Aug/Sep, grey above with many buff
fringes; later, as ad winter (sometimes
through 1st summer). VOICE Low croak.
HABITAT Marsh, mud. FOOD Invertebrates.
RANGE 134: May–Nov (esp Aug–Oct), all
since 1954, widely scattered. (N America.)

Black-winged Stilt

♂ summer

juv

ad

Cream-coloured Courser

ad

ad

1st winter

Wilson's Phalarope

1st winter

♂ summer

♀ summer

1st winter

Black-winged Pratincole

ad

juv

♂ summer

Collared Pratincole

ad

♂ summer

PLOVERS (Charadriidae)

Semipalmated Plover *Charadrius semi-palmatus* 17–19 cm (*c*7 in). Very like Ringed Plover (122), but neater, slimmer, with stubbier bill, smaller rounded head; webbing both sides of middle toes (not just outer); breast-band and white collar narrower, wing-bar shorter and less distinct (esp at base), head-markings less clear, secondaries darker, legs duller; call distinct. Differs also as follows. *Ad* Less white behind eyes (sometimes almost missing in summer), bill-base with less orange; in winter, mask/breast-band always largely brown. *Juv/1st winter* Supercilia more obscure, buff edges to wing-coverts clearer, bill blackish with little yellow-pink at base, legs duller greenish to yellowish-flesh. VOICE Plaintive *chur-wit*, piping *chip*. RANGE 1: Oct–Nov, Scilly. (N America.)

Killdeer *Charadrius vociferus* 23–25 cm (*c*9½ in). Much larger than Ringed Plover (122) with longer black bill, smaller head, long wedge-tail, longer legs; 2 black chest-bands, orange rump, black on tail, bold white wing-bar. *1st winter* Till *c*Jan some scapulars/inner medians fringed pale (ad rufous). VOICE Loud repeated *killdea*. HABITAT Grass or ploughed fields, gravel pits, reservoirs, coasts. FOOD Insects, crustaceans. RANGE 33: Nov–Mar, widely scattered. (N/S America.)

Greater Sand Plover *Charadrius leschen-aultii* 22–24 cm (*c*9 in). Thickset, hunched, with heavy bill, biggish head, longish (usually grey) legs; brown and white, with white wing-bar and tail-sides, brownish patches at breast-sides in winter, no white collar. *Ad summer* Black forecrown/mask, rufous nape and breast-band; ♀ often duller. *Ad winter* Grey-brown above, pale forehead and supercilia; brown breast-patches, often joined by thin line. *1st winter* As ad, but inner medians fringed buff; breast-patches warmer buff. VOICE Short trilling *chirrirrip*. HABITAT Mud/sand by fresh or salt water. FOOD Invertebrates. RANGE 3: Nov–Feb, Jun, Sussex/Avon/Orkney. (S Asia.)

Lesser Golden Plover *Pluvialis dominica* 23–25 cm (*c*9½ in). Smaller, slighter than Golden Plover (124), with longer bill and legs, narrower wings extending beyond tail; underwings buff-grey. *Ad summer* Black below to flanks/undertail, ♀ with some white speckling. *Ad winter* American race *(P.d. dominica)* greyer and Asiatic race *(P.d. fulva)* more buff, both lightly mottled on breast, with blackish crown and clearer supercilia (*cf* winter Dotterel, 126). *Juv/1st winter* As ad, but brown-speckled belly/flanks to at least Dec, more marked on American race; Asiatic race much yellower on head and body. VOICE Flight-call soft *quee*, whistled *queedel-oo*. HABITAT Fields, marshes, mud. RANGE 66: Apr–Feb (esp Sep–Oct), scattered, most SIr, SW/EBr. (N America, NE Asia.)

Sociable Plover *Chettusia gregaria* 28–31 cm (*c*11½ in). Size of Lapwing (126), but longer black bill and legs, less rounded narrower wings; grey-brown, with dark cap, pale supercilia meeting on nape, white tail with black patch near tip, white secondaries, black primaries. *Ad summer* Black crown, white supercilia; ♂ belly black and chestnut, ♀'s often greyer and speckled white. *Ad winter* With moult in Jun–Nov, crown brown, supercilia buff, breast mottled, belly white. *Juv/1st winter* Buff fringes above (many kept to spring) and breast distinctly streaked till *c*Nov. VOICE Short whistle, harsh *etch-etch-etch*. HABITAT Grassy/sandy areas, near water. FOOD Insects. RANGE 24: Jul–May, esp Oct, E/SBr. (SE Russia, W/Cent Asia.)

White-tailed Plover *Chettusia leucura* 26–28 cm (*c*10¾ in). Slimmer than Sociable, longer legs yellow; grey-brown above, pale face; white belly, tail and black-edged band from secondaries to base of primaries. Elegant, stretches neck when alert; stoops on long legs. *Ad* Breast rufous and grey; mantle/coverts tinged mauve, belly pinkish. *Juv* Blotched black and buff above; breast browner. *1st winter* As ad from *c*Oct, but inner medians buff-fringed. VOICE Loud *kee-wik*. HABITAT Marshy shallows. FOOD Insects. RANGE 2: Jul, Warwicks/Dorset. (SW/Cent Asia.)

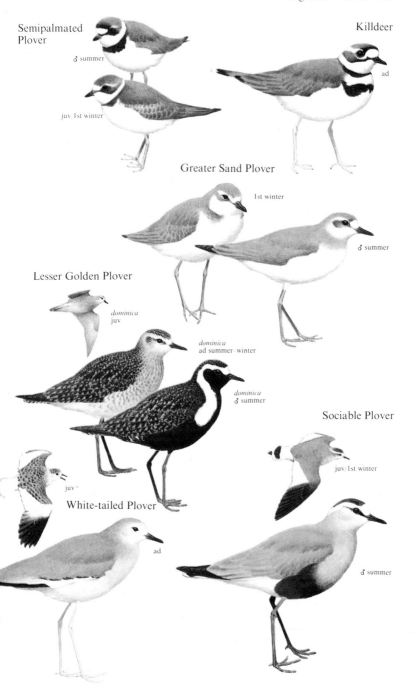

Semipalmated Plover

♂ summer

juv/1st winter

Killdeer

ad

Greater Sand Plover

1st winter

♂ summer

Lesser Golden Plover

dominica juv

dominica ad summer-winter

dominica ♂ summer

Sociable Plover

juv/1st winter

juv

White-tailed Plover

ad

♂ summer

TYPICAL WADERS (Scolopacidae)

Broad-billed Sandpiper *Limicola falcinellus* 16–17 cm (*c*6½ in). Smaller than Dunlin (132), with long broad kink-tipped bill, abrupt forehead, shorter legs looking set far back; summer/juv very dark above with double supercilia; in winter, blackish shoulders (*cf* Sanderling, 128), at least traces of head-pattern, often green tinge to dark legs and paler-based bill. Very sluggish. *Ad summer* By May, blackish above with bold buff/whitish fringes, much blacker with wear; white below with heavy streaks on throat/chest, arrows on flanks. *Ad winter* With moult in Aug–Jan, grey-brown above, coverts fringed white, lessers blackish; double supercilia often still clear; breast thinly streaked grey-brown. *Juv* As ad summer above, but coverts edged pale buff, cheeks/breast buffish with faint brown streaks; as ad winter after moult in *c*Sep–Dec, but buff-fringed inner medians. VOICE Dry trilled *tirrreek*. HABITAT Saltmarshes, creeks, pools. RANGE 65: May–Sep, also Oct–Nov, scattered, esp E/SBr. (N Eurasia.)

Semipalmated Sandpiper *Calidris pusilla* 14–15.5 cm (*c*5¾ in). Very like Little Stint (128), but slightly bulkier, with blunter-tipped and stouter-based bill, and partly webbed toes; much overlap in pattern and only juv reliably separable by colour (rather drab above with less chestnut, no whitish V lines). Plumage sequence similar. VOICE Low husky *chirrp*. RANGE 27: Jul–Dec, esp SWIr/SWBr. (N America.)

Western Sandpiper *Calidris mauri* 15.5–17 cm (*c*6½ in). Larger than Little Stint (128), with character more of small Dunlin (132), including usually longer, more droop-tipped and stouter-based bill, longer-looking legs; much like Semi-palmated, even to partly webbed toes, but summer/juv more rufous above (often partly retained into winter on head/scapulars) and stronger-streaked below, with broader supercilia. Plumage sequence similar. Wades much more than stints. VOICE High thin *cheet*. RANGE 6: most Jul–Oct, SIr/SBr. (N America, NE Asia.)

Least Sandpiper *Calidris minutilla* 13.5–14.5 cm (*c*5½ in). Smaller than Little Stint (128) with thinner bill, smaller squarer head, shorter wings, shorter and usually greenish or yellowish legs (*cf* Temminck's, 128); clearer breast-band of brown streaks, summer/juv much darker. HABITAT Grassy marshes, pools, less on open mud. VOICE High grating *kreeet*. RANGE 23: most Aug–Oct, esp Ir, WBr. (N America.)

White-rumped Sandpiper *Calidris fuscicollis* 16–18 cm (*c*6¾ in). Slim with short straight bill, long wings projecting beyond tail, short legs, horizontal stance; white above tail, very faint wing-bar (*cf* Curlew Sandpiper, 132). *Ad summer* Black-brown above streaked with chestnut, buff, grey and whitish; white below with brown-streaked breast/flanks. *Ad winter* After moult in *c*Aug–Oct, grey-brown above and on streaked breast, coverts still fringed whitish. *Juv* As ad summer, but bolder-marked above with more whitish fringes; coverts broadly fringed buff and whitish; streaked breast/flanks tinged grey-buff; much as ad winter with moult in Sep–Jan, but mantle more mixed with brown, inner medians fringed buff. VOICE Thin squeaky *jeet*. HABITAT Mud-flats, beaches, lagoons, marshy pools. RANGE 199: most months, esp Aug–Nov, widely scattered, most SIr, SW/EBr. (N America.)

Baird's Sandpiper *Calidris bairdii* 17–19 cm (*c*7 in). Shape and stance as White-rumped Sandpiper (only similar wader with wings projecting well beyond tail; distinctively buffish head/breast, bold supercilia, blotched or scaled mantle, dark rump/uppertail, short thin wing-bar. *Ad summer* Blackish and buff blotches on mantle; coverts grey-brown fringed pale buff. *Ad winter* With moult in *c*Aug–Oct, mottled grey-brown and buff above; coverts fringed whitish. *Juv* Blackish mantle scaled whitish; coverts fringed tawny; breast brighter buff, less streaks; as ad winter by *c*Nov, but inner medians still fringed tawny. VOICE Trilled *krreep*. HABITAT Stony and grassy pools. RANGE 88: Aug–Oct (May–Nov), scattered, most SIr, SW/EBr. (N America, NE Asia.)

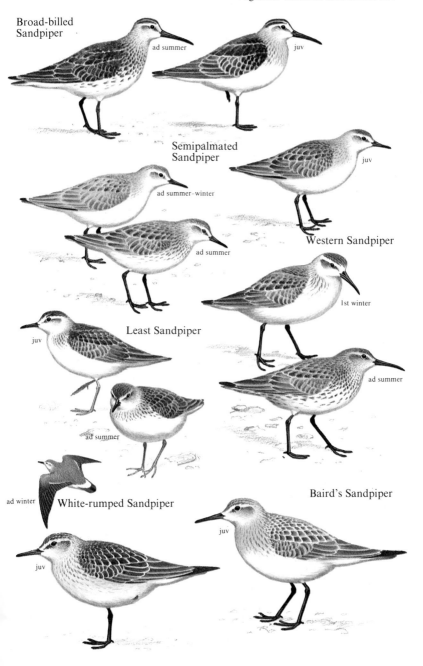

Broad-billed
Sandpiper

ad summer

juv

Semipalmated
Sandpiper

juv

ad summer-winter

ad summer

Western Sandpiper

1st winter

Least Sandpiper

juv

ad summer

ad summer

ad winter White-rumped Sandpiper

Baird's Sandpiper

juv

juv

Sharp-tailed Sandpiper *Calidris acuminata* 17–21 cm (*c*7 in). Like Pectoral (130), inc tail-pattern, but rather portlier with slightly shorter straighter bill, flatter crown; whiter supercilia wider behind eyes, cap more rufous than mantle, no clear-cut gorget, streaked under tail. *Ad summer* Dark brown above, fringed tawny and grey-buff; scalloped/V-marked on buff breast/white flanks. *Ad winter* Grey-brown coverts whitish-edged; breast grey-buff, lightly marked, merging into white belly. *Juv* Bolder cap/supercilia, whitish face; blackish above, fringed rufous and cream; orange-buff breast, streaked necklace; as ad by *c*Nov, but buff-edged brown inner medians. VOICE Soft *weep* or *trrt*. RANGE 15: Aug–Oct (Jan, Apr), most E/Cent/SBr. (NE Siberia.)

Buff-breasted Sandpiper *Tryngites subruficollis* 19–21 cm (*c*8 in). Short bill, small head, longish neck; scaly above, all buff below; pale eye-rings (bare-faced look), plain rump, no wing-bar, white on underwings, yellow legs (*cf* juv Ruff). Flight low, twisting; erect stance, high steps; tame. *Ad* Blackish above, scaled buff; dark spots at chest-sides. *Juv* Browner above, scaled creamy; spots paler; as ad after moult in Oct–Dec, but worn coverts with dark subterminal band. VOICE Trilled *pr-r-r-reet*, sharp *tik*. HABITAT Short grass. FOOD Insects. RANGE 388: Sep–Oct (Apr–Nov), esp Ir, SWBr. (NW America.)

Stilt Sandpiper *Micropalama himantopus* 20–22 cm (*c*8¼ in). Slender with longish droop-tipped bill, long spindly greenish or green legs; bold supercilia, white rump, plain wings with darker flight-feathers. Actions recall Curlew Sandpiper (132). *Ad summer* Blackish above with pale fringes, chestnut cheeks/nape; barred black-brown below. *Ad winter* Brown-grey with white fringes; white below. *Juv* Dark brown with grey-brown coverts, fringed pale buff; whitish below with buff throat/chest, few dark streaks. *1st winter* As ad winter, but some dark juv feathers remain. VOICE Low husky *chu*. HABITAT Marshes, mudflats. FOOD Invertebrates. RANGE 13: Jul–Oct (Apr), SE/N/WBr, SIr. (N America.)

Great Snipe *Gallinago media* 27–29 cm (*c*11 in). Bulkier than Snipe (136), shorter stouter bill, bigger head, broader wings; less striped above, largely barred below, with mealy head, white-edged dark central wing-panel and obscure pale rear edge. Flight slower, straighter, usually brief, with bill more level, like small Woodcock (136). *Ad* Coverts broadly tipped white; tail-corners white. *Juv* Thin covert-tips, tail more as Snipe; as ad by *c*Dec. VOICE Silent, or gruff croak. HABITAT/FOOD As Snipe; more in dry grass/heather. RANGE 226: Aug–May, most EBr. (N Eurasia.)

Long-billed Dowitcher *Limnodromus scolopaceus* 27–31.5 cm (*c*11½ in). Chunky, with Snipe-like bill (5½–8 cm), shortish legs; whitish supercilia, tips to secondaries, wedge on back; tail-bars blackish, wider than white between. Feeds with sewing-machine action. *Ad summer* Blackish above, fringed pink-buff, but many coverts greyish; all brick-red below, well marked, chest-sides barred. *Ad winter* After moult in Aug–Sep, grey-brown, fringed white on inner medians; grey neck/chest finely streaked, white below. *Juv* Dark brown, fringed red-buff; tertials plain; crown and neck/breast greyish, obscurely speckled, belly buff; as ad after moult in Sep–Dec, but worn juv wings/tail, buff-tipped inner medians. VOICE High *keek*, 1–3 times; other mono/polysyllabic calls. HABITAT More by fresh water. FOOD Invertebrates. RANGE 71 + (? nearly all) of 185 dowitchers: all months (esp Sep–Nov), scattered Br/Ir. (N America, NE Asia.)

Short-billed Dowitcher *Limnodromus griseus* 26–30 cm (*c*11 in). *Very* like Long-billed, overlapping bill-length (5–7 cm); tail-bars browner, usually narrower than white between; summer/juv distinct. *Ad summer* Paler orange-red below, less marked, chest-sides spotted, belly whitish; moult in Jul–Aug. *Juv* Fringes above wider/paler buff; tertials tiger-striped; crown brown, neck/breast buff, more spotted; moult in *c*Oct. VOICE Soft rattled *tu-tu-tut*; other mono/polysyllabic calls. HABITAT More on coastal flats. RANGE 2 + (see above): Oct–Nov, SEBr. (N America.)

Sharp-tailed Sandpiper

juv

ad summer

Buff-breasted Sandpiper

Stilt Sandpiper

ad winter

1st winter

ad

ad summer

Great Snipe

ad

Long-billed Dowitcher

ad winter

ad

ad summer

Short-billed Dowitcher

ad winter

ad summer

juv

juv

Upland Sandpiper *Bartramia longicauda* 25–28 cm (*c*10½ in). Short thin bill, small head, long thin neck, long wings, longish wedge-tail; head/body pattern like tiny Whimbrel (140), but rump and tail-centre dark, whitish underwings boldly barred, legs yellow. Flight low, flicking like Common Sandpiper (144), or high with strong beats, head withdrawn; runs plover-like; readily perches on posts; shy. *Ad* Scapulars/coverts barred blackish. *Juv/1st winter* Scapulars darker/unbarred, coverts paler/scaled brown. VOICE Mournful whistle. FOOD Grass, stubble. FOOD Insects. RANGE 33: Sep–Dec, scattered, esp SWBr/SIr. (N America.)

Marsh Sandpiper *Tringa stagnatilis* 22–24 cm (*c*9 in). Like small, slender Greenshank (142), with needle-bill, long spindly green legs. Active, graceful. *Ad summer* Boldly spotted blackish. *Ad winter* Paler, more uniform, coverts scaled white; white face and underparts. *Juv* Mantle/coverts dark brown heavily marked buff; usually as ad by Oct, but many brown coverts. VOICE Weak *teu*, sharp *chik*. HABITAT Marshes. FOOD Invertebrates. RANGE 33: Apr–Oct, esp E/SBr. (SE Europe, Asia.)

Greater Yellowlegs *Tringa melanoleuca* 30–33 cm (*c*12½ in). Shape as Greenshank (142); paler above, more barred tail, square whitish rump, bright yellow legs projecting beyond tail. Actions similar. Plumage sequences as smaller slighter Lesser Yellowlegs, but ad more boldly marked below in summer, head more streaked in winter, juv darker above. VOICE Greenshank-like *teu* 3–5 times. HABITAT/FOOD As Lesser Yellowlegs, but more by salt water. RANGE 24: esp Jul–Oct, mainly Ir, S/WBr. (N America.)

Lesser Yellowlegs *Tringa flavipes* 24–27 cm (*c*10 in). Smaller, slimmer than Redshank (142), with thin black bill, long spindly yellow legs projecting well beyond tail; pale-spotted above, squared whitish rump, barred tail. Actions like Wood Sandpiper (144), but flight slower. *Ad summer* Black-brown above, spotted whitish; breast/flanks streaked and

barred. *Ad winter* Grey-brown above with fewer spots, tertials barred; thin breast-streaks. *Juv* Browner with pale spots, inc tertials; breast greyer, streaked. *1st winter* As ad with moult in Aug–Jan, but scapulars and tertials brown with buff notches. VOICE Flat *tu* 1–2 times. HABITAT Marshes. FOOD Invertebrates. RANGE 151: all months, esp Ir, S/NEBr. (N America.)

Solitary Sandpiper *Tringa solitaria* 19–21 cm (*c*7¾ in). Like small Green Sandpiper (144), also with dark underwings, but paler olive-brown above, obvious white eye-rings, dark rump, barred tail-sides whiter; wings extend beyond tail. Actions/plumage sequences similar; juv chest more buff. VOICE Thin *pzik*, piping *pit-weet-weet*. HABITAT Muddy streams, marshes, pools. FOOD Insects. RANGE 20: Jul–Oct, esp SIr, SBr. (N America.)

Terek Sandpiper *Xenus cinereus* 22–24 cm (*c*9 in). Like large Common Sandpiper (144), but long tapering upcurved bill, short orange-yellow legs; greyer-brown above, dark 'shoulders', white trailing edge to wings. Similar bobbing; rushes around, seems to trip on to bill as it picks food. *Ad summer* Blackish bands on scapulars; bill dark. *Ad winter* Uniform above; bill orange-based. *Juv* Scapulars streaked blackish, coverts fringed buff; as ad with moult in Sep–Jan. VOICE Sharp whistled *wit-e-wit*. HABITAT Mud-flats. FOOD Invertebrates. RANGE 18: May–Sep, esp E/SBr. (NE Europe, Siberia.)

Spotted Sandpiper *Actitis macularia* 18–20 cm (*c*7½ in). Shape as Common Sandpiper (144), but shorter tail; in autumn/winter, greyer above, shoulders more barred, wing-bar shorter, tail-sides less white, usually yellowish bill-base and legs. *Ad summer* Spotted below; bill-base/legs flesh-pink. *Ad winter* Brown-grey above, indistinct blackish bars on wing-coverts (*cf* juv). *Juv* More uniform greyish above, tertials plain with thin buff tips and coverts boldly barred blackish and buff; as ad with moult in Sep–Jan. VOICE Sharp *peet-weet*. RANGE 53: all months, most SW/SBr; nested NBr 1975. (N America.)

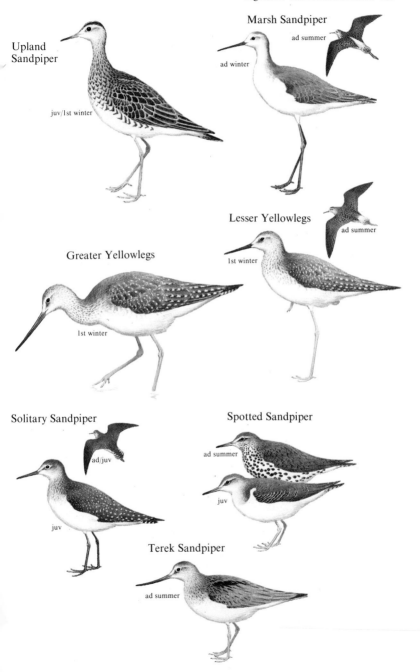

Upland
Sandpiper

juv/1st winter

Marsh Sandpiper

ad summer

ad winter

Lesser Yellowlegs

ad summer

1st winter

Greater Yellowlegs

1st winter

Solitary Sandpiper

ad/juv

juv

Spotted Sandpiper

ad summer

juv

Terek Sandpiper

ad summer

GULLS (Laridae)

Laughing Gull *Larus atricilla* 37–41 cm
(*c*15½ in). Just smaller than Common Gull
(156), longer droop-tipped bill, thinner
wings, longer legs; ad back/wings slate-
grey, almost plain black wing-tips, black
hood in summer; 1st year has much dark
grey on head and underparts, brown and
blackish wings, white rump, grey tail with
broad black band. Flight light, graceful.
Ad Neat black wing-ends, small white tips
to inner primaries; in *c*Feb–Oct, head
black (white eye-crescents at all ages),
bill/legs dull red; in *c*Aug–Mar, hindhead
grey with blackish eye/ear-marks, bill
legs blackish. *1st year* Head, breast and
flanks with much dark grey, but whitish
face and belly (head variably hooded in
summer); outer wings/secondaries mainly
blackish, coverts brown; bill/legs black.
2nd year More as ad, but wing-tips black
almost to carpal joint, traces of tail-band
and bar on secondaries, summer hood
often incomplete. HABITAT Coasts. FOOD
Fish, aquatic invertebrates. RANGE 28:
Feb–Dec, widely scattered. (N America.)

Franklin's Gull *Larus pipixcan* 33–36 cm
(*c*13 in). Smaller, rounder-winged than
Black-headed (154); dark grey Laughing,
but smaller, dumpier, with shortish
wings, tail and legs, shorter bill, ad
differing in pied wing-tips and grey-
centred tail, winter/imms in half-hood,
thicker white eye-crescents and white-
tipped primaries, 1st winter also in whiter
underparts/underwings, grey inner
primaries, narrower tail-band not reaching
corners. Flies buoyantly, hawks insects,
picks from surface, follows plough. *Ad*
Black on wing-tips surrounded by white;
in *c*Apr–Sep, head black, rosy tinge
below; in *c*Aug–May, half-hood, bill/legs
blackish or still red. *1st winter* Blackish
half-hood, white underparts tinged grey at
breast-sides, brown wing-coverts, blackish
flight-feathers and tail-band, white-tipped
primaries; bill/legs blackish. *1st summer*
Full or partial hood, dark grey wings with
blackish ends like 2nd year Laughing but
for white-tipped primaries; sometimes
faint tail-band and bar on secondaries;

bill/legs blackish or bill red-based. *2nd
winter* As ad, but more black on wing-tips,
no whitish line on inside edge. HABITAT
Coasts, lakes, fields. FOOD Insects. RANGE 6:
Oct–May, Jul, most S/EBr. (N America.)

Bonaparte's Gull *Larus philadelphia* 30–33
cm (*c*12½ in). Like small Black-headed
(154); similar pattern on less pointed
wings, but white below on primaries, and
always largely black bill; whole ad head
grey-black with bold white eye-crescents
in *c*Mar–Oct, more orange-red legs;
winter plumages with blacker ear-spot,
grey nape; 1st year also has darker brown
carpal bar, inner primaries with neater
black border and white tips. Plumage
sequence as Black-headed. Flight more
tern-like, with quicker beats, dipping to
surface to feed. HABITAT As Black-headed.
FOOD Invertebrates. RANGE 34: Jun–Apr,
scattered, most S/EBr. (N America.)

Slender-billed Gull *Larus genei* 41–45 cm
(*c*17 in). Larger than Black-headed (154)
with longer bill, flat forehead, long neck;
wings similar, but more white on outer
primaries at all ages, paler carpal bar
on 1st year; head all white (except juv),
obscure eye/ear-marks in winter; ad pink-
tinged in summer, bill/legs dark red/
orange-red (bill looking black), eyes pale,
1st year bill/legs paler. Plumage sequence
(except head) as Black-headed. Head/neck
droop in low flight, tilted forward on
water. HABITAT Coasts. FOOD Fish,
invertebrates. RANGE 4: Apr, Jun–Sep,
SBr. (N Africa, S Europe, S/Cent Asia.)

Ring-billed Gull *Larus delawarensis* 43–47
cm (*c*17½ in). Like large Common (156),
bulkier with stouter bill, flatter head; ad
paler grey with faint eyebrows, fiercer
expression (like Herring), less white on
folded tertials, clear black band on yellow
bill, pale eyes; 1st year more spotted on
nape and flanks, blacker outerwings and
secondaries, grey greater coverts, less
distinct tail-band, bill dark-tipped but
band appearing in 1st summer, eyes dark
until 2nd winter. Plumage sequence and
HABITAT/FOOD As Common. RANGE 37:
Nov–Sep, esp SWBr, WIr. (N America.)

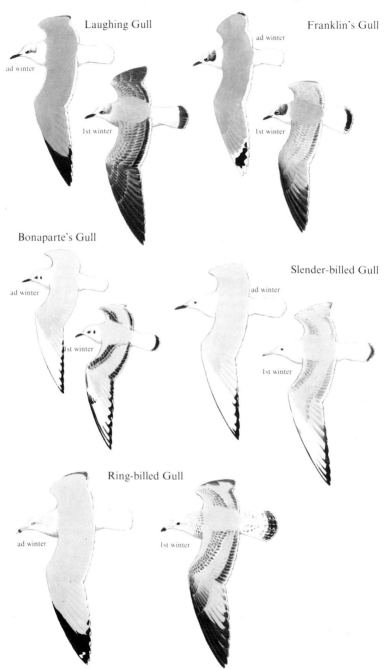

Laughing Gull

ad winter

1st winter

Franklin's Gull

ad winter

1st winter

Bonaparte's Gull

ad winter

1st winter

Slender-billed Gull

ad winter

1st winter

Ring-billed Gull

ad winter

1st winter

Great Black-headed Gull *Larus ichthyaetus*
60–67 cm (*c*25 in). Near size of Great
Black-backed (162), but slighter, with flat
forehead, peaked hindcrown, longer wings,
tertials often humped; ad pale grey back,
much white on outer wings, black summer
hood, dark winter mask, in 1st year wide
clear tail-band and wings of imm Common
Gull type, with grey mantle and white
underparts like small gulls. *Ad* Jagged
black band near wing-tips; in *c*Jan–Sep,
head black (white eye-crescents at all
ages), bill yellow with black band and
red tip, legs yellow; in *c*Aug–Feb, head
white with dark mask behind eyes, bill/
legs duller. *1st year* Head/body much as
ad winter, but nape/breast-sides mottled
blackish; wings banded brown/grey-
brown/blackish; legs and black-tipped bill
grey-flesh. *2nd year* More as ad (mainly
pale grey wings, variable hood in summer),
but largely black outer primaries, narrow
tail-band. *3rd year* Blacker wing-ends
than ad, often faint tail-band. HABITAT
Coasts, lakes. FOOD Fish. RANGE 6: Aug–
May, esp SBr. (S Russia, W/Cent Asia.)

Ross's Gull *Rhodostethia rosea* 30–33 cm
(*c*12½ in). Size much as Little Gull (152);
tiny bill, dove-like head, short legs,
long pointed wings, wedge-tail; ad pinkish below, grey underwings; 1st year dark
tail-band, W on wings/rump (*cf* Little
Gull, Kittiwake). Flight buoyant, shear-
ing, or pigeon-like with deep beats;
hovers to pick from water; walks with
short steps, nodding head. *Ad* Thin black
leading edge to outer wings, secondaries
white; in *c*Feb–Oct, thin neck-ring, rich
pink below, orange-red legs; in *c*Aug–
Apr, eye/ear-marks, greyish hindneck,
duller legs. *1st year* Dusky W on wings/
rump, black tail-band, both brownish by
summer, when neck-ring and pink often
develop; more white on hindwing than
Little Gull. HABITAT Coasts. FOOD
Invertebrates, fish. RANGE 25: all months,
esp Nov–Jan, Apr–May, most N/EBr, but
even SIr. (NE Siberia, arctic America.)

Ivory Gull *Pagophila eburnea* 42–47 cm
(*c*17 in). Plump, pigeon-like, with short
neck, short blackish legs, pointed wings;

all white, with dark marks in 1st year.
Flight strong, tern-like; rolling walk. *Ad*
Bill greyish tipped yellow-orange, eye-
rings red. *1st year* Blackish face and
spotting on wings/upperbody, all less or
lost by summer; black-tipped primaries,
broken tail-band; bill duller, eye-rings
black. HABITAT Coasts. FOOD Invertebrates, fish, carrion. RANGE 98: Aug–Jun,
esp Oct–Feb, esp N/EBr. (High Arctic.)

TERNS (Sternidae)

Caspian Tern *Sterna caspia* 48–56 cm
(*c*20½ in). Near size of Herring Gull (156),
with huge orange-red bill, shallow tail-
fork, longish legs; primaries blackish
below. Flight gull-like. *Ad* Black cap in
*c*Feb–Sep, closely streaked crown and
blackish eye-patch in *c*Aug–Feb; bill
orange-red. *Juv* Crown more buff than ad
winter; upperbody mottled dark brown;
wings as ad but dusky lesser coverts, tail
with dusky end; bill orange with dark tip.
1st summer As ad winter. VOICE Harsh
kraaa. HABITAT Coasts. FOOD Fish. RANGE
147: Apr–Nov, esp S/EBr. (Most world.)

Royal Tern *Sterna maxima* 45–51 cm (*c*19
in). Near size of Caspian; less stout bill
orange to orange-yellow, longer deeper-
forked tail, shorter legs; head more
crested, winter crown much whiter, forehead white in Jun–Feb, upperparts paler,
primaries less dark below. *Juv* Wings
more contrasted than Caspian (primaries
darker than ad, lesser coverts dark,
median whitish, greater dusky), tail-tip
dusky; bill duller than ad or pinkish. *1st
summer*. More like ad winter. VOICE High
chirrip. HABITAT Coasts. FOOD Fish, crabs.
RANGE 4: most Jul–Sep, S/WBr (Mar, dead,
EIr). (N America, W Indies, W Africa.)

Forster's Tern *Sterna forsteri* 34–37 cm
(*c*14 in). Like Common (162), but longer
tail/legs, heavier bill; silvery panel on
outer wings (esp ad), white sides to grey
tail; ad winter/imm head white with black
mask-patches, grey nape; ad summer bill-
base more orange; 1st winter much fainter
carpal bar. Shallower wing-beats. VOICE
Soft low *krurr*. HABITAT/FOOD As Common.
RANGE 1: Jan–Mar, Cornwall. (N America.)

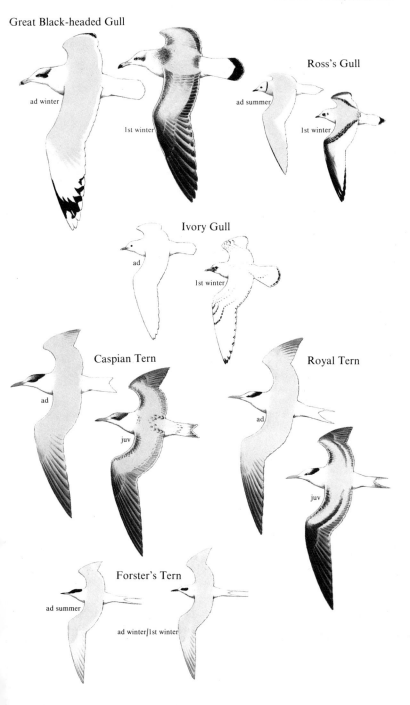

Great Black-headed Gull

ad winter

1st winter

Ross's Gull

ad summer

1st winter

Ivory Gull

ad

1st winter

Caspian Tern

ad

juv

Royal Tern

ad

juv

Forster's Tern

ad summer

ad winter/1st winter

Gull-billed Tern *Gelochelidon nilotica*
35–39 cm (*c*14½ in). Stockier than Sandwich Tern (166); shorter stouter all-black
bill, shorter broader wings, less forked
tail and longer legs; wing-tips paler, tail
grey, head largely white in winter. Flight
heavier, seldom plunges, dips down to
water or ground. *Ad summer* Black cap,
black legs. *Ad winter* With moult in Jul–
Oct, head white but for blackish round
eyes, greyish crown/nape. *Juv* As ad
winter, but above tinged buff and mottled
brown; also darker primaries, brown-
tipped tail, red-brown legs. *1st winter and
summer* With moult in Sep–Feb, as ad
winter but outer primaries dark. VOICE
Throaty *ka-huk*. HABITAT Coasts, marshes,
lakes. FOOD Insects, voles. RANGE 206:
Mar–Oct, esp May–Sep, most S/EBr.
(Cosmopolitan.)

Aleutian Tern *Sterna aleutica* 33–36 cm
(*c*13½ in). Like Bridled Tern but slate-grey
above, white forehead to over eyes, rump/
tail white, dark secondaries below; juv
brown-grey above, tail greyish. VOICE Soft,
4–5 note, wader-like whistle. HABITAT
Oceanic. RANGE 1: May, NEBr. (N Pacific.)

Bridled Tern *Sterna anaethetus* 34–37 cm
(*c*14 in). Dark grey-brown above, white
forehead to behind eyes, pale collar,
palish-tipped underwings. Deep stiff beats
of broadish wings; settles on water,
perches. *Ad summer* Grey-brown above;
black crown, white-sided tail. *Ad winter*
Mantle tipped whitish; black on head
browner, streaked white. *Juv* Dark brown
above with creamy tips, crown streaked
black and white; tail shorter, no white on
sides. *1st winter.* As ad, but worn juv wings/
tail. VOICE Harsh calls. HABITAT Oceanic.
FOOD Fish, invertebrates. RANGE 7: Apr,
Aug–Nov, widely scattered. (Tropics.)

Sooty Tern *Sterna fuscata* 39–43 cm (*c*16
in). Larger than Bridled. Slow fluid beats
of narrowish wings; rarely settles,
snatching food from surface. *Ad* Black
above (fringed white in winter) with white
forehead to eyes, tail-sides; white below
with blackish wing-tips and trailing edges.
Juv/1st winter All sooty-brown, greyer

below, with buff or, in 1st winter, white
flecks above; whitish-grey vent and underwings. As ad by 3–5 years old. VOICE Nasal
waaki-waak. HABITAT Oceanic. FOOD Fish.
RANGE 25: Apr–Oct, esp E/SBr. (Tropics.)

Whiskered Tern *Chlidonias hybridus* 26–29
cm (*c*10¾ in). More like Common (164)
than Black Tern (166), with more forked
tail than Black; in summer white cheeks,
dusky underparts; in autumn silvery grey
and white without contrasting collar,
rump or dark breast-patches (but
variegated saddle on juv). Actions as
Black Tern. *Ad summer* Black cap, white
cheeks; dark grey shading to blackish
below; bill/legs dark red. *Ad winter* With
moult in Jul–Dec, grey above and white
below but for black-streaked white crown,
blackish U from eyes round nape; bill
blackish. *Juv* As ad winter, but for mottled
brown/buff/greyish mantle, slaty
shoulders; as ad winter with moult in Jul–
Oct. RANGE 71: Apr–Sep, esp May–Jun,
most SBr. (S Eurasia, Africa, Australia.)

White-winged Black Tern *Chlidonias
leucopterus* 22–24 cm (*c*9 in). Stockier than
Black Tern (166), with stubbier bill and
broader-based wings. Actions as Black
Tern; slower, shallower wing-beats. *Ad
summer* Glossy black but for white
shoulders, rump and tail (last greyer on
♀); bill red-black, legs red. *Ad winter* With
moult in *c*Jul–Nov, as Black Tern, also
with white collar, but isolated black ear-
coverts, white-flecked crown/nape, no
dark breast-patches, paler grey rump,
white underwing; bill black. *Juv* As ad
winter, but blackish saddle, white rump;
bill blackish, legs red-brown; as ad winter
with moult in Aug–Feb. *1st summer*
Usually as ad winter. RANGE 436: Mar–
Nov, most SEBr. (E Europe, Asia.)

AUKS (Alcidae)

Brünnich's Guillemot *Uria lomvia* 40–44
cm (*c*16½ in). As Guillemot (168), but
almost black above; shorter stouter bill,
pale line at base; in winter black of crown
down over ear-coverts (*cf* juv Razorbill,
168); imm not separable until Nov.
RANGE 14: Jul–Apr, NBr/EIr. (Arctic.)

Gull-billed Tern

ad summer

juv

ad summer

1st summer

Aleutian Tern

Sooty Tern

1st autumn

ad

Bridled Tern

ad summer

Whiskered Tern

1st autumn

juv

ad summer

ad winter

White-winged Black Tern

Brünnich's Guillemot

ad summer

juv

ad summer

ad summer

ad winter

ad winter

ad summer

SANDGROUSE (Pteroclididae)

Pallas's Sandgrouse *Syrrhaptes paradoxus* 33–41 cm (13–16 in). Plump, pigeon-like, but with very long and thin pointed tail, long curved wings, and short legs; sandy-buff, spotted/barred black above, with orange head, grey breast and primaries, black belly-patch. Flight fast with flicked beats, rising awkwardly with pigeon-like clatter; otherwise always on ground, waddling with tiny steps; gregarious, but recent vagrants singly; shy. *Ad/1st year ♂* Head orange-buff with greyish crown/nape and curve behind eyes to grey breast with band of black crescents; wing-coverts almost plain sandy-buff; wings and tail needle-pointed. *Ad/1st year ♀* Head paler with black band on throat (but none on breast); crown, neck and wing-coverts spotted; wings and tail less pointed. VOICE Repeated *cu-reru.* HABITAT Vagrants on dunes, stubble, dry marshes. FOOD Seeds, grain. RANGE Several invasions 1859–1909 (some nested), only 6 birds since: May, Sep, Dec, EBr. (W/Cent Asia.)

PIGEONS, DOVES (Columbidae)

Rufous Turtle Dove *Streptopelia orientalis* 32–34 cm (c13 in). Patterned like Turtle Dove (174), but larger, bulkier, darker; heavier black marks on mantle/coverts and less grey on outer coverts, back/rump bluer, breast darker pink-brown and belly hardly paler; grey (not white) on undertail-coverts, tail-border and neck-patches. Flight/gait heavier than Turtle Dove. *Ad* Strongly rufous above, with black and blue-grey neck-patches, slate-blue back and rump, and pink-brown below. *Juv* Paler, browner: rufous-buff above, no neck-patches, browner back/rump, and dull grey below tinged pink-buff; as ad after moult in Sep–Jan. VOICE Dull sleepy *croo croo-croo croooo.* HABITAT Woods, fields, scrub. FOOD Seeds, grain. RANGE 8: Oct–Nov, May (Jan), E/SWBr. (Asia.)

CUCKOOS (Cuculidae)

Great Spotted Cuckoo *Clamator glandarius* 38–41 cm (c15½ in). Larger than Cuckoo (174), crested, with graduated tail half total length; dark brown above with greyer cap, orange eye-rings, boldly spotted wings, white-edged tail, and creamy below with yellower throat. Flight slightly dipping. *Ad* Cap blue-grey with crest; large white spots on scapulars/wing-coverts, long white tail-tips; primaries brown. *Juv* Cap black, less crested; smaller creamier spots above and short white tail-tips; primaries largely rufous. *1st summer* Intermediate after moult in Jan–Mar: cap blackish-grey; smallish white spots above; primaries mixed rufous and brown. VOICE Harsh *keeow* and repeated chattering *kittera.* HABITAT Wood-edges, bushy areas with scattered trees. FOOD Insects. RANGE 24: Mar–May, Aug–Oct, esp SWBr spring, EBr autumn. (S Europe, SW Asia, Africa.)

Black-billed Cuckoo *Coccyzus erythrophthalmus* 27–29 cm (c11 in). As Yellow-billed, but little or no rufous on wings, no black and much less white on tail; black bill, red or yellow eye-rings. *Ad* Glossy brown above with narrow white tips on graduated tail; eye-rings red. *Juv/1st winter* Speckled whitish above till Sep–Oct moult; tail faintly tipped buff-white, rufous fringes on wings; eye-rings yellow. VOICE/HABITAT/FOOD As Yellow-billed. RANGE 7: Sep–Nov, scattered but most SW/NEBr, 1 Ir. (N America.)

Yellow-billed Cuckoo *Coccyzus americanus* 27–29 cm (c11 in). Smaller, slimmer, more dove-like than Cuckoo (174), with curved bill, shorter wings, longer graduated tail; brown above, whitish below, with much black and white in tail, rufous primaries, yellow bill-patch, grey or yellow eye-rings. Actions as Cuckoo, but flight weaker; secretive, usually in cover, often low. *Ad* Slightly glossy brown above; boldly white-tipped blackish edges and underside of tail; eye-rings greyish. *Juv/1st winter* Duller; tail browner with less clear white tips; more rufous on wing-coverts and primaries; eye-rings yellow. VOICE Vagrants silent. HABITAT Wood-edges, bushy areas, scrub. FOOD Insects; berries in autumn. RANGE 38: Oct–Nov (end Sep–Dec), well scattered but most S/W/NBr, Ir. (N America.)

Pallas's Sandgrouse

♂   ♀

♂

Rufous Turtle Dove

juv

ad

Great Spotted Cuckoo

juv   ad

juv

ad

1st summer

Black-billed Cuckoo

ad

juv/1st winter

ad

Yellow-billed Cuckoo

ad

juv/1st winter

ad

OWLS (Strigidae)

Scops Owl *Otus scops* 18–20 cm (*c*7½ in). Strictly nocturnal; smaller, slimmer and longer-winged than Little Owl (176), with ear-tufts forming concave top to thinner head; brown-grey to rufous, delicately marked. Flight wavering; roosts by day against trunk or in cover. *Ad = 1st year.* VOICE Monotonous whistled *pew*. HABITAT Woods, parks, avenues. RANGE 77: esp Apr–Jun, also Jul–Nov, most SBr, also Ir/NBr. (S Europe, W Asia, NW Africa.)

Hawk Owl *Surnia ulula* 35–41 cm (*c*15 in). Diurnal; big head, shortish pointed wings, long tail; brown and white, barred below, with black face-edge. Flight low, dashing, hawk-like; perches in open, leaning forwards, jerking tail. *Ad = 1st year.* VOICE Chattering *kikikiki*. HABITAT Conifers, birches. FOOD Mammals, birds. RANGE 10: Aug–Mar, most SW/NBr, inc 3 of American race. (N Eurasia, N America.)

Tengmalm's Owl *Aegolius funereus* 24–27 cm (*c*10 in). Mainly nocturnal; longer-tailed than Little Owl (176), with large rounded head and 'surprised' look, shorter shaggy legs; chocolate and white, mottled below, with black face-edge. Flight wavering. *Ad = 1st year.* VOICE Soft liquid *poo-poo-poo.* . . . HABITAT Conifers. FOOD Mammals, birds. RANGE 53, but only 4 since 1950: Oct–Jan, May, all Orkney. (E Europe, N Asia, N America.)

BEE-EATERS (Meropidae)

Blue-cheeked Bee-eater *Merops superciliosus* 28–31 cm (*c*11½ in). Shape and actions as Bee-eater but with longer tail-points; mainly green, with blue surrounding black mask, and coppery throat and underwings. *Ad* Bright green, blue across forecrown; ♂ longer tail-points. *Juv* Duller green, no blue across forecrown, throat paler, no tail-points; as ad after moult in Dec–Mar. VOICE Throaty *pruuk*. RANGE 2: Jun–Jul, Scilly. (SW Asia, N Africa.)

Bee-eater *Merops apiaster* 27–29 cm (*c*11 in). Long curved bill, triangular wings, projecting tail-points; chestnut and turquoise, with gold V above, yellow

throat, pale chestnut underwings. Flight graceful, mixing quick beats with gliding, wheeling, not unlike large House Martin; perches in open. *Ad summer* Chestnut and gold above, with greenish tail; blue-green below, with black-edged yellow throat; ♀ tinged greenish on back and wings, with tail-points shorter. *Ad winter* After moult in Aug–Sep, more green (esp ♀) or blue-green above, almost no black throat-band. *Juv/1st winter* As ad winter, but still less chestnut; greyer scapulars, paler throat, tail-points hardly projecting. VOICE Liquid *pruup*. HABITAT Open country, scattered trees. FOOD Insects, on wing. RANGE 266: Apr–Nov, esp S/EBr; nested 1920, 1955. (S Europe, SW Asia, NW Africa.)

ROLLERS (Coraciidae)

Roller *Coracias garrulus* 29–32 cm (*c*12 in). Rather Jay-like, but heavier bill, longer pointed wings; turquoise and chestnut with blackish flight-feathers, but juv much duller. Flight Jackdaw-like but more floppy; 'rolls' in display; waits on trees, wires, swooping on to prey; hops heavily. *Ad summer* Turquoise and chestnut. *Ad winter* With moult in Jul–Nov, crown and breast dull brownish-green, mantle duller brown. *Juv* Still duller and paler till moult during Nov–Dec; wings and tail tipped with brown, latter without pointed black corners. VOICE Loud harsh *krrak-ak*. HABITAT Open country, scattered trees. FOOD Large insects. RANGE 199: Apr–Nov (esp May–Jul), scattered, most S/EBr. (S/Cent Europe, W Asia, NW Africa.)

KINGFISHERS (Alcedinidae)

Belted Kingfisher *Ceryle alcyon* 30–34 cm (*c*12½ in). Jackdaw-sized, with long thick bill, large head, double crest, rounded wings, longish tail; mainly blue-grey and white. Actions as Kingfisher (180), but wing-beats deeper, less regular, floppier; often hovers; very noisy. *Ad* ♂ Blue-grey chest-band. *Ad* ♀ Also rusty breast-band. *Juv/1st winter* Chest-band tipped rufous, only flanks rusty (both more on ♀); crest darker; more white tips on wings, central tail spotted as ad ♀. VOICE Harsh rattle. HABITAT Fresh water. FOOD Fish. RANGE 3: Nov–Aug, Cornwall/Mayo. (N America.)

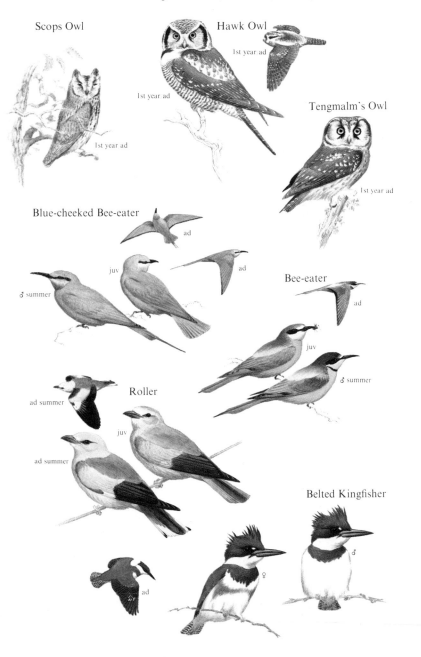

Scops Owl

Hawk Owl

1st year ad

1st year ad

1st year ad

Tengmalm's Owl

1st year ad

Blue-cheeked Bee-eater

ad

juv

ad

♂ summer

Bee-eater

ad

juv

♂ summer

Roller

ad summer

juv

ad summer

Belted Kingfisher

♀

♂

ad

NIGHTJARS (Caprimulgidae)

Common Nighthawk *Chordeiles minor*
21–25 cm (*c*9 in). Smaller, darker and
greyer than Nightjar (180) with long,
pointed, white-banded wings and notched
tail. Crepuscular, but also hunts by day;
flight buoyant, tern-like. *Ad ♂* White
throat and band across tail. *Ad ♀* Throat-
patch smaller, more buff; no tail-band.
Juv As ♀, but mottled greyer, throat
obscured by barring. VOICE Nasal *peent*.
HABITAT Pinewoods, fields, moors, towns.
FOOD Insects, on wing. RANGE 8: Sep–Oct,
most Scilly, also Cent/NEBr. (N America.)

SWIFTS (Apodidae)

Needle-tailed Swift *Hirundapus caudacutus*
19–21 cm (*c*7¾ in). Body size of Alpine
Swift but stouter, wings broader-based;
tail very short, squarish ('needle' points
usually invisible); dark brown with green
gloss (purple or mat when abraded), esp
on wings; white throat and U under tail,
grey-brown triangle on back (fading to
whitish). Flight slower, more fluttery

than Swift (186). *Juv/1st winter* As ad,
but white undertail-coverts dark-tipped.
VOICE Vagrants silent. HABITAT Aerial.
FOOD Insects, on wing. RANGE 3: Jun–Jul,
Essex/Hants/Cork. (E Asia.)

Pallid Swift *Apus pallidus* 16–17 cm (*c*6½
in). *Very* like Swift (186), but wings
broader-based, blunter; paler, scalier,
with rather larger whitish face and throat
(emphasising dark eye-mark); light inner
wings contrast with darker back, breast
and outer primaries. Flight more deliberate, more gliding. RANGE 1: May, Kent.
(S Europe, SW Asia, N Africa.)

Alpine Swift *Apus melba* 20–22 cm (*c*8¼
in), wingspan 50–55 cm (*c*21 in). Much
larger and paler than Swift (186), with
white throat and belly, brown breast-
band. *Juv* White edgings to wing-feathers
(but ad has thin fringes in fresh plumage).
VOICE Vagrants silent. HABITAT Aerial,
often near coast. FOOD Insects, on wing.
RANGE 302: mid Apr–Oct (Mar–Nov),
scattered, esp S/EBr. (S Eurasia, Africa.)

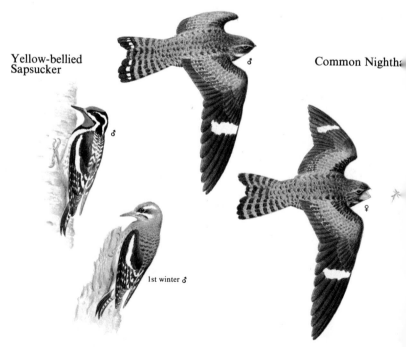

Yellow-bellied
Sapsucker

♂

1st winter ♂

Common Nightha[

♂

♀

Little Swift *Apus affinis* 12–13 cm (c5½ in). Smaller, more compact than Swift (186) with shorter, broader-based wings, square-ended tail and square white rump. *Juv/1st winter* Whitish edgings to wing-feathers. VOICE Vagrants silent. HABITAT Aerial. FOOD Insects, on wing. RANGE 2: Jun, Nov, Cork/Gwynedd. (S Asia, Africa.)

WOODPECKERS (Picidae)

Yellow-bellied Sapsucker *Sphyrapicus varius* 19–23 cm (c8¼ in). Smallish woodpecker with mottled/barred back, white rump, wing-patches, and bands behind and below eyes on black head-sides. *Ad ♂* Black-bordered red forecrown and throat. *Ad ♀* Less red on forecrown (or all-black), throat white. *Juv* Brown and buff; whitish traces of ad pattern on head, whitish throat. *1st winter ♂* assumes some red and black in Aug–Sep, ♀ not before Oct. VOICE Nasal mew; migrants usually silent. HABITAT Woods, orchards; vagrants in coastal areas with few trees. FOOD Drills rows of holes in trees, returns to feed on

sap, insects. RANGE 1: Sep–Oct, Scilly. (N America.)

SWALLOWS, MARTINS (Hirundinidae)

Red-rumped Swallow *Hirundo daurica* 17–18.5 cm (c7 in). Longer-bodied than Swallow (186), with thicker incurved tail-streamers, broader wings; chestnut supercilia and nape, chestnut to buff (often 2-tone) rump, black undertail-coverts; no breast-band or tail-spots. Flight slower, more deliberate, more as House Martin. *Ad* Glossy blue-black above, faintly streaked below. *Juv* Tail shorter; faint buff fringes above, little gloss; collar and rump paler; no streaks below. *1st winter* More as ad after moult in Jul–Sep, but still duller above, and still unstreaked below. VOICE Drawn-out soft *chirrup*, longer and softer than Swallow. HABITAT Open country. FOOD Insects, on wing. RANGE 74: Mar–Jun (esp Apr–May), also end Aug–early Nov, most S/EBr, with some north to Yorks., few Ir/NBr. (S Eurasia, Africa.)

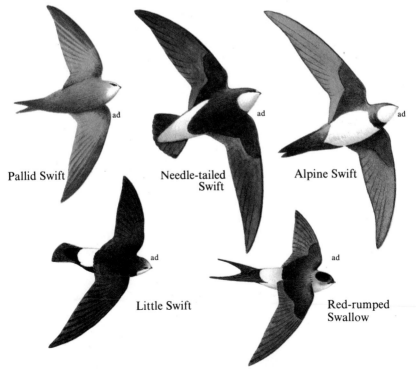

Pallid Swift   ad

Needle-tailed Swift   ad

Alpine Swift   ad

Little Swift   ad

Red-rumped Swallow   ad

LARKS (Alaudidae)

Calandra Lark *Melanocorypha calandra*
18–20 cm (*c*7½ in). Stout with pale bill,
heavy head, bulky body, short tail, no
crest; whitish underparts contrast with
bold black neck-patches (look narrow
when hunched) and dark upperparts; tail-
sides white; broad triangular wings look
black from below in flight, and dark above
with paler coverts, narrow white trailing
edges. Does not crouch flat like Skylark
(184). *Juv* Scaled above with buff feather-
edges, tail-sides tinged buff; black spots
on breast and ear-coverts; neck-patches
partly obscured; as ad after moult end
Jul–Sep. VOICE Nasal rippling *chrrreet*.
HABITAT Open wastes, farmlands. FOOD
Seeds, insects. RANGE 2: Apr, Dorset/
Shetland. (Mediterranean east to Iran.)

Bimaculated Lark *Melanocorypha bimaculata* 16.5–17.5 cm (*c*6¾ in). Like small
Calandra, but more rufous with whiter
supercilia, narrower and less clear neck-
patches, and buff sides but white tips to
tail; wings lack white trailing edges in
flight. HABITAT Mountain fields, deserts in
winter. FOOD As Calandra. RANGE 3:
May–Jun, Oct, Devon/Scilly/Shetland.
(SW Asia north to Kirghiz Steppes.)

White-winged Lark *Melanocorypha
leucoptera* 17–18.5 cm (*c*7 in). Shape as
Calandra, but more rufous above, white
on wings, no neck-patches; in flight wings
narrower with wide white trailing edges
divided from chestnut forewings by black
stripe. *Ad ♂* Cap, lesser and median
coverts, and sides of breast all chestnut,
clearer in summer when also fainter chest-
spots. *Ad ♀* Crown as mantle, only tinged
chestnut; wing-coverts paler than ♂; sides
of breast more streaked, less chestnut.
Juv Crown and wing-coverts brown;
upperparts scaled with buff fringes, breast
and cheeks spotted blackish; tail-sides
and less extensive white in wings all tinged
buff; as ads after moult end Jul–Sep.
HABITAT Dry grassland. FOOD Seeds,
insects. RANGE 6: Aug–Nov, SBr. (SE
Russia to Cent Asia.)

Calandra Lark   Bimaculated Lark

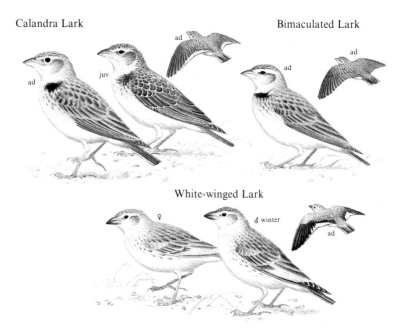

White-winged Lark

Short-toed Lark *Calandrella brachy-dactyla* 13.5–14.5 cm (*c*5½ in). Small, pale, sandy above and whitish below; dark bar on median coverts, but patch at sides of neck often obscure; short yellowish bill, rather flat head; white-sided dark tail in flight. *Ad S races* Sandy-buff to pale grey-brown above, often reddish cap (esp summer); unstreaked below, but sides of throat finely spotted above neck-patch, sandy wash on chest. *Ad E races* Paler and greyer above; no rufous cap. *Juv* Rather spotted above; irregular narrow band of obscure blotches across chest, rarely on upper flanks; as ad after moult in late Jul–Sep, but chest-marks may sometimes remain into 1st winter. VOICE Short hard *chichirrp*. HABITAT Sandy wastes, fields. FOOD Seeds, insects. RANGE 227: Apr–Dec, esp May (S races) and Sep–Oct (mainly E races), wide-scattered but majority Shetland/Scilly. (S Eurasia, Africa.)

Lesser Short-toed Lark *Calandrella rufescens* 13.5–14.5 cm (*c*5½ in). Like grey Short-toed (see 1st winter), but regular streaks on breast, throat-sides, usually flanks (all much less on juv); no covert-bar or neck-patches; rounder head. VOICE Distinctive *prrt*. HABITAT Dry marsh to desert. RANGE 4 records of 42 birds: Jan–May, all Kerry/Wexford/Mayo. (Spain and N Africa east to Manchuria.)

Crested Lark *Galerida cristata* 16.5–17.5 cm (*c*6¾ in). Sometimes confused with Skylark (184), but plumper, with pointed crest, longer bill and much shorter buff-sided tail; diffusely streaked breast and, in flight, buff undersides to broader wings. *Juv* Crest less pointed; upperparts more spotted and scaly, 2 thin whitish wing-bars (tips of greater and median coverts); less heavily marked below; as ad after moult, end Jul–Sep. VOICE Liquid whistle *whee-wheeoo*. HABITAT Farmland, waste ground, roadsides. FOOD Seeds, insects. RANGE 20: Mar–Jun, Sep–Jan, most SBr but also north to Shetland. (Temperate Eurasia, Africa.) NOTE Thekla Lark *G. theklae*, of Mediterranean area, is very similar, has bold breast-streaks, grey underwings.

Short-toed Lark

Lesser Short-toed Lark

E races
ad

E races
juv–1st winter

S races
ad

ad

Crested Lark

juv

ad

PIPITS, WAGTAILS (Motacillidae)

Richard's Pipit *Anthus novaeseelandiae*
17–18.5 cm (*c*7 in). Largest pipit, with
stout bill, white-sided tail, long stout
legs, large feet, upright stance; brown
above, heavily streaked, and boldly
marked on breast; whitish supercilia,
black moustaches. *Juv* Blacker above,
scaled with buff; whiter below, but well-
streaked; moults in Aug–Dec, still many
pale-edged juv feathers. VOICE Explosive
schreep. HABITAT Wet grassland. FOOD
Insects, worms, seeds. RANGE 1064: Aug–
May, esp Sep–Nov, most coastal E/S/
WBr, rare Ir. (Asia, Africa, Australasia).
NOTE Blyth's Pipit *A. godlewskii* (Sussex,
Oct 1882) is very like Richard's, but in
autumn more intermediate between it and
imm Tawny, with some orange-buff below.

Tawny Pipit *Anthus campestris* 16–17 cm
(*c*6½ in). Large, slim, wagtail-like, with
slender bill, longish tail. *Ad* Sandy above,
creamy below, almost unstreaked; creamy
supercilia, line of dark spots on median

coverts. *Juv* Streaked above and boldly
spotted on breast, like Richard's Pipit, but
greyer, slimmer, less erect, with thinner
bill and legs; moults in Aug–Nov, still
streaked to Sep–Oct. VOICE Wagtail-like
tseep, more metallic *tseuk*. HABITAT Sandy
ground, farmland. FOOD Insects. RANGE
583: mainly end Jul–early Nov (esp Sep–
Oct), also Apr–mid Jun, most coastal S/
SEBr; rare NBr, Ir. (Eurasia, N Africa.)

Olive-backed Pipit *Anthus hodgsoni* 14.5–
16 cm (*c*6 in). Size of Tree Pipit (188);
olive and whitish with bold breast-spots;
black-edged buff and white supercilia;
white patch and black mark at rear
cheeks. Skulks; pumps tail. VOICE Hoarse
tseep. HABITAT Typically trees. FOOD
Insects. RANGE 18: Sep–Nov, Apr–May,
mainly S/E/NEBr. (NE Russia, Asia.)

Pechora Pipit *Anthus gustavi* 14–15 cm
(*c*5¾ in). Like Tree Pipit (188) but shorter
tail; whiter wing-bar/underparts, 2 whitish
lines on back, buffish tail-sides, boldly
streaked rump. Very skulking. VOICE Loud

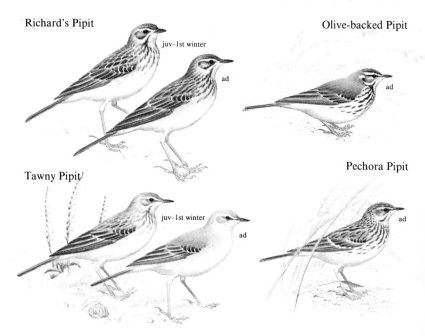

Richard's Pipit

juv–1st winter

ad

Olive-backed Pipit

ad

Tawny Pipit

juv–1st winter

ad

Pechora Pipit

ad

hard *pwit*. HABITAT Swamps; migrants in crops. FOOD Insects. RANGE 24: end Aug–Nov (Apr), N/EBr. (NE Russia, Asia.)

Red-throated Pipit *Anthus cervinus* 14–15 cm (*c*5¾ in). Darker, browner than Meadow Pipit (186); heavier streaking extends to rump. *Ad summer* Pink to brick-red throat, usually supercilia, sometimes breast/forehead (♂ often redder but sexing unsure); streaks below mainly on flanks. *Ad winter* May show pinkish throat; breast boldly streaked. *Juv* Throat streaked, yellower below; as ad after moult in Aug. VOICE High drawn-out *psssss*, more hissing than Tree Pipit. HABITAT Marshes, wet fields. FOOD Insects, also molluscs, worms, seeds. RANGE 144: mid Apr–mid Jun, mid Aug–Nov, mainly coastal E/SBr, also SIr. (N Eurasia.)

Citrine Wagtail *Motacilla citreola* 16–17 cm (*c*6½ in). Like Yellow Wagtail (190) from front, White Wagtail (192) from rear; grey back and 2 white wing-bars at all ages. ♂ *summer* Yellow head and under-parts, black half-collar. ♂ *winter*/♀ Crown and nape grey; forehead, supercilia and underparts dull yellow. *Juv* Forehead buff, crown and ear-coverts grey, supercilia white or yellowish, throat white, breast buff (often indistinctly spotted gorget), underparts brownish-white; as ad winter by end of moult in Sep–Oct. VOICE Hard *tsreep*. HABITAT/FOOD As Yellow Wagtail. RANGE 26: most imms, Sep–Nov, NE/EBr; 2 ♂s, May/Jul, EBr. (E Russia, Asia.)

ACCENTORS (Prunellidae)

Alpine Accentor *Prunella collaris* 17–18.5 cm (*c*7 in). Larger than Dunnock (196); dark patch between 2 whitish wing-bars, buff tips to tail. *Ad* Throat white with black spots, flanks streaked chestnut. *Juv* Duller with plain buff-grey throat, dark-streaked flanks and underparts; as ad after moult in Jul–Oct. VOICE Lark-like *chirrirrip*. HABITAT Mountains; vagrants on rocky ground. FOOD Insects, seeds, berries. RANGE 35: Mar–Jun, Aug–Jan, most SBr. (Cent/S Eurasia, NW Africa.)

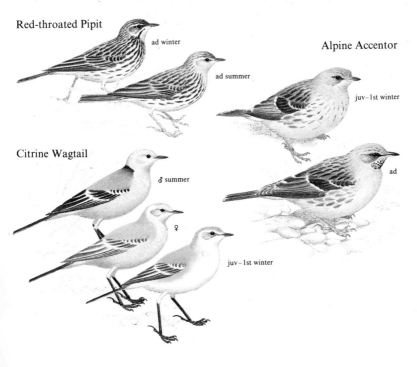

Red-throated Pipit

ad winter

ad summer

Alpine Accentor

juv–1st winter

Citrine Wagtail

♂ summer

ad

♀

juv–1st winter

THRASHERS (Mimidae)

Brown Thrasher *Toxostoma rufum* 26.5–29.5 cm (*c*11 in). Rather thrush-like, but slimmer, with long tail, slightly curved bill; bright rufous above with greyish cheeks, 2 pale wing-bars; whitish below with heavy brown streaks. Flight slow, heavy, low; much on ground in or near cover; walks, runs, hops; cocks and thrashes tail about; hammers seeds; unobtrusive. *Ad* Greater and median coverts tipped whitish; eyes yellow. *1st winter* As ad if no buff-tipped juv coverts left; eyes may still be grey as juv. VOICE Explosive *chak*, huskier *chaaak*. HABITAT Wood-edges, thickets. FOOD Insects, acorns, berries. RANGE 1: Nov–Feb, Dorset 1966/67. (N America.)

CHATS, THRUSHES (Turdidae)

Rufous Bush Robin *Cercotrichas galactotes* 14.5–16 cm (*c*6 in). Near size of Nightingale (198), but slimmer, with longer bill, longer graduated tail tipped with white and black; more or less rufous above, with creamy supercilia. Perches in open, hops on ground, cocking and fanning tail. *W race (C.g. galactotes)* Wholly rufous above; creamy below. *E races (C.g. syriacus/familiaris)* Head/back grey-brown; tinged greyish below. *Ad = 1st winter*. VOICE Hard *tek tek*. HABITAT Scrub, bushy areas. FOOD Insects. RANGE 10: end Aug–Oct (Apr), most SBr, SIr. (Iberia, N Africa, S Asia.)

Thrush Nightingale *Luscinia luscinia* 16–17 cm (*c*6½ in). Very like Nightingale (198), but dark olive-brown above, tail darker rufous, breast mottled grey-brown. Actions and plumage sequence similar; much louder song lacks crescendo. RANGE 41: most May–Jun, also end Jul–Oct, esp E/NBr. (E Europe, W Asia.)

Siberian Rubythroat *Luscinia calliope* 15–16.5 cm (*c*6¼ in). Near size of Nightingale (198), but character more like Robin or Bluethroat (196); rufous wing-panel and rump, brown back/tail, with whitish

Brown Thrasher

Rufous Bush Robin

galactotes ad

syriacus ad

ad

ad

♀

1st winter ♂

♂

Thrush Nightingale

Siberian Rubythroat

supercilia, eye-rings, moustaches and belly, red or white throat. *Ad ♂* Throat ruby-red, edged black; breast greyish; supercilia/moustaches white. *Ad ♀* Throat whitish (rarely little red), edged grey-brown; breast buff; supercilia/moustaches whitish. *1st winter* As ad ♀, but greater coverts tipped buff; ♂ obscure red traces on white throat. VOICE Plaintive *chee-wee*, churr. HABITAT/FOOD Much as Bluethroat. RANGE 2: Oct, Shetland/Lincs. (Asia.)

Red-flanked Bluetail *Tarsiger cyanurus* 13.5–14.5 cm (*c*5½ in). Build of Robin (196); rump and tail (at least) blue or grey-blue (but tail often simply looks dark), flanks orange-rufous. Jerks (not shivers) tail; often on ground. *Ad ♂* Grey-blue above with bluer supercilia, bright blue shoulders, rump and tail-coverts; creamy-white below; blue partly obscured by grey-brown tips in autumn/winter. *Ad ♀/1st year* Olive-grey above but for dull blue rump/tail; pale eye-rings; centre of throat whitish, surrounded by defined brown-grey. VOICE Short *tik tik*.

HABITAT Trees with undergrowth. FOOD Insects, berries. RANGE 8: most Oct (Sep/May-Jun), EBr. (NE Europe, Asia.)

Isabelline Wheatear *Oenanthe isabellina* 16–17 cm (*c*6½ in). Larger than Wheatear (202), with longer heavier bill, bigger rounder head, shorter-looking tail; pale sandy-brown above, creamy-buff below, thin dark eye-line, usually more blackish on tail (forming square with projection towards white rump, rather than inverted T), whitish underwings in flight (not mottled black and white); in autumn/winter, creamy-edged primary coverts isolate black-brown alula from dark primaries. Upright stance, bounding gait; often tame. Sexes indistinguishable but for extremes: ♂ black lores, clear whitish supercilia, black-ended tail; ♀ grey-speckled lores, obscure creamy supercilia, brown-ended tail. *Ad = 1st winter*. VOICE Quiet *cheep*, whistled *weet-wit*. HABITAT Open sandy areas, short grass. FOOD Insects. RANGE 4: Sep–Nov, May, most EBr. (SE Europe, Cent/S Asia.)

Red-flanked Bluetail

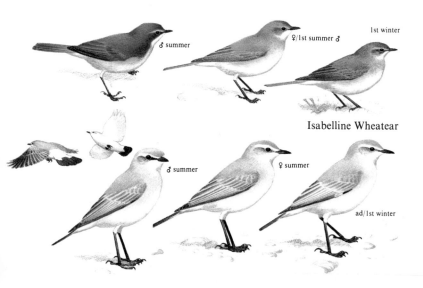

♂ summer

♀/1st summer ♂

1st winter

Isabelline Wheatear

♂ summer

♀ summer

ad/1st winter

Pied Wheatear *Oenanthe pleschanka*
14–15.5 cm (*c*5¾ in). Smaller, slimmer, and
less upright than Wheatear (202); longer
tail has similar pattern, but more black
at sides, and tip often broken by white;
♂ has dark mantle, wings and (usually)
throat, and whitish crown/shawl, variably
obscured by brown-buff in autumn; ♀ very
like some other ♀ wheatears, esp E race of
Black-eared, though darker above, with
distinct pale fringes in autumn, and more
defined tawny chest-band. Perches on
bushes and trees, dropping to ground and
flying up again. ♂ *summer* Mantle, wings
and throat black, crown/nape whitish.
♂ *winter* After moult in Jun–Sep, looks
generally darkish above, with crown/nape
mainly grey-brown mottled buff, and
black areas broken by brown and creamy
fringes. ♀ *summer* Grey-brown above and
brownish-white below; throat often
mottled darker, chest tawny. ♀ *winter* Bold
pale fringes above, throat brownish-white.
1st year ♂ As ad, but mantle/wings much
browner; in autumn, fringes buffer and
wider, dark throat also obscured. VOICE
Harsh *zack-zack*. HABITAT Sandy/stony
areas, open or with thin scrub. FOOD
Insects. RANGE 8: Sep–Nov (May), most
E/SBr, 1 SWIr. (SE Europe, S Cent Asia.)

Black-eared Wheatear *Oenanthe hispanica*
14–15.5 cm (*c*5¾ in). Shape, actions and
tail-pattern like Pied Wheatear; ♂ buff,
pale grey-brown or white above, with
black wings, scapulars and either mask or
whole throat; ♀ has darker cheeks and
scapulars than ♀ Wheatear (202), wings
more fringed buff in summer than Pied,
but mantle lacks Pied's pale fringes in
autumn. ♂ *W race (O.h. hispanica)* Crown
and mantle buff (paler with wear); mask
hardly extends above bill; after moult
in Jul–Aug, wings more fringed buff.
Ad ♀ Pale sandy-buff above, throat
whitish-buff or mottled grey-brown; ear-
coverts brown, wings brown with buff
fringes. ♂ *E race (O.h. melanoleuca)* As
W race, but crown/mantle pale grey-brown
(white with wear); mask crosses forehead;
if present, black throat extends farther
down. *Ad* ♀ As W race, but darker grey-
buff above, looking more like ♀ Pied. *1st*

year ♂ *(both races)* As ad ♂s, but wings
much browner, and more obscured by buff
fringes in autumn (as is throat of black-
throated birds); mask of E race may not
cross forehead. VOICE Grating *zerrk*,
plaintive whistle. HABITAT/FOOD As Pied.
RANGE 34: Mar–Nov, most Apr–Jun/Sep
in E/SBr. (S Europe, SW Asia, NW Africa.)

Desert Wheatear *Oenanthe deserti* 14–15.5
cm (*c*5¾ in). Shape and actions much as
Pied Wheatear, but rump buff-white, most
of tail black (white only at basal corners);
♂ otherwise much as black-throated
Black-eared Wheatear, but with sandy
(not black) scapulars and much white on
inner wing-coverts; ♀ like dull ♂ with
whitish throat (sometimes blackish in
summer), but usually more buff rump,
more pale fringes on wings. *Ad* ♂ Ear-
coverts, throat and wings black; throat
tipped with white and wings fringed
whitish after moult in Jul–Aug. *Ad* ♀ Ear-
coverts and wings browner; throat buff-
white, mottled with or even largely blackish through wear by summer. *1st year* ♂
As ad ♂, but wings much browner, with
broad buff fringes as ♀; throat obscured
more by whitish in autumn/winter. VOICE
Mournful grating whistle. HABITAT/FOOD
Much as Pied. RANGE 20: Aug–Apr (Jun),
all E/SBr. (SW/Cent Asia, N Africa.)

Black Wheatear *Oenanthe leucura* 17–19
cm (*c*7 in). Larger, more thrush-like; all
blackish but for white rump, undertail-
coverts and tail with black inverted T at
end (tip rather narrow). *Ad* ♂ Glossy black.
Ad ♀ Sooty-blackish, barely glossed;
tinged rufous below after moult in Jul–
Oct, duller brown by summer. *1st year*
Much as ads (♂s tinged brown), but flight-
feathers/outer coverts browner, contrasting with blackish inner/smaller coverts.
VOICE Slurred *chak*, piping *pee-pee*.
HABITAT Usually cliffs, mountains. FOOD
Insects. RANGE 5: Jun, Aug–Oct, NE/SE/
WBr, WIr. (SW Europe, N Africa.)

NOTE But for summer ♂s, wheatears can
be hard to identify. Look at colours of
mantle/rump/underparts, exact pattern of
tail and markings of head/throat/wings.

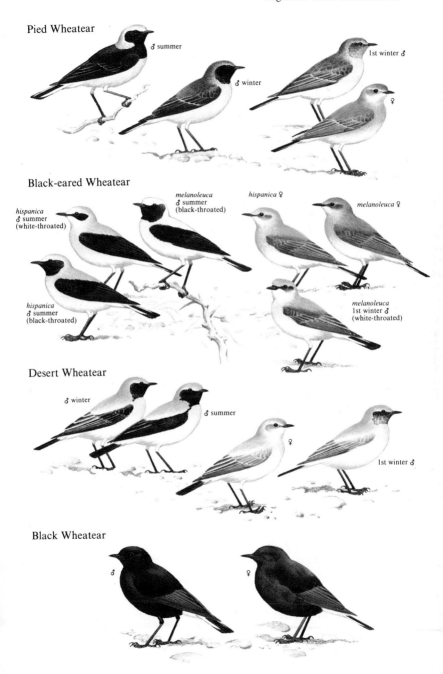

Pied Wheatear

♂ summer

♂ winter

1st winter ♂

♀

Black-eared Wheatear

hispanica
♂ summer
(white-throated)

melanoleuca
♂ summer
(black-throated)

hispanica ♀

melanoleuca ♀

hispanica
♂ summer
(black-throated)

melanoleuca
1st winter ♂
(white-throated)

Desert Wheatear

♂ winter

♂ summer

♀

1st winter ♂

Black Wheatear

♂

♀

Rock Thrush *Monticola saxatilis* 18–20 cm
(*c*7½ in). About size of fat Song Thrush,
with much shorter, mainly orange tail and
more wheatear-like stance; summer ♂
grey-blue and orange with variably white
back, but other plumages mottled above
and crescent-marked below. Flight low,
usually from rock to rock, often tending to
dive round corners; also perches on trees,
wires, buildings; hops on ground, either
erect or crouching, and jerks and flirts tail;
shy. ♂ *summer* Grey-blue head, at least
some white on back, blackish wings,
orange below. ♂ *winter* After moult in
Jul–Sep, buff-speckled blackish-brown
above (blue and white largely hidden);
wing-feathers edged buff-white; central
throat whitish to pale blue, otherwise
orange below, all with whitish tips and
dark crescents. *Ad/1st winter* ♀ As ♂
winter, but paler brown above and pale
buff to orange-buff below (more orange
in summer); little bluish, no pure white.
1st winter ♂ As ♂ winter, but not so dark
above, paler orange below; almost no
blue, but clearly distinct from ♀ if traces of
pure white on back. VOICE Soft *chak chak*.
HABITAT Rocks, grassland. FOOD Insects,
also snails, worms, berries. RANGE 13:
most May–Jun (also Oct–Nov), scattered
S/E/NBr. (Cent/S Eurasia, NW Africa.)

Hermit Thrush *Catharus guttatus* 17–19
cm (*c*7 in). Much smaller than Song
Thrush (206); pattern not dissimilar, but
thin buff-white eye-rings, rusty rump/tail.
Shy, skulking; habitually slowly raises and
lowers tail. *Ad* Olive-brown above, but for
rufous rump/tail; whitish below, tinged
buff on breast, with blackish spots
strongest on chest and throat-sides. *1st
year* As ad but for buff-tipped greater
coverts. VOICE Low *chuk*. HABITAT Damp
woods, thickets. FOOD Insects, berries.
RANGE 1: Jun, Shetland. (N America.)

Swainson's Thrush *Catharus ustulatus*
17.5–19.5 cm (*c*7¼ in). Hardly larger than
Hermit Thrush, without rufous; very
much like Grey-cheeked, but creamy-buff
throat and breast, usually bold eye-rings.
Skulks in ground cover, also high in trees.

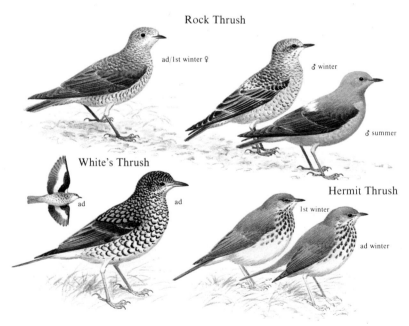

Rock Thrush

ad/1st winter ♀

♂ winter

♂ summer

White's Thrush

ad

ad

Hermit Thrush

1st winter

ad winter

Ad Brownish-olive above with more or less grey tinge; eye-rings and line in front yellow-buff, throat/breast similar and spotted blackish, rest of underparts whitish. *1st year* As ad but for buff-tipped greater coverts. VOICE High *whit*. HABITAT/FOOD As Hermit Thrush. RANGE 8: most Oct (May), W/SIr, S/NEBr. (N America.)

Grey-cheeked Thrush *Catharus minimus* 17.5–19.5 cm ($c7\frac{1}{4}$ in). Very like Swainson's Thrush, but greyer cheeks and breast, obscure eye-rings. Usually in ground cover. *Ad* Greyish-olive above; cheeks greyish, faint eye-ring whitish; whitish throat and greyer breast spotted blackish. *1st year* As ad but for buff-tipped greater coverts. VOICE High nasal *kwee-a*. HABITAT/FOOD. As Hermit. RANGE 14: Oct–Nov, esp W/NBr. (N America, NE Asia.)

Veery *Catharus fuscescens* 17–19 cm (*c*7 in). Warm brown (not really rufous) above, no eye-rings, only ill-defined smudges on breast. Usually in ground cover; often stands still, rather upright.

Ad Warm brown to rich tawny above; buff and whitish below, with indistinct grey-brown spots. *1st year* As ad but for buff-tipped greater coverts. VOICE Low *phew*. HABITAT/FOOD As Hermit Thrush. RANGE 1: Oct, Cornwall. (N America.)

White's Thrush *Zoothera dauma* 25–28 cm ($c10\frac{1}{2}$ in). Size of Mistle Thrush (206), but bill longer; yellow-brown and whitish, with bold black crescents all over head/body, white and black bands on underwings. Flight undulating; mostly skulks in undergrowth with crouched stance; shy. *Ad* Yellow-brown above, tinged olive in winter but greyer in summer, and yellowish-white below, all boldly scaled black; brown and yellow-olive pattern on upperwings; central tail-feathers brown, rest blackish with white tips. *1st winter* As ad but for yellow-buff tips to central tail. VOICE Monotonous and tuneless whistle. HABITAT Woods with dense undergrowth. FOOD Insects, berries. RANGE 38: most Oct–Feb (also May, Sep), widely scattered but most E/SBr. (Cent/E Asia, Australia.)

Swainson's Thrush

Grey-cheeked Thrush

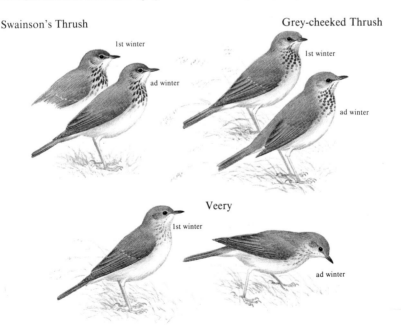

1st winter

ad winter

1st winter

ad winter

Veery

1st winter

ad winter

304 Turdidae

Siberian Thrush *Zoothera sibirica* 22–24 cm (*c*9 in). Slightly smaller, flatter-headed than Blackbird (204); black with white supercilia, or brown with buff eyebrows and crescent-marked underparts; white tail-corners, bands on underwings (*cf* White's Thrush, 302). Actions as Blackbird, but shy, skulking. *Ad* ♂ Slate-black but for supercilia, tail-corners, grey or whitish belly. *Ad* ♀ Olive-brown above, with buffish supercilia, pale-speckled cheeks, whitish throat, extensive brown crescent-marks below. *1st winter* ♂ Duller: throat buff, less uniform below; retained juv wings and tail olive-brown. VOICE Soft *zit*. HABITAT Woods, thickets, esp near water. FOOD Insects, worms. RANGE 3: Oct–Dec, scattered E/SBr. (Cent/E Asia.)

Eye-browed Thrush *Turdus obscurus* 20–22 cm (*c*8¼ in). Size, actions and (whiter) supercilia as Redwing (206), but longer bill, plain orange-buff chest/flanks, white belly, pale grey underwings. *Ad* ♂ Head (and variably lower throat) greyish; white under eyes and on upper throat;

chest/flanks orange-rufous. *Ad* ♀ Head grey-brown to olive-brown, no patch under eyes, dark streaks on throat; chest/flanks duller orange-buff. *1st winter* Duller than ads, with buff-tipped greater coverts; chest/flanks often only warm buff, little or no grey about head. VOICE Thin *tlip-tlip*, loud *keuk*. HABITAT Woods, fields. FOOD Insects, worms, berries. RANGE 4: Oct–Dec, scattered W/CentBr. (Cent/E Asia.)

Dusky Thrush *Turdus naumanni* 22–24 cm (*c*9 in). Size of Song Thrush (206), but with heavy bill; dark above, variously marked chestnut, with broad whitish supercilia, blackish ear-coverts, breast-patches and flanks. Actions recall Fieldfare (204), esp erect stance with bill up; not skulking. *Ad* ♂ Black-brown above, with variable chestnut on back, rump, tail-base, scapulars, and esp coverts/secondaries; cheeks/throat creamy and underparts white with blackish on breast and flanks (more uniform in summer, scaled white in winter). *Ad* ♀ Usually, browner above with less and paler chestnut, breast-patches

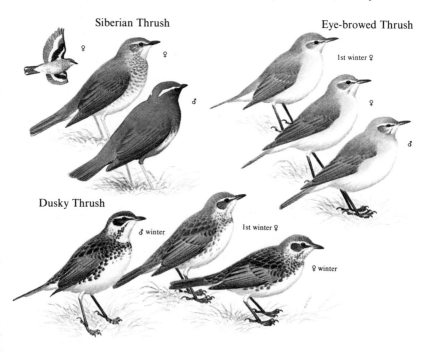

Siberian Thrush

Eye-browed Thrush

Dusky Thrush

browner, flanks rustier. *1st winter* Imm ♂ intermediate between ads, ♀ duller than ad ♀ with buff on wings and rusty-brown on breast/flanks; paler edges and shaft-streaks on some coverts. VOICE Blackbird-like clucking, wheezy flight-call. HABITAT Wood-edges, grassland. FOOD Insects, worms, berries. RANGE 6: Sep–Mar, N/CentBr. (Cent/E Asia.)

Black-throated Thrush *Turdus ruficollis* 23–25 cm (*c*9½ in). Just larger than Song Thrush (206); black or densely spotted throat/chest, orange-buff axillaries, yellow-based bill. Actions as Blackbird (204). *Ad* ♂ Brown-grey above with blackish streaks on crown/nape; black supercilia and throat/chest, thinly scaled whitish in winter; dull white below with greyer flanks. *Ad* ♀ Olive-brown above; faint supercilia grey-buff, throat white with blackish streaks, chest blackish with broad grey-buff fringes; more grey-brown below. *1st winter* As ad ♀, but ♂ face to chest more as ad ♂ winter; grey-white tips to any unmoulted outer greater coverts.

VOICE Blackbird-like chuckle, thin *tseep*. HABITAT Open woods, fields. FOOD Insects, worms, berries. RANGE 10: Oct–Apr, most NE/EBr. (Cent Asia.)

American Robin *Turdus migratorius* 24–27 cm (*c*10 in). Typical thrush, size and shape of Blackbird (204) with mainly yellow bill, brick-red breast; grey to blackish above, with white eye-crescents, throat (streaked black), tail-corners and lower belly. Actions much as Blackbird; restlessly flicks wings and tail. *Ad* ♂ Dark grey above, head and tail blacker; breast rich orange-red, with whitish feather-fringes in winter. *Ad* ♀ Browner-grey above, head/tail less contrasting; breast paler, often fringed whitish all year. *1st winter* As ads, but browner above, with buff-tipped outer greater coverts, and duller rufous below. VOICE Anxious *tcheep* and *tut-tut-tut*, often combined; flight-note very like Blackbird. HABITAT Woods, fields. FOOD Insects, worms, snails, berries. RANGE 23: Sep–May (esp Oct–Feb), most Ir, SBr, also NBr. (N America.)

Black-throated Thrush

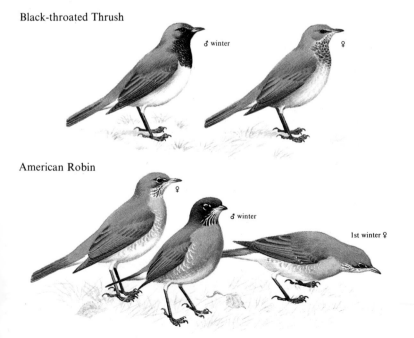

♂ winter   ♀

American Robin

♀   ♂ winter   1st winter ♀

306 Sylviidae

WARBLERS (Sylviidae)

Fan-tailed Warbler *Cisticola juncidis* 9–11 cm (*c*4 in). Tiny, with longish bill but short rounded wings and tail; tawny-buff above with bold dark streaks (more blotched in summer), whitish below with warm buff breast/flanks; beady eyes in pale face, rufous rump, black and whitish tips to all but central tail (esp underside). Flight weak, jerky, but high in undulating display; skulking, but also perches in open and often cocks thin or fanned tail, looking like minute Sedge Warbler (208) or scruffy Wren (194). *Ad = 1st winter.* VOICE Short *zip*, explosive *tew*; song sharp penetrating *zeep . . . zeep . . . zeep . . .* in time with dips in display-flight or from perch. HABITAT. Rushy marshes, rank grassland, cornfields. FOOD Insects. RANGE 3: Apr–Sep, Cork/Dorset/Norfolk; is spreading north in Europe, may colonise. (W/S Europe, S Asia, Africa, Australia.)

Pallas's Grasshopper Warbler *Locustella certhiola* 13–14 cm (*c*5¼ in). Shape/actions as Grasshopper Warbler (208), but larger, more striated above and whiter below, with thin creamy supercilia and rufous rump (*cf* Sedge Warbler, 208), contrasting dark tail shading to blackish near end with grey-white tips on all but central feathers (esp underside). *Ad* White throat and belly, plain warm buff breast and flanks; wings worn in autumn. *1st winter* Creamy below, chest dark-spotted; wings fresh. VOICE Double *chirr* or *cherk*. HABITAT/FOOD As Lanceolated. RANGE 5: Sep–Oct, NE/EBr, EIr. (Cent/E Asia.)

Lanceolated Warbler *Locustella lanceolata* 11–12 cm (*c*4½ in). Shape/actions as Grasshopper Warbler (208), but smaller, darker, heavier-streaked; faint buff-white supercilia, necklace of bold short streaks, usually also longer streaks on flanks, sometimes spots on throat. *1st winter* As ad, but wings fresh. VOICE Chuckled churr. HABITAT Reeds, swamps, thick cover. FOOD Insects. RANGE 28: Sep–early Nov (May), most NE/EBr (esp Shetland). (E Russia, Asia.)

Fan-tailed Warbler

Pallas's Grasshopper Warbler

song-flight

ad

ad

juv–1st winter

ad (worn plumage)

Lanceolated Warbler

juv–1st winter

ad (worn plumage)

River Warbler *Locustella fluviatilis* 13.5–14.5 cm (c5½ in). Shape/actions as Grasshopper Warbler, but larger, longer-winged, with unstreaked upperparts (cf Savi's, 208); faint off-white supercilia, blurred grey-brown streaks on whitish throat/chest, broad whitish tips to brown undertail-coverts. *Ad* Dark olive-brown above but for slightly warmer tail, much whitish below; wings worn. *1st winter* Slightly tinged rufous above (esp scapulars, wing/tail-coverts), more creamy-buff below; wings fresh. VOICE Low harsh churr. HABITAT Damp tangles, thickets. FOOD Insects. RANGE 3: Sep, NE/WBr. (E Europe, W Asia.)

Moustached Warbler *Acrocephalus melanopogon* 12–13 cm (c5 in). Very like Sedge Warbler (208), but shorter wings, more rounded tail, pure white supercilia broader behind eyes and square-ended; crown blacker (esp in summer), cheeks duskier, upperparts/flanks more rufous, mantle bolder-streaked, underparts whiter. *Ad* Wings/tail worn until moult in Aug–Oct. *1st winter* Wings/tail fresh. VOICE Calls as Sedge, but harsher *chuk*. HABITAT Reeds. FOOD Insects. RANGE Pair bred Cambs 1946; 5 others; Apr–Aug, all SEBr. (S Europe, SW Asia, NW Africa.)

Aquatic Warbler *Acrocephalus paludicola* 12–13 cm (c5 in). Like spiky-tailed Sedge Warbler (208), but head striped with creamy crown-band and long supercilia, blackish crown-sides (but cf ill-defined crown-stripe of juv Sedge); bolder black streaks above extend thinly on to rump. Skulking, often on or near ground. *Ad* Ground-colour above greyish in summer, then tawnier with moult in cAug–Oct but worn wings/tail faded grey-brown; creamy below, thinly streaked (esp in summer). *Juv/1st winter* Ground-colour above bright sandy-buff with tawny-buff fringes on fresh wings/tail; more buff below, usually unstreaked. VOICE Calls resemble Sedge Warbler. HABITAT Sedgy marshes; reeds on passage. FOOD Insects. RANGE 569: Apr–Nov, most Aug–early Oct, esp SBr, few EBr and SIr. (Cent/E Europe.)

River Warbler

Moustached Warbler

Aquatic Warbler

Paddyfield Warbler *Acrocephalus agricola* 12–13 cm (*c*5 in). Looks smaller than Reed Warbler (210), with shortest bill, shortest roundest wings, and longest tail of any unstreaked *Acrocephalus*; often brighter rufous above (esp rump) and sandy-buff below, with creamy supercilia broadest behind eyes, legs pale brown to flesh. Flight more whirring than Reed; cocks tail on landing, often flicks tail and raises crest. *Ad* Usually rufous above, but sometimes greyer (except rump); wings/tail worn in autumn. *1st winter* Sandier-brown above; wings/tail fresh with rufous fringes. VOICE Hard *chik*. HABITAT Reeds, waterside cover. FOOD Insects. RANGE 5: Sep–Oct, NE/SWBr. (SE Europe, Asia.)

Blyth's Reed Warbler *Acrocephalus dumetorum* 12–13 cm (*c* 5 in). Very like Marsh Warbler (210), but more peaked crown, shorter rounder wings, longer-looking tail; brown or grey-brown above, with 'spectacled' appearance and supercilia indistinct at rear, legs grey-brown. Flight like Paddyfield; rather deliberate creeping movements; flicks tail. *Ad* Greyish olive-brown above, wearing to grey-brown or brown; wings/tail worn in autumn. *1st winter* Warmer brown, tinged rufous on rump; wings/tail fresh with rufous fringes. VOICE Harsh *tak* and trill, soft *tup tup*. HABITAT Trees, tangles, swamps. FOOD Insects. RANGE 11: Aug–Oct, most N/EBr. (NE Europe, Asia.)

Great Reed Warbler *Acrocephalus arundinaceus* 18–20 cm (*c*7$\frac{1}{2}$ in). Much as Reed Warbler (210), but far larger, twice as bulky, much stouter longer bill, angular head, bold supercilia, dusky lores (*cf* Thick-billed). Flight heavy with rounded tail often fanned, crashing into reeds; actions more lumbering. *Ad* Warm olive-brown above and orange-buff below, wearing greyer and whiter by autumn; faint streaks on throat. *1st winter* More rusty-buff above, esp rump and fresh wings; orange-buff below, no streaks. VOICE Harsh *chak*, churring croak; song loud raucous creaking *karra-karra-karra-gurk-gurk-gurk*. HABITAT Reeds, osiers. FOOD Insects. RANGE 123: May–Nov, esp May–Jun (sometimes in song), most S/EBr. (Cent/S Europe, Asia, NW Africa.)

Thick-billed Warbler *Acrocephalus aedon* 18.5–20.5 cm (*c*7$\frac{3}{4}$ in). Size of Great Reed; shorter thicker bill (clearly curved on top), much shorter rounded wings, longer and more graduated tail; plumage similar, but no supercilia or throat-streaks, lores whitish, rump redder, legs blue-grey. Flight looks weak; raises crest, moves tail like shrike; hops in cover rather than creeping and sidling. *Ad* Olive-brown above; wings/tail worn in autumn. *1st winter* More rufous above, richer buff below; wings/tail fresh. VOICE Loud *chook-chook* and *tak-tak*. HABITAT Trees, scrub, not always near water. FOOD Insects. RANGE 2: Sep–Oct, Shetland. (Asia.)

Olivaceous Warbler *Hippolais pallida* 12–14 cm (*c*5$\frac{1}{4}$ in). Like non-yellow form of Icterine (210), but flatter crown, shorter wings (as Melodious, 210), fatter belly, more rounded tail, W race also longer bill; olive-grey to brown above, buffish-white below, with thin whitish supercilia, eye-rings (often obvious) and tail-sides, bluish to brownish-flesh legs (*cf* Garden Warbler, 214). Flight fluttery, as Melodious. *Ad W race (H.p. opaca)* Larger, with longer tail and esp bill; olive-grey above. *Ad E race (H.p. elaeica)* Smaller, more grey-brown, with shorter bill and tail (*cf* Booted Warbler). *1st winter* As ad, but wings fresh in autumn. VOICE Calls as Melodious. HABITAT Trees, scrub. FOOD Insects. RANGE 12: Aug–Oct, most SBr. (SW Europe/NW Africa, SE Europe/SW Asia.)

Booted Warbler *Hippolais caligata* 11–12 cm (*c*4$\frac{1}{2}$ in). Smaller than Olivaceous (not unlike *Phylloscopus*), with shorter finer bill, rounder head, squarer tail, short wings; brown, greyish, even sandy above, creamy below, with longer supercilia and faint dusky eye-stripes (otherwise similar eye-rings, tail-sides, legs). Flight fluttery. *Ad winter* Warm brownish-olive above; wings worn or moulting in autumn. *1st winter* Greyer or sandier and whiter; wings fresh. VOICE Sharp *tic*, quiet *chuk*. HABITAT/FOOD As Olivaceous. RANGE 12: Aug–Oct, N/E/SBr. (E Europe, Asia.)

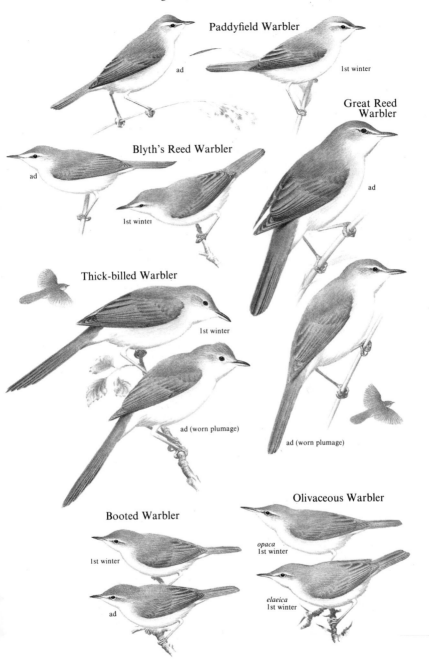

Paddyfield Warbler

ad

1st winter

Great Reed
Warbler

Blyth's Reed Warbler

ad

1st winter

ad

Thick-billed Warbler

1st winter

ad (worn plumage)

ad (worn plumage)

Olivaceous Warbler

Booted Warbler

opaca
1st winter

1st winter

ad

elaeica
1st winter

Spectacled Warbler *Sylvia conspicillata*
11.5–12.5 cm (*c*4¾ in). Like tiny slim
Whitethroat (212) with shorter rufous
wings; whitish spectacles often inconspicuous, legs pale red-brown to yellowish.
Very lively; shy. *Ad ♂* Head slate-grey
with darker lores/ear-coverts, browner
nape; bold white throat shades down into
grey; breast pink, flanks brownish-pink.
Ad ♀ Head browner, often with greyish
lores/ear-coverts; throat tinged buff;
breast dull pink, flanks pink-buff. *1st
winter ♂♀* As dull ad ♀, no greyish. VOICE
Sharp *tek tek*, rattling alarm call.
HABITAT Low scrub. FOOD Insects. RANGE
3: Oct/Jun, SW/NEBr. (SW Europe,
Middle East, NW Africa.)

Subalpine Warbler *Sylvia cantillans*
11.5–12.5 cm (*c*4¾ in). Shape as tiny Lesser
Whitethroat (212) with longish tail; ♂
grey and pinkish with white moustaches;
♀ smaller, slimmer, paler, buffer than ♀
Sardinian, with more white on tail-sides,
sometimes rusty-buff (not bright rufous)
fringes on wings (*cf* Spectacled), legs pale
ochre. Cocks tail. *Ad ♂* Blue-grey above
with pale-fringed brown wings, pink to
orange-brown below with bold moustaches; eye-rings red. *Ad ♀* Brown above,
greyer on head; pink-buff (variably
showing moustaches) to pale buff below;
eye-rings red or yellowish, often whitish
circle outside. *1st winter* As ads, but wings
browner (less grey), tail-sides brownish-
white, eye-rings yellowish; ♀ creamier
below. VOICE Sharp *tek tek*, chatter.
HABITAT Scrub, trees. FOOD Insects. RANGE
90: Apr–Nov (esp May–Jun), most NE/
E/SBr. (S Europe, Turkey, NW Africa.)

Sardinian Warbler *Sylvia melanocephala*
12.5–14 cm (*c*5¼ in). Shape as smallish
Whitethroat (212) but short wings, rounded tail; darkish above with dark hood,
white cornered tail, whitish underparts,
dark flanks, brown legs, often red eye-
rings (*cf* Subalpine, Orphean, Rüppell's).
Cocks and fans tail; skulking. *Ad ♂* Hood
black, mantle dark grey, flanks grey; eye-
rings red. *Ad ♀* Hood dark grey-brown,
mantle brown, flanks dull brown; eye-
rings reddish to brown. *1st winter* As ads,

but ♂ browner above (esp nape and
wings), ♀ hood brown; tail-corners
brownish-white, eye-rings brownish.
VOICE Harsh stutter. HABITAT Scrub, trees.
FOOD Insects, seeds, berries. RANGE 8:
Apr–May, Aug–Oct, most SBr (2 NEBr).
(S Europe, Middle East, N Africa.)

Rüppell's Warbler *Sylvia rueppelli* 13.5–
14.5 cm (*c*5½ in). Larger than Sardinian
with longer wings; paler above (not tail),
black or creamy throat, whitish moustaches, red-brown eye-rings and legs.
Ad ♂ Crown, face and throat black,
moustaches white; blue-grey above, pink-
white below with greyer flanks. *Ad/1st
winter ♀* Crown grey-brown, throat
creamy (both often mottled black on ad),
moustaches whitish; brown above, buff
below with browner flanks. *1st winter ♂*
Browner above; white fringes on throat.
VOICE Harsh chatter, *tak tak*. HABITAT
Scrub, trees. FOOD Insects. RANGE 2: Jun–
Sep, Shetland/Devon. (E Mediterranean.)

Desert Warbler *Sylvia nana* 11–12 cm (*c*4½
in). Tiny, wings/tail longish; sandy with
white-edged brown tail, yellowish eyes,
bill and legs. Often on ground by scrub.
Asian race (S.n. nana) Greyish sandy-
brown above, with warm buff rump;
creamy to greyish below with buff flanks.
N African race (S.n. deserti) Pale sandy
and whitish with rufous rump. VOICE
Sharp *wee-churr*. HABITAT Low scrub.
FOOD Insects. RANGE 3: Oct–Jan, S/EBr
(all Asian). (Cent Asia, N Africa.)

Orphean Warbler *Sylvia hortensis* 14.5–16
cm (*c*6 in). Larger than Lesser Whitethroat
(212), with heavy bill, squared tail; dark
hood (crown browner, cheeks blacker)
merging into grey-brown or brown mantle,
white-sided tail, greyish legs, usually
yellow-white eyes (*cf* Sardinian). Mainly
arboreal. *Ad ♂* Crown brown-black
(spring) to dark brown-grey (autumn);
breast/flanks pink-white. *Ad ♀* Crown
duller grey-brown; breast/flanks buff-
white. *1st winter ♂♀* As ad ♀, but crown
brown as mantle (*cf* Barred, 212). VOICE
Hard rattle, *tak tak*. HABITAT Trees, tall
scrub. FOOD Insects, berries. RANGE 3:
Jul–Oct, SW/EBr. (S Eurasia, N Africa.)

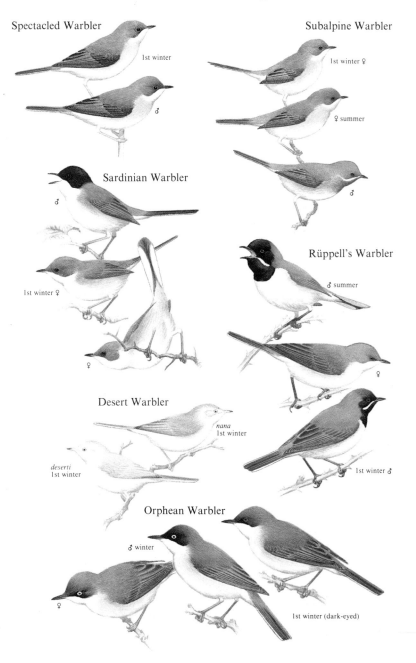

Spectacled Warbler

1st winter

♂

Subalpine Warbler

1st winter ♀

♀ summer

♂

Sardinian Warbler

♂

1st winter ♀

♀

Rüppell's Warbler

♂ summer

♀

1st winter ♂

Desert Warbler

nana
1st winter

deserti
1st winter

Orphean Warbler

♂ winter

♀

1st winter (dark-eyed)

Greenish Warbler *Phylloscopus trochiloides* 10–11 cm (*c*4¼ in). Size/shape of Chiffchaff (216); greyish-olive and whitish, with clear creamy supercilia, usually 1 short whitish wing-bar (but *cf* E Chiffchaff); bill-base pinkish, legs brown-grey. *Ad summer/1st winter* Brighter, greener; wing-bar clear on greater coverts, sometimes trace of 2nd on medians. *Ad winter* Greyer; wings/tail worn; wing-bar faint or missing. VOICE Penetrating *chee-wee*; song short high shrill phrase ('full of saliva') or Wren-like trill. HABITAT Trees, bushes. FOOD Insects. RANGE 133: Aug–Jan, May–Jul (sometimes in song), esp E/SBr, SIr. (E Europe, Asia.)

Arctic Warbler *Phylloscopus borealis* 11.5–12.5 cm (*c*4¾ in). Robust, larger than Greenish, with heavier bill, flatter forehead; olive and whitish, with long upturned creamy supercilia, 1–2 thin whitish wing-bars; bill-base orange-yellow or yellow-brown as legs. *Ad winter* Wings/tail faded brown; often median wing-bar missing, rarely both; whitish below. *1st winter* Wings/tail dark brown; median wing-bar present till *c*Sep; darker greenish above, yellower-white below. VOICE Husky *tssik*, hoarse *tswee-ip*. HABITAT/FOOD As Greenish. RANGE 105: Aug–Oct (Jul), esp EBr. (N Eurasia, Alaska.)

Pallas's Warbler *Phylloscopus proregulus* 8.5–9.5 cm (*c*3½ in). Tiny, like Goldcrest (236); bright green and whitish, with long yellow supercilia, crown-stripe, 2 wing-bars, rump. Hovers among leaves. *Ad = 1st winter*. VOICE Shrill *sweep* and *choo-ee*. HABITAT Trees. FOOD Insects. RANGE 146: Oct–Nov, esp E/SBr. (Cent/E Asia.)

Radde's Warbler *Phylloscopus schwarzi* 12–13 cm (*c*5 in). Larger, bulkier than Chiffchaff (216), with longer thicker bill, longer tail, stout legs, similar shortish rounded wings; brownish- to greenish-olive and buff-white, with browner head, long broad upturned creamy supercilia edged with black, rusty vent; bill-base pink to orange, legs pinkish-yellow. Skulks; much on ground. *1st winter* More

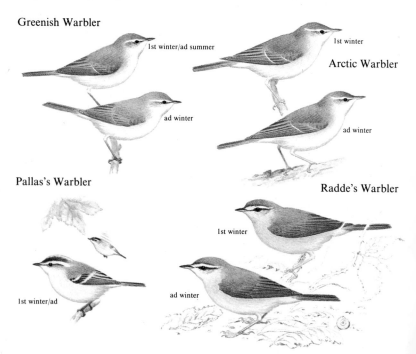

Greenish Warbler

1st winter/ad summer

ad winter

1st winter

Arctic Warbler

ad winter

Pallas's Warbler

1st winter/ad

Radde's Warbler

1st winter

ad winter

buff throat(?). VOICE Soft *tchwit*, harder *tchwik* and *chirp trok-trok*. HABITAT Wood-edges, scrub. FOOD Insects. RANGE 28: end Sep–Oct, esp E/SBr. (Cent/E Asia.)

Dusky Warbler *Phylloscopus fuscatus* 11.5–12.5 cm (*c*4¾ in). Slighter than Radde's with finer bill, shorter tail; brown and creamy-grey, with longish rusty-white supercilia, rusty cheeks and flanks; bill-base and legs yellow-brown. Skulks; much on ground; cocks tail and flicks wings. *Ad winter* Brown above, no yellow below. *1st winter* Olive-brown above, some yellow on belly. VOICE Loud *tak*, *chik*, chattering *tsek-tsek*. HABITAT Scrub, reeds. FOOD Insects. RANGE 29: Aug–Nov (May), esp E/SBr. (Cent/E Asia.)

Bonelli's Warbler *Phylloscopus bonelli* 11–12 cm (*c*4½ in). Just larger, bigger-headed than Chiffchaff (216), wings less rounded; grey-brown above with greyer head, yellowish wing-panel, rump, and tail-fringes, white below; bill-base pinkish, legs dark pink-brown. *Ad* Rump yellow-

green; wings/tail faded by autumn. *1st winter* Mantle greyer, rump pale olive-brown; wings/tail fresh, bright-edged. VOICE Loud *hoo-eet*; song short even trill. HABITAT Trees, bushes. FOOD Insects. RANGE 68: Aug–early Nov, also Apr–Jun (sometimes in song), esp S/E/WBr, SIr. (Cent/S Europe, NW Africa, SW Asia.)

FLYCATCHERS (Muscicapidae)

Collared Flycatcher *Ficedula albicollis* 12–13 cm (*c*5 in). Like long-winged Pied (218); differs as follows. ♂ *summer* White collar, whitish rump, more white on fore-head and base of primaries, little or none on tail-sides. *Ad* ♀ Greyer above, usually white patch on primaries, often hint of pale collar and rump. ♂ *winter* As ♀ from *c*Aug–Sep but for black flight-feathers, outer wing-coverts and central tail. *1st winter* As ad ♀ unless pale spots on some or all median coverts. VOICE Drawn-out *wheee*. HABITAT Trees, scrub. FOOD Insects. RANGE 10: May–Jun (Sep), most N/EBr. (Cent/SE Europe, W Asia.)

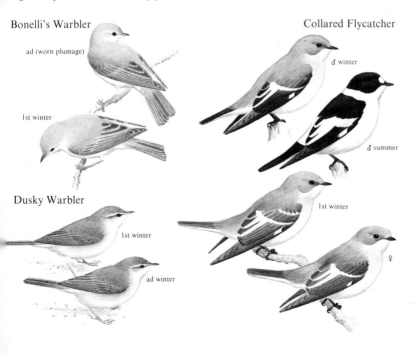

Bonelli's Warbler — ad (worn plumage) — 1st winter
Dusky Warbler — 1st winter — ad winter
Collared Flycatcher — ♂ winter — ♂ summer — 1st winter — ♀

WALLCREEPERS (Tichodromadidae)

Wallcreeper *Tichodroma muraria* 16–17 cm (*c*6½ in). Long curved bill, long broad rounded wings narrowing at base; largely grey with crimson patches and white spots on blackish wings, white-edged dark tail. Flits jerkily like butterfly; climbs rock faces with small hops, leisurely flicking wings, and probes into crevices. ♂ *summer* Throat to breast black *c*Apr–Aug. ♀ *summer* Throat whitish with small black patch, or no black (probably 1st year), and breast grey. *Ad winter* Throat whitish. *Juv* Bill straighter at first, all underparts brown-grey; as ad winter after moult in Aug–Nov. VOICE Thin high piping. HABITAT Cliffs, ruins. FOOD Insects. RANGE 10: Sep–Jun, most SBr; wintered Nov–Apr in 3 years 1969–78. (S/Cent Eurasia.)

TREECREEPERS (Certhiidae)

Short-toed Treecreeper *Certhia brachydactyla* 12–13 cm (*c*5 in). *Very* like Treecreeper (226): tends to be duller/greyer above with less rusty rump, shorter/less distinct supercilia, and less white below with rufous-tinged flanks; on average, bill longer/more curved, hind-claws shorter, but much overlap. Calls similar, but include loud *chink*, Dunnock-like *zeet*. RANGE 7: Sep–Oct, Apr–May, SE/EBr. (W/Cent/S Europe, Turkey, NW Africa.)

PENDULINE TITS (Remizidae)

Penduline Tit *Remiz pendulinus* 10.5–11 cm (*c*4¼ in). Tiny with prominent tail; grey head, black mask, rusty back, white-edged blackish flight-feathers and tail, and buff underparts tinged pinkish on breast and flanks. Flight more fluttery than Blue Tit (224); flicks tail. *Ad* ♂ Mask black, crown to upper mantle grey, lower mantle chestnut, back rufous. *Ad* ♀ Mask smaller and not solid black, crown to nape grey-brown, mantle pale chestnut. *Juv* Duller, browner, no mask; as ad after moult in Aug–Sep. VOICE Thin plaintive *tsee*, rather Robin-like. HABITAT Waterside thickets; vagrants in coastal bushes. FOOD Insects, seeds. RANGE 3: Oct/May, Humberside/Scilly/Kent. (S/Cent Eurasia.)

SHRIKES (Laniidae)

Isabelline Shrike *Lanius isabellinus* 16–18 cm (*c*6¾ in). Shape as Red-backed Shrike (228), but grey-buff above, with rusty rump and tail, white bar on base of primaries (S/E races sandier above, browner mask, often no wing-bar). *Ad* ♂ Grey-buff above in summer, paler in winter; narrow black mask; white below with pink-buff flanks. *Ad* ♀ Even paler above; mask not pure black on lores; greyish crescent bars on breast-sides. *1st winter* Duller, barred additionally on wing-coverts and flanks. VOICE/HABITAT/FOOD Much as Red-backed. RANGE 15: Aug–Oct (Mar–May), most E/SBr (1 SWIr). (S/Cent Asia.)

Lesser Grey Shrike *Lanius minor* 19–21 cm (*c*8 in). Like small Great Grey (228), with stubbier bill, longer wings, shorter tail; mask over forehead, no white supercilia, less white on scapulars, bolder wing-bar. Flight straighter; perches more upright. *Ad* ♂ Deep mask black; pink tinge below. *Ad* ♀ Narrower mask blackish, mottled grey on forehead; creamier below. *Juv–1st winter* Brown-grey above, with varying dark bars, greyish forehead, brown-black wings and tail; traces of faint bars on flanks. VOICE/HABITAT As Great Grey. FOOD Esp insects. RANGE 112: May–Nov, esp EBr, only 2 Ir. (S Europe, SW Asia.)

Woodchat Shrike *Lanius senator* 16–18 cm (*c*6¾ in). Size of Red-backed Shrike (228), but larger head, broader wings, shorter tail; pied, with chestnut crown/nape, white scapulars, wing-bar and rump, bold white underparts. Perches more unobtrusively. *Ad* ♂ Mask black, mantle blackish, wings/tail black. *Ad* ♀ Narrower mask mixed with brown and whitish, mantle brown, wings/tail brown, some crescents on breast/flanks. *Juv–1st winter* Greyish to rufous above, and paler and more scaly than imm Red-backed, with pale scapulars, rump and wing-bar; creamy below, barred with black crescents. VOICE Hard chatter. HABITAT Trees, scrub. FOOD Birds, insects. RANGE 402: Apr–Oct, esp SW/EBr, SIr. (Cent/S Europe, SW Asia, NW Africa.)

Wallcreeper

♀ summer

♂ summer

ad/1st winter

Short-toed Treecreeper

ad

Penduline Tit

juv

♂

Isabelline Shrike

ad

1st winter

♂

Lesser Grey Shrike

ad

♂

juv–1st winter

Woodchat Shrike

♂

juv–1st winter

♀

♂ summer

CROWS (Corvidae)

Nutcracker *Nucifraga caryocatactes* 30–33 cm (*c*21½ in). Shape closest to small Jay (228), but longer pointed bill, short tail; chocolate speckled with white, but plain cap, blacker wings/tail, bold white on undertail-coverts, white tail-end (obvious from below). Actions much as Jay, with rather slow jerky flight; perches more in open (often on tree-tops); hops clumsily. *1st winter* Tends to be browner than ad, less glossy wings with more spots on coverts. VOICE Harsh high *kraak*. HABITAT Conifers; vagrants in any woods, fields. FOOD Conifer seeds, hazel nuts, berries. RANGE 399 (315 in 1968): most Aug–Jan, esp SEBr. (Eurasia.)

STARLINGS (Sturnidae)

Rose-coloured Starling *Sturnus roseus* 20.5–22.5 cm (*c*8½ in). Shape/actions as Starling (234), but bill more thrush-like; ad pink and black with crest; juv sandy. *Summer* Ad ♂ brighter pink, glossier black, crest fuller; ♀/1st summer ♂ duller, pink variably obscured by grey-brown. *Winter* After moult in Aug–Oct, pattern variably obscured by grey-buff tips, esp on pink upperparts and more so on ♀/1st winter ♂, while 1st winter ♀ brown, dull, short-crested, almost no pink above. *Juv* Sandy-fawn with paler throat/rump, dark wings/tail, dark-tipped yellowish bill; moults in *c*Aug–Nov. VOICE Starling-like but higher, harsher. HABITAT Fields, open country. FOOD Insects, fruit. RANGE 267: all months, esp Jun–Oct, wide-scattered, esp NE/SBr. (SE Europe, SW Asia.)

SPARROWS (Passeridae)

Spanish Sparrow *Passer hispaniolensis* 14–15.5 cm (*c*5¾ in). As House Sparrow (234), but ♂ has chestnut crown, whiter cheek-patches, more black on breast, heavily streaked shoulders/flanks; other plumages show traces of this pattern in paler cheeks, more striped and contrasted back, faint flank-streaks. VOICE Similar, but richer, less harsh. HABITAT Scrub, trees, woods. FOOD Seeds. RANGE 3: Jun, Oct, Devon/Scilly. (Mediterranean, SW Asia.)

FINCHES (Fringillidae)

Serin *Serinus serinus* 11–12 cm (*c*4½ in). Tiny, with stubby bill, longish wings, short notched tail; streaky, yellowish, with yellow rump (not juv), no yellow in tail. Flight fast, undulating; often in trees, but feeds much by hopping on ground. ♂ *summer* Forecrown, hindneck, throat/breast unstreaked yellow. ♂ *winter* After moult in Aug–Sep, yellow of forecrown, supercilia and hindneck more or less obscured, throat/breast greener-yellow, flanks less clearly streaked. *Ad ♀* Crown/hindneck yellow-green, heavily streaked; supercilia and throat/breast yellow-white streaked dark. *Juv* Brown-buff above, rump barely paler, all streaked dark; yellow-buff below streaked brown; as ads after moult in Aug–Sep. VOICE Flight-call liquid twittering trill; other calls include weak *chip-chip*, sharp tit-like *chirr*, anxious *tsooeet*; song rapid hissing jangle like miniature Corn Bunting (248). HABITAT Gardens, parks, wood-edges, esp near weedy ground. NEST In trees, tall bushes, 3–5 eggs, end Apr–Jul; 2 broods. FOOD Seeds of weeds, alder, birch. RANGE 397: all months, esp Feb–Jun, Oct–Nov, mainly SBr; nested 1967, 1969, 1978. (Europe, Asia Minor, NW Africa.)

Arctic Redpoll *Carduelis hornemanni* 12–13.5 cm (*c*5 in). Like Mealy race of Redpoll (240), not always separable; typically shows clear white rump and paler head with contrasting grey back, bolder wing-bars, whiter underparts with few thin streaks on breast-sides/flanks, but rather variable (*eg* rump and flanks may be tinged buff). *Ad ♂* Variably tinged pink on cheeks, breast, esp rump. ♀/*1st year ♂* No pink (except red crown), but some 1st year ♂s slightly pink on rump. *Greenland (C.h. hornemanni) and N Eurasian (C.h. exilipes) races* Many inseparable, but Greenland ♂ typically bigger, whiter, less streaked, often with 'hoar-frosted' face. VOICE Flight-note slower, sharper than Redpoll. HABITAT/FOOD Much as Redpoll, but less linked with trees. RANGE 89: Jul–Apr, most Oct–Feb, esp N/EBr. (Circumpolar Arctic.)

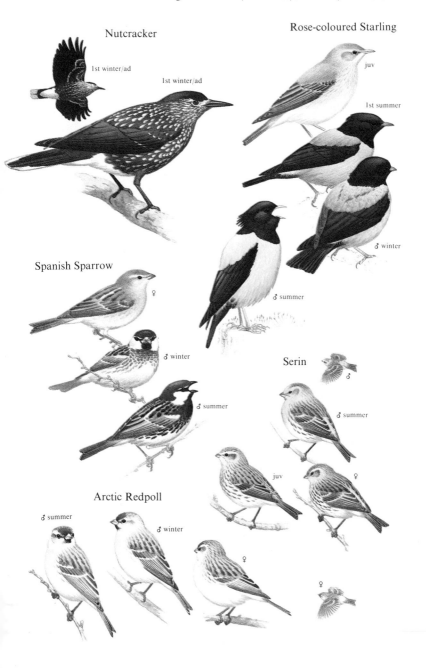

Nutcracker

1st winter/ad

1st winter/ad

Rose-coloured Starling

juv

1st summer

♂ winter

♂ summer

Spanish Sparrow

♀

♂ winter

♂ summer

Serin

♂

♂ summer

juv

♀

Arctic Redpoll

♂ summer

♂ winter

♀

♀

Two-barred Crossbill *Loxia leucoptera*
14–15 cm (*c*5¾ in). Like small Crossbill
(242), but rather brighter, with 2 white
wing-bars, white-tipped inner secondaries.
Habits as Crossbill. *Ad ♂* Red areas
uniform bright scarlet-carmine. *Ad ♀*
Yellower-green than Crossbill with
yellower rump; streaks on crown and
mantle stand out more. *1st year ♂* Colours
mixed as Crossbill, but paler, brighter;
white wing-marks smaller than ad. VOICE
Less emphatic Crossbill-like *jip jip*,
drier *jif jif* not unlike Redpoll (240).
HABITAT Conifers, esp larches. FOOD
Conifer seeds. RANGE 63: most Jul–Feb,
scattered, esp EBr. (N Eurasia, America.)

Parrot Crossbill *Loxia pytyopsittacus*
16.5–17.5 cm (*c*6¾ in). Differs from Crossbill and Scottish Crossbill (242) in larger,
deeper, stouter bill giving top-heavy look;
plumages and habits similar. VOICE
Deeper, stronger *jop jop*. HABITAT
Conifers, esp pines. FOOD Pine seeds.
RANGE Over 70: mostly Sep–Mar, esp
1962/63, mainly EBr. (N Europe.)

Trumpeter Finch *Bucanetes githagineus*
12–13 cm (*c*5 in). Linnet-sized (240), but
dumpier, shorter-tailed, with big head and
stout, round-tipped, red or yellowish bill,
often pinkish legs; sandy-brown with
darker wings/tail, more or less tinged
pink. Inconspicuous ground-feeder, often
crouched, upright when alert; suddenly
flies off high. *♂ summer* Bill orange-red
like blob of sealing wax; much pink, esp
on face, rump, wing-edges and underparts; head grey. *♂ winter* Bill orange-
brown; body duller, pink obscured by
buff. *Ad ♀* Bill pink-orange to yellowish;
body much less bright, but usually faint
pink wash in summer. *Juv/1st winter* Bill
yellow-brown; yellow-buff cheeks; pink
first on rump. VOICE Flight-call nasal
buzzing note, far-carrying. HABITAT
Desert, stony uplands; vagrants in dunes,
fields. FOOD Seeds. RANGE 2: May–Jun,
Suffolk/Sutherland. (N Africa, SW Asia.)

Scarlet Rosefinch *Carpodacus erythrinus*
14–15 cm (*c*5¾ in). Dumpy, with stout
conical bill, rounded head, beady black

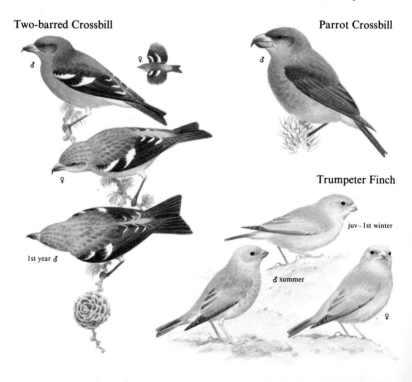

Two-barred Crossbill

Parrot Crossbill

Trumpeter Finch

eyes; carmine-pink, or brown and streaky; 2 faint bars on darker wings. Settles on bushes or ground. *Ad ♂* Head, rump and breast carmine-pink, brighter in summer; otherwise brown with whitish belly, variably tinged pink. *♀/1st year ♂* Olive-brown to grey-brown above and whitish-buff below, streaked esp on breast. VOICE Soft *teu-ik*. HABITAT Marshy woods, scrub; migrants in fields. FOOD Seeds. RANGE 750 + : most Aug-Oct, few May-Jun, esp N/EBr. (E Europe, Asia.)

Pine Grosbeak *Pinicola enucleator* 20–22 cm (*c*8 in). Starling-sized finch with heavy bill, flat crown, stout body, longish tail; mainly rose-pink or greenish-gold with 2 white bars on brown wings. Flight strong, undulating; clambers in trees like Crossbill (242), much on ground; tame. *Ad ♂* Rose-pink to scarlet, with greyish back, scapulars and belly, dark brown wings and tail with pink-white edges and wing-bars. *Ad ♀* Greenish-gold where ♂ pink, esp on head and breast, wearing to duller yellow-green in summer. *1st year ♂* As ad ♀, but

often pinker-yellow on head/breast. VOICE Low whistling *tee-tee-tew*. HABITAT Coniferous/mixed woods, scrub. FOOD Berries, seeds, buds. RANGE 9: Apr–May, Oct–Nov, EBr. (N Eurasia, N America.)

Evening Grosbeak *Hesperiphona vespertina* 20–22 cm (*c*8 in). Shape of big Hawfinch (242) with huge bill, short tail; mainly yellow or greyish, with much black on wings/tail, and white inner secondaries. On trees or ground; tame. *Ad ♂* Primarily yellow with bold U back from forehead showing against olive-brown head and forebody; tail all black; white on secondaries tinged yellow in winter, whitish-horn bill turns green in spring. *Ad ♀* Greyish, tinged yellow on nape and flanks, with whitish throat, dirty white on secondaries, other white marks on wings and tail. *1st winter* As ads, but white inner secondaries edged buff. VOICE Harsh penetrating chirp. HABITAT Conifer forests; seeding trees in winter. FOOD Seeds (esp maple), berries, buds, insects. RANGE 2: Mar, St Kilda/Highland. (N America.)

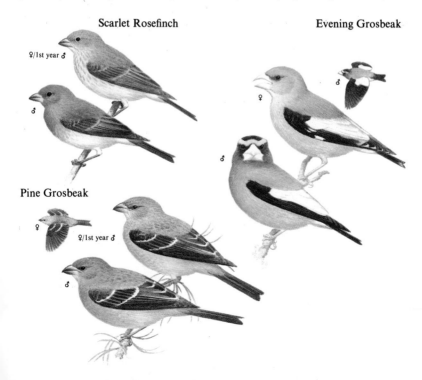

Scarlet Rosefinch

Evening Grosbeak

Pine Grosbeak

AMERICAN WARBLERS (Parulidae)

Black-and-white Warbler *Mniotilta varia*
13–14 cm (*c*5¼ in). Striped black and
white; white crown-stripe and supercilia.
Creeps up and down trunks and branches;
moves slowly, often hops from side to
side; catches flies. *Ad ♂* Cheeks black;
throat black in summer, streaked black in
winter. *Ad ♀* Cheeks whitish, throat white,
flanks less streaked; blacks browner, esp
in winter when flanks washed buff. *1st
winter ♂* Cheeks and throat as ad ♀, but
body blacker and whiter, clearer flank-
streaks. *1st winter ♀* Browner still than ad
♀ with dull white stripes, very obscure
flank-streaks. VOICE Weak *chip*, louder
chink, buzzing notes. HABITAT Woods,
trees. FOOD Insects. RANGE 6: Sep–Oct
(1 Mar), SW/NEBr, SWIr. (N America.)

Tennessee Warbler *Vermivora peregrina*
12–13 cm (*c*5 in). Winter plumages like
stocky Willow Warbler (216), but bright
green above, 0–2 pale wing-bars, white
undertail-coverts, grey legs. *♂ summer*
Grey crown, white supercilia, black eye-
stripes, green above with no wing-bars,
whitish below. *♀ summer* Crown washed
green; yellowish below. *Ad/1st winter*
Bright olive-green above, yellow below
but for white at rear; yellowish supercilia/
eye-rings, 1–2 pale wing-bars. VOICE
Firecrest-like *zit-zit*. HABITAT Tree-tops;
migrants in bushes. FOOD Insects. RANGE
2: Sep, Shetland. (N America.)

Parula Warbler *Parula americana* 11–12
cm (*c*4¾ in). Bluish and yellow with white
broken eye-rings, wing-bars, belly. Clings
to trunks, hangs from twigs like tit. *Ad ♂*
Blue above with green patch, breast-band
blackish/chestnut; in winter, blue tinged
green, less breast-band. *Ad ♀* Duller; little
or no breast-band. *1st winter* As ads, but
greener above, duller below; *♂* traces of
breast-band. VOICE Soft *weet*, buzzy trill.
HABITAT Trees, bushes. FOOD Insects.
RANGE 3: Oct–Nov, SWBr. (N America.)

Yellow Warbler *Dendroica petechia* 12–13
cm (*c*5 in). Mainly yellow; 2 yellow wing-
bars, yellow-edged wing/tail-feathers, bold
black eyes. *Ad ♂* Very yellow, but greener

above, with chestnut-tinged crown,
chestnut streaks below; duller, less
streaked in winter. *Ad ♀* Duller, head less
yellow; few streaks below, none in winter.
1st winter Pale greenish above, dull yellow
below; *♂* lightly streaked. VOICE Sharp
chip, thin *tsee*. HABITAT Trees, bushes, esp
by water. FOOD Insects. RANGE 1: Aug,
Gwynedd. (N America.)

Cape May Warbler *Dendroica tigrina*
12–13 cm (*c*5 in). Mainly greenish above,
with yellowish rump and neck-sides, 2
white wing-bars, white near tips of outer
tail; yellow or whitish below with dark
streaks. *Ad ♂* Blackish crown, chestnut
cheeks, white shoulder-patches, and much
yellow, boldly streaked above and below;
in winter, much duller (no chestnut),
obscured by grey and whitish edgings, but
crown still blackish, back streaked. *Ad ♀*
More uniform above, but for wing-bars
and rump, with yellowish supercilia and
neck-sides, yellowish throat/breast
streaked blackish-grey; duller in winter.
1st winter ♂ As ♀ winter, and scarcely
streaked above, but yellower below with
heavier streaks. *1st winter ♀* Duller,
browner above; dull whitish below with
smudgy grey streaks. VOICE Song of high
thin *seet* notes. HABITAT Spruce forests;
trees, bushes. FOOD Insects. RANGE 1: ♂
singing, Jun, Strathclyde. (N America.)

Yellow-rumped Warbler *Dendroica
coronata* 13.5–14.5 cm (*c*5½ in). Yellow
patches on rump, breast-sides and crown,
2 white wing-bars, white in outer tail.
Clings to trunks, often feeds on ground.
Ad ♂ Blue-grey, streaked black, with
whitish supercilia, black cheeks; whitish
below, with black on breast/flanks; in
winter, browner above, no black on
cheeks, less heavily marked below. *Ad ♀*
Duller, browner, less yellow, less boldly
marked below. *1st winter* Duller brown
and less streaked above with obscure
crown- and breast-patches (esp ♀); dull
white below, buff throat and flanks,
faintly streaked. VOICE Loud *chek*.
HABITAT Conifers; trees, bushes. FOOD
Insects; berries, seeds. RANGE 7: Oct–Feb
(1 May), most SWBr/SIr. (N America.)

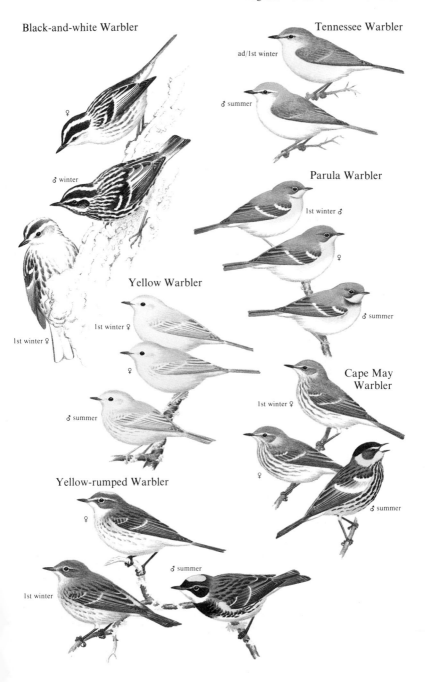

Black-and-white Warbler

Tennessee Warbler

ad/1st winter

♂ summer

♀

♂ winter

Parula Warbler

1st winter ♂

♀

Yellow Warbler

♂ summer

1st winter ♀

1st winter ♀

♀

♂ summer

Cape May
Warbler

1st winter ♀

♂ summer

♀

♂ summer

Yellow-rumped Warbler

♀

♂ summer

1st winter

Blackpoll Warbler *Dendroica striata* 13–14 cm (*c*5¼ in). Streaky grey-green and yellowish (but summer ♂ black, grey and white), with 2 wing-bars, white vent and undertail-patches, and legs brownish or yellowish with yellow feet. *♂ summer* Black cap/moustaches, white cheeks/underparts, black streaks on flanks and greyish mantle. *♀ summer* Grey-green above, whitish below, streaked blackish on mantle/flanks. *Ad winter* After moult in Jul–Aug, greener and yellow-white, with thinner streaks. *1st winter* Yellower below, all streaking obscurer; tertials edged whiter. VOICE High *zit*, louder *chik*. HABITAT Trees, scrub. FOOD Insects. RANGE 15: Sep–Nov, all SW/WBr. (N America.)

American Redstart *Setophaga ruticilla* 12–13 cm (*c*5 in). Butterfly-like warbler; black with white belly, or olive-brown and white, with orange or yellow patches on breast-sides, wings and tail. Flits, flycatches, droops wings, fans tail. *Ad ♂* Black and orange; buff fringes in autumn. *Ad ♀* Olive-brown, white and yellow with grey head, white eye-rings. *Imm ♂* As ♀, but greener and duller white, with grey-buff throat, orangy breast-sides; little black by 1st summer, all by 2nd winter when wing/tail-patches sometimes still yellow. *1st winter* ♀ Browner above, less yellow on wings and breast-sides. VOICE Clear *tseet*, short *chip*. HABITAT Trees, bushes. FOOD Insects. RANGE 2: Oct, Cork/Cornwall. (N America.)

Ovenbird *Seiurus aurocapillus* 14.5–16 cm (*c*6 in). Portly, terrestrial warbler ('ovenlike' nest on ground); olive-green above with black-edged orange crown, white eye-rings, creamy below with stripes of black spots, pink legs. Walks and runs like pipit or tiny thrush, quivers and cocks tail. *Ad* Crown pale orange; mainly white below. *1st winter* Crown greenish-orange; creamier below with more buff flanks. VOICE Sharp *chik*. HABITAT Undergrowth. FOOD Insects, berries. RANGE 2: Oct/Dec, Shetland/Mayo. (N. America.)

Northern Waterthrush *Seiurus noveboracensis* 14.5–16 cm (*c*6 in). Plump, pipit-like warbler with short tail; olive-brown above with bold yellowish to buff supercilia, yellowish below with lines of brown streaks, spotted throat, dirty pink legs. Walks and runs with constant teetering and tail-wagging. *Ad* White inner tips to outer 2–4 tail-feathers. *1st winter* No white tips. VOICE Sharp *spink*, *pweet*. HABITAT Low cover by water. FOOD Insects. RANGE 2: Sep–Oct, Scilly. (N America.)

Yellowthroat *Geothlypis trichas* 12–13 cm (*c*5 in). Olive-brown above, yellow throat, whitish belly; ♂ has black mask. Dodges Wren-like in and out of cover; cocks tail; often on ground. *Ad ♂* Grey band above mask; yellow below, white belly, brown flanks. *Ad ♀* Throat yellow, breast/flanks buff, belly whitish. *1st winter ♂* Variable grey-black traces of mask on cheeks, throat paler yellow. *1st winter ♀* Browner above, throat buff. VOICE Hoarse *chep*. HABITAT Thickets by water. FOOD Insects. RANGE 1: Nov, Devon. (N America.)

Hooded Warbler *Wilsonia citrina* 13–14 cm (*c*5½ in). Plain olive and yellow with yellow face, ♂ black 'hood'; longish tail often flicked or fanned, showing white on outer 3 feathers. *Ad ♂* Black head, yellow mask. *Ad ♀* Yellow face/underparts; often traces of (sometimes much) black on crown/neck-sides. *1st winter ♂* Yellow fringes on black of head, esp throat. *1st winter ♀* As ad ♀, but greenish cheeks below yellow supercilia, no black, browner wings/tail. VOICE Metallic *chink*. HABITAT Damp thickets. FOOD Insects. RANGE 1: Sep, Scilly. (N America.)

VIREOS (Vireonidae)

Red-eyed Vireo *Vireo olivaceus* 14.5–16 cm (*c*6 in). Like largish thickset warbler with stout bill, short tail, thick grey legs; olive-green and whitish, with blue-grey crown, bold white supercilia edged with black (*cf ♂* Tennessee Warbler, 320). Movements deliberate. *Ad* Eyes red. *1st autumn* Eyes brown. VOICE Whining nasal *chway*. HABITAT Woods, tall cover. FOOD Insects, berries. RANGE 11: Oct, all SWBr, SIr. (N America.)

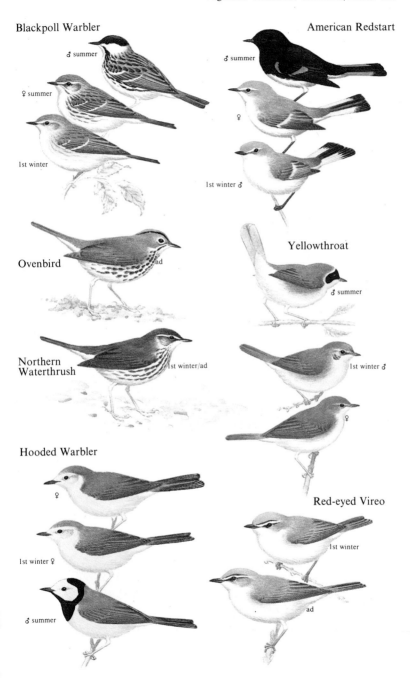

Blackpoll Warbler

♂ summer

♀ summer

1st winter

American Redstart

♂ summer

♀

1st winter ♂

Ovenbird

ad

Northern
Waterthrush

1st winter/ad

Hooded Warbler

♀

1st winter ♀

♂ summer

Yellowthroat

♂ summer

1st winter ♂

♀

Red-eyed Vireo

1st winter

ad

TANAGERS (Thraupidae)

Summer Tanager *Piranga rubra* 17.5–19.5 cm (*c*7¼ in). Like big finch with heavy pale bill; red, or olive and orange-yellow with yellow underwings, no black. Flight fast, also flycatches; arboreal, actions rather deliberate, shy. *Ad* ♂ All rose-red, bill whitish. *Ad* ♀ Brownish-olive and dull gold, bill yellowish; old ♀s have some red feathers. *1st winter* As ad ♀, but ♂ all tinged orange, ♀ yellower. *1st summer* ♂ Red or mottled, but wings still greenish. VOICE Low rattling *piki-tuki-tuk*. HABITAT Trees. FOOD Insects (*eg* bees), berries. RANGE 1: Sep, Gwynedd. (N America.)

Scarlet Tanager *Piranga olivacea* 17–19 cm (*c*7 in). Shape/actions as Summer Tanager, smaller bill often darker; red, or green and yellow with whitish underwings, black or grey-brown wings/tail. ♂ *summer* Scarlet and black, bill whitish. ♂ *winter* Blotched during moult in Jul–Sep, then yellow-green above, yellow below, wings/tail still black. *Ad* ♀ As winter ♂, but olive-green above with dark grey-brown wings/tail fringed greenish, duskier shoulders; bill pink-grey. *1st winter* ♂ As ad ♀, but variably black wing-coverts. *1st winter* ♀ Duller, less yellow, no black. *1st summer* ♂ Scarlet or orange with black coverts/tail, brown flight-feathers. VOICE Low *chik-kurr*. HABITAT/FOOD As Summer Tanager. RANGE 2: Oct, Scilly. (N America.)

BUNTINGS, AMERICAN SPARROWS (Emberizidae)

Rufous-sided Towhee *Pipilo erythroph-thalmus* 19–21.5 cm (*c*8 in). Big 'sparrow' with long rounded tail; dark head/upper-parts, white wing-patches/tail-corners/belly, rufous flanks, usually red eyes. Flight jerky, with pumping tail; much on ground, rummages in dead leaves, cocks/fans tail. *Ad* ♂ Dark parts black. *Ad* ♀ Rich brown instead. *1st year* As ads, but ♂ primary-coverts brownish; eyes brown at first. VOICE Loud *cheweek*. HABITAT Thick scrub. FOOD Seeds, berries, insects, snails. RANGE 1: Jun, Devon. (N/Cent America.)

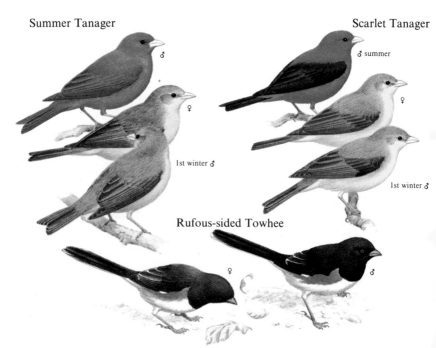

Summer Tanager

Scarlet Tanager

♂

♀

1st winter ♂

♂ summer

♀

1st winter ♂

Rufous-sided Towhee

♀

♂

Fox Sparrow *Zonotrichia iliaca* 17–19 cm (*c*7 in). Size of Corn Bunting; grey-buff above, white below, all heavily streaked chestnut; 2 buff bars on rufous wings, plain foxy-red rump/tail, often breast-smudge. Rummages about like Towhee; skulks. *Ad/1st year* Very chestnut above in autumn, greyer by summer. VOICE Loud *chek*, thin *tseep*. HABITAT Woods, thickets. RANGE 1: Jun, Co Down. (N America.)

Song Sparrow *Zonotrichia melodia* 15–16.5 cm (*c*6¼ in). Dunnock-like, but with bunting bill, and longish rounded tail; dark-streaked grey-brown above with striped head, and whitish below with heavy rufous-black streaks, breast-smudge. Pumps tail in flight and perched; skulks. *Ad = 1st year*. VOICE Nasal *chip*, high *tseet*. HABITAT Thickets. RANGE 5: Apr–Jun, N/WBr. (N America.)

White-crowned Sparrow *Zonotrichia leucophrys* 16–18 cm (*c*6¾ in). Larger, bulkier than Yellowhammer, with high puffy crown; bold-striped head, 2 wing-bars, greyish above with dark streaks, grey below with whitish chin, yellow-pink bill (*cf* White-throated). Perches erect; much on ground in open. *Ad* Cap white with black stripes meeting at front. *1st winter* Head-stripes buff and chestnut, body more buff-grey; as ad after moult in Mar–May. VOICE Metallic *chink* and *peet*. HABITAT Open scrub areas. RANGE 2: May, Shetland/Humberside. (N America.)

White-throated Sparrow *Zonotrichia albicollis* 16–18 cm (*c*6¾ in). More compact/Dunnock-like than White-crowned; more chestnut above, black-edged white throat, yellow front to supercilia, dark bill. Flicks wings, skulks. *Ad* Head-stripes either white and black in summer (white usually tinged buff in *c*Aug–Apr) or much as 1st winter all year. *1st winter* Stripes tawny and black-brown (crown sometimes grey or white); throat duller, browner-grey below with variable thin streaking. VOICE Hard *pink*, high *tseet*. HABITAT Forest undergrowth, thickets. RANGE 12: Apr–Jun, Oct–Nov, scattered. (N America.)

Fox Sparrow

ad summer

White-crowned Sparrow

1st winter

ad summer

1st winter/
tawny-striped ad

Song Sparrow

1st winter
variant

ad summer

white-striped
ad summer

White-throated Sparrow

Slate-coloured Junco *Junco hyemalis*
15–16.5 cm (*c*6¼ in). Neat bunting; slate
or brown with bold white belly/tail-sides,
pink-white bill. Much on ground, flicking
tail; not shy. *Ad ♂* Slate-grey, darkest on
head, with grey-edged blackish wings;
brown fringes after moult in Aug–Sep.
Ad ♀ Paler browner-grey. *1st year* As ads,
but broader brown fringes on ♂ (esp
mantle, flanks), browner worn juv flight-
feathers (tertials with faded tawny fringes)
and tail (2 rather than 3 white outer
feathers), bill often duller flesh. VOICE
Twittering *tit-it-it*, abrupt *chet*, smacking
tack. HABITAT Scrub, untended fields.
FOOD Seeds, insects. RANGE 9: Apr–May
(Jan), N/E/WBr, WIr. (N America.)

Pine Bunting *Emberiza leucocephalos* 16–
17 cm (*c*6½ in). Like Yellowhammer (246)
in many ways, inc rump/tail, but white
instead of yellow, lesser coverts brown.
Ad ♂ White, chestnut and black on head,
chestnut streaks on white breast/flanks;
all partly obscured by grey-buff after
moult in Aug–Sep. *Ad ♀* Dark-streaked

brown-grey head, buff-white to white
below with blackish streaks on breast/
flanks. *1st winter ♂* As ad, but black
streaks on crown. VOICE Calls softer in
tone. RANGE 7: esp Oct–Nov (Jan, Apr,
Aug), most NBr. (NE Russia, N Asia.)

Rock Bunting *Emberiza cia* 15–16.5 cm
(*c*6¼ in). Black-striped grey head, grey
throat/chest, orange-buff below, chestnut
rump, white-edged tail. Much on ground,
but also in bushes, trees; wary. *Ad ♂* Head
cold grey (tinged buff after moult in Aug–
Oct), all stripes black; flanks unmarked.
Ad ♀ Head browner-grey, lores blackish-
brown; flanks often thinly streaked. *1st
winter* Much as ♀, but eyes brown (ad red-
brown), no white on 3rd tail-feathers;
imm ♀ has more buff head, more streaked
chest/flanks. VOICE Thrush-like *zit*, thin
tsee. HABITAT Rocks, scrub. FOOD Seeds,
insects. RANGE 5: Feb–Oct, S/W/EBr.
(S Eurasia, NW Africa.)

Cretzschmar's Bunting *Emberiza caesia*
15–16.5 cm (*c*6¼ in). Like Ortolan (248),

Slate-coloured Junco

Pine Buntin

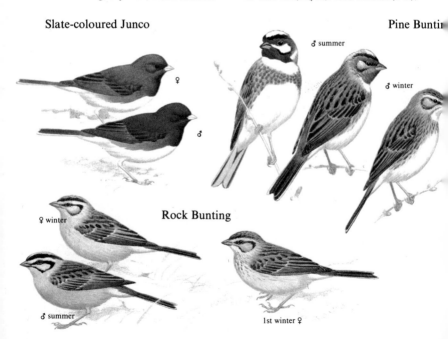

♂ summer

♀

♂

♂ winter

♀ winter

Rock Bunting

♂ summer

1st winter ♀

but smaller, dumpier, shorter-winged, with grey head/chest, orange-buff throat, rufous rump, whitish underwings. *Ad ♂* Blue-grey crown (may be faintly streaked) and chest. *Ad ♀* Crown/chest duller grey, finely streaked blackish. *1st year* Much as ad ♀, but more buff and streaked (more chestnut-buff upperparts and orange-buff throat, less clear eye-rings and wing-bars than imm Ortolan). VOICE Hard *tsyip*. HABITAT/FOOD As Rock Bunting. RANGE 2: Jun, Shetland. (Balkans, Middle East.)

Rustic Bunting *Emberiza rustica* 14–15 cm ($c5\frac{3}{4}$ in). Shorter-tailed than Reed Bunting (248); white throat, stripe behind eyes, and belly, and more or less chestnut nape, scapulars, rump and blotches on chest/flanks. Often raises crown-feathers. *♂ summer* Crown/cheeks jet-black; stripe behind eyes, throat and belly silky white; chestnut areas nearly uniform. *♀ summer* Crown/cheeks brown, generally streaked black; clear broken moustaches, often some dark brown streaks on chest; whites and chestnuts variably tinged buff. *Ad/1st*

winter Much as dull ♀ summer; some ad/imm ♂s have jet-black rear cheek-patch and crown-marks. VOICE High sharp *tsip*, *tsip*. HABITAT Swampy thickets, wood-edges, fields. FOOD Seeds, insects. RANGE 142: Sep–Nov, May–Jun (few Mar–Apr), most NE/E/SWBr. (NE Europe, N Asia.)

Little Bunting *Emberiza pusilla* 13–14 cm ($c5\frac{1}{4}$ in). Like small compact ♀ Reed Bunting (248) with short tail, straight (not convex) culmen; uniform chestnut cheeks with black lower edge not reaching bill, brown (not rufous) lesser coverts, whiter below with neater black streaks, usually bold creamy eye-rings, pinker legs. Jerks closed tail. *Ad summer ♂♀* alike except bright ♂s (face and broadly black-edged crown rich chestnut), dull ♀s (cheeks and brown-edged dark-streaked crown pale). *Ad/1st winter* Crown obscured by buff; ad head usually more rufous (esp lores), imm whiter throat. VOICE Hard sharp *zik*. HABITAT Scrub, fields. FOOD Seeds, insects. RANGE 268: Sep–Oct (few Nov–May), most NE/E/SWBr. (NE Europe, N Asia.)

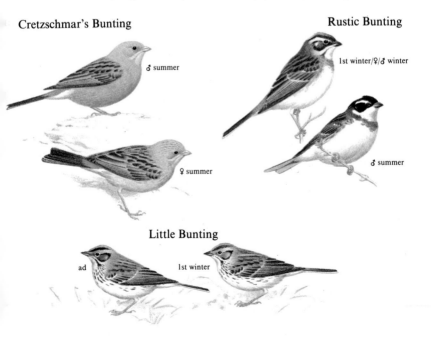

Cretzschmar's Bunting

♂ summer

♀ summer

Rustic Bunting

1st winter/♀/♂ winter

♂ summer

Little Bunting

ad   1st winter

Yellow-breasted Bunting *Emberiza aureola*
13.5–14.5 cm (*c*5½ in). Clearly smaller
than Yellowhammer (246); yellow below,
buff under tail, streaked flanks. 2 wing-
bars, some white on tail-sides; ♀/imm
striped head. *Ad* ♂ Chestnut and yellow;
chest-band, black face, white shoulders;
all partly obscured by buff after moult in
Aug–Oct. *Ad* ♀ Dark-streaked tawny
above, tinged grey to chestnut; striped
crown; pale buff-yellow below. *1st winter*
As ♀, but fresh wings/tail. *1st summer* ♂
Dark-streaked brown, tinged chestnut
(esp rump, crown), and pale yellow; chest-
band thin, face blackish, wings as ♀. VOICE
Robin-like *tik*, nasal *tsit*. HABITAT Scrub,
marshes. FOOD Seeds, insects. RANGE 94:
most Aug–Oct, esp NEBr. (N Eurasia.)

Pallas's Reed Bunting *Emberiza pallasi*
13–14 cm (*c*5¼ in). Like small Reed (248),
but lesser coverts greyish (not rufous),
rump paler, almost unstreaked below (*cf*
Little, 326). *Ad* ♂ As ♂ Reed, but striped
black and grey above, whitish rump, nape
yellow in spring; much obscured by buff

in winter, no bib or white nape, thin
supercilia. *Ad/imm* ♀ More buff above,
whiter below than ♀ Reed with clear pale
'braces', almost no dark edges to cheeks,
thin moustaches ending in hook or blob;
in summer greyish collar/rump. VOICE
Sparrow-like *chireep*, shrill *peeseeoo*.
HABITAT Scrub, reeds. FOOD Seeds, insects.
RANGE 1: Sep–Oct, Shetland. (Asia.)

Black-headed Bunting *Emberiza melanocephala* 16–17 cm (*c*6½ in). Bulkier than
Yellowhammer (246); all unstreaked
yellow or pale buff below, yellow undertail-coverts, no pure white on tail. *Ad* ♂
Plain chestnut and yellow, black hood; all
partly obscured by grey-buff after moult
in Jul–Aug but face/cheeks still blackish.
Ad ♀ Dark-streaked grey-brown, tinged
rufous, and pale or dingy yellow, more
buff on breast; sometimes blackish crown,
wings/tail worn by autumn. *1st winter*
All more buff (yellow under tail as ads);
wings/tail fresh. VOICE Loud *zit*, soft *chup*.
HABITAT Fields, scrub. RANGE 58: Apr–
Oct, esp NE/SBr. (SE Europe, SW Asia.)

Yellow-breasted Bunting

Pallas's Reed Bunting

Black-headed Bunting

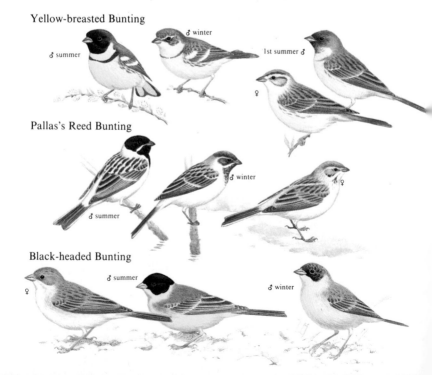

Rose-breasted Grosbeak *Pheucticus ludovicianus* 19–21 cm (*c*7¾ in). Size of small fat thrush with big head, huge pale bill; black, white and rosy, or streaked with striped head, 2 wing-bars. Flight undulating; often furtive. *Ad ♂* Black head/ upperparts, white on wings, rump, tail-corners; white below, breast and underwings rose-red; body (not wings/tail) variably browner in winter, often much as ♀ but rosy throat/breast. *Ad ♀* Brown and whitish, all streaked, with white-striped head, eye-crescents, wing-bars, plain tail, yellow underwings. *1st winter* Markings/ underbody more buff; ♂ less pinkish, rump buff, wings and plain tail browner. VOICE Sharp *keek*. HABITAT Trees, thickets. FOOD Seeds, berries, insects. RANGE 9: Oct–Jan, most Ir/SWBr. (N America.)

AMERICAN ORIOLES (Icteridae)

Bobolink *Dolichonyx oryzivorus* 17–19 cm (*c*7 in). Conical bill, flat forehead, long body, pointed tail-feathers; yellowish, streaked above, with striped head; summer ♂ all black below. Flight direct, fans tail.

♂ summer Black face/underparts, yellowish nape, whitish scapulars/rump. *♂ winter* As ♀ after moult in Jul–Aug, but odd black feathers on throat/breast. *♀/imm* Yellow-buff with blackish stripes on head, streaks on back/flanks. VOICE Soft *cheek*, clear *pink*. HABITAT Fields, marshes. FOOD Seeds, insects. RANGE 7: Sep–Oct, most SWBr. (N America.)

Northern Oriole *Icterus galbula* 18–20 cm (*c*7½ in). Starling-shaped head; black and orange, or olive and yellow, with bluish bill, bold wing-marks, coloured rump/ tail-sides. Flight direct; secretive, in high cover. *Ad ♂* Orange with black head, back, tail-centre and white-edged wings. *Ad ♀* Olive-grey and orange-yellow, 2 wing-bars; often traces of black on head/throat. *1st winter* Much as ad ♀, but no black; ♂ browner above, more orange below; as ads after spring moult, but worn brown juv flight-feathers. VOICE Low whistled *kew-li*. HABITAT Esp trees. FOOD Insects, nectar, seeds, berries. RANGE 12: Sep–Oct, May, S/W/NEBr. (N America.)

Rose-breasted Grosbeak

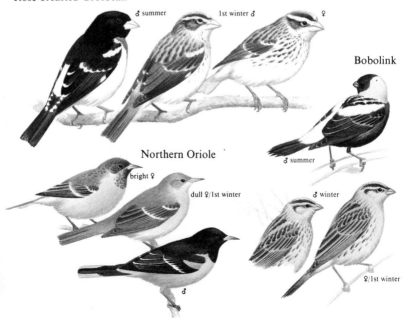

Bobolink

Northern Oriole

Bibliography

Many of the following books which have been used for reference in the preparation of this guide make valuable further reading. In addition to these are countless notes and papers in *British Birds*, which also publishes annual reports on rare birds. These have enabled the totals and patterns of vagrants to be given in this book.

Bent, A. C. *Life Histories of North American Birds*. Dover Pubns., Washington 1919–68 (23 vols).

Campbell, B., and Ferguson-Lees, I. J. *A Field Guide to Birds' Nests*. Constable, London 1972.

Cramp, S., Simmons, K. E. L., and others. *The Birds of the Western Palearctic*. Oxford, London 1977 onwards (1st 2 vols).

Dementiev, G. P., and Gladkov, N. A. *Birds of the Soviet Union*. Moscow 1951–54 (Israel translation: Jerusalem 1966–68).

Grant, P. J. *Gulls: A Guide to Identification*. Poyser, Calton (Staffs) 1982.

Hollom, P. A. D. *The Popular Handbook of Rarer British Birds*. Witherby, London 1980 (revised edition).

King, B., Woodcock, M., Dickinson, E. C. *A Field Guide to the Birds of South-East Asia*. Collins, London 1975.

Peterson, R. T. *A Field Guide to the Birds of Eastern and Central North America*. Houghton Mifflin, Boston 1980.

Peterson, R., Mountfort, G., and Hollom, P. A. D. *A Field Guide to the Birds of Britain and Europe*. Collins, London 1974 (revised edition in collaboration with I. J. Ferguson-Lees and D. I. M. Wallace).

Porter, R. F., Willis, I., Christensen, S., and Nielsen, B. P. *Flight Identification of European Raptors*. Poyser, Berkhamsted 1980 (3rd revised edition).

Prater, A. J., Marchant, J. H., and Vuorinen, J. *Guide to the Identification and Ageing of Holarctic Waders*. British Trust for Ornithology, Tring 1977.

Records Committee of British Ornithologists' Union. *The Status of Birds in Britain and Ireland*. Oxford, London and Edinburgh 1971.

Robbins, C. S., Bruun, B., and Zim, H. S. *A Guide to Field Identification: Birds of North America*. Golden Press, New York 1966.

Sharrock, J. T. R. *The Atlas of Breeding Birds in Britain and Ireland*. Poyser, Tring and Berkhamsted 1976.

Sharrock, J. T. R. and E. M. *Rare Birds in Britain and Ireland*. Poyser, Berkhamsted 1976.

Svensson, L. *Identification Guide to European Passerines*. Naturhistoriska Riksmuseet, Stockholm 1975 (revised edition).

Tuck, G., Heinzel, H., *A Field Guide to the Seabirds of Britain and the World*. Collins, London 1978.

Williamson, K. *Identification for Ringers: 1–3* (warblers). British Trust for Ornithology, Tring 1967–68 (revised editions).

Witherby, H. F., Jourdain, F. C. R., Ticehurst, N. F., and Tucker, B. W. *The Handbook of British Birds*. Witherby, London 1938–41 (5 vols).

This book covers all the species recorded wild or breeding ferally in Britain and Ireland in the 50 years 1931–80 (except for Yellow-browed Bunting *Emberiza chrysophrys* which occurred in 1980 but was accepted too late for inclusion). Thus, it excludes a few vagrants which have been found here for the first time since 1980, and also the following 14 from before our period:

Capped Petrel *Pterodroma hasitata*; White-faced Petrel *Pelagodroma marina*; Green Heron *Butorides striatus*; Egyptian Vulture *Neophron percnopterus*; Griffon Vulture *Gyps fulvus*; Spotted Eagle *Aquila clanga*; Allen's Gallinule *Porphyrula alleni*; Sandhill Crane *Grus canadensis* (also recorded 1981); Caspian Plover *Charadrius asiaticus*; Eskimo Curlew *Numenius borealis*; Eagle Owl *Bubo bubo*; Red-necked Nightjar *Caprimulgus ruficollis*; Egyptian Nightjar *Caprimulgus aegyptius*; Citril Finch *Serinus citrinella*.

Index

Accentor, Alpine, 296
Accipiter gentilis, 98
 nisus, 98
Acrocephalus aedon, 308
 agricola, 308
 arundinaceus, 308
 dumetorum, 308
 melanopogon, 306
 paludicola, 306
 palustris, 210
 schoenobaenus, 208
 scirpaceus, 210
Actitis hypoleucos, 144
 macularia, 280
Aegithalos caudatus, 220
Aegolius funereus, 290
Aix galericulata, 68
 sponsa, 68
Alauda arvensis, 184
Albatross, Black-browed, 250
Alca torda, 168
Alcedo atthis, 180
Alectoris rufa, 112
Alle alle, 170
Alopochen aegyptiacus, 66
Anas acuta, 74
 americana, 258
 clypeata, 76
 crecca, 72
 discors, 260
 formosa, 260
 penelope, 70
 platyrhynchos, 72
 querquedula, 74
 rubripes, 258
 strepera, 70
Anser albifrons, 62
 anser, 60
 brachyrhynchus, 60
 caerulescens, 62
 erythropus, 258
 fabalis, 60
 rossii, 62
Anthropoides virgo, 270
Anthus campestris, 296
 cervinus, 296
 gustavi, 296
 hodgsoni, 296
 novaeseelandiae, 296
 pratensis, 188
 spinoletta, 188
 trivialis, 188
Apus affinis, 292
 apus, 186
 melba, 292
 pallidus, 292

Aquila chrysaetos, 102
Ardea cinerea, 56
 purpurea, 256
Ardeola ralloides, 254
Arenaria interpres, 140
Asio flammeus, 178
 otus, 178
Athene noctua, 176
Auk, Little, 170
Avocet, 120
Aythya collaris, 260
 ferina, 78
 fuligula, 80
 marila, 80
 nyroca, 78

Bartramia longicauda, 280
Bee-eater, 290
 Blue-cheeked, 290
Bittern, 56
 American, 254
 Little, 254
Blackbird, 204
Blackcap, 214
Bluetail, Red-flanked, 298
Bluethroat, 196
Bobolink, 328
Bombycilla garrulus, 194
Botaurus lentiginosus, 254
 stellaris, 56
Brambling, 236
Branta bernicla, 64
 canadensis, 64
 leucopsis, 64
 ruficollis, 258
Bubulcus ibis, 254
Bucanetes githagineus, 318
Bucephala albeola, 262
 clangula, 88
 islandica, 88
Bufflehead, 262
Bullfinch, 236
Bulweria bulwerii, 252
Bunting, Black-headed, 328
 Cirl, 246
 Corn, 248
 Cretzschmar's, 326
 Lapland, 244
 Little, 326
 Ortolan, 248
 Pallas's Reed, 328
 Pine, 326
 Reed, 248
 Rock, 326
 Rustic, 326
 Snow, 244
 Yellow-breasted, 328
Burhinus oedicnemus, 120

Bustard, Great, 270
 Houbara, 270
 Little, 270
Buteo buteo, 100
 lagopus, 100
Buzzard, 100
 Honey, 92
 Rough-legged, 100

Calandrella brachydactyla, 294
 rufescens, 294
Calcarius lapponicus, 244
Calidris acuminata, 278
 alba, 128
 alpina, 132
 bairdii, 276
 canutus, 130
 ferruginea, 132
 fuscicollis, 276
 maritima, 130
 mauri, 276
 melanotos, 130
 minuta, 128
 minutilla, 276
 pusilla, 276
 temminckii, 128 .
Calonectris diomedea, 50
Capercaillie, 110
Caprimulgus europaeus, 180
Carduelis cannabina, 240
 carduelis, 238
 chloris, 238
 flammea, 240
 flavirostris, 240
 hornemanni, 316
 spinus, 238
Carpodacus erythrinus, 318
Catharus fuscescens, 302
 guttatus, 302
 minimus, 302
 ustulatus, 302
Cepphus grylle, 170
Cercotrichas galactotes, 298
Certhia brachydactyla, 314
 familiaris, 226
Ceryle alcyon, 290
Cettia cetti, 208
Chaffinch, 236
Charadrius alexandrinus, 122
 dubius, 122
 hiaticula, 122
 leschenaultii, 274
 morinellus, 126
 semipalmatus, 274
 vociferus, 274

Chettusia gregaria, 274
  leucura, 274
Chiffchaff, 216
Chlamydotis undulata, 270
Chlidonias hybridus, 286
  leucopterus, 286
  niger, 166
Chordeiles minor, 292
Chough, 230
Chrysolophus amherstiae,
  114
  pictus, 114
Ciconia ciconia, 256
  nigra, 256
Cinclus cinclus, 194
Circus aeruginosus, 94
  cyaneus, 96
  macrourus, 264
  pygargus, 96
Cisticola juncidis, 306
Clamator glandarius, 288
Clangula hyemalis, 84
Coccothraustes
  coccothraustes, 242
Coccyzus americanus, 288
  erythropthalmus, 288
Columba livia, 172
  oenas, 172
  palumbus, 172
Coot, 118
  American, 118
Coracias garrulus, 290
Cormorant, 54
Corncrake, 116
Corvus corax, 232
  corone, 232
  frugilegus, 232
  monedula, 230
Coturnix coturnix, 112
Courser, Cream-coloured,
  272
Crake, Baillon's, 268
  Little, 268
  Spotted, 116
Crane, 270
  Demoiselle, 270
  Sandhill, 270
  Sarus, 270
Crex crex, 116
Crossbill, 242
  Parrot, 318
  Scottish, 242
  Two-barred, 318
Crow, Carrion/Hooded,
  232
Cuckoo, 174
  Black-billed, 288
  Great Spotted, 288
  Yellow-billed, 288

Cuculus canorus, 174
Curlew, 140
Cursorius cursor, 272
Cygnus columbianus, 58
  cygnus, 58
  olor, 58

Delichon urbica, 186
Dendrocopos major, 182
  minor, 182
Dendroica coronata, 320
  petechia, 320
  striata, 322
  tigrina, 320
Diomedea melanophris, 250
Dipper, 194
Diver, Black-throated, 42
  Great Northern, 42
  Red-throated, 42
  White-billed, 250
Dolichonyx oryzivorus, 328
Dotterel, 126
Dove, Collared, 172
  Rock, 172
  Rufous Turtle, 288
  Stock, 172
  Turtle, 174
Dowitcher, Long-billed,
  278
  Short-billed, 278
Duck, Wood, 68
  Black, 258
  White-headed, 68
  Ferruginous, 78
  Long-tailed, 84
  Ring-necked, 260
  Ruddy, 68
  Tufted, 80
Dunlin, 132
Dunnock, 196

Eagle, Golden, 102
  White-tailed, 264
Egret, Cattle, 254
  Great White, 256
  Little, 256
Egretta alba, 256
  garzetta, 256
Eider, 82
  King, 260
  Steller's, 260
Emberiza aureola, 328
  caesia, 326
  cia, 326
  cirlus, 246
  citrinella, 246
  hortulana, 248
  leucocephalos, 326
  melanocephala, 328

  pallasi, 328
  pusilla, 326
  rustica, 326
  schoeniclus, 248
Eremophila alpestris, 184
Erithacus rubecula, 196

Falco columbarius, 104
  eleonorae, 266
  naumanii, 266
  peregrinus, 106
  rusticolus, 264
  sparverius, 266
  subbuteo, 106
  tinnunculus, 104
  vespertinus, 266
Falcon, Eleonora's, 266
  Red-footed, 266
Ficedula albicollis, 312
  hypoleuca, 218
  parva, 218
Fieldfare, 202
Finch, Trumpeter, 318
Firecrest, 220
Flycatcher, Collared, 312
  Pied, 218
  Red-breasted, 218
  Spotted, 218
Fratercula arctica, 170
Fregata magnificens, 250
Frigatebird, Magnificent,
  250
Fringilla coelebs, 236
  montifringilla, 236
Fulica americana, 118
  atra, 118
Fulmar, 48
Fulmarus glacialis, 48

Gadwall, 70
Galerida cristata, 294
  theklae, 294
Gallinago gallinago, 136
  media, 278
Gallinula chloropus, 118
Gallinule,
  American Purple, 268
  Purple, 268
Gannet, 48
Garganey, 74
Garrulus glandarius, 228
Gavia adamsii, 250
  arctica, 42
  immer, 42
  stellata, 42
Gelochelidon nilotica, 286
Geothlypis trichas, 322
Glareola nordmanni, 272
  pratincola, 272

Godwit, Bar-tailed, 138
  Black-tailed, 138
Goldcrest, 220
Goldeneye, 88
  Barrow's, 88
Goldfinch, 238
Goosander, 90
Goose, Barnacle, 64
  Bean, 60
  Brent, 64
  Canada, 64
  Egyptian, 66
  Greylag, 60
  Lesser White-fronted, 258
  Pink-footed, 60
  Red-breasted, 258
  Ross's, 62
  Snow, 62
  White-fronted, 62
Goshawk, 98
Grebe, Black-necked, 46
  Great Crested, 44
  Little, 46
  Pied-billed, 250
  Red-necked, 44
  Slavonian, 46
Greenfinch, 238
Greenshank, 142
Grosbeak, Evening, 318
  Pine, 318
  Rose-breasted, 328
Grouse, Black, 110
  Red, 108
Grus antigone, 270
  canadensis, 270
  grus, 270
Guillemot, 168
  Black, 170
  Brünnich's, 286
Gull, Black-headed, 154
  Bonaparte's, 282
  Common, 156
  Franklin's, 282
  Glaucous, 160
  Great Black-backed, 162
  Great Black-headed, 284
  Herring, 156
  Iceland, 160
  Ivory, 284
  Laughing, 282
  Lesser Black-backed, 158
  Little, 152
  Mediterranean, 152
  Ring-billed, 282
  Ross's, 284

Sabine's, 154
Slender-billed, 282
Gyrfalcon, 264

Haematopus ostralegus, 120
Haliaeetus albicilla, 264
Harlequin, 262
Harrier, Hen, 96
  Marsh, 94
  Montagu's, 96
  Pallid, 264
Hawfinch, 242
Heron, Grey, 56
  Night, 254
  Purple, 256
  Squacco, 254
Hesperiphona vespertina, 318
Himantopus himantopus, 272
Hippolais caligata, 308
  icterina, 210
  pallida, 308
  polyglotta, 210
Hirundapus caudacutus, 292
Hirundo daurica, 292
  rustica, 186
Histrionicus histrionicus, 262
Hobby, 106
Hoopoe, 180
Hydrobates pelagicus, 52

Ibis, Glossy, 256
Icterus galbula, 328
Ixobrychus minutus, 254

Jackdaw, 230
Jay, 228
Junco hyemalis, 326
Junco, Slate-coloured, 326
Jynx torquilla, 180

Kestrel, 104
  American, 266
  Lesser, 266
Killdeer, 274
Kingfisher, 180
  Belted, 290
Kite, Black, 264
  Red, 94
Kittiwake, 162
Knot, 130

Lagopus lagopus, 108
  mutus, 108
Lanius collurio, 228

excubitor, 228
  isabellinus, 314
  minor, 314
  senator, 314
Lapwing, 126
Lark, Bimaculated, 294
  Calandra, 294
  Crested, 294
  Lesser Short-toed, 294
  Shore, 184
  Short-toed, 294
  Thekla, 294
  White-winged, 294
Larus argentatus, 156
  atricilla, 282
  canus, 156
  delawarensis, 282
  fuscus, 158
  genei, 282
  glaucoides, 160
  hyperboreus, 160
  ichthyaetus, 284
  marinus, 162
  melanocephalus, 152
  minutus, 152
  philadelphia, 282
  pipixcan, 282
  ridibundus, 154
  sabini, 154
Limicola falcinellus, 276
Limosa lapponica, 138
  limosa, 138
Limnodromus griseus, 278
  scolopaceus, 278
Linnet, 240
Locustella certhiola, 306
  fluviatilis, 306
  lanceolata, 306
  luscinioides, 208
  naevia, 208
Loxia curvirostra, 242
  leucoptera, 318
  pytyopsittacus, 318
  scotica, 242
Lullula arborea, 184
Luscinia calliope, 298
  luscinia, 298
  megarhynchos, 198
  svecica, 196
Lymnocryptes minimus, 136

Magpie, 230
Mallard, 72
Mandarin, 68
Martin, House, 186
  Sand, 186
Melanitta fusca, 86
  nigra, 86
  perspicillata, 262

Melanocorypha
  bimaculata, 294
  calandra, 294
  leucoptera, 294
Merganser, Hooded, 262
  Red-breasted, 90
Mergus albellus, 88
  cucullatus, 262
  merganser, 90
  serrator, 90
Merlin, 104
Merops apiaster, 290
  superciliosus, 290
Micropalama himantopus,
  278
Miliaria calandra, 248
Milvus migrans, 264
  milvus, 94
Mniotilta varia, 320
Monticola saxatilis, 302
Moorhen, 118
Motacilla alba, 192
  cinerea, 192
  citreola, 296
  flava, 190
Muscicapa striata, 218

Netta rufina, 76
Nighthawk, Common, 292
Nightingale, 198
  Thrush, 298
Nightjar, 180
Nucifraga caryocatactes,
  316
Numenius arquata, 140
  phaeopus, 140
Nutcracker, 316
Nuthatch, 226
Nyctea scandiaca, 176
Nycticorax nycticorax, 254

Oceanites oceanicus, 252
Oceanodroma castro, 252
  leucorhoa, 52
Oenanthe deserti, 300
  hispanica, 300
  isabellina, 298
  leucura, 300
  oenanthe, 202
  pleschanka, 300
Oriole, Golden, 226
  Northern, 328
Oriolus oriolus, 226
Osprey, 102
Otis tarda, 270
Otus scops, 290
Ouzel, Ring, 204
Ovenbird, 322
Owl, Barn, 176

Hawk, 290
  Little, 176
  Long-eared, 178
  Scops, 290
  Short-eared, 178
  Snowy, 176
  Tawny, 178
  Tengmalm's, 290
Oxyura jamaicensis, 68
  leucocephala, 68
Oystercatcher, 120

Pagophila eburnea, 284
Pandion haliaetus, 102
Panurus biarmicus, 220
Parakeet, Ring-necked,
  174
Partridge, Grey, 112
  Red-legged, 112
Parula americana, 320
Parus ater, 222
  caeruleus, 224
  cristatus, 224
  major, 224
  montanus, 222
  palustris, 222
Passer domesticus, 234
  hispaniolensis, 316
  montanus, 234
Perdix perdix, 112
Peregrine, 106
Pernis apivorus, 92
Petrel, Bulwer's, 252
  Leach's, 52
  Madeiran, 252
  Storm, 52
  Wilson's, 252
Phalacrocorax aristotelis,
  54
  carbo, 54
Phalarope, Grey, 146
  Red-necked, 146
  Wilson's, 272
Phalaropus fulicarius, 146
  lobatus, 146
  tricolor, 272
Phasianus colchicus, 114
Pheasant, 114
  Golden, 114
  Lady Amherst's, 114
Pheucticus ludovicianus,
  328
Philomachus pugnax, 134
Phoenicurus ochruros, 198
  phoenicurus, 198
Phylloscopus bonelli, 312
  borealis, 312
  collybita, 216
  fuscatus, 312

inornatus, 216
  proregulus, 312
  schwarzi, 312
  sibilatrix, 216
  trochiloides, 312
  trochilus, 216
Pica pica, 230
Picus viridis, 182
Pigeon, Feral, 172
Pinicola enucleator, 318
Pintail, 74
Pipilo erythrophthalmus,
  324
Pipit, Meadow, 188
  Olive-backed, 296
  Pechora, 296
  Red-throated, 296
  Richard's, 296
  Rock, 188
  Tawny, 296
  Tree, 188
Piranga olivacea, 324
  rubra, 324
Platalea leucorodia, 56
Plectrophenax nivalis, 244
Plegadis falcinellus, 256
Plover, Golden, 124
  Greater Sand, 274
  Grey, 124
  Kentish, 122
  Lesser Golden, 274
  Little Ringed, 122
  Ringed, 122
  Semipalmated, 274
  Sociable, 274
  White-tailed, 274
Pluvialis apricaria, 124
  dominica, 274
  squatarola, 124
Pochard, 78
  Red-crested, 76
Podiceps auritus, 46
  cristatus, 44
  grisegena, 44
  nigricollis, 46
Podilymbus podiceps, 250
Polysticta stelleri, 260
Porphyrio porphyrio, 268
Porphyrula martinica, 268
Porzana carolina, 268
  parva, 268
  porzana, 116
  pusilla, 268
Pratincole, Black-winged,
  272
  Collared, 272
Prunella collaris, 296
  modularis, 196
Psittacula krameri, 174

Ptarmigan, 108
Puffin, 170
Puffinus assimilis, 252
   gravis, 50
   griseus, 50
   puffinus, 52
Pyrrhocorax pyrrhocorax, 230
Pyrrhula pyrrhula, 236

Quail, 112

Rail, Water, 116
Rallus aquaticus, 116
Raven, 232
Razorbill, 168
Recurvirostra avosetta, 120
Redpoll, 240
   Arctic, 316
Redshank, 142
   Spotted, 142
Redstart, 198
   American, 322
   Black, 198
Redwing, 206
Regulus ignicapillus, 220
   regulus, 220
Remiz pendulinus, 314
Rhodostethia rosea, 284
Riparia riparia, 186
Rissa tridactyla, 162
Robin, 196
   American, 304
   Rufous Bush, 298
Roller, 290
Rook, 232
Rosefinch, Scarlet, 318
Rubythroat, Siberian, 298
Ruff, 134

Sanderling, 128
Sandgrouse, Pallas's, 288
Sandpiper, Baird's, 276
   Broad-billed, 276
   Buff-breasted, 278
   Common, 144
   Curlew, 132
   Green, 144
   Least, 276
   Marsh, 280
   Pectoral, 130
   Purple, 130
   Semipalmated, 276
   Sharp-tailed, 278
   Solitary, 280
   Spotted, 280
   Stilt, 278
   Terek, 280
   Upland, 280

Western, 276
   White-rumped, 276
   Wood, 144
Sapsucker,
   Yellow-bellied, 292
Saxicola rubetra, 200
   torquata, 200
Scaup, 80
Scolopax rusticola, 136
Scoter, Common, 86
   Surf, 262
   Velvet, 86
Seiurus aurocapillus, 322
   noveboracensis, 322
Setophaga ruticilla, 322
Shag, 54
Shearwater, Cory's, 50
   Great, 50
   Little, 252
   Manx, 52
   Sooty, 50
Shelduck, 66
   Ruddy, 258
Shoveler, 76
Shrike, Great Grey, 228
   Isabelline, 314
   Lesser Grey, 314
   Red-backed, 228
   Woodchat, 314
Siskin, 238
Sitta europaea, 226
Skua, Arctic, 150
   Great, 148
   Long-tailed, 150
   Pomarine, 148
Skylark, 184
Smew, 88
Snipe, 136
   Great, 278
   Jack, 136
Somateria mollissima, 82
   spectabilis, 260
Sora, 268
Sparrow, Fox, 324
   House, 234
   Song, 324
   Spanish, 316
   Tree, 234
   White-crowned, 324
   White-throated, 324
Sparrowhawk, 98
Sphyrapicus varius, 292
Spoonbill, 56
Starling, 234
   Rose-coloured, 316
Stercorarius longicaudus, 150
   parasiticus, 150
   pomarinus, 148

skua, 148
Sterna albifrons, 166
   aleutica, 286
   anaethetus, 286
   caspia, 284
   dougallii, 164
   forsteri, 284
   fuscata, 286
   hirundo, 164
   maxima, 284
   paradisaea, 164
   sandvicensis, 166
Stilt, Black-winged, 272
Stint, Little, 128
   Temminck's, 128
Stonechat, 200
Stone-curlew, 120
Stork, Black, 256
   White, 256
Streptopelia decaocto, 172
   orientalis, 288
   turtur, 174
Strix aluco, 178
Sturnus roseus, 316
   vulgaris, 234
Sula bassana, 48
Surnia ulula, 290
Swallow, 186
   Red-rumped, 292
Swan, Bewick's, 58
   Mute, 58
   Whooper, 58
Swift, 186
   Alpine, 292
   Little, 292
   Needle-tailed, 292
   Pallid, 292
Sylvia atricapilla, 214
   borin, 214
   cantillans, 310
   communis, 212
   conspicillata, 310
   curruca, 212
   hortensis, 310
   melanocephala, 310
   nana, 310
   nisoria, 214
   rueppelli, 310
   undata, 212
Syrrhaptes paradoxus, 288

Tachybaptus ruficollis, 46
Tadorna tadorna, 66
   ferruginea, 258
Tanager, Scarlet, 324
   Summer, 324
Tarsiger cyanurus, 298
Teal, 72
   Baikal, 260

Blue-winged, 260
Tern, Aleutian, 286
  Arctic, 164
  Black, 166
  Bridled, 286
  Caspian, 284
  Common, 164
  Forster's, 284
  Gull-billed, 286
  Little, 166
  Roseate, 164
  Royal, 284
  Sandwich, 166
  Sooty, 286
  Whiskered, 286
  White-winged Black, 286
Tetrao tetrix, 110
  urogallus, 110
Tetrax tetrax, 270
Thrasher, Brown, 298
Thrush, Black-throated, 304
  Dusky, 304
  Eye-browed, 304
  Grey-cheeked, 302
  Hermit, 302
  Mistle, 206
  Rock, 302
  Siberian, 304
  Song, 206
  Swainson's, 302
  White's, 302
Tichodroma muraria, 314
Tit, Bearded, 220
  Blue, 224
  Coal, 222
  Crested, 224
  Great, 224
  Long-tailed, 220
  Marsh, 222
  Penduline, 314
  Willow, 222
Towhee, Rufous-sided, 324
Toxostoma rufum, 298
Treecreeper, 226
  Short-toed, 314
Tringa erythropus, 142
  flavipes, 280
  glareola, 144
  melanoleuca, 280
  nebularia, 142
  ochropus, 144
  solitaria, 280
  stagnatilis, 280
  totanus, 142
Troglodytes troglodytes, 194
Tryngites subruficollis, 278

Turdus iliacus, 206
  merula, 204
  migratorius, 304
  naumanni, 304
  obscurus, 304
  philomelos, 206
  pilaris, 202
  ruficollis, 304
  torquatus, 204
  viscivorus, 206
Turnstone, 140
Twite, 240
Tyto alba, 176

Upupa epops, 180
Uria aalge, 168
  lomvia, 286

Vanellus vanellus, 126
Veery, 302
Vermivora peregrina, 320
Vireo olivaceus, 322
Vireo, Red-eyed, 322

Wagtail, Citrine, 296
  Grey, 192
  Pied, 192
  Yellow, 190
Wallcreeper, 314
Warbler, Aquatic, 306
  Arctic, 312
  Barred, 214
  Black-and-white, 320
  Blackpoll, 322
  Blyth's Reed, 308
  Bonelli's, 312
  Booted, 308
  Cape May, 320
  Cetti's, 208
  Dartford, 212
  Desert, 310
  Dusky, 312
  Fan-tailed, 306
  Garden, 214
  Grasshopper, 208
  Great Reed, 308
  Greenish, 312
  Hooded, 322
  Icterine, 210
  Lanceolated, 306
  Marsh, 210
  Melodious, 210
  Moustached, 306
  Olivaceous, 308
  Orphean, 310
  Paddyfield, 308
  Pallas's, 312
  Pallas's Grasshopper, 306
  Parula, 320

Radde's, 312
Reed, 210
River, 306
Rüppell's, 310
Sardinian, 310
Savi's, 208
Sedge, 208
Spectacled, 310
Subalpine, 310
Tennessee, 320
Thick-billed, 308
Willow, 216
Wood, 216
Yellow, 320
Yellow-browed, 216
Yellow-rumped, 320
Waterthrush, Northern, 322
Waxwing, 194
Wheatear, 202
  Black, 300
  Black-eared, 300
  Desert, 300
  Isabelline, 298
  Pied, 300
Whimbrel, 140
Whinchat, 200
Whitethroat, 212
  Lesser, 212
Wigeon, 70
  American, 258
Wilsonia citrina, 322
Woodcock, 136
Woodlark, 184
Woodpecker, Great Spotted, 182
  Green, 182
  Lesser Spotted, 182
Woodpigeon, 172
Wren, 194
Wryneck, 180

Xenus cinereus, 280

Yellowhammer, 246
Yellowlegs, Greater, 280
  Lesser, 280
Yellowthroat, 322

Zonotrichia albicollis, 324
  iliaca, 324
  leucophrys, 324
  melodia, 324
Zoothera dauma, 302
  sibirica, 304